THE SCRIBES OF ROME

In a society in which only a fraction of the population was literate and numerate, being one of the few specialists in reading, writing and reckoning was to possess an invaluable asset. The fact that the Roman state heavily relied on these professional scribes in financial and legal administration led to their holding a unique position and status. By gathering and analysing the available source material on the Roman *scribae*, Benjamin Hartmann traces the history of Rome's public scribes from the early Republic to the Later Roman Empire. He tells the story of men of low social origin who, by means of their specialised knowledge, found themselves at the heart of the Roman polity, in close proximity to the powerful and responsible for the written arcana of the state – a story of knowledge and power, corruption and contested social mobility.

BENJAMIN HARTMANN is a former Research and Teaching Assistant in Ancient History at the University of Zurich. His research focuses on the role of literacy in the ancient world, ancient cultural and social history, and Latin epigraphy. He has published mainly on writing on everyday objects and small finds from the Roman world.

THE SCRIBES OF ROME
A Cultural and Social History of the Scribae

BENJAMIN HARTMANN
University of Zurich

CAMBRIDGE
UNIVERSITY PRESS

University Printing House, Cambridge CB2 8BS, United Kingdom

One Liberty Plaza, 20th Floor, New York, NY 10006, USA

477 Williamstown Road, Port Melbourne, VIC 3207, Australia

314–321, 3rd Floor, Plot 3, Splendor Forum, Jasola District Centre, New Delhi – 110025, India

79 Anson Road, #06-04/06, Singapore 079906

Cambridge University Press is part of the University of Cambridge.

It furthers the University's mission by disseminating knowledge in the pursuit of education, learning, and research at the highest international levels of excellence.

www.cambridge.org
Information on this title: www.cambridge.org/9781108493963
DOI: 10.1017/9781108656917

© Benjamin Hartmann 2020

This publication is in copyright. Subject to statutory exception and to the provisions of relevant collective licensing agreements, no reproduction of any part may take place without the written permission of Cambridge University Press.

First published 2020

A catalogue record for this publication is available from the British Library.

Library of Congress Cataloging-in-Publication Data
NAMES: Hartmann, Benjamin, author.
TITLE: The Scribes of Rome : A Cultural and Social History of the Scribae / Benjamin Hartmann.
DESCRIPTION: Cambridge, United Kingdom ; New York, NY : Cambridge University Press, 2020. | Includes bibliographical references and index.
IDENTIFIERS: LCCN 2020002811 | ISBN 9781108493963 (hardback) | ISBN 9781108713740 (paperback)
SUBJECTS: LCSH: Scribes–Rome. | Rome–Officials and employees.
CLASSIFICATION: LCC DG83.3 .H37 2020 | DDC 937–dc23
LC record available at https://lccn.loc.gov/2020002811

ISBN 978-1-108-49396-3 Hardback

Cambridge University Press has no responsibility for the persistence or accuracy of URLs for external or third-party internet websites referred to in this publication and does not guarantee that any content on such websites is, or will remain, accurate or appropriate.

This work was accepted as a PhD thesis by the Faculty of Arts and Social Sciences, University of Zurich, in the spring semester 2018 on the recommendation of the Doctoral Committee consisting of Professor Dr Anne Kolb (University of Zurich, main supervisor), Professor Dr Beat Näf (University of Zurich) and Professor Nicholas Purcell (University of Oxford).

to my parents Annemarie and Josef
to Esther

sine quibus non

Er hat einen Sturm in einem Wasserglase beobachtet und dabei noch Verschiedenes mehr entdeckt als nur Eigenschaften eines Sturmes.

He observed a storm in a teacup and thereby discovered much more than just the characteristics of a storm.

Ludwig Hohl, *Die Notizen*

Epigraph excerpt from: Ludwig Hohl, Die Notizen oder Von der unvoreiligen Versöhnung. © Suhrkamp Verlag Frankfurt am Main 1981. All rights reserved Suhrkamp Verlag Berlin.

Contents

List of Figures and Tables		*page* xi
Acknowledgements		xiii
Abbreviations		xv
1	Imagining the Roman *Scriba*	1
	Knowledge Is Power	1
	Scribal Capital	3
	Evidence Lost	5
	Images of *Scriba*-ship	9
2	The Human Archive	13
	Consequences of Literacy	13
	Scribal Education	16
	Two Cultures	19
	Roman Literate Practice	24
	A Culture of Documentation	27
	The Public Repository	31
	Archives and Archival Practice	36
	Guardians of the Written	44
	Scriptum Facere	48
3	The Attendant	61
	Roman Civil Servants	61
	Origins	63
	Association	68
	Hierarchy	75
	Diversity	80
	Model	84
	Human Relations	88
4	The Profiteer	94
	Thieves and Opportunities	94
	A Matter of Trust	98
	Under Suspicion	103
	Making a Living	106

5	**The Parvenu**	111
	An *Ordo* of *Scribae*	111
	Humble Beginnings	114
	Contested Mobility	120
	Imperial Careers	124
	Local Notables	130
	The Tale of a *Scriba*	136
6	**The Roman *Scriba* Reimagined**	140
	A Classical Model	140
	Remnants and Revivals	142
	The Legacy of an Idea	146

Appendix The Roman *Scribae* — 150

    A.1 Roman State — 150
    A.2 Cities and Communities — 164
    A.3 Associations — 169
    A.4 Naval Forces — 173
    A.5 Unassigned — 174
    A.6 *Falsi* — 175

Bibliography — 176
Index Locorum — 201
General Index — 216

Figures and Tables

Figures

2.1 Via Appia, 'vigna Casali', Porta S. Sebastiano, Rome. So-called Ara degli Scribi, upper relief. Occupational scene. Museo Nazionale Romano, Terme di Diocleziano, Rome, Inv. nr. 475113. Benjamin Hartmann. By permission of The Ministry of Cultural Heritage and Activities – National Roman Museum. *page* 40

2.2 Forum Romanum, Curia Iulia, Rome. So-called Plutei Traiani, stone balustrade with bas-relief of Hadrian's general debt relief. Antonio Cederna. Archivio Cederna, 1206.3_000_000_011. By permisson of the Archivio Cederna – Capo di Bove, Parco Archeologico dell'Appia Antica, MiBAC. 42

2.3 Campus Martius, temple of Neptune, Rome. So-called Altar of Domitius Ahenobarbus, left side, relief, detail. Marie-Lan Nguyen / Wikimedia Commons. Louvre, Paris. Inv. nr. LL 399. By permission of the photographer. 50

2.4 Paestum, Capaccio (Seliano). Marble plaque, funerary inscription with relief depiction. Umberto Soldovieri. By permission of the photographer. 53

3.1 Clevsins, Chiusi. Etruscan funerary relief, bas-relief. Museo Archeologico *Antonino Salinas*, Palermo, Cippo (N.I.8385), Collezione Casuccini. By permission of the Archivio Fotografico del Museo Archeologico Regionale *Antonino Salinas* di Palermo. 64

3.2 Forum Romanum, behind the *rostra*. Marble tablet, 27 × 14.5 × 3.5 cm. Fragment of an *album* of the *scribae quaestorii* (*CIL 6, 37145*). Museo Nazionale Romano, Parco Archeologico del Colosseo, Chiostro S. Francesca Romana, Rome. Inv. nr. ep. 5213. By permission of the

	Ministero dei Beni e delle Attività Culturali e del Turismo – Parco Archeologico del Colosseo.	79
5.1	Via Appia, 'vigna Casali', Porta S. Sebastiano, Rome. So-called Ara degli Scribi, front view. Museo Nazionale Romano, Terme di Diocleziano, Rome, Inv. nr. 475113. By permission of The Ministry of Cultural Heritage and Activities – National Roman Museum.	118
5.2	Ostia, Porta Romana, via Ostiense. Remains of the tomb of C. Domitius Fabius Hermogenes. Luciano Morpurgo. ICCD – Gabinetto Fotografico Nazionale, Fondo GFN, E038116. By permission of the Istituto Centrale per il Catalogo e la Documentazione – MiBAC.	137

Table

3.1	Hierarchy of *apparitores* of the *colonia Iulia Genetiva* (Urso) according to annual wages, with number of yearly assignments to municipal officials.	85

Acknowledgements

Historical research is a joint effort. I am indebted to those who have gone before me, who have been engaged with the same questions and who have made invaluable headway in the search for answers. I join their ranks in the hope that my own questions and provisional answers may be of use and be an incentive for further scientific inquiry.

Books and ideas will only take one so far, however. I would like to thank, first and foremost, Anne Kolb (Zurich) for her continuous and unabated generous support and promotion; Beat Näf (Zurich) for his trust and confidence, for his generosity, for new perspectives and approaches; Hans-Jörg Brem (Frauenfeld) with his team at the Amt für Archäologie Thurgau for his faith in and encouragement of a novice; Regula Frei-Stolba (Fribourg, Aarau) for her inspiration, assistance and collaboration; Ulrich Eigler (Zurich) for his continued interest and mindfulness. I am, furthermore, indebted to the members – former and current – of the Fachbereich Alte Geschichte of the University of Zurich, in particular Jens Bartels, Ursula Kunnert and Marie-Louise von Wartburg; to the participants of the Forschungskolloquium of the Fachbereich, who patiently endured many a trial run for ideas and exploratory work for the study at hand; to the eager students of the spring term of 2016, who helped in shaping a better understanding of the subject matter.

I owe special thanks to Jose Cáceres Mardones (Zurich), who has always been a most authoritative companion, both scientific and mundane; to Nikolas Hächler (Zurich), the most well-mannered scientific disputant, colleague and friend; to Anna Willi (Zurich, London), Roman Wild (Zurich), Cornelia Ritter-Schmalz (Zurich), Adrian Brändli (Oxford, Zurich), Matthias Zimmermann (Zurich, Fribourg), Konradin Eigler (Zurich, Freiburg), Marco Vitale (Oxford, Zurich) for their conversations, interest and help; to Fritz Hartmann (St Gallen), who generously facilitated my scientific and literary curiosity; to all the individuals who have helped in making this become reality. Family and friends have been invaluable in reminding me of life beyond the ivory tower and historical research. Thank you.

That this book sees the light of day is due to Michael Sharp, who kindly accepted my work for publication by Cambridge University Press. I am thankful for his knowledgeable and protective editorship.

In having incessantly fostered and enabled my pursuit of my own interests and choices, my parents, Josef and Annemarie, are a significant part of this endeavour. Esther has not only been a model of patience and understanding, but also the dependable and loving centre of my life. This book is dedicated to them, without whom nothing.

Abbreviations

The abbreviations of the names of ancient writers and their works adopted here are the ones used in the index of the *Thesaurus Linguae Latinae*[1] and Liddell-Scott-Jones' *Greek–English Lexicon*.[2] Short forms of epigraphic *corpora* follow the usage of Clauss-Slaby's *Epigraphik-Datenbank*.[3] Journals are abbreviated according to the usage of *L'Année Philologique*. For the sake of convenience, the abbreviations of epigraphic corpora and reference works used in the text are reproduced below.

Acquasparta	P. Bruschetti and R. Pastura (2005). 'Acquasparta. Iscrizioni in Palazzo Cesi'. In: *Epigraphica* 67, pp. 473–485.
AE	*L'Année épigraphique* (1889–). Paris.
Aesernia	Marco Buonocore (2003). *Molise. Repertorio delle iscrizioni latine. Le iscrizioni. 5, 2: Le iscrizioni di Aesernia*. Ed. by Gianfranco De Benedittis. Campobasso: Palladino.
Allifae	Nicola Mancini (2005). *Allifae*. Piedimonte Matese: Tip. Bandista.
CAG	Michel Provost, Jean-Marie Pailler, et al. (2017). *Carte archéologique de la Gaule. Toulouse. 31/3*. Paris: Académie des Inscriptions et Belles Lettres.
CartNova	Juan Manuel Abascal Palazón and Sebastián F. Ramallo Asensio, eds. (1997). *La ciudad de Carthago Nova. 3: La documentación epigráfica*. Murcia: EDITUM.

---

[1] Thesaurus linguae Latinae, ed. (1990). *Index librorum scriptorum inscriptionum ex quibus exempla afferuntur*. Editio altera. Leipzig: Teubner.
[2] H. G. Liddell and R. Scott (1996). *Greek–English Lexicon*. Revised and augmented by H. S. Jones with the assistance of R. McKenzie and with the cooperation of many scholars. With a revised supplement. Oxford: Clarendon Press.
[3] www.manfredclauss.de.

CCCA	Maarten Jozef Vermaseren (1977–1989). *Corpus Cultus Cybelae Attidisque (CCCA)*. Leiden: Brill.
CCID	Monika Hörig and Elmar Schwertheim (1987). *Corpus Cultus Iovis Dolicheni (CCID)*. Leiden: Brill.
CEACelio	Gian Luca Gregori, ed. (2001). *La collezione epigrafica dell'Antiquarium Comunale del Celio. Inventario generale, inediti, revisioni, contributi al riordino*. Rome: Quasar.
CECapitol	Silvio Panciera (1987). *La collezione epigrafica dei musei Capitolini*. Rome: Ed. di storia e letteratura.
CECasapulla	Laura Chioffi (2007). *La collezione epigrafica di Camillo Pellegrino a Casapulla*. Rome: Quasar.
CEL	Paolo Cugusi, ed. (1992, 2002). *Corpus Epistularum Latinarum Papyris Tabulis Ostracis servatarum. Vol. I Textus, Vol. II Commentarius, Vol. III Addenda, Corrigenda, Indices rerum, Index verborum omnium*. Florence: Gonnelli.
ChLA	Albert Bruckner and Robert Marichal, eds. (1954–1998). *Chartae Latinae Antiquiores. 1–49*. Dietikon, Zurich: Urs Graf Verlag.
CIG	August Boeck et al., eds. (1828–1877). *Corpus Inscriptionum Graecarum*. Berlin: Akademie.
CIL	*Corpus Inscriptionum Latinarum* (1862–). Berlin: de Gruyter.
CIMRM	Maarten Jozef Vermaseren (1956–1960). *Corpus Inscriptionum et Monumentorum Religionis Mithriacae, 2 Vols.* The Hague: Martinus Nijhoff.
CLE	Franz Bücheler and Ernst Lommatzsch, eds. (1895–1926). *Carmina Latina Epigraphica*. Leipzig: Teubner.
CSIR	*Corpus Signorum Imperii Romani* (1964–).
Devijver	Hubert Devijver (1976–2001). *Prosopographia militarium equestrium quae fuerunt ab Augusto ad Gallienum*. Ed. by Ségolène Demougin and Marie-Thérèse Raepsaet-Charlier. Leuven: Universitaire Pers.
EAOR	Patrizia Sabbatini Tumolesi, ed. (1988–). *Epigrafia anfiteatrale dell'Occidente Romano*. Rome: Quasar.
EE	*Ephemeris Epigraphica. Corporis Inscriptionum Latinarum Supplementum edita iussu Instituti archeologici Romani* (1872–1913). Berlin.
ERAlavesa	Juan Carlos Elorza (1967). *Ensayo topografico de epigrafia romana Alavesa*. Vitoria: Dip. Foral da Alava.

EURom	Heikki Solin (1975). *Epigraphische Untersuchungen in Rom und Umgebung*. Helsinki: Soumalainen Tiedeakatemia.
FCap	Attilio Degrassi, ed. (1954). *Fasti Capitolini*. Turin: Paravia.
FIRA	Salvator Riccobono et al., eds. (1968). *Fontes iuris Romani anteiustiniani*. 2nd edn. Florence.
Franchetti	Maryline G. Parca (1995). *The Franchetti Collection in Rome. Inscriptions and Sculptural Fragments*. Rome: Quasar.
GLIA	Stephen Mitchell and David French (2012). *The Greek and Latin Inscriptions of Ankara (Ancyra)*. Munich: C. H. Beck.
GLISwedish	Bengt E. Thomasson (1997). *A Survey of Greek and Latin Inscriptions on Stone in Swedish Collections*. Stockholm: Åström.
IAnkara	David French (2003). *Roman, Late Roman and Byzantine Inscriptions of Ankara. A Selection*. Ankara: Museum of Anatolian Civilizations.
IATrebula	Heikki Solin, ed. (1993). *Le iscrizioni antiche die Trebula, Caiatia e Cubulteria*. Caserta: Associazione Storica del Caiatino.
ICUR	*Inscriptiones Christianae urbis Romae. Nova series* (1922–). Rome.
IDR	*Inscriptiones Daciae Romanae* (1975–). Bucharest.
IDRE	Constantin C. Petolescu (1996–). *Inscriptiones Daciae Romanae. Inscriptiones extra fines Daciae repertae*. Bucharest: Editura enciclopedică.
I.Ephesos	Hermann Wankel et al., eds. (1979–1984). *Die Inschriften von Ephesos*. Inschriften griechischer Städte aus Kleinasien 11–17.4. Bonn: Habelt.
IG	*Inscriptiones Graecae* (1902–). Berlin.
IGI-Napoli	Elena Miranda (1990–1995). *Iscrizioni greche d'Italia. Napoli*. Rome: Quasar.
IGLFriuli	Fulvia Mainardis (2004). *Aliena saxa. Le iscrizioni greche e latine conservate nel Friuli-Venezia Giulia ma non pertinenti ai centri antichi della regione*. Rome: Accademia Nazionale dei Lincei.
IGLMessina	Irma Bitto (2001). *Le iscrizioni greche e latine di Messina*. Messina: DiScAM.

IGRRP	René Cagnat (1901–1927). *Inscriptiones Graecae ad Res Romanas Pertinentes*. Paris: Laroux.
IGUR	Luigi Moretti (1968–1990). *Inscriptiones Graecae Urbis Romae*. Rome: Istituto Italiano per la Storia Antica.
IK	Kommission für die Archäologische Erforschung Kleinasiens, ed. (1972–). *Inschriften griechischer Städte aus Kleinasien*. Bonn: Habelt.
IKöln	Brigitte Galsterer and Hartmut Galsterer (2010). *Die römischen Steininschriften aus Köln. IKöln.* 2nd ed. Mainz: Philipp von Zabern.
ILAfr	René Cagnat (1923). *Inscriptions latines d'Afrique (Tripolitaine, Tunisie, Maroc)*. Paris.
ILAlg	*Inscriptions latines d'Algérie* (1922–2003). Paris: H. Champion.
ILBulg	Boris Gerov (1989). *Inscriptiones Latinae in Bulgaria repertae*. Sofia: Kliment Ohridski.
ILCV	Ernst Diehl, ed. (1925–1967). *Inscriptiones Latinae Christianae Veteres*. Berlin: Weidmann.
ILD	Constantin C. Petolescu (2005). *Inscripții latine din Dacia (ILD). Inscriptiones latinae Daciae*. Bucharest: Editura Academiei Române.
ILJug	Anna Šašel and Jaro Šašel (1963–1986). *Inscriptiones latinae quae in Iugoslavia inter annos MCMXL et MCMLX repertae et editae sunt*. Ljubljana: Narodni muzej.
ILLRP	Attilio Degrassi (1937–1963). *Inscriptiones Latinae liberae rei publicae*. Göttingen: Vandenhoeck & Ruprecht.
ILLRP-S	Silvio Panciera et al. (1991). 'Inscriptiones Latinae liberae rei publicae'. In: *Epigrafia. Actes du colloque international d'épigraphie latine en mémoire de Attilio Degrassi pour le centenaire de sa naissance. Actes du colloque de Rome (27–28 mai 1988)*. Rome: École Française de Rome, pp. 241–491.
ILLRP.Imagines	Attilio Degrassi (1965). *Inscriptiones Latinae liberae rei publicae. Imagines*. Berlin: de Gruyter.
ILMN	Giuseppe Camodeca (2000). *Catalogo delle iscrizioni latine del Museo nazionale di Napoli, ILMN*. Naples: Loffredo.
ILN	*Inscriptions Latines de Narbonnaise (I. L. N)* (1985–). Paris: CNRS.

ILPBardo	Zeïneb Benzina Ben Abdallah (1986). *Catalogue des Inscriptions latines païennes du Musée du Bardo*. Rome: École Française de Rome.
ILS	Hermann Dessau, ed. (1892–1916). *Inscriptiones latinae selectae*. Berlin.
ILSanMichele	Hilding Thylander (1962). 'Inscriptions latines de San Michele d'Axel Munthe'. In: *Opuscula Romana* 4, pp. 129–157.
ILTun	Alfred Merlin (1944). *Inscriptions latines de la Tunisie*. Paris: Presses Universitaires de France.
IMCCatania	Kalle Korhonen (2004). *Le iscrizioni del museo civico di Catania*. Helsinki: Societas Scientiarum Fennica.
InscrAqu	Johannes Baptista Brusin (1991–1993). *Inscriptiones Aquileiae*. Pubblicazioni della Deputazione di Storia Patria per il Friuli 20. Udine: Deputazione di Storia Patria per il Friuli.
InscrIt	*Inscriptiones Italiae* (1931–). Rome.
IPOstia	Hilding Thylander (1951–1952). *Inscriptions du port d'Ostie*. Lund: Gleerup.
IRComo	Antonio Sartori (1994). *Le Iscrizioni Romane. Guida all'esposizione*. Como: Musei Civici.
IRPAlicante	Manuel Abilio Rabanal Alonso and Juan Manuel Abascal Palazón (1985). 'Inscripciones Romanas de la provincia de Alicante'. In: *Lucentum* 4, pp. 191–244.
IScM	*Inscriptiones Scythiae Minoris Graecae et Latinae* 2 (1980–). Bucharest.
ISIS	Anne Helttula (2007). *Le iscrizioni sepolcrali latine nell' Isola sacra*. Rome: Institutum Romanum Finlandiae.
LapSav	Tóth Endre (2011). *Lapidarium Savariense*. Szombathely.
LIKelsey	Steven L. Tuck (2005). *Latin Inscriptions in the Kelsey Museum. The Dennison and De Criscio Collections*. Ann Arbor: University of Michigan Press.
LMentana	Guido Barbieri, ed. (1982). *Il lapidario Zeri di Mentana*. Rome: Istituto italiano per la storia antica.
P. Mich.	Herbert Chayyim Youtie and John Garrett Winter, eds. (1951). *Papyri and Ostraca from Karanis. Second Series*. Ann Arbor: University of Michigan Press.
Pflaum	Hans-Georg Pflaum (1960–1982). *Les carrières procuratoriennes équestres sous le Haut-Empire romain*. Paris: Geuthner.

PIR¹	Elimar Krebs et al., eds. (1897–1898). *Prosopographia Imperii Romani I. II. III.* Berlin: G. Reimer.
PIR²	Klaus Wachtel et al., eds. (1933–). *Prosopographia Imperii Romani saec. I. II. III.* Editio altera. Berlin: de Gruyter.
RDGE	Robert K. Sherk, ed. (1969). *Roman Documents from the Greek East. Senatus consulta and epistulae to the Age of Augustus.* Baltimore: The Johns Hopkins Press.
RECapua	Laura Chioffi (2005). *Museo provinciale Campano di Capua. La raccolta epigrafica.* Capua: Museo provinciale campano.
RIB II	R. G. Collingwood et al., eds. (1990–1995). *The Roman Inscriptions of Britain. Volume II. Instrumentum Domesticum.* Oxford: Alan Sutton.
RICIS	Laurent Bricault (2005). *Receuil des inscriptions concernant les cultes isiaques (RICIS).* Paris: De Boccard.
RIU	*Die römischen Inschriften Ungarns* (1972–). Budapest: Enciklopédia Kiadó.
Roman Statutes	Michael H. Crawford, ed. (1996). *Roman Statutes.* 2 Volumes. Bulletin of the Institute of Classical Studies. Supplement 64. London: University of London.
Schiavi	Marco Buonocore (1984b). *Schiavi e liberti dei Volusi Saturnini. Le iscrizioni del colombario sulla via Appia antica.* Rome: Bretschneider.
SCPP	Werner Eck, Antonio Caballos, and Fernández Fernando (1996). *Das senatus consultum de Cn. Pisone patre.* Vestigia 48. Munich: C. H. Beck.
SEG	*Supplementum epigraphicum Graecum* (1923–). Leiden: Brill.
Sinn	Friederike Sinn (1987). *Stadtrömische Marmorurnen.* Mainz: von Zabern.
SIRIS	Ladislav Widman (1969). *Sylloge inscriptionum religionis Isiacae et Sarapiacae.* Berlin: de Gruyter.
SupIt	*Supplementa Italica* (1981–). Rome: Quasar.
tab. Vindon.	Michael A. Speidel (1996). *Die römischen Schreibtafeln von Vindonissa. Lateinische Texte des militärischen Alltags und ihre geschichtliche Bedeutung.* Veröffentlichungen der Gesellschaft Pro Vindonissa 12. Brugg: Gesellschaft Pro Vindonissa.
Thomasson	Bengt E. Thomasson (1972–2009). *Laterculi Praesidum.* Goteborg: Bokförlaget Radius.

TitAq	Péter Kovács and Ádám Szabó, eds. (2009–2011). *Tituli Aquincenses I–III*. Budapest: Pytheas.
WT	Roger S. O. Tomlin (2016). *Roman London's First Voices: Writing Tablets from the Bloomberg Excavations, 2010–14*. MOLA Monograph 72. London: Museum of London Archaeology MOLA.

*A*gain *his eyes were drawn to the* comitium *lying beneath him on the forum. Again he felt the anxiety that had haunted him since before dawn. He wasn't even sure if he had slept at all, kept awake by wheels clattering on the cobblestones, the muted sounds of the sleepless city. Any other night he would have been able to ignore the noise, but this night was different. It didn't help that he was now engaged in preparing the very event that was the source of his disquiet. Again he stole a glance at the circular enclosure where the tribes used to elect the magistrates. For a moment he saw himself standing in the midst of the crowd, his white toga resplendent in the blinding summer sun, donned with the broad purple band of the aedile-elect. Among the people stood his father, Annius, in sheer disbelief that his own son, the son of a freedman, could make it as far as the Roman senate. His father had already been more than content when he had aspired to become an* apparitor *of the Roman magistrates. 'Cnaeus Flavius,* scriba *of the Roman people'. It had a certain ring to it. Things started to happen very fast when he was allotted to serve Appius Claudius. Looking back, the random lot that was picked that early December morning didn't seem entirely coincidental now. He didn't even consider himself a revolutionary. Sure, he knew the hardships of the common people from personal experience. But he had considered the order to be God-given. Appius had opened his eyes, an experience he shared with so many others. Change was possible. He himself was living proof of it. He had learnt the legal calendar by heart, betrayed the priests, smuggled their jealously guarded treasure out of their precinct. Sure, he had become a* scriba *on Appius' behalf, the publication of the priestly arcana had been his idea. He couldn't have done it without the protection of his patron, who had assumed responsibility. The duped aristocrats would have eaten him alive. But now, some years later, he couldn't help but accept it as his own achievement. Not for no reason had he become a favourite of the plebs. And they had vowed to help him on even further. — Clamour from the entrance area of the* aerarium *suddenly pulled him back from his reverie. Startled, his otherwise steady hand slipped and left a deep impression in the wax surface of the writing tablet that lay before him. It was the tablet that was supposed to receive the results of the election later that day. He smiled.*

CHAPTER I

Imagining the Roman Scriba

Knowledge Is Power

The history of the Roman *scribae* is best characterised by a Republican hero. While the prototypical Republican hero was a man of war, Cnaeus Flavius (A.73), our scribal hero, wielded a sharp pen rather than an edged sword. His conquest was not territory, but knowledge. We owe the most picturesque version of Flavius' heroic deeds to Cicero.[1] Flavius, in defiance of his post as a subaltern clerk of the Republican state, discloses to the people legal documents jealously guarded by a small elite. On a daily basis, Flavius diligently learns parts of the texts by heart and subsequently commits them to writing. By eventually publishing the legal rules he manages to trick his superordinates and, in Cicero's words, 'peck out the eyes of the raven'. Flavius' release of the *fasti* and *legis actiones* – later aptly known as the *ius civile Flavianum*[2] – publicised knowledge pivotal for the initiation of legal action. This knowledge was power and thanks to the *scriba* it finally left the hands of the privileged few.

Cn. Flavius' motives and, in fact, even the particulars of his life are obscured by conflicting narratives of the Republican annalistic tradition. It may come as no surprise that the story of our scribal hero was politically charged. Set at the very end of the fourth century BC, Flavius' career had by the Middle Republic become an epitome of the Struggle of the Orders. The son of a freedman, backed by the *plebs* and through his apparitorial post as *scriba* closely associated with its champion, the *censor* Appius Claudius Caecus, managed to snatch the *ius civile* from the aristocracy, and later be elected curule aedile and tribune of the plebs himself only to be despised as a social and political upstart by his new peers in the Roman senate.[3]

---

[1] Cic. *Mur.* 25.
[2] Dig. 1. 2. 2. 7.
[3] The analysis of the annalistic tradition in Wolf (1980). Cn. Flavius mentioned in Piso *frg.* F29 (FRH) = Gell. 7. 9. 1–6; D.S. 20. 36. 6; Cic. *Mur.* 25; Cic. *de orat.* 1. 186; Cic. *Att.* 6. 1. 8; Liv. 9. 46. 1–12; Liv. *perioch.* 9; V. Max. 2. 5. 2; 9. 3. 3; Plin. *nat.* 33. 17–19; Dig. 1. 2. 2. 7; Macr. 1. 15. 9.

Regardless of whether we consider the persona of Cn. Flavius to be historical or merely a convenient product of annalistic fiction, it is certainly no coincidence that we find him to be a *scriba*. As such he plausibly fitted the narrative, political colour notwithstanding. By stripping the various narrative strands of their factionist embellishment, J. G. Wolf has convincingly shown that the main theme of Flavius' story was the political and social advancement of a man of humble origins to the heights of the Roman magistracy and the senate.[4] Indeed, the 'appritorial world was the world of the social climber', as N. Purcell has put it with regard to the *scribae*.[5] Yet, it was not only this main theme that made a *scriba* a plausible figure for this specific scenario. Social mobility was only a consequence of the *scriba*'s place in the Roman world in general. In a world in which literacy and power were aristocratically monopolised, the *scriba* was able to participate in both – even though his low social origin and his ancillary profession did not initially allow for such influence. His scribal post brought him close to the powerful. His role as an expert in literate practice set the arcana of the state in the form of legal and financial documents at his disposal. Admittedly, the *scriba*'s power was collateral[6] and precarious, and influence and money often came at a price: abuse of position.

Cn. Flavius, in this sense, serves as the quintessential prototype, exemplifying the world of the Republican *scriba* in a nutshell.[7] The implications of his humble origins and subordinate profession contrast and clash with the potential of his specialised skills, his social and political affiliations and, as a consequence, his position of intimate knowledge and trust. It is obvious that the annalistic vignette of the *scriba* Flavius is an exaggerated one. Flavius, as the first Roman *scriba* we know by name, already represents the apex of his kind, both in terms of social mobility and political power. Nevertheless, his legacy lived on. The key issues raised by Flavius' life and deeds echo through the entire history of the Roman *scriba*-ship.

It is these key issues of Roman *scriba*-ship that I will explore in the course of this study to arrive at a history of the Roman *scribae*. The study is, thus, much less chronological than it is thematic. I do not, in the first place, aim to write an institutional history of the appritorial office of the Roman *scriba*. I am much more interested in the societal and cultural implications of the *scriba*'s professional expertise and his consequent position in the

---

[4] Wolf (1980) 28.
[5] Purcell (1983) 136.
[6] This characterisation with regard to the appritorial *accensi* by Stefano Manzella (2000).
[7] Purcell (2001) 637.

Roman apparatus of state. I aim, therefore, to place the Roman *scriba* in Roman society and culture. What did it mean to be a Roman *scriba* – both in terms of professional skill as well as social status and public prestige?

Scribal Capital

Roman society was predominantly hierarchical. As such, social rank and social status were two parts of the same equation.[8] However, status was not a fixed entity in Roman society, it was alterable and negotiable. Status changes and thus social mobility were a reality, especially for the Roman *scribae*.[9] As I will try to show, a crucial factor in the prospects of social advancement and change of social status of the *scribae* was their professional expertise, their mastery of literate practices.

What empowered *scribae* was what the French anthropologist and sociologist Pierre Bourdieu has categorised as 'cultural capital'. As part of his larger theory of social class negotiated by 'taste'-distinctions ('habitus'), Bourdieu postulated different forms of capital at play.[10] In marked contrast to Marxist and economic class theory and following Max Weber,[11] Bourdieu sought to incorporate non-economic factors into his explanation of the workings of societal stratification and social status. He thus defined capital more broadly as 'accumulated labor'.[12] Besides 'economic capital' (wealth) he established the categories of 'social capital' (social connections) and 'cultural capital' (cultural and intellectual assets). In Bourdieu's model, these forms of capital may appear as either 'materialised' (objects) or 'embodied' (knowledge), enabling social actors to 'appropriate social energy in the form of reified or living labor'.[13] This 'social energy' may be transformed into one of the three forms of capital or, ultimately, into the fourth form of 'symbolic capital', i.e. prestige and status. In Bourdieu's system, 'cultural capital' and social origin together form the nucleus on which the accumulation of the other forms of capital depends, thus stressing the importance of birth and socialisation – a concept very familiar to Roman society.

---

[8] See the overview of the relevant research by Peachin (2011); on the question of the general characterisation of Roman society see the discussion in Alföldy (2011), especially 197–205 with a discussion of the critique on his 'soziale Pyramide' 196; on the disputed question of a Roman middle class most recently Mayer (2012) 1–21.
[9] On the *scribae* and the other *apparitores* already Purcell (1983).
[10] Most concisely Bourdieu (1986).
[11] Weber's theory of stratification postulated, in addition to economic classes, status ('Stand'), which was defined by non-economic factors, (2002) 534–8.
[12] Bourdieu (1986) 46.
[13] Bourdieu (1986) 46.

I intend to make use of Bourdieu's framework of different 'capitals' to systematise and rationalise my argument about the role and place of the *scribae* in Roman society. Bourdieu's model naturally allows us to adequately incorporate the aspect that defined Roman *scribae* the most: their skill in reading, writing and reckoning, which set them apart from a major part of Roman society. As obsessed as Romans (or rather the elite) were with social origin and property, individual skill and prowess carried weight nonetheless. I will argue that it was the *scriba*'s 'embodied cultural capital', his expertise in literacy and numeracy, which allowed him, by way of his public office, to attain important social connections ('social capital') in the first place. These social connections eventually entailed the possibility of the accumulation of wealth ('economic capital'). All three 'capitals' bore the possibility of a change in status, i.e. the acquisition of 'symbolic capital'. Literacy skills, social connections and wealth were prerequisites for the *scriba*'s social mobility, his place in Roman society.

The study is divided along the lines of these different prerequisites. A first part deals with the *scriba* in his role as an expert in literacy and literate practice. Being able to read, write and reckon was an undeniable asset in a society only partially literate and numerate, even more so when the state eventually came to rely heavily on this knowledge for its functioning in financial and legal administration. A look at Roman literacies in general and Roman literate administrative and archival practice in particular reveals the importance of the Roman *scribae* for the functioning of Roman administration. The *scribae* were strongly linked to the *tabulae publicae*, the repository of knowledge of the Roman state, archived on large-format wax tablets. They were the veritable guardians of these *tabulae*, of the knowledge they contained and of what they stood for symbolically.

A second part is dedicated to the structure and workings of the apparitorial system of the *scribae*. The system as such, as well as the recruitment and assignment of *scribae*, was well-regulated. The apparitorial system was, after all, a substantial part of the Roman constitutional state. This system, however, was susceptible to the peculiarities of Roman social relations. Patronage and partisanship played a significant part in the world of the *scribae*. The appointment of a *scriba* was not an apolitical, bureaucratic act, but instead was highly politicised. After all, installing a confidant as *scriba* could mean influence and access to power – not only for the patron, but also for the protégé.

A third part addresses the subversive side of the role of the *scribae* in the Roman state. The combination of expertise, position and socio-political enmeshment discussed in the preceding parts opened the doors to abuse and embezzlement. *Scribae*, in their role as bookkeepers and archivists, stood with their own social reputation for the integrity of the records they administered. As a result, they were the ones to bribe and, indeed, frequently lined their own pockets. The discourse of malpractice is a constant in the history of the Roman *scribae*. The position was, in general, a financially lucrative one, attractive to both honest and less honest characters.

A fourth part investigates the Roman *scribae* and their place in Roman society, both as individuals and as a social group. Social mobility was a constant in the history of the Roman *scribae*. It was the combination of stereotypically low social origin with the prestige and the social and financial possibilities opened up by the scribal post that resulted in social advancement and made for truly extraordinary careers. Besides legendary Republican tales of *scribae* become senators, the social reality of most Roman *scribae* was the aspiration towards the equestrian order.

A final, fifth part serves at the same time as a conclusion and as an epilogue to *scriba*-ship in the Later Roman Empire. The Roman *scriba*-ship did not just cease to exist with Diocletian's reordering of the Roman state. The idea of the *scriba* lived on, albeit in various forms.

Evidence Lost

The scope of this book is – naturally – limited by our sources on the Roman *scribae*. And limited it is indeed. We are seemingly confronted with a paradox. Although we are dealing with a group of people that was tasked with the making, keeping and using[14] of an enormous body of written text in antiquity, we are completely deprived of the day-to-day work of the *scribae*. Not a single scrap of what *scribae* have written survives.[15] The peculiarities of the support material ensured that nothing would ever reach modern times. The Roman state mainly made use of wooden wax tablets (*tabulae ceratae*) and, to a lesser extent, sheets of papyrus (*chartae*) whenever it chose to document its administrative activities.[16] Unfortunately, organic material is prone to decay and decompose; only specific, anaerobic

---

[14] The idea of these three different and not necessarily consequential steps in dealing with written documents in Clanchy (1993) 154.
[15] See the survey of Roman archives and archival practice aptly named *la mémoire perdue* in Nicolet (1994), continued in Moatti (1998), Moatti (2000), and Moatti (2001); with respect to the *scribae* emphatically Purcell (2001) 634.
[16] Only a small percentage of text shelved in the archives, especially legal texts, made it onto more durable materials such as stone and especially metal. Their durability was limited as well, see Williamson (1987), Eck (2014), and Kolb (2015).

conditions preserve these precious ancient documents[17] – conditions not met in the Roman capital. More importantly, what was recorded were administrative legal and financial procedures. The fate of these documents was closely connected to the political system they documented. They were, thus, bound to become obsolete. The nature of the documents, especially the financial ones, made sure that their end would come sooner rather than later. There are few things more prone to catch fire than debts recorded on waxed wood.[18]

A look over the *scriba*'s shoulder on the basis of his own professional writings is thus not possible. What we are left with are images of the *scriba*'s labour in the texts of other writers. Unfortunately, our literary sources are not specifically interested in the work and life of *scribae* as such. Rather, *scribae* mainly fill the role of supernumeraries in the plays of – in the eyes of the upper-class authors – more important actors. As a result, the corpus of sources on *scribae* mainly consists of short mentions, allowing the occasional glimpse of their regular professional or private lives. It is only in special cases such as the tale of Cn. Flavius that *scribae* steal the spotlight. In these cases, as we have seen, their role most often becomes controversial: they act, in the words of N. Purcell, as 'paragons of the problematic'.[19] Naturally, the obvious and regular did not need telling. The exceptional was deemed much more interesting by our historical informants and their audience. One of the most prominent ancient *scribae*, the Augustan poet Q. Horatius Flaccus (A.88), may serve as a case in point. While his extensive œuvre paints a vivid picture of his life and times, his activities as *scriba* are mentioned only at the sidelines and very sparingly. Work to rule was beneath notice. Much more interesting was behaviour out of the ordinary, when *scribae* transgressed professional or social boundaries, such as M. Claudius Glicia (A.42), who was named *dictator* by P. Claudius Pulcher in 249 BC, or the infamous Maevius (A.109), who was C. Verres' accomplice in plundering the province of Sicily in the late seventies of the first century BC, to name just two of the most prominent.

What we know about the *scribae* from literary sources is, as a result, very often a picture in the negative, documenting the extraordinary. The

---

[17] See for example the case of *tabulae ceratae* in Hartmann (2015).
[18] A certain Q. Sosius is said to have set alight the central archive, the *tabularium*, in the first quarter of the first century BC; CIC. *nat. deor.* 3.74. Hadrian's general debt relief is later achieved by officially and publicly burning the respective *tabulae ceratae*; see the relief depiction on the so-called Plutei Traiani (Fig. 2.2), Koeppel (1986) 21–3 no. 2, cf. *CIL* 6, 967; DIO 69.8.1². Cf. the debt relief by Aurelian, HIST. AUG. *Aurelian.* 39.1. On the deliberate destruction of compromising documentary evidence in general see Moreau (1994) 141–3.
[19] Purcell (2001) 638.

ordinary is not completely lost to us, however. In describing the overstepping of the accepted bounds, these negatives can show us the professional, social and cultural limits of *scriba*-ship. They convey idealised pictures of *scribae* and their role in Roman political, social and cultural life as they were seen at any given time. This outside view is mainly limited to the Roman Republic, however. Not very surprisingly, Cicero is our main source. His intimate knowledge and analysis of the political and administrative system as well as his interest in Roman social relations make his writings a treasure chest for the history of the late Republican *scribae*. In particular, his speeches against C. Verres and his partners in crime, among them *scribae*, constitute an invaluable resource. *Scribae* and scribal matters mentioned by later writers, such as Dionysius of Halicarnassus, Livy, Plutarch or Cassius Dio, in many cases make reference to Republican times. For the imperial period, literary evidence is scarce; attestations are few and far between. Looking at our narrative sources, one could thus easily take the Roman *scriba* as a Republican phenomenon.

Fortunately, abundant epigraphic evidence supplements our knowledge and greatly expands our picture of imperial *scribae*. While we lack narrative accounts involving *scribae* for the greater part of imperial times, inscriptions provide us with a different access to our subject. Rather than giving an outside view they often let us get closer to the persona behind the label *scriba*, telling us about the individual's career and life as well as – owing to the peculiarities of the epigraphic medium – his self-perception and self-representation. This peculiar historical tradition results in the fact that we know more than 300 imperial *scribae* by name, while our knowledge of Republican ones is restricted to approximately one-sixth of that number. What is more, legal texts pertaining to *scribae*, such as the Sullan *lex Cornelia de XX quaestoribus*, the Caesarian *lex Iulia municipalis* or the *leges coloniae* of *Urso* and *Irni*, survive in epigraphic form and further our understanding of, above all, organisational aspects of Roman *scriba*-ship.

Pictorial testimonies complement the literary and epigraphic sources. Relief representations of *scribae* can be found on sarcophagi and other funerary monuments of magistrates, both in Rome and in the provinces. In such cases, *scribae* are most often depicted as part of a magisterial following of *apparitores*, which was meant to emphasise the importance of the deceased in his public role.[20] Reliably identifying *scribae* in pictorial representations other than such 'Beamtenaufzüge' and *sella curulis* reliefs

---

[20] In general Wrede (1981); Schäfer (1989) nos. 2, 11, 24, 70, 71, 73, 74, 75, 78, 79, C53; Wrede (2001) 71f.

is difficult, however. Contextual information is key as depictions of men holding writing material were a popular motive even outside the circles of writing professionals.[21] Conclusive identification is only possible in two instances. The so-called Ara degli Scribi (see Fig. 5.1), unearthed in the year 2000 at 'vigna Casali' near the Porta S. Sebastiano in Rome, preserves the *memoria* of the two Fulvii brothers (A.81, A.82), who had both been *scribae* of the *aediles curules*. The marble altar is spectacularly decorated, allowing us to envision the *scribae* at their workplace.[22] Another occupational scene is depicted on the funerary inscription of a local *scriba* from the Lucanian colony of Paestum (see Fig. 2.4). The marble slab, only recently found as a spolium in a farmstead outside the limits of the city, shows a certain [Ca]murtius [Se]verus (A.242) busy with the administration of the city's finances.[23] Both monuments allow us to catch rare glimpses of *scribae* in their element. At the same time they represent outstanding testimonies of scribal self-perception of the first decades of the first century AD.

While conclusive identification of depicted *scribae* is difficult, our written sources are more precise. The denomination of *scriba* was an official one. As it entailed privileges and duties it was sanctioned by the Roman state. It is true that there were many other specialists of writing in Roman public and private life. Yet, despite the fact that the word *scriba* itself is of a most unspecific nature, derived from the Latin verb *scribere*, it was used exclusively for people occupying a place as a Roman *apparitor*. By analogy, it was later carried over to designate officially employed or assigned scribal officials in provincial cities in the West, in *collegia* and the Roman fleet. These positions shared the original characteristics of their counterparts in the Roman state: they were bestowed with privileges and duties; they were official functionaries of their respective bodies (see Chapter 3). The fixity of the term is best illustrated by its translation into Greek. *Scriba* was merely transliterated: σκρ(ε)ίβα(ς) became the official denomination. The term γραμματεύς would have been the obvious choice had it not already identified a distinct office of the Greek *poleis* for a long time and continued to do so in Roman times.[24] In fact, Greek writers nevertheless often employed the term γραμματεῖς for Roman *scribae*, yet only when contexts were obvious. Inscriptions speak exclusively of σκρ(ε)ίβαι to avoid confusion with the office of the Eastern *poleis*.

[21] E. A. Meyer (2009).
[22] Rotondi (2010) 136–40; Zevi and Friggeri (2012).
[23] Mello (2012).
[24] Schulte (1994).

This official title makes it relatively easy to keep track of the office of the Roman *scriba* through the ages, from its mythical beginnings at the birth of the Roman Republic at the end of the sixth century BC, to the turmoil of the late Republic and the onset of the Empire, to the Later Roman Empire through to Ostrogothic Italy of the sixth century AD, where we meet with a seeming relict of a distant past. Yet, in tracing the evolution of Roman *scriba*-ship and its consequences for the individual *scriba*'s role in the Roman state and society, we are bound to focus mainly on the late Republic and the early and high Empire. It is the time span for which our sources are most numerous and consistent. At both ends of the spectrum, the testimonies become fewer and more isolated, complicating the acquisition of reliable historical knowledge.

Images of *Scriba*-ship

The scientific quest for historical knowledge on the Roman *scribae* is inextricably linked with the name of the great Theodor Mommsen. It is true that researchers have been interested in the history of writing and thus of scribes in general and *scribae* in particular before Mommsen, especially so since the seventeenth century.[25] Yet, it was the German historian who put the scientific inquiry on this topic on a new footing. Not only did he base his studies on ancient evidence, first and foremost epigraphic testimonies, which he was set on seeking out and editing in his newly created mammoth project of the *Corpus Inscriptionum Latinarum (CIL)*. He also sought to incorporate the Roman *scriba* in the greater context of the organisation of the Roman state and organisation. Already his dissertation of 1843 at the University of Kiel touched upon the subject in an analysis of Sulla's *lex Cornelia de XX quaestoribus*.[26] Five years later, he expanded on organisational questions related to the *apparitores* of the Roman state, especially the *scribae*, on the basis of an analysis of inscriptions of the city of Rome.[27] These studies, substantial as they were in themselves, were mere spadework for his monumental *Römisches Staatsrecht* published in 1871. In a desire to systematise and explain the Roman state in its structure and workings, he covered the Roman *scribae*, together with the remaining 'Dienerschaft der Beamten', as he called it, in the first volume of his opus,

---

[25] Hergött and Bürger (1668); Eschenbach and Spies (1687); C. H. Trotz in Hugo (1738) 451–513.
[26] Mommsen (1843).
[27] Mommsen (1848).

which was devoted to the Roman magistrature.[28] His intimate knowledge of the ancient evidence and its thorough treatment set the benchmark for the next century of scientific research[29] and still represents the foundation of scientific inquiry into the Roman *scribae* today.

Mommsen set out to write the history of Roman Republican institutions according to – as the title *Staatsrecht* suggests – a construed constitutional law.[30] As a result, he treated the *scribae* in the organisational framework of the Roman state. He was interested mainly in the institutionalised office of the Roman *scriba* and its embedding in the apparitorial and magisterial system. He thus portrayed the Roman *scribae* as essential, yet lesser institutional entities tasked with higher scribal duties in a well-ordered apparatus governed by rule of law. The people fulfilling these duties were of secondary importance. After all, Mommsen was a child of his times; he himself would not witness the orientation of historical scholarship towards social history by a fair margin. Nevertheless, to him belongs the credit for drawing attention to the function and importance of the Roman *scribae* in the Roman state. His well-founded and thorough analysis set the unsurpassed standard for similar studies devoted to Roman institutional history for decades to come. The Roman *scribae* were now an integral part of Roman history.[31]

With the advent of social history in the second half of the twentieth century, the Roman *scribae* became the subject of new questions. They were still treated only in relation to other contexts, however. The common focus of historical scholarship now lay on the question of social groups and their access to political power and wealth and, as a consequence, social mobility, be it in the context of Roman freedmen,[32] senators,[33] *apparitores*,[34] or knights.[35] It was as late as 1989 that Ernst Badian offered an exclusive treatment of *scribae*, looking at the prosopography and the social relations of

---

[28] Mommsen (1887) I 346–55. The page numbers are those of the final third edition, which will be cited throughout this study.
[29] August Krause's very similar and by no means less scientific and thorough study (1858) on the Roman *scribae* that preceded Mommsen's by more than ten years was made obsolete and is mainly forgotten today.
[30] Rebenich (2002) 118.
[31] Mostly dependent on or heavily influenced by Mommsen Herzog (1884–1891) I 855–8, 863–6; Karlowa (1885–1901) I 193–200; Kornemann (1921); Cencetti (1940) 40–2; A. H. M. Jones (1949); still Muñiz Coello (1982).
[32] Treggiari (1969) 153–9.
[33] Wiseman (1971) 70–4.
[34] Purcell (1983) and Cohen (1984).
[35] Demougin (1988) 707–12.

the Republican holders of the post.³⁶ What emerged from all these studies was the picture of a self-conscious and confident, yet heterogenous group of skilled professionals, most often tied to powerful patrons, with considerable access to both power and wealth through their occupation – a position that enabled them to challenge established structures and climb socially. Mommsen's orderly and somewhat static image had become more organic and historical. A look at the scientific successor of Mommsen's *Staatsrecht* in the Handbuch der Altertumswissenschaft by Wolfgang Kunkel and Roland Wittmann, published at the end of the twentieth century, exemplifies these changes in the research landscape. In their understanding of the Roman Republic, the post of *scriba* in theory held significant responsibility and power, requiring substantial professional knowledge. In reality, however, *scribae* are portrayed as corrupt, professionally unfit owners of sinecures, who were mainly interested in the furthering of their own financial and social standing.³⁷

Already in his important study of apparitorial social mobility of 1983, Nicholas Purcell had drawn attention to the connection of the Roman *scriba* with the 'world of literary culture' and learning.³⁸ Finally, in his seminal 2001 paper, suggestively titled 'The *Ordo Scribarum*: A Study in the Loss of Memory', Purcell brought this aspect to the fore and specifically asked for the role of literacy in the history of the Roman *scriba*.³⁹ As a result, he characterised the history of Republican *scribae* as an episodic struggle for the precarious control of knowledge against (and with) members of the aristocracy, who sought to preserve their monopoly. His image of the *scribae* is a rather dark and pessimistic one of people with access to knowledge and power neglecting their primary duty out of partisan motives and self-enrichment. He defines the *scribae* by their 'apparent incompetence and corruption' while acknowledging their importance and merits for the Republican administration.⁴⁰ Focusing on the primary duty and practical work of the *scribae*, Adalberto Giovannini, on the other hand, has painted a slightly brighter picture. He characterises the *scribae* as knowledgeable archivists, savant in handling documents and their content and filling an intermediary role between document and

---

³⁶ Badian (1989). An earlier treatment of the Roman *scribae* by Muñiz Coello (1982) was conceptually very much based on Mommsen's effort and did not succeed in going much beyond its model.
³⁷ Kunkel and Wittmann (1995) 116–19.
³⁸ Purcell (1983) 142–6.
³⁹ Purcell (2001).
⁴⁰ Purcell (2001) 634 (quotation), 663.

public.⁴¹ I intend to try to expand on these broad outlines of Roman *scriba*-ship.⁴²

It is the question of literacy that, I believe, defined the Roman *scribae* the most – our skewed historical tradition notwithstanding. It will thus stand, as outlined above, at the beginning of the following inquiry into the history of the Roman *scribae*. A scrutiny and re-evaluation of the available source material will yield new results with regard to the Roman *scribae* and their role in literate practices in particular and their position in the Roman literate landscape in general. Attitudes towards literacy and the written must inevitably have had consequences for one of its main representatives. Or put differently: what was the role of literacy in the making of the Roman *scriba*? This search for the cultural history of the Roman *scriba* will help to contrast and understand the other aspects of Roman *scriba*-ship that rank much higher in our body of sources and have thus been more obvious starting points of scientific enquiry in the past.

As scientific research has, naturally, been guided by the body of source material, and especially so by the literary sources, the Roman Republic has been the obvious focal point for enquiries into the history of the Roman *scribae*. Admittedly, as will become clear, the Roman Republic constituted the 'classical' phase in the history of this institution, as the office had evolved out of the necessities of the Roman Republican state. With the Augustan *res publica restituta* and its imperial successors, the functions of the office of *scriba* were bound to change together with its altered place in the structure of the reconstituted state. Its history did not end then and there, however. The Republican institutions were, at least at face value, still intact. And the office of *scriba* was more than a mere husk of its classical model.

---

[41] Giovannini (1998) 117–22.
[42] For some preliminary considerations see Hartmann (2018).

CHAPTER 2

The Human Archive

The same steady adherence to principle, and correct regard for truth, which always marked my conduct, marks it still. I am call'd Old Honesty; sometimes Upright Telltruth, Esq., and I own it tickles my vanity a little.
                                Charles Lamb, Letter to John Chambers, *1818*

Consequences of Literacy

The history of the Roman *scriba* begins with an Etruscan scribe. When, in 507 BC, the Etruscan king Lars Porsenna besieged the city of Rome, a young Roman nobleman named C. Mucius set out to relieve the city and save the young Republic. He planned on murdering Porsenna in cold blood. Yet, it was the king's scribe who took the blow. It was not an act of loyal selflessness from the scribe that caused the incident, however, but rather mere ignorance. Mucius failed to correctly identify the Etruscan king. He had caught Porsenna and his scribe in the act of paying the soldiers. It was the scribe's busyness and the soldiers' interaction with him that deceived Mucius. As both the king and the scribe were very similarly clad, the young Roman picked the wrong target.

The historian Livy, who vividly depicts the scene almost half a millennium later,[1] uses the term *scriba* to denominate the Etruscan scribe. Obviously, Livy had updated an earlier account of the legendary subject for his late Republican audience.[2] Yet, the update must have been a fitting one. The Romans apparently believed they had adopted an Etruscan model of the apparitorial posts for their own magistrates.[3] And in fact, scribes and other magisterial personnel can be found on Etruscan relief depictions from

---

[1] Liv. 2. 12. 1–16.
[2] The earliest extant fragment of the episode from the second century BC in Cass. Hem. *frg.* F20 (FRH).
[3] Liv. 1. 8. 3.

the fifth century BC, which are in striking agreement with Livy's account.⁴ It is, after all, a truism that the social and political system of the Romans developed alongside and under the influence of the Etruscans.⁵ Livy's approximation of the Roman *scriba* to its Etruscan counterpart might thus very well have had a basis in early history (see Chapter 3).⁶

Unfortunately, reconstructing early Republican *scriba*-ship is a near impossibility. We lack reliable and conclusive evidence. Livy's episode is a case in point. If we were to believe Livy's account, the Roman apparitorial post must have constituted a marked departure from its Etruscan predecessor. Mucius' deception is made possible, in the first place, by the misreading of Etruscan conditions by application of a Roman model. Mucius correctly deduced from the situation that the one Etruscan besides the king involved in handing out stipends was bound to be what Romans called a *scriba*. Yet, this *scriba* neither acted nor looked like in the style of a Roman *scriba* but instead played the part of a superior, the Etruscan king, as imagined by the young Roman nobleman.⁷ Livy's characterisation of the Etruscan scribe evokes what William Harris, with respect to the literocratic ancient civilisations of Egypt and the Near East, in which the mastery of literate practices and the exercise of power went hand in hand, has called 'scribal literacy'.⁸ Yet, already the little we know of Etruscan scribes in particular and Etruscan literacy in general paints a different, more nuanced picture.⁹ Livy's main theme is one of oppositions, his tale one of a marked contrast between the young Roman republican state and the monarchic Etruscan kingdom in all their symbolic attributes. His image of the *scriba* is a projection of his own, late Republican times rather than a reliable reconstruction of the scribal office in the late sixth century BC.

Livy's construed vignette of the powerful and king-like Etruscan scribe was no mere narrative tool, however. Rather, the question of the *scriba*'s position and, subsequently, his power was of great consequence in Livy's time and, in fact, relevant for the better part of the Republic and beyond. What defined the Roman *scriba*, as I will try to show, was his mastery of

---

4 The evidence in Colonna (1976); a survey of Etruscan magistrates and their personnel in Lambrechts (1959), 193f. for the scribes; cf. Fioretti (2014) 351.
5 Cornell (1995) 164.
6 Lambrechts (1959) 203.
7 The Greek historian Dionysius of Halicarnassus, writing shortly after Livy, depicts Mucius' misstep as deception without any alternative. In his version of the heroic tale, the Etruscan scribe is a man of impressive stature, clad in purple and sitting on the king's seat on a tribunal surrounded by armed guards; D.H. *ant.* 5. 28. 2; 5. 29. 1.
8 Harris (1989) 7.
9 Haynes (2000) 64–9; Lambrechts (1959) 203.

literate and numerate practices. The *scriba*'s expertise in literacy was his cultural capital. Not by chance do we find the Etruscan scribe administering financial matters, one of the main duties of the *scribae* in Livy's time. In a society in which only a fraction of the population was literate and numerate, being able to read, write and reckon was a specialised asset. That the Roman state relied on this human resource in financial and legal administration, setting the arcana of the state at the *scriba*'s disposal, bore potential for influence on the part of the specialist and thus for conflict. Literacy has consequences – for the individual and society as a whole. And it is these consequences, as I will argue, that are a defining part of what constituted a Roman *scriba*.

It seemed like scholarship of the early 1960s had found a straightforward answer to the question of the consequences of literacy. Anthropologist Jack Goody and literary scholar Ian Watt, in a highly influential analysis of early alphabetic writing and ancient Greek literacy, argued that the presumed rationality of alphabetic writing and its alleged wide diffusion in ancient Greek society had effected a rationalisation of thought, giving rise to Greek democracy, philosophy and historiography.[10] They propagated what has come to be known as the 'autonomous model' of literacy, which attributes to literacy inherent qualities of autonomous efficacy.[11] This perception of literacy as a mainly cognitive phenomenon was heavily challenged in the following decades. The supposition of literacy as the defining factor in social, cultural and political change was criticised. Literacy was no longer seen as an abstract civilising force but rather as one highly versatile cultural tool among others. In this 'ideological model', what defined literacy's historical importance were the 'conventions of literate practice' in any given society.[12] Socio-historical context became paramount in the analysis of literacy and its consequences for a society and the individual within.[13] Evidently, literacy and being literate, respectively, meant different things in different societies. Literacy levels, measured against a modern standard, were thus reduced to mere numbers with very restricted explanatory value. Being one of the few experts on literacy in a sea of non-experts could mean

---

[10] Goody and Watt (1963).
[11] On a characterisation of the model see Street (1984) esp. ch. 1 and 2; in Goody and Watt's footsteps Ong (2012) and Havelock (1986); for a recent assessment of ancient Greek literacy and a correction of Goody and Watt's view Thomas (1992) esp. ch. 2.
[12] Street (1984) 4 and Chapter 4.
[13] Graff (1986) 62–5; cf. Graff (1987). This strand of literacy studies is now referred to as 'The New Literacy Studies' (NLS), Gee (2015).

everything or nothing, depending on context. Livy's tale of the Etruscan *scriba*, evoking its differently natured Roman counterpart, is a case in point.

As a result, an assessment of the cultural, social and political consequences of the literate skills of the *scribae* must try to place them in the broader framework of Roman literate practice and culture. The uses and functions of literacy in particular as well as attitudes towards literacy in general defined the importance and perception of what *scribae* did for a living and, subsequently, influenced their position in Roman society and the state.

Scribal Education

While studying philosophy in Athens, Q. Horatius Flaccus (A.88)[14] was recruited by one of the murderers of Caesar, M. Iunius Brutus, to fight for his Republican cause. As *tribunus militum*, we eventually find Horace on the loser's side in the battle of Philippi in 42 BC. He survived and was pardoned by the triumvirs, but stripped of his sizeable patrimony in his native town of Venusia. About two years later, at the age of 25 and in financial difficulties, we find him buying a place as a *scriba quaestorius*.[15] Shortly afterwards, he would meet Maecenas and join his literary circle, which catapulted him to riches and fame and into the immediate proximity of Augustus himself. In 40 BC, however, a place as Roman *scriba* seemed adequate for a degraded son of an Italian freedman. It was an opportunity for financial betterment. And without doubt he possessed the skills necessary for the post.

In many ways, Horace might not have been the most prototypical of *scribae*, however. His education was geared towards a place among the educated Roman elite. His well-off freedman father had made sure that his son got the best education possible.[16] He thus sent him to school in Rome, together with the capital's well-to-do.[17] When we meet Horace in Athens on the eve of the battle of Philippi, he is putting the finishing touches to his higher grammatical and rhetorical education with a stay abroad, a practice common among the Roman elite.[18] We may safely assume that

---

[14] What we know about Horace's life stems from his own writings as well as a later biography by Suetonius. See still essential Fraenkel (1957) 1–23; most recently Nisbet (2007); with regard to his social standing Armstrong (2010).
[15] SUET. *vita Hor.* 24.
[16] Horace's father most likely had not been a Greek slave but rather a Samnite who had been enslaved during the Social War, G. Williams (1995); Nisbet (2007) 7.
[17] HOR. *sat.* 1.6.71–78.
[18] Bonner (1977) 90.

Horace was highly overeducated for the tasks required from a Roman *scriba*. While he had acquired artistic proficiency in language and literature, scribal work was much more clerical. Indeed, Horace himself was not very fond of the obligations of *scriba*-ship, which he associated with laborious *negotium* rather than artistic *otium*.[19]

Unfortunately, our sources do not provide us with any formal professional requirements for the post. It is debatable whether such requirements existed at all. As a matter of fact, we find no trace of such regulations where we would expect them, such as in the surviving charters of Roman *coloniae* and *municipia*, which were modelled on the city of Rome. Granted, these texts are fragmentary. Yet, what survives gives the impression that legal status and moral suitability were deemed more important than professional knowledge. The *lex Irnitana* of the early 90s of the first century AD dedicates a separate rubric to the *scribae* of the *municipium*.[20] Those eligible to fill the post needed to be *municipes*[21] of the city and had to be approved by the majority of the *decuriones*, the city's council.[22] Accordingly, professional fitness seems to have been controlled implicitly by those authorised to appoint the *scribae*. What was more important, apparently, was the candidates' moral suitability. The relevant parts of the *lex Irnitana* as well as of the earlier, Caesarian, colonial charter of *Iulia Genetiva*, the so-called *lex Ursonensis*, centre around an oath of due diligence that every *scriba* had to take before his admission.[23]

Evidently, a *scriba*'s professional skill was assumed as given. This becomes clear when we look at what *scribae* were tasked with. In a convenient characterisation of the fields of activity of the *scribae*, Cicero concludes that the *scribae* were occupied, together with the senatorial magistrates, with the public accounts and the written documents of the state.[24] We find the same characterisation in the aforementioned city legislation. Here, the *scribae* are writing and handling the public accounts and documents.[25] Apparently, Roman *scribae* were required to master as a minimum the basic triad of reading, writing and arithmetical reckoning in order to fulfil their duty. What we know of Roman public accounting and documentation suggests

---

[19] HOR. *sat*. 2.6.36.
[20] *lex Irn*. 73.31–47.
[21] *lex Irn*. 73.35–36.
[22] *lex Irn*. 73.34–35.
[23] *lex Irn*. 73.32–42; *lex Urson*. 81.14–25. See also CIC. *Verr*. 2.3.183. It is this very subjectivity in the assessment of a *scriba*'s suitability that was a recipe for the abuse of the system, see Chapter 4.
[24] CIC. *dom*. 74: *scribae, qui nobiscum in rationibus monumentisque publicis versantur*.
[25] *lex Urson*. 81.14–25: '*scribere*', '*referre*', '*tractare*', '*habere*' the '*rationes*' and '*tabulae publicae*'; *lex Irn*. 73.31–47: '*scribere*', '*ordinare*', '*inspicere*' and '*referre in*' the '*tabulae libri rationes communes*'.

that this might have sufficed to start with.[26] A look at Roman education in general reveals that it was exactly this triad that stood at the beginning of education in schools.[27]

Although the Romans must have known elementary education outside of aristocratic households at least since the third century BC,[28] learning to read, write and reckon remained a matter of individual choice – a choice that was most often dictated by financial rather than cultural constraints. The Roman state knew neither compulsory nor subsidised education.[29] Accordingly, for a great part of Roman society, formal education was an unaffordable and even unnecessary luxury. That is not to say that the middle and lower strata of Roman society were uneducated and ignorant.[30] Rather, without formal education, for most Romans literacy and numeracy were a highly functional affair. One would learn what was needed to cope in everyday life and professional occupation from family, friends or colleagues.[31] The higher education of the noble and wealthy, which aimed to produce an elite fit for ruling, was out of bounds.[32] We may certainly expect from a Roman *scriba* that he had spent more time being trained in literacy and numeracy skills than the average Roman. After all, reading, writing and reckoning were part of his everyday business. What exactly the professional education of a *scriba* looked like, we unfortunately do not know. We certainly have no evidence for any specialised educational institution of the state that would have prepared aspirants for the post. We must assume that candidates came with at least the basic skills, which were then refined on the job.[33]

Given that there existed no standardised and prescribed scribal education, levels of proficiency of *scribae* must have varied greatly. Horace may serve as a case in point. The acquisition of the basic skills in reading, writing and reckoning had marked only the starting point of his learning. Horace had, in addition, acquired the culturally and socially superior and far less clerical education of the senatorial upper class, notwithstanding his low social origins – his father, after all, was wealthy enough to make it possible. What is more, Horace might have had the opportunity to acquire advanced

---

[26] On the limited nature of accounting in general and the methods of accounting see Ste Croix (1956) 33–50; Fallu (1979) 100–2. See also below.
[27] Bonner (1977) 165–88; Cribiore (2001) 167–84.
[28] Vössing (2003) 460.
[29] Cic. *rep.* 4. 3; Cribiore (2001) 3f.; Vössing (2003) 485.
[30] Horsfall (2003) esp. 48–63.
[31] Meissner (1997) 59f.
[32] Vössing (2003) 483.
[33] Rankov (1999) speaks of 'experienced amateurs'.

skills in accounting, as his father had earned his wealth as a *coactor*, a professional money-receiver in auctions.³⁴ As such he was obliged to keep his own registers of the transactions.³⁵ We might very well picture the young Horace making his first foray into the the world of numbers and accounting by looking over his father's shoulder. That said, Horace most certainly was not representative of his co-*scribae*. The average *scriba* might not have had the monetary and thus educational background of the Venusian poet. The range of educational careers must have been as varied as the social backgrounds of the known *scribae* (see Chapter 5). Unfortunately, none are quite as well documented as that of Horace.

Two Cultures

The Roman *scribae* did not possess the same education as the senatorial superiors they had been sworn in to serve. Yet, that is not to say that the *scribae* were under- or uneducated, unfit to practise their duty. Although their superiors could boast a culturally prized higher education, *scribae* were still considered to be the experts on literate administrative practice. This is exemplified by an episode in the life of M. Porcius Cato Uticensis, recounted by Plutarch. Cato the Younger, renowned for being a paragon of Roman tradition and the republican state, had hesitated to become *quaestor* and thus head of the state archive and the *scribae quaestorii*. Before finally acceding in 65/4 BC, he had seen the need to educate himself on the details of the office. Allegedly, the *scribae* were notorious for patronising their superiors, who were, as a rule, less knowledgeable than themselves. According to Plutarch, it was their broad experience, their daily handling of the documents, that made the *scribae* the experts in what they were doing.³⁶ This condition denounced by Cato was far from being specific to his situation, however. It was inherent in the system.

Roman literate culture was basically divided into two groups. For the elite, literate learning and education was a means of ascertaining their social status. Higher education in the liberal arts sought to raise the individual towards *humanitas*, the Roman adaptation of the Greek concept of παιδεία. The notion of an ideal education, producing ideal human beings fit to rule and lead, marked the boundary between the elite and the rest of

---

[34] HOR. *sat.* 1. 6. 86; cf. Andreau (1987) 717–20.
[35] Andreau (1999) 38f., so-called *tabulae auctionariae* or *auctionales*.
[36] PLUT. *Cat. Mi.* 16. 1–2. The scribae (γραμματεῖς) are described as being διὰ χειρὸς ἀεὶ τὰ δημόσια γράμματα καὶ τοὺς νόμους ἔχοντες.

Roman society.[37] Higher education was an exclusive status marker. As such it was associated with the upper-class lifestyle of *otium* – literate education was a calling. For literate experts, such as the *scribae*, on the other hand, literacy was a profession, *negotium*. The *scribae* were, in their capacity as *apparitores*, employees of the Roman state. They worked for wages, the *aes apparitorium*,[38] *salarium*[39] or *merces*.[40]

As it happens, *mercennarii* were in no good odour, at least not with the highly educated. According to Cicero, wage labour was incompatible with the status of a free man and was instead a sign of slavery.[41] We learn from the first-century BC biographer and historiographer Cornelius Nepos – a friend of Cicero – that the Roman *scribae* were among those manual wage labourers who were scorned by the elite. In an aside on Eumenes, the chancellor of Philip II of Macedon and his son Alexander the Great, Nepos explains the difference between Greek and Roman public scribes. He highlights the fact that the Greek '*scribae*' were deemed much more honourable than their Roman counterparts and identifies the reason as the Roman status of the Roman *scribae* as mercenaries. He goes on to contrast this status with the Greek scribe's position of honour, loyalty and diligence.[42] That is not to say that the *scribae* as individuals were perceived as dishonourable or that their work was felt to be dispensable. In fact, Cicero, in his indictment of C. Verres, argues for the exact opposite. Except for some allegedly degenerate subjects, who are the targets of his charge, he portrays the *scribae* as proper Roman *patres familias*, virtuous and honourable men, to whose integrity the public documents were entrusted.[43] The salient point made by both Roman writers was that the literate occupation of the *scribae* was paid, very much in contrast to the elite's engagement with literacy. In a situation in which *scribae* not only participated in domains predestined to be the prerogative of the educated elite, namely literacy and the exercise of office, but eventually even contested their superiors, the 'response was to limit the damage by emphasizing how lowly the jobs were'.[44]

While the institutional aspect of *scriba*-ship bore the stigma of employed labour, the work itself was ennobled by the general status of literate and literary practice and its close affiliation with the ideal lifestyle of the

---

[37] See Cicero's first letter to his brother Quintus, esp. CIC. *ad Q. fr.* 1.1.29. Cf. Morgan (1998) 245f., 268–70.
[38] *lex Irn.* 73.31.
[39] PLIN. *ep.* 4.12.2.
[40] *lex Urson.* 62.31; CIC. *Verr.* 2.3.182.
[41] CIC. *off.* 1.150; cf. Lis and Soly (2012) 78–87.
[42] NEP. *Eum.* 1.5.
[43] CIC. *Verr.* 2.3.182–184.
[44] Purcell (2001) 665; cf. Cuomo (2011) 180–2.

elite.⁴⁵ Granted, the clerical work in public service was seen as tedious and much less intellectually rewarding than any literary pursuit. Indeed, clerical writing involved repetition and was technical. Yet it was perceived as no less noble and, in fact, marked an integral part of a magistrate's daily duty. Pliny the Younger, for example, may have complained about the amount of clerical work in his days as *praefectus aerarii Saturni* – an office at the heart of administrative literate practice, of which the *scribae* were part. However, at the same time, he himself distinctly marked it as a most important and noble duty.⁴⁶ Literate activity, even if it was clerical, was not stigmatised per se. As a result, it was most probably no coincidence that a literary figure(-to-be) like Horace chose to buy a place in the *decuriae* of the *scribae quaestorii* rather than pursuing other sources of income. Being a *scriba* paid very well (see Chapter 4), and there was the added bonus that Horace was already well versed in literate practice. Socially, he did not have much to lose – quite the contrary, in fact. He had been stripped of his inheritance and status and was in dire straits. However stigmatised and thus unappealing the post would have been to a well-to-do member of the aristocracy, an upstart from an Italian town was likely to find an opportunity for social advancement in the position of a quaestorian *scriba* (see Chapter 5). In addition, his literary ambitions were certainly not hindered by his choice of employment. Writing, even if it was clerical writing, must have been seen as an obvious fit for a non-aristocratic man of letters.

As a rule, we might be well advised not to take Horace's life as prototypical or even as a model of something we would call a 'literary *scriba*'. Nevertheless, evidence suggests that the specific conditions at the end of the Republic and the beginning of the Principate might have furthered the concurrence of literary talents and the clerical profession of the *scriba*. The literary patronage in Augustus' ambit and the influx of non-aristocratic, young literary upstarts from Italian communities into these circles is characteristic of the times.⁴⁷ It might, thus, not surprise us to find in the entourage of the Julio-Claudian family other young poets employed as *scribae* who had a social background similar to that of Horace. Two fellow poets of Horace, a certain Iulius Florus (A.92), who '*scriba fuit saturarum scriptor*',⁴⁸ as well as Albinovanus Celsus (A.10), referred to as '*comes scribaque*' of the later emperor Tiberius,⁴⁹ appear on the staff of the

---

⁴⁵ Pliny the Younger gives vivid examples of an idealised life with literature, PLIN. *ep.* 3.1; 3.5.
⁴⁶ PLIN. *ep.* 1.10. 9–10; cf. Corbier (1974) 671–92 on the office, no. 32 on Pliny's term AD 98–100.
⁴⁷ Fantham (1996) 68f.; cf. Purcell (1983) 143.
⁴⁸ PORPH. *Hor. ep.* 1.3.1; cf. HOR. *epist.* 1.3; 2.3; on the controversial question of the identification of Iulius Florus see most recently H. Koch (2014).
⁴⁹ HOR. *epist.* 1.8.1–2; cf. HOR. *epist.* 1.3.15–20; 1.8.

latter during his Armenian campaign of 20 BC.⁵⁰ It is difficult to say whether this phenomenon was a corollary of traditional ties of the *scribae* with the literary world or just a coincidence of primarily social factors at the end of the Republic, when these posts were a feasible opportunity for social advancement for young and well-educated men of Italian cities.

At first sight, we might be wary of drawing an overly clear line between the literary and clerical uses of literacy in a society in which being able to read and write was considered to be expert knowledge to begin with. Yet, what we have established above in relation to the early days of the Roman Republic and the Etruscan scribes suggests that a distinction between clerical writing and literary ambitions must have existed at a very early date. The scant evidence we have concerning the Republic is notoriously difficult to interpret. Our key witness is the second-century AD lexicographer Sex. Pompeius Festus. In a famous passage on the third-century BC poet Livius Andronicus, Festus, most probably relying on the Augustan grammarian M. Verrius Flaccus, explains to his reading public why, during the Republic, the poet had been honoured by the association of the *scribae histrionesque*, which met in the temple of Minerva on the Aventine.⁵¹ The question is – as we would expect – one of semantics. He explains that

> scribas proprio nomine antiqui et librarios et poetas vocabant; at nunc dicuntur scribae equidem librari, qui rationes publicas scribunt in tabulis.⁵²

Obviously, it must have puzzled a reader of Festus (and Flaccus, for that matter) that *scribae* would have associated with actors to honour a poet. The obvious answer was that, in Andronicus' time and beyond, not only the apparitorial writers (now *scribae librarii*) were called *scribae* but also the poets (*poetae*). The word *scriba* had, evidently, not yet become a technical term used exclusively for the apparitorial writers of the state, the *scribae librarii*.⁵³ According to Festus, the puzzling statement that *scribae* had associated with actors was not due to the fact that they had shared some professional trait or point of interest in ancient times. Quite the opposite: the *scribae* who associated with actors in Andronicus' times were,

---

⁵⁰ On the question of their role as *scribae* see Chapter 3.
⁵¹ The date given by the historian Livy for the composition of Andronicus' *carmen* is 207 BC; LIV. 27.37.7.
⁵² FEST. 446.26–29 (333M): '*The ancients used the formal appellation* Scriba *for both* poetae *and* librarii*; but now those who write down the financial accounts of the state on tablets are known as* Scribae Librarii', transl. Purcell (2001) 644f.
⁵³ The same reading in Jory (1970) 226; Horsfall (1976) 79, 90; Pennitz (1993) 683.

despite their denomination, not actual *scribae*, but rather *poetae*.⁵⁴ Among *scribae*, *poetae* and *histriones*, *scribae* were, and always had been, the odd ones out.⁵⁵ This, naturally, does not mean that it was out of the question that a *scriba* could also have been literarily gifted or that a *poeta* could become a *scriba*. Horace and his friends Florus and Celsus are evident examples. However, the two professions and their fields of activity were apparently separate and distinct.

It is as late as the year AD 357 that we find another point of contact of *scribae* with the literary world. In a rescript of the emperors Constantius and Julian we find regulations about the requirements on the *primus ordinis*, the head of the clerical *decuriae* of the *librarii*, *fiscales* and *censuales* (see Chapter 6), who together formed an *ordo*. The candidate should be well versed in the study and practice of the liberal arts and literature. However, the candidate apparently was not recruited from the pool of the members of the *decuriae*, but was an outsider.⁵⁶ That members of the *decuriae* were similarly gifted is, thus, at least very doubtful. The requirements were most probably rather aimed at emphasising the educational ethos of high-ranking, senatorial candidates⁵⁷ than connected with the everyday tasks of the members of the *decuriae* who were, according to their denomination, mainly occupied with financial matters and bookkeeping.

Arguing for a close connection between clerical and literary writing would mean stretching the very little evidence we possess.⁵⁸ The liaison of literary

---

54 Festus' *collegium scribarum histrionumque* is commonly identified with the *collegium poetarum* mentioned by V. MAX. 3.7.11. A certain freedman Cornelius Surus, who had held several lesser apparitorial posts but no *scriba*-ship, had been *mag(ister) scr(ibarum) poetar(um)*, most probably of the same *collegium*; *AE* 1959, 147; see More (1975) 248, contra Horsfall (1976) 91, who postulates an association of apparitorial *scribae* with lesser poets; cf. Panciera (1986) 39f.; Romano (1990) 19–23. On the general question of the *collegium / collegia* of poets Crowther (1973).

55 See in addition Horsfall (1976) 90, who notes that poets themselves never, even at such an early date, spoke of themselves as *scribae*, but rather *poetae*, and, 80, highlights the fact that the wording in Festus' passage closely resembles the language of *senatus consulta*, thus proposing 'a designation imposed by an unsympathetic administration, quite possibly lumping authors and government clerks together in a single category'; cf. on the other hand Kunihara (1963) 85f., who does not consider the term *scriba* to denote anything other than 'poet' for the time Festus is speaking about; contra Fioretti (2014) 345, who assumes a common social and professional background of *poetae* and *librarii* for Andronicus' times; cf. Romano (1990) 19–27.

56 COD. Theod. 14.1.1: *In decuriarum ordine insigni, cui librariorum vel fiscalium sive censualium nomen est, nequaquam aliquis locum primi ordinis adipiscatur nisi is, quem constiterit studiorum liberalium usu adque exercitatione pollere et ita esse litteris expolitum, ut citra offensam vitii ex eodem verba procedant: quod cunctis volumus intimari.*

57 The likely successor of the *primus ordinis* in the Ostrogothic Kingdom, the *rector decuriarum*, mentioned by Cassiodorus in his *Variae*, was a senator in the rank of a *vir spectabilis*; CASSIOD. *Var.* 5.21.1–3; 5.22.1–5; cf. Sinnigen (1957) 78–82.

58 Contra Purcell (1983) 142, who argues for a a connection of the *scribae* with the literary world.

figures with the *scriba*-ship at the transition from Republic to Empire was, most likely, a singular event and had less to do with the question of literacy than with socio-political realities. Already at an early date, clerical writing must have been perceived as separate from literary pursuits, creating different trajectories. Clerical writing thereby took the ancillary position while the occupation with literature became the prerequisite of the ruling elite. We are dealing with two literate cultures that eventually became as distinct enough to provoke serious disruption in their mutual understanding.[59] Plutarch's portrayal of the common practice in the *aerarium* at the time of Cato the Younger illustrates this state of affairs.

Roman Literate Practice

Latin literate practice had made only slow headway into Roman society since the early years of the Roman Republic.[60] Oral practice prevailed. The first written documents are found almost exclusively in the legal and religious domains. Although written practice gradually expanded during the fourth and third century BC as a result of Roman military and colonising activity, the importance of the written word in the Roman public must have remained marginal.[61] Cn. Flavius' publication of legal procedures at the end of the fourth century BC, discussed above, was unprecedented after all. His case exemplifies one of the key features of early Roman literacy that would have a formative influence on the coming centuries of Roman literacy history: the monopolisation of literacy by the educated elite. It was the topmost echelon of Roman society that had first made use of literate practice both in private and in governing the Republic. And it was the same small group that had subsequently adopted Greek literary culture and education, discussed above, as their own since the third century BC, when the Romans had gradually conquered the Eastern Mediterranean.[62] The aristocratic household, gradually employing written practice to meet

---

[59] Cf. the similarities to the concept of 'The Two Cultures' by Snow (1998), who observed a knowledge and communication rift between scientists and literary intellectuals of the twentieth century, which was bound to cause a lack of mutual intellectual understanding and even hostility between the two groups.

[60] The classic exposition of ancient literacy by Harris (1989) is still valid, although his 'primitivistic' image of Roman literacy has faced criticism and additions; for an overview of the debate see Werner (2009).

[61] Harris (1989) 149–59; an overview of the evidence for the use of writing in the first centuries of the Republic in Poucet (1989).

[62] Cf. Horace's famous dictum *Graecia capta ferum victorem cepit et artis intulit agresti Latio*, epist. 2.1.156–157.

various challenges from the administration of estates to Republican politics, marked the nucleus of expanding Roman literacy.[63] 'In this world, after the archaic period, the entire elite relied heavily on writing, and the entirety of the rest of the population was affected by it.'[64] As a result, Roman culture was, by the end of the second century BC, in many ways a literate culture. Written practice and thus contact with the written became more common, especially in the domains of literary production, government, military, personal accounting and the commemoration of the dead.[65] The first century BC eventually saw a further expansion of these writing practices, most obviously in quantitative terms as a result of the incorporation of the Western provinces into the growing empire.[66] It is true that at the end of the Roman Republic '[l]iteracy, in public or in private, was a way of living, a way of working and a way of thinking'.[67] Yet, Roman society had not become a literate society per se. Literate practice was socially and functionally confined. Oral practice coexisted with and in most cases even obviated the need for literate practice. There was never a mass of literate Romans able to read, write and reckon.

The degree to which the non-elite participated in this literate culture throughout the late Republic and the Empire is a matter of debate. Harris' conservative evaluation of the extent of literacy, which mainly highlighted its limitations, has not gone unopposed. Yet, its central points still stand. The peculiarities of Roman education as well as the lack of a practical necessity for literacy for most inhabitants of the Roman world must have greatly hindered widespread literacy.[68] It is true that with the onset of the Empire we witness a veritable explosion of written testimonies. The most evident case is the unfolding of an 'epigraphic habit' throughout the Mediterranean with Augustus, which caught not only the members of the (local, regional, imperial) elite but also various groups from lower strata of society.[69] In addition, writing on *instrumentum domesticum* and small finds becomes, it seems, ubiquitous, and attests to the use of writing in day-to-day religious, legal, commercial, artisanal and private practice.[70] However, the contexts of these testimonies are, owing to their often

---

[63] Woolf (2009) 51f.
[64] Harris (1989) 327.
[65] Harris (1989) 159–74.
[66] Harris (1989) 196.
[67] Morgan (1998) 3.
[68] A synoptic overview of the body of research in Werner (2009); most recently Woolf (2009) and Häussler (2013) and Woolf (2015).
[69] Most recently Beltrán Lloris (2015).
[70] For an exemplary cross-section of the possible types of such writing see *RIB II*.

fragmentary nature and our frequently limited knowledge of the processes they were part of, notoriously difficult to assess.[71] Determining their quantitative representativity is made difficult by their often very fragile and ephemeral support media, such as wood and other organic material.[72] We may certainly establish that – concrete literacy levels aside – the average inhabitant of the Roman Empire, at least one living in an urban area, was confronted with such writing on a daily basis.[73] As already discussed in connection with the elite conception of literacy, and as will become even clearer when we look at the literate practice of the Roman state, Roman society was 'a society in which people were expected to cope with writing'.[74] Again, this does not imply that the vast majority of people were literate in the traditional sense. Depending on context and demands, coping with writing allowed for a wide variety of proficiencies in writing, reading and reckoning or a combination of the three skills. Even people completely lacking any of these skills were able to participate in literate practices via the help of a knowledgeable aide. A big portion of the inhabitants of the growing empire, especially in the West, were native speakers of neither Greek nor Latin, after all.[75] Roman literacy might, thus, best be understood in terms of a continuum rather than the traditional strict division between literate and illiterate. Greg Woolf has recently proposed understanding Roman literacy as a 'semiological competence', including 'a broad set of graphic sign systems that included – but were not limited to – signs used to encode speech'.[76] Our literary sources and the elite educational ideas they represent have taught us to think of ancient literacy in very modern terms: of literacy as a sharp dichotomy. However, the very context-driven (and often enigmatic) writings on *instrumentum domesticum*, in particular, show a very different picture. Somebody like Cicero might not have regarded, for example, a fuller from a provincial backwater as being literate. Granted, the fuller might not have been able to read and understand Cicero's latest opus. But the same might be said for Cicero's ability to readily decipher the tiny, cryptically inscribed lead labels that

---

[71] For an overview of some of these issues see the collaborative effort of the association *Ductus. Association internationale pour l'étude des inscriptions mineures* in Fuchs, Sylvestre and Heidenreich (2012) and Scholz and Horster (2015).
[72] General reflections on the importance of wood as a support material by Eck (1998); a case study of surviving wooden wax tablets (*tabulae ceratae*) showing the pivotal importance of the conditions of transmission by Hartmann (2015).
[73] Corbier (1987).
[74] Häussler (2013) 4108.
[75] Woolf (2000) 878f.
[76] Woolf (2015) 38.

were part of the daily business of the craftsman.[77] Literacy was, in any case, a specialised expertise.[78]

A Culture of Documentation

Literate practice was never a mere end in itself; it suited needs, served purposes. Thus, in the same way that Cicero and his educated peers distinguished themselves by literate culture and the ordinary craftsman made use of literate routines in the manufacture and marketing of his product, the Roman state relied on literate practice for its functioning and its self-conception. Thereby, the *scribae* took the role of literate administrative experts, making, keeping and using documents central to the conception and working of the Roman state, the *tabulae publicae*.

Tracing Roman literate administrative practice is a challenging endeavour. Romans mainly used waxed wooden tablets (*tabulae ceratae*) as their preferred writing material for administrative and archival purposes. They took advantage of the fact that – as the raw material was readily available – wooden tablets were cheap, reusable and sufficiently hard-wearing to be used in administrative writing and archiving. Wood is durable enough to survive for decades, even centuries if properly stored and cared for; wax, which bore the writing, was thought to be a lasting medium.[79] The Romans' short-term benefit is the modern historian's long-term loss, however. Besides the generally ephemeral nature of administrative legal and financial documentation, which made it prone to being discarded on occasion, archaeological survival of wood over longer periods of time is only given under specific anaerobic conditions not usually found in the Roman capital. The buildings and places that once housed archives of countless *tabulae* – the *tablina* of the aristocratic households and the *tabularia* of the state – are now devoid of documentary evidence. It is this complete lack of first-hand evidence that has shaped our image of Roman administrative practice and its use of written documents. It has always been obvious that, in this case, absence of evidence was not evidence of absence. Yet, although traces of the lost documentary evidence can be found in epigraphic, literary and pictorial sources, the scarcity of evidence has

---

[77] The biggest find of such labels from *Siscia* (Zagreb) in Radman-Livaja (2014).
[78] Woolf (2015) 41; on the problematics of dichotomies and the importance of context in literacy studies in general Graff (1986) 65–9.
[79] E. A. Meyer (2004) 35.

made it easy to argue for the marginal importance of written procedures.[80] The classic narrative of Roman administrative practice is one of increasing complexity and mounting personal resources from the Republic through to the Later Roman Empire: from a slim state managed by few magistrates with minimal staff to the gradual separation and differentiation of political, military and administrative power during the Empire to the development of a highly branched, professional administrative apparatus under the Later Roman Empire.[81] While extensive use of written practice is generally perceived as a feature of late Roman times,[82] the Roman Republic especially is traditionally not credited with a documentary mentality.[83] It was not until the last decade of the twentieth century that this notion was challenged. A research project initiated by Claude Nicolet, continued by his pupil Claudia Moatti, has shed light on the lost evidence – 'la mémoire perdue' – for Republican (and imperial) administrative literate practice.[84] Nicolet's conclusion of the project's early findings already re-characterised the Roman Republic since the second century BC as 'fortement "paperassière"', thus suggesting a backdating of Roman 'bureaucratie' for several centuries.[85]

The Roman Republic was certainly no bureaucracy in the strict sense. Max Weber's highly rational, hierarchical and professional ideal type bureaucracy[86] is a far cry from what we know of Roman Republican, imperial and even late imperial administration.[87] Yet, Nicolet's allusion to Roman red tape draws attention to what I would call the Roman culture of documentation. As it turns out, this culture of documentation is at the centre of the work and self-conception of the Roman *scribae*.

Leaving a paper trail of one's actions and practices is a matter of accountability. A Republic managed by a few aristocratic families, which ruled *inter pares*, was certainly not fertile soil for such demands. At least in the early Republic, the state had no interest in documenting its workings and operations outside of the aristocratic circle. We have to assume that everything that was written down and archived either catered to the immediate needs of the correct exercise of the office or were private records

---

[80] See already Mommsen (1887) esp. II.1, who covers the evidence while discussing the different magistrates; a thorough assessment of the main sources by Cencetti (1940) 34–8; building on the former with a rather pessimistic conclusion in the classic account of Posner (1972) 184f.
[81] Eck (2002).
[82] Kelly (1994).
[83] A characterisation of the very pessimistic scientific tradition in Rankov (1999) 15.
[84] Nicolet et al. (1994), Moatti et al. (1998), Moatti et al. (2000), and Moatti et al. (2001).
[85] Nicolet (1994) XIf.
[86] Weber (2002) 126–30.
[87] An overview in Eich (2005) 21–32.

of the office holder. There was, in the first place, no need to either publish or publicly safeguard these documents. In fact, as the members of the aristocratic families constituted the state, they themselves were entrusted with the custody and passing on of knowledge pertaining to the governance of the Republic.[88] Even in Cicero's time it was still common practice and according to the *mos maiorum*, the ancestral customs, that magistrates kept written documents that were, technically, of a public nature.[89] The Greek historian Dionysius of Halicarnassus, for example, while looking for information on the year 392 BC, had to consult the private archives of former censors, which had been kept and passed on exclusively within censorial families.[90] In this sense, administrative documents formed a natural part of the aristocratic household. The *tablinum* functioned, as its name suggests, as a repository for the *tabulae* that recorded the *res gestae* of the magistrate's terms of office.[91]

The aristocratic household was the nucleus of Roman literate practice. As such, it served as a model for the state as a whole. It is not by accident that the second-century AD author P. Annius Florus, in an epitome of Livy, compares the Roman state with an aristocratic household when it comes to literate administrative practice. The results of the legendary *census* of the sixth king of Rome, Servius Tullius, were allegedly committed to tablets (*in tabulas referre*), 'with the exactitude of a small household'.[92] We later find the censors depositing their *tabulae censoriae* not in their private homes but in the *aedes Nympharum* in the vicinity of their premises at the *villa publica* on the Campus Martius[93] as well as in the *aerarium* on the Capitolium[94] close to their headquarters, the *Atrium Libertatis*.[95] Questions about the historicity of Tullius' *census* aside, the episode, most certainly in a later retrojection, illustrates the practical constraints which led a state such as the Roman Republic to rely on public records in addition to private initiative. The registration of its people and their financial as well as their legal status – Florus speaks of *patrimonium, dignitas, aetas, ars* and *officium* – lies at the heart of a functioning body politic. The *tabulae censoriae* provided the basis for the right to citizenship, military conscription and taxation.

---

[88] Culham (1989) 104.
[89] CIC. *Sul.* 42.
[90] D.H. *ant.* 1.74.5.
[91] PLIN. *nat.* 35.7; cf. FEST. 490.28–31 (395M).
[92] FLOR. *epit.* 1. 6. 3: *in tabulas referrentur, ac sic maxima civitas minimae domus diligentia contineretur*, transl. E. S. Forster.
[93] CIC. *Mil.* 73; cf. Manacorda (1996).
[94] LIV. 29.37.12–13.
[95] Mommsen (1887) II.1, 359f.

Their non-partisan archival and management must thus have constituted a common desire. Tampering with the records by individuals became much more difficult; extinguishing one's bad record was much more momentous when it required setting fire to a public temple rather than to a private *tablinum*.⁹⁶ Livy, who reports the creation of the censorial office for the year 443 BC, not only assigns the holding of the *census* to its authority but fittingly also the supervision of the *tabulae* as well as of the *scribae* ('*scribarum ministerium custodiaeque tabularum cura*').⁹⁷ The censors, in their function as the highest moral authority, were thus in charge of the most sensitive data and of the people managing it.

In similar fashion to the *censores*, the other Roman magistrates were expected to produce writing in order to properly administer their office. From a *senatus consultum* of the year 11 BC on the endowment of the *curatores aquarum publicarum* we learn about what was considered essential for the exercise of the office. Not only were the *curatores* given a staff of *apparitores* – among them *scribae* – but also '*tabulas, chartas ceteraque quae eius curationis causa opus essent*'. Funds were allocated for these expenses by the *aerarium*, i.e. the state treasury.⁹⁸ Such provisions for magistrates were no new phenomenon. In the case of the *curatores aquarum publicarum* they were explicitly modelled on existing ones for the *praefecti frumenti dandi*,⁹⁹ which in turn might have been based on these of the preceding aedilician office. Thanks to recent research on the documentary practice of the *cura annonae* we now know that wooden and papyrus writing material was indeed necessary for keeping track of the highly complex operations of the agency.¹⁰⁰ Lists of those eligible as well as lists of actual beneficiaries had to be drawn up, maintained and regularly revised and brought up to date with the basic lists of citizens.¹⁰¹ The year-round distribution of grain itself had to be monitored, the recipients checked against the lists. If the extant papyrological evidence from Roman Egypt for municipal *frumentationes* is anything to go by, the *cura annonae* of the capital must inevitably have been forced to maintain administrative archives in order to keep up with the paperwork needed to fulfil its duties.¹⁰²

---

⁹⁶ This is what Cicero accused Clodius of, CIC. *Mil.* 73.
⁹⁷ LIV. 4. 8. 4.
⁹⁸ FRONTIN. *Aq.* 2. 100.
⁹⁹ FRONTIN. *Aq.* 2. 100.
¹⁰⁰ On the evidence for the documentary practice Virlouvet (1998); on the general workings of the public distribution of grain Virlouvet (1995).
¹⁰¹ Provided either by the *tribus*, Virlouvet (1998) 253–8, or the *vici*, Tarpin (1998) 406–9.
¹⁰² Carrié (1998) 280, 287.

The administrative practice of other magistrates might not be as well documented and studied as that of the office of the *praefecti frumenti dandi*. Yet, the little we know suggests similar documentary procedures. According to their range of duties, the different magistrates and their staff were bound to produce distinct documentation. The legal, financial and military assessment of the people (*census*) by the *censores* resulted, as already discussed, in the *tabulae censoriae*.[103] The *praetores* and *iudices quaestionum* produced a mass of minutes and other documentation belonging to judicial hearings.[104] The *quaestores*, concerned with the financial administration of the empire, managed the books of account in the provinces as well as in the city.[105] The *tribuni plebis* and *aediles*, initially the plebeian counterparts to the patrician magistrates, performed similar functions, which must have entailed appropriate documentary practice in the areas of tribunician legislation and jurisdiction as well as the aedilician *curae annonae*, *urbis* and *ludorum* – at least they possessed their own *scribae* and archive.[106] Other official charges, such as agrarian commissions, relied heavily on written documentation to administer their responsibilities.[107] At least from the Late Republic, magistrates chronicled their day-to-day activities in so-called *commentarii*, daybooks to be used for future reference.[108] And as a body, the magistrates produced *senatus consulta* and *commentarii* of their council, the *acta senatus*.[109] All in all, there existed a culture of documentation that was, by the time of Cicero, taken for granted.[110]

The Public Repository

By the Late Republic at the latest, documenting one's administrative actions and achievements had undoubtedly become an integral part of a Roman magistrate's office. Yet, the state's interest did not lie in complete documentation of either its magistrates' activities or its people's lives. What was publicly archived were documents that had an immediate

---

[103] Lo Cascio (2001); cf. in general Moatti (2001).
[104] Mantovani (2000) 668; cf. L. Piso's ample documentation (*multi codices*) of legal cases, in which he disagreed with his co-*praetor* C. Verres, CIC. *Verr.* 2.1.119.
[105] PLUT. *Publ.* 12.2; cf. Mommsen (1887) II.1, 525f.
[106] LIV. 3.55.13; cf. Culham (1989) 103.
[107] Moatti (1993) 49–78; Moatti (1994) 112.
[108] Haensch (1992) 230–45; cf. *CIL* 10, 7852 for a possible example of such a *codex ansatus*; the example of Frontinus' *de Aquis urbis Romae* in Peachin (2004) 24f.
[109] Coudry (1994) 77–84.
[110] See the considerable range of written documents consulted and adduced by Cicero in his denunciation of C. Verres in 70 BC, Butler (2002) 35–60.

bearing on the state's past, present, or future financial and legal affairs.[111] What the state archived entered the so-called *tabulae publicae*. And unlike modern archives, which triage and incorporate into their holdings the very documents a certain agency delivers, Roman archives did not file the 'originals' produced by the magistrates. Rather, they incorporated into the *codices* of the *tabulae publicae* transcriptions of relevant documents. The technical term, ubiquitous in the sources, is *referre in tabulis publicis*.[112] An example may illustrate the procedure. When, in 55 BC, L. Calpurnius Piso Caesoninus returned from his governorship of the province of Macedonia, he delivered, as had become common practice, his provincial accounts to the *aerarium*. In Cicero's mocking invective,[113] Piso praises himself for his sense of duty and diligence. Rather than enter the city in triumph, he had hastened to the Capitol to fulfil his official duty. Piso goes on to describe the procedure at the *aerarium*:

> Quas rationes si cognoris, intelleges nemini plus quam mihi litteras profuisse. Ita enim sunt perscriptae scite et litterate ut scriba ad aerarium qui eas rettulit perscriptis rationibus secum ipse caput sinistra manu perfricans commurmuratus sit: ratio quidem hercle apparet, argentum 'οἴχεται'.[114]

Piso's self-praise and Cicero's scorn aside, we learn from the passage that, at the *aerarium*, a *scriba* accepted and filed (*referre*) a governor's *rationes* by copying them down (*perscribere*). Handing in one's accounts was no mere deposition. Instead, the *scriba* registered the relevant documents by making a copy. Such a procedure not only reduced the holdings of the state archives to the absolutely necessary, but also introduced an element of control. While copying them, the *scriba* at the same time audited the accounts. He could obviously confirm Piso's claim that his accounts were drafted '*scite et litterate*' – even if, according to Cicero, all the money had run out on Piso.[115] It is clear that this last step was, in theory, not in the *scriba*'s authority and responsibility. It was for the heads of the archiving institution to verify the documents about to be registered. Cato the Younger's refusal to file a *senatus consultum* without previous verification of its authenticity by the *consules* during his infamous quaestorship bears testimony to these usual

---

[111] See E. A. Meyer (2004) 38f. on the close affiliation of legal practice and documents, and 29 for the *tabulae*'s association with the 'propitious or desired order of Rome'; cf. Cencetti (1940) 42.
[112] On the terminology cf. Bats (1994) 28 n. 45.
[113] On Cicero's stratey to discredit Piso see Pap (2016).
[114] Cic. *Pis.* 61: *And if you study those accounts, you will find that no one has profited more highly from his learning than myself. In so acute and scholarly fashion are they made out, that the clerk who made the return to the treasury, having completed his copy of them, murmured while he scratched his head with his left hand – The count indeed is plain, the coin – is gone!*, transl. N. H. Watts.
[115] The phrase '*ratio quidem hercle apparet, argentum* οἴχεται' borrowed from PLAUT. *trin.* 419.

The Public Repository 33

responsibilities.[116] Yet, exactly Cato's complaints about the accepted inner workings of the *aerarium* and the power of *scribae*, which I have discussed above, show that, for all practical purposes, Piso's version might not have been far from the truth. All things considered, what the Roman state chose to archive were very specific documents only: the final products of a longer chain of writings produced by the individual magistrate. The magistrate himself, on the other hand, committed his paperwork to his private *tablinum* as desired. It is these idiosyncrasies of Roman documentary culture that made Dionysius of Halicarnassus frequent private censorial archives while researching for his *Roman Antiquities*. Consulting a public *tabularium* and a private *tablinum* would inevitably have yielded very different results.[117]

What one would find in the *tabulae publicae* was, above all, information that was of communal interest – *tabulae publicae* also went by the name of *tabulae communes*.[118] As already mentioned, the results of the *census*, i.e. lists of citizens[119] with listings of their property,[120] were an important section of the archived records. Another core part were public finances:[121] revenues[122] and expenditures,[123] the acquisition[124] and sale[125] of public property, provincial *rationes*,[126] debts of citizens due to the state[127] and of the state due to citizens[128] as well as public contracts.[129] Laws in general[130] and legislation by individual magistrates,[131] the senate[132] and the *comitia*[133] in particular were included. Court proceedings were recorded in detail and the minutes transferred into the official public records.[134] The daybooks (*commentarii*)

---

[116] Plut. *Cat. Mi.* 17. 3–4.
[117] See e.g. Cic. *Balb.* 11 for a *causa* in which *tabulae publicae* as well as corresponding private *tabulae* of a magistrate are adduced and compared to prove a point.
[118] *lex Irn.* 73. 32–39.
[119] Liv. 29. 37. 7; Cic. *Balb.* 8.
[120] Liv. 2. 27. 6; Cic. *Mil.* 73; Dig. 50. 15. 4. 1; extraordinary declarations (*professiones*), *Tab. Heracl.* 14, in *municipia*, which were then transferred to Rome, *Tab. Heracl.* 148–156.
[121] Urso, *lex Urson.* 81. 15–17.
[122] Tarentum, *lex agr.* 13, 20; 10: *pequnia pulic[a sa]cra religiosa*.
[123] Sen. *dial.* 1. 3. 8.
[124] Liv. *perioch.* 57; including spoils of war, Cic. *Verr.* 2. 1. 57.
[125] Cic. *S. Rosc.* 128.
[126] Cic. *Balb.* 11.
[127] *lex agr.* 70; *Tab. Heracl.* 39–40; Cic. *Font.* 2; Tac. *ann.* 13. 28. 2; Hist. Aug. *Aurelian.* 39. 1.
[128] Liv. 26. 36. 11.
[129] Frontin. *Aq.* 2. 96. 1.
[130] Sen. *dial.* 4. 28. 2.
[131] V. Max. 9. 2. 1.
[132] Cic. *leg. agr.* 2. 3/; Cic. *Sest.* 129; *SCPP* 176. Decuriones of Urso, *lex Urson.* 130. 42, 131. 3, 134. 41–44; Pisae, *CIL* 11, 1421.
[133] Cic. *Pis.* 36.
[134] Cic. *Cluent.* 62; Cic. *Vat.* 34; Cic. *Verr.* 2. 2. 104–105.

of the magistrates also found their way into the public repository.[135] This list of references to explicit mentions of the *tabulae publicae*'s content gives a necessarily lacunary yet apt characterisation of what the Romans deemed worthy and necessary of documentation in the name of the public. What was officially archived was, evidently, information pertaining to public legal and financial affairs.

Determining a precise dividing line between *tabularium* and *tablinum*, in other words knowing the criteria for the selection of specific pieces of information produced by the magistrates to be included in the *tabulae publicae*, is difficult, however. What, at first sight, seems to be a stable inventory must have come together only successively. Without knowing the exact timeline we may imagine a conflict-laden process to make 'private' documentation of magistrates accessible to a broader 'public'. Reasons may have been mainly political, accountability and peer control among the ruling class more important than any (modern) idea of general administrative transparency. It is highly likely, to take an example, that the deposition of provincial accounts at a public rather than a private archive was called for as a result of accusations of magistrates' plundering of provinces and abuse of provincials, which led to the *lex Calpurnia de repetundis* of 149 BC and later legislation of the same kind, and made it necessary to substantiate accusations of financial irregularities with tangible evidence in court, the *quaestio de repetundis*.[136] Yet, still in 70 BC, when Cicero brought a charge *de repetundis* against Verres, the public accessibility of the culprit's detailed *rationes* was not yet taken for granted. Cicero had to draw on private copies of Verres' accounts.[137] It is only some years later, as we learn from the case of L. Calpurnius Piso Caesoninus, which I have already covered, that the deposition of provincial accounts had been made compulsory by C. Iulius Caesar, most likely through his *lex Iulia de repetundis* of 59 BC.[138] Archival policy was intertwined with the general political tug-of-war. Cn. Flavius' battle for the control of legal information during the Struggle of the Orders is a telling early incident. Caesar's legislation during his first consulate that dictated the publication of the *acta diurna* – most likely the minutes

---

[135] Cic. *Verr.* 2. 2. 101–106.
[136] On the introduction of these permanent courts and their evolution Rosillo-López (2010a) 119–23; Lintott (1981); see Chapter 4. Cf. the mention of written evidence in the Gracchan *lex repetundarum*, Roman Statutes no. 1, l. 34: *tabulas libros leiterasue pop[licas preiuatasue pos]cere proferrequ[e uolet, ad praetorem deferto - - -]*.
[137] Cic. *Verr.* 2. 1. 60. Verres had only deposited an extremely brief, general total of revenues and expenditures; Cic. *Verr.* 2. 1. 36.
[138] Cic. *Pis.* 61. See also Cato the Younger, who returns from his pro-praetorial quaestorship in Cyprus in 58 BC with detailed accounts of his tenure in duplicate. Both copies eventually perish due to unfortunate coincidences before he reaches Rome; Plut. *Cat. Mi.* 38. 2–3.

of the senate's sessions – had been equally politically motivated (and was subsequently rolled back under Augustus).[139] What constituted the public repository of knowledge at any given time is, thus, difficult to say with certainty. We may discern the broader picture; the details are mostly lost.

What is clear is the fact that the *tabulae publicae* constituted the veritable Roman repository of public knowledge. What was entered in the public tablets became – in Cicero's words – '*memoria publica*',[140] stored 'for the eternal remembrance of future ages'.[141] Words carved into the wax surface of the *tabulae publicae* assumed authoritative power. Referral to the public repository was no act of mere copying, but legal validation. *Senatus consulta* only became legally binding if and when inscribed into the *tabulae publicae*.[142] The same was true for the other legal or financial information in the *tabulae*. What was on record in the public repository was official knowledge and legally valid. The *tabulae publicae* were the touchstone of truthfulness as demonstrated by Cicero's use of and reference to the official repository in court.[143] The authority of the *tabulae publicae* is hard to underestimate: knowingly introducing into the *tabulae* anything false was deemed to be high treason from the last decades of the first century BC at the latest.[144] Accordingly, expectations were high. Even if Cicero's claim to eternity may have been hyperbolical, he himself and Cato the Younger assume, and in the latter case even attest to, gapless financial records going back at least one generation.[145] The minutes of more recent trials[146] as well as the *commentarii* of magistrates[147] were extant. Censorial lists were kept for at least five years as they were brought up to date and were archived again with every new censorial period. And *senatus consulta*

---

[139] SUET. *Iul.* 20. 1; SUET. *Aug.* 36. 1; on the *acta diurna / senatus* see Bats (1994).
[140] CIC. *Mil.* 73.
[141] CIC. *Sest.* 129: *ad memoriam posteri temporis sempiternam*, transl. R. Gardner.
[142] The most instructive example TAC. *ann.* 3. 51. 2 (AD 21); cf. Coudry (1994) 66f.
[143] A telling case is CIC. *Arch.* 8–9, in which Cicero argues for the validity of trustworthy witnesses in the case of Heraclia, where the local *tabularium* had burned down during the Social War, and documents could thus not be produced. He argues for trusting the Heracleians' word about what had been written in the local *tabulae publicae* based on their '*ius iurandum fidesque*', which is a reference to the oath magistrates and *scribae* swore in order to be allowed to write and manage the *tabulae publicae* (see Chapter 4). Cicero reverts to providing documentary proof rather than witnesses immediately after this argument. It shows that written documents had become the preferred means of evidence, despite the fact that they could be tampered with with relative ease and were susceptible to destruction. Other instances CIC. *Balb.* 8; CIC. *Font.* 2; CIC. *S. Rosc.* 128; CIC. *Verr.* 2. 2. 104–105; CIC. *Verr.* 2. 5. 10.
[144] DIG. 48. 4. 2. 1; cf. Williamson (2016) 339f.
[145] CIC. *S. Rosc.* 128; PLUT. *Cat. Mi.* 18. 2. Both cases make reference to Sullan times
[146] CIC. *Cluent.* 62; CIC. *Vat.* 34; CIC. *Verr.* 2. 2. 104–105; CIC. *Verr.* 2. 5. 10.
[147] CIC. *Verr.* 2. 2. 106.

were expected to be retrievable from the *tabulae* even after a century.¹⁴⁸ It is worth noting that these were the standards that Cicero presupposed for the *tabulae publicae*. We are, unfortunately, a far cry from having a complete picture of Roman documentary culture during imperial times. The very little we know does not, however, suggest a regression of archival practice.¹⁴⁹ It is for the provinces that we have the most conclusive evidence and it shows a vivid production and use of official documentation of a financial and legal nature that eventually led to the establishment of official provincial archives.¹⁵⁰ Attitudes to documentation and archiving seem to have persisted. At the end of the second century AD, in his role as an official in the provincial administration of Egypt, Lucian of Samosata recorded court proceedings and rescripts of the emperor with the notion that these were to be archived 'for all time', thus echoing the words of Cicero.¹⁵¹

Archives and Archival Practice

By AD 16, the archived *tabulae publicae* were in a state of disorder. We learn from Cassius Dio that Tiberius instated three senators assigned with the task of retrieving and copying parts of the public records because they 'had either perished completely or at least become illegible with the lapse of time'.¹⁵² The measure was, evidently, much needed. Thirty years later, in AD 46, we still find mention of these *curatores tabularum publicarum*.¹⁵³ The oversight of the public records, the *cura tabularum publicarum*, which in the Republic had been a responsibility of the *censores*,¹⁵⁴ had obviously been left uncared for. The issue was resolved in AD 56, when the *cura* was assigned to the *praefecti*, who had then been given the supervision of the *aerarium*.¹⁵⁵ Nero's decision marked the end of an archival reform that had been underway since Augustus and eventually concentrated the *tabulae publicae* under the sole responsibility of the head of the public treasury.¹⁵⁶

---

¹⁴⁸ CIC. *Att.* 13. 3. 33.
¹⁴⁹ Cencetti (1940) 46; Cencetti (1953).
¹⁵⁰ Haensch (1992) 219–37.
¹⁵¹ LUK. *Apol.* 12: πρὸς τὸν ἀεὶ χρόνον.
¹⁵² DIO 57. 16. 2: ἐπεί τε πολλὰ τῶν δημοσίων γραμμάτων τὰ μὲν καὶ παντελῶς ἀπωλώλει, τὰ δὲ ἐξίτηλα γοῦν ὑπὸ τοῦ χρόνου ἐγεγόνει, τρεῖς βουλευταὶ προεχειρίσθησαν ὥστε τά τε ὄντα ἐκγράψασθαι καὶ τὰ λοιπὰ ἀναζητῆσαι, transl. E. Carey.
¹⁵³ *CIL* 6, 916; on the evidence on the *curatores tabularum publicarum* see Hammond (1938).
¹⁵⁴ LIV. 4. 8. 4.
¹⁵⁵ TAC. *ann.* 13. 28. 3.
¹⁵⁶ A concise overview over the steps taken to reform the *aerarium* since Augustus in Millar (1963) 33f.; cf. Coudry (1994) 77; Corbier (1974) 676.

When the Romans had first begun archiving documents of public importance, they had used the facilities of temples. Temples, priests and writing had formed a natural alliance since the early Republic.[157] As a result, Roman temples had soon become 'both generators and storehouses of documents'.[158] The temple of Saturn housed the treasury (*aerarium*), which was administered by the *quaestores*.[159] As such it had always been the most important repository of financial and legal documents. It was at the *aerarium* that Polybius found early treaties between Rome and the Carthaginians.[160] It is where provincial *rationes* and *consulta* of the senate were deposited. The *aedes Nympharum*[161] as well as the *Atrium Libertatis*[162] housed the documents of the *censores*. At the *aedes Cereris* we find the *aediles* and *tribuni plebis* depositing their documents, including copies of senatorial decrees, most likely in an attempt to counter the monopoly of the senate.[163] As a result, the *tabulae publicae* must have been distributed over several differently located *tabularia*. What finally brought them together under the guise of the *aerarium* is difficult to assess.

The developments in the archival landscape of the Late Republic are only partially known. What we can discern is that *tabulae publicae* and the involved parties moved closer together. We find not only the *quaestores* but also the *aediles* and *tribuni* working at the *aerarium* during the Late Republic. We learn that, prior to 11 BC, the *tribuni plebis* and the *aediles* had been charged with the keeping of the *senatus consulta*, a task that was then transferred to the *quaestores* as the former authorities had neglected their duty.[164] As early as 202 BC, we find the *aediles* associated with the *aerarium*, when some of their *scribae* and *viatores* embezzled money from the treasury.[165] We may assume that, as a result of the Struggle of the Orders, what had once constituted the 'archive of the plebs' was subsequently incorporated into the general financial and legal archive of the *aerarium*, whereby the aediles and tribunes were granted the oversight of the *senatus consulta*.[166] Already in pre-Sullan times, the Romans were most likely used

---

[157] North (1998) 45.
[158] Beard (1998) 76.
[159] On the *aerarium* in general Millar (1964).
[160] Plb. 3.26.1.
[161] Cic. *Mil.* 73.
[162] Liv. 43.16.13.
[163] Liv. 3.55.13; cf. Culham (1989) 109.
[164] Dio 54.36.1.
[165] Liv. 30.39.7. Plb. 3.26.1 even associates the ταμιεῖον (*aerarium*) on the Capitol with the ἀγορανόμοι, i.e. the *aediles*, not with the *quaestores*; cf. Walbank (1957–1979) II 353f., who thus assumes a second treasury.
[166] See already Mazzei (2009) 333 w. n. 205. According to Dio 43.48.3, Julius Caesar even appointed two *aediles* to head the *aerarium* in 45 BC.

to referring to one most important archive as *the* archive. At least this is what is suggested by Cicero's remark that it had been a Roman knight named Q. Sosius who '*tabularium incenderit*'.[167] In 83 BC, another fire that devastated the Capitoline Hill and completely destroyed the Temple of Jupiter was set to radically change the Roman archival landscape.[168] Although the details are still hotly debated,[169] it is undisputed that a new *tabularium* had been built as part of the huge new structure that included the new Capitoline temple and dominates the Campidoglio to this day (the so-called Tabularium).[170] We do not know its exact place or its dimensions in relation to the whole complex.[171] The erection of a dedicated *tabularium* in the vicinity of the temple of Saturn and the *aerarium* might very well have met demands for an expanding and more centralised archival practice. N. Purcell's hypothetical, yet intriguing identification of parts of the structure of the 'Tabularium' with the construction of the *Atrium Libertatis* in 39 BC would also tie the censors and their documentary practice to the Capitoline Hill.[172] Virgil's evocative image of life in the capital consisting of '*ferrea iura insanumque forum aut populi tabularia*' might have been influenced by this new Capitoline archive.[173] Virgil's late-fourth-century commentator Servius identified his '*populi tabularia*' with the place where the '*actus publici*' were archived, i.e. the complex comprised of the temple of Saturn and the *aerarium*.[174] Servius' explanation might not have been unfounded. At least since AD 88, the *tabularium* on the Capitoline Hill was officially known as the *tabularium publicum*, making it the prime

---

[167] CIC. *nat. deor.* 3. 74; cf. CIC. *Rab. perd.* 8, a certain C. Curtius acquitted of the same charge; Moreau (1994) 141f. w. n. 89.
[168] PLUT. *Sull.* 27. 6; TAC. *hist.* 3. 72. 3.
[169] The most recent reconstruction of the whole complex with a discussion of earlier proposals in Tucci (2014).
[170] The inscription mentioning the building by Q. Lutatius Catulus, is now lost; *CIL* 6, 1314: *Q(uintus) Lutatius Q(uinti) f(ilius) Q(uinti) [n(epos)] Catulus co(n)s(ul) / substructionem et tabularium / de s(enatus) s(ententia) faciundum coeravit [ei]demque / pro[bavit]*.
[171] The classic account with its influential identification of the extant structure as the *substructio* and the localisation of the *tabularium* above it, now lost, by Delbrueck (1907–1912) I 23–46; an overview over more recent research in Mura Somella (1999) 19, who follows Delbrueck's interpretation; Coarelli (2011) 33–9 imagines that the *tabularium* occupied the whole structure of the 'Tabularium' and had, technically, been an extension of the *aerarium* and the temple of Saturn; Tucci (2005) assigns only small parts of the structure to a minor *tabularium* (no central archive), identifying the construction as the new building of the mint and the temple of Iuna Moneta; contra Culham (1989) 102f., who completely denies the building complex of the 'Tabularium' the use as *tabularium*; cf. a thorough review of the available sources and possibilities of interpretation by Mazzei (2009).
[172] Purcell (1993).
[173] VERG. *georg.* 2. 501–502.
[174] SERV. *georg.* 2. 502: '*Populi tabularia' ubi actus publici continentur. Significat autem templum Saturni, in quo et aerarium fuerat et reponebantur acta, quae susceptis liberis faciebant parentes*'.

candidate to house the *tabulae publicae* under the oversight of the head of the *aerarium*.[175]

With the Empire, a second strand of Roman archival practice came into being, a strand independent of the archive of the people and the senate, which housed the *tabulae publicae*. The political and administrative apparatus of the *princeps* generated its own documentation that was archived on its own. The *tabularium publicum* found its match in one or several archives of the *princeps* – among them the *tabularium principis* – that accommodated the output of the imperial financial and legal administration as well as the imperial chancery.[176] The *scribae*, as the Republican institution they were, had nothing to do with this part of the administration of the Roman state. They were left with their role in the Republican state, whose relics were incorporated into the new constitutional order of the Empire.

What a public archive, a *tabularium*, looked like, we do not know with certainty. Despite the fact that they were an essential part of a city's administrative practice and must, thus, have been a given, archaeological identification of *tabularia* is, to this date, only hypothetical. The problems surrounding the architectural complex of the 'Tabularium', discussed above, are a case in point. While *tabularia* are attested epigraphically, their localisation in the field remains difficult. Archaeologists have tended to identify *tabularia* as part of building complexes associated with or belonging to municipal administration (most often incorporating a *curia* or other assembly places). Prime candidates have usually been buildings featuring wall niches as part of their architecture.[177] By analogy with what we know of libraries and the keeping of tablets in general, the niches are expected to have been fitted with shelves and cabinets (*armaria*) to house the *tabulae publicae*.[178] We have no direct, positive evidence, however. The rare glimpses of the workplace of the *scriba*, which may, in the best case, give us an understanding of the interior of a *tabularium*, focus on the working with, rather than the storing of the writing tablets. Our prime example is the upper relief from the early imperial 'Ara degli Scribi', a funerary altar for two *scribae* of the *aediles curules*, showing the *scribae* at work (see Fig. 2.1).[179] The focus lies on the tablets placed on a table in the

---

[175] Two military diplomas dated to AD 88 are '*descriptum et recognitum ex tabula aenea quae fixa est Romae in Capitolio in latere sinistro tabulari publici*', CIL 16, 35; AE 1974, 655.
[176] In general Cencetti (1953); Moatti (1993) 63–9; on archival infrastructure Gros (2001) 113–16.
[177] On evidence for *tabularia* in general Balty (1991) 151–61; Mazzei (2009) 294–317.
[178] Houston (2014) 180–97.
[179] Zevi and Friggeri (2012).

Figure 2.1 So-called Ara degli Scribi, upper relief. Occupational scene, Roman *scribae* of the *aediles* together with assistants handling large-format *tabulae ceratae*. Via Appia, 'vigna Casali', Porta S. Sebastiano, Rome. Early 1. c. AD. (Benjamin Hartmann)

centre of the scene and the people working with them.[180] The architecture of the workspace is of secondary importance, in fact it is almost completely hidden. Such a characterisation of the interior of a *tabularium* may seem odd to a modern observer, who most likely associates a still life of racks full of documents with the concept of an 'archive'. Yet, it is quite possible that, on the contrary, the active aspects of documentary culture were at the heart of a Roman *tabularium*. Keeping documents was surely one purpose of such a dedicated building, but making and using them might have been at least equally important. *Tabularia* were not only storage rooms but above all workrooms. If we are to believe Tacitus, *tabularia* were, in his time, genuinely used as places of trial.[181]

The *tabulae publicae*, which the *tabularia* housed, were – as the denomination of *tabulae* suggests – wooden wax tablets. Tablets made from fir wood, recessed on one or both sides and filled with black or red wax to form a writing surface, were joined together to a so-called *codex*, which had become the prototypical form of *tabulae publicae*.[182] While we possess ample testimony for the form and typological range of wax tablets (*tabulae*

---

[180] Cf. the fragmentary bas-relief of a very similar scene, kept in the Museo Nazionale Romano, Terme di Diocleziano, Sala IV (without inv. nr.).
[181] TAC. *dial.* 39. 1.
[182] SEN. *dial.* 10. 13. 4.

ceratae) in private and professional use,¹⁸³ evidence for the *codices* used as *tabulae publicae* is much more limited. We lack any physical remains. What we are left with are, on the one hand, pictorial representations. Although clearly assignable depictions are few, we are lucky enough to possess evidence for a cross-section of *tabulae publicae*, namely such used to document the *census*, the finances of the state as well as legal matters.¹⁸⁴ These representations suggest that the *tabulae publicae* likely were of a much bigger size than the handy tablets used for domestic purposes. Measured against the people handling them, the wax tablets used as *tabulae publicae* must have had a page length of more than 50 centimetres. While ordinary writing tablets usually fit a hand (they also went by the name *pugillares*), these large-format tablets were bulky and heavy armfuls. The depiction of *scribae* at work on the 'Ara degli Scribi' vividly exemplifies this fact (see Fig. 2.1). At least three of the five people involved in working in the office of the *aediles curules* conveniently carry one or more ordinary writing tablet in their hands or their garb (*sinus*). Meanwhile, the *tabulae publicae* lie heavily on a stack on a table before them and are handled with both hands. The heaviness and bulkiness of these wooden wax tablets is physical on the 'Plutei Traiani', the bas-relief showing Hadrian's debt relief, where soldiers amass these huge tablets on the *forum* in order to burn them (see Fig. 2.2). The main advantage of such large-format tablets was that they provided a multiple of the writing surface of an ordinary writing tablet, which made them an ideal medium of archival. Unity of subject matter was much more important than portability when it came to keeping documents.

On 10 December AD 20, the Roman senate debated the case of Cn. Calpurnius Piso, who had been accused of poisoning the heir to the throne Germanicus and who had, in anticipation of the inevitable verdict, taken his own life. The *senatus consultum* passed by the assembly under the supervision of the emperor Tiberius recapitulates the hearing as well as the measures taken against the perpetrators and in favour of the *memoria* of Germanicus. We learn from the resolution that it was recorded by A. Plautius,¹⁸⁵ the *quaestor* of Tiberius, on fourteen wax tablets ('*in tabellis XIIII*') and was designated to be archived in the *tabulae publicae* ('*referre in tabulas*

---

[183] An overview in Ammirati (2013); a typology in Speidel (tab. Vindon.) 23–8; most recently Tomlin (WT) 22–30; an overview of known extant tablets in Hartmann (2015).
[184] A *census* in the bas-relief of the so-called altar of Domitius Ahenobarbus, H. Meyer (1993), (see Fig. 2.3); financial documents in the depiction of Hadrian's debt relief on the so-called Plutei Traiani, Koeppel (1986) nos. 1–2, (see Fig. 2.2); *scribae* of the *aediles curules* handling *tabulae publicae* on the 'Ara degli Scribi', Zevi and Friggeri (2012) (see Fig. 2.1).
[185] Eck, Caballos, and Fernando (SCPP) 104f.

42   The Human Archive

Figure 2.2   Stone balustrade, so-called Plutei Traiani, depicting Hadrian's general debt relief. Roman soldiers bringing together large-format *tabulae ceratae* containing financial documentation to burn them. Forum Romanum, Curia Iulia, Rome. After AD 118. (Antonio Cederna)

publicas').[186] The wording is the same as that used for the registration of the provincial *rationes*: the *senatus consultum* was referred to the public tablets, i.e. copied into the *tabulae publicae*. What had filled the pages of fourteen ordinary writing tablets could likely have been accommodated on one large-format tablet of the *tabulae publicae*.[187] Ordinary small-format wax tablets could fit up to thirty characters per line of ten centimetres and ten lines per ten centimetres of tablet height.[188] The two sides of a *tabula publica* of even modest size would have provided enough space to receive the whole text of the *senatus consultum*, which amounts to approximately 12,500 characters[189] and occupies a bronze tablet of ca. 120 × 45 centimetres in its published form (using double the letter size of wax tablets).[190] It is evident that the process of copying the text of several ordinary wax tablets onto one large-format tablet of the *tabulae publicae* significantly simplified the process of archival and retrieval. Building a dossier of related documents, e.g. of resolutions of the senate in a so-called *liber sententiarum in senatu*

---

[186] *SCPP* 175.
[187] See for a similar instance the Aphrodisian inscription Reynolds (1982) no. 8, ll. 1–3, which mentions different sources for the text of the *senatus consultum de Aphrodisiensibus* which is cited. One, the ταμιακαὶ δέλτοι, i.e. the *tabulae publicae*, had the text on one δέλτος, the other, a σύνκλητος (*codex*), perhaps a *commentarius* of a magistrate, used as many as six individual tablets to accommodate the same text.
[188] The measurements from *tab. Vindon.* 1, a military certificate of discharge on a wax tablet. The document, clearly written by a trained hand, might come close in character to what we have to expect from writing on *tabulae publicae*.
[189] Eck, Caballos and Fernando (1996) 277.
[190] Eck, Caballos and Fernando (1996) 7.

dictarum[191] was more feasible and easier to handle in one large-format 'codex' than as a heap of small tablets.

What such a *codex* might have looked like is recorded in an inscription from the Etrurian municipality of Caere.[192] In the year AD 113, Ulpius Vesbinus, an imperial freedman and *sevir Augustalis* was set on establishing a club-house for the *Augustales* at his own expense. As the plot of land was public, a decision had to be made by the local senate, and as the colony was under the watch of a *curator* of the state, the local senate had to appeal to a certain Curiatius Cosanus first. Vesbinus' request was eventually granted and, perhaps due to the fact that the assessment of his project had been very favourable, he decided to include the decisions made by the *curator* as well as the *decuriones* in the inscription that remembered his generous donation. The documents are quoted as certified copies from the '*commentarium cottidianum municipi(i) Caeritum*'. It becomes clear that this *commentarium* must have been the daybook of the municipality's senate. The instances cited are referenced by *paginae* (pages) and *capita* (headings), suggesting two-sided large-format tablets suited to incorporate extensive amounts of text. The *commentarium* was organised by year, naming the consuls of Rome as well as the highest municipal official (*dictator*) and the *aedilis iure dicundo* in his role as *praefectus aerarii*, i.e. the magistrate charged with the oversight of the archive and the *commentarium*. The discussion of Vesbinus' request by the *decuriones* is recorded on the twenty-seventh *pagina*, under the sixth header. The assembly's letter to the *curator*, dated to the ides of August, follows under the first header on the '*pagina altera*', i.e. the twenty-eighth. Under the same header, thus most probably subsequent, the commentary contained Curiatius Cosanus' answer to the Caerites, dated to the day before the ides of September of the same year (the inscription was manufactured and dedicated in the following year AD 114). Unless we assume that the Caerite summer of AD 113 was utterly uneventful, the dates of the letters cited and their subsequent arrangement on the pages suggest that the *commentarium* on large tablets represented a fair copy, which was established in the aftermath and with a certain thematic order in mind.

---

[191] In the *senatus consultum de nundinis saltus Beguensis*, CIL 8, 23246; cf. Cic. *Att*. 13. 33. 3, which mentions a '*lib[er] in quo sunt senatus consulta Cn. Cornelio, L. Mummio coss*'. Contra Culham (1989) 113 n. 61, who argues that these *libri* were not part of the *tabulae publicae*. However, at least in the case of the *senatus consultum de nundinis saltus Beguensis*, we are explicitly dealing with a certified copy on a diptychon of wax tablets, attested by Roman *scribae*, which makes it almost certain that *tabulae publicae* were used.

[192] CIL 11, 3614; 4347.

Financial documents must have been of very similar appearance. A fragmentary inscription from the Sabine town of Trebula Suffenas dated to Trajanic times cites passages from two *codices accepti et expensi*[193] archived in the *tabularium* of the town, which testify to the payment of debts by a certain A. Furius some forty years earlier. The passages are cited by yearly dated *codices*, tablets (*tabulae*) and pages (*cerae*).[194]

Documentary practice at a local level was no different from at the state level. The characteristics of the medium to a great extent determined the systematics of the documents themselves. The *commentarii* of the magistrates seem to have followed the same regime as the *commentarium cottidianum* of Caere. A *codex ansatus* of L. Helvius Agrippa, *proconsul* of *Sardinia* in AD 69, recorded his decisions on *tabulae* under *capita*.[195] Very similarly, *senatus consulta* were archived according to *consules*,[196] i.e. organised per year and likely divided further per month[197] or as required. Senatorial decrees and daybooks of magistrates are usually cited per *codex* and wax page.[198]

Guardians of the Written

The documentary and archival practice of the Republican state was geared towards uniformity and continuity. The information that made up the *tabulae publicae* was purposefully picked and carefully recorded onto a uniform medium. The *tabulae* were intended to be diligently stored for lasting reference. The most important and at the same time most limiting factor in this procedure was, I would argue, the personnel employed to ensure these principles, i.e. the people making, keeping and using the documents. It is certainly true that the existence of a dedicated institution such as the *scriba*-ship as such shows a certain Roman appreciation for written procedure. At the same time it blatantly reveals the limitations of the documentary culture of the Roman Republican state. The *scribae* were

---

[193] A synonym of *rationes*, Ste Croix (1956) 41.
[194] *AE* 1999, 571b. On the limited nature of accounting in general and the methods of accounting see Ste Croix (1956) 33–50; Fallu (1979) 100–2.
[195] *CIL* 10, 7852; cf. Haensch (1992) 222f., n. 36.
[196] Cic. *Att.* 13. 33. 3: *lib[er] in quo sunt senatus consulta Cn. Cornelio, L. Mummio coss* (146 BC); *CIL* 8, 23246, the *senatus consultum de nundinis saltus Beguensis*: '*ex libro sententiarum in senatu dictarum Kani Iuni Nigri C. Pomponi Camerini coss*' (AD 138).
[197] Attested by the *senatus consultum de Aphrodisiensibus* RDGE no. 29, ll. 1–3; Reynolds (1982) no. 8, 65f.
[198] In Greek δέλτος (*tabula*) and κήρωμα (*cera*); a *commentarius* of a magistrate in 129 BC, RDGE no. 12, l. 20; a *commentarius* of L. Calpurnius Piso in 112 BC, RDGE no. 14, l. 75; a *senatus consultum* of 80 BC, RDGE no. 23, ll. 58–9; a *senatus consultum* of 44 BC, J. *AJ* 14. 219; a *senatus consultum* of 39 BC, Sherk (RDGE) no. 28, ll. 1–3.

the only senior officials explicitly dedicated to documenting and archiving in the Republican administrative framework. Our sources are surprisingly secretive when it comes to other personnel apart from *scribae* assisting the magistrates in this domain. We know only of public slaves.[199] We find them working in the *tabularium* of the censors as well as transcribing the financial documents in the *aerarium*.[200] The lean apparitorial system, of which the *scribae* were part, had been in place since the early Republic. And it is easy to recognise that such a system must have been stretched to its limits when faced with the expansive documentary practice I have sketched above. Indeed, it is the notion that the endeavour of public documentation had begun to suffer from being notoriously undermanned on which Plutarch could draw for his topic characterisation of Cato the Younger's term as *quaestor urbanus* of 65/4 BC. Cato had seen the need to knock the *aerarium* into shape and bring in his own household slaves to cope with the daily business of copying financial documents. And he ended up leaving them at the treasury even after he had finished his term of office.[201]

This systematic shortage of manpower seems to have been tackled not long after Cato's term. As far as we can discern, the Republican apparitorial system had, by design, known no additional clerical officials apart from the *scribae*.[202] Yet, it is clear from our imperial epigraphic record that such a charge had eventually been introduced. Not only do we still find the official title of *scriba* but also a second, subordinate category, the one of *scriba librarius*. Our prime source is, once again, the late Augustan to early Tiberian 'Ara degli Scribi'. Faustus (A.81), one of the two Fulvii brothers honoured with the funerary altar, is designated as both '*scriba et scriba librarius aedilium curulium*', clearly showing both specific scribal posts side by side for the first time.[203] Aristocratic households had long made use of *librarii* for a wide range of clerical and secretarial duties, above all

---

[199] Nollé (1982) 115 has argued that the five *signatores* following the two *scribae* in the *senatus consultum de nundinis saltus Beguensis* (CIL 8, 270, 11451, 23246) might be identified with lesser officials working at the *aerarium*. Their identity remains unclear, however.

[200] LIV. 43.16.13: *censores extemplo in atrium Libertatis escenderunt et ibi obsignatis tabellis publicis clausoque tabulario et dimissis servis publicis [...]*; *Frat. Arv.* 80, 61–65: *[D. Rupilio ?] Seuero, L. Iulio Seuero co(n)s(ulibus) / (ante diem tertium) idus Decembr(es) (vacat) / [in locum Ca]rp[i] publici Corneliani promoti ad tabulas quae/storias transscribendas substitu<tu>s est Epictetus Cuspianus publi/cus ex litteris M. Fului Aproniani promagistri*. The slave of a quaestorian *scriba* mentioned in PLIN. *ep.* 6. 22. 4 might have been a public slave.

[201] PLUT. *Cat. Mi.* 18. 5.

[202] Already Mommsen (1887) I 354.

[203] Cf. A.141 for a slightly later second holder of both scribal posts.

the transcription and copying of texts.[204] It is in this capacity that we eventually find them associated with Roman magistrates. At the peak of the Catiline conspiracy in 63 BC, Cicero let fellow senators keep the minutes of the session of the senate and subsequently had the minutes manifolded at the hands of *librarii* in order to publish them state-wide.[205] It is quite likely that these *librarii* were already institutionalised *apparitores* rather than his private scribes. In his oration of the same year against the agrarian legislation of P. Servilius Rullus, Cicero counts *librarii* among the prototypical apparitorial entourage of Roman office holders.[206] The assignment of additional clerical manpower must have been the new reality.[207] The earliest extant colonial charter, the almost contemporaneous Caesarian *lex coloniae Genetivae Iuliae*, quite symptomatically allowed for two clerical apparitorial posts: the major *scribae* as well as the minor *librarii*.[208] This is the division we subsequently find in large cities as well as in Rome itself (see Chapter 3). By the end of the 50s of the first century BC, Cicero naturally associates the *librarii* with the public repository.[209] The official denomination of *librarius* must have been adjusted to *scriba librarius* in the following years, most likely to differentiate the holders of the apparitorial post from private *librarii*. The new title is first attested for a certain M. Seius (A.156), who had been the *apparitor* of M. Terentius Varro and subsequently managed his estate.[210] At least by the mid 30s, when Varro wrote his treatise on agriculture, the denomination must have become established. The *Tabula Heracleensis*, difficult to date but most likely pertaining to the same age, also uses the new terminology.[211] The picture finally becomes clear in imperial times. Besides private *librarii*[212] there were now two apparitorial clerical categories: *scribae* and *scribae librarii*.

From an institutional perspective we may characterise the *scribae librarii* as junior partners to the *scribae*. The clauses of the *lex coloniae Genetivae Iuliae* show the *librarii* at the bottom of the apparitorial pay scale of the city,

---

[204] The term denominated both booksellers as well as private clerks and copyists, Collassero (1985) (*TLL*); the range of clerical work exercised by *librarii* in Haines-Eitzen (2000) 30f.
[205] Cic. *Sul.* 42.
[206] Cic. *leg. agr.* 2. 32.
[207] Contra Purcell (2001) 645f., who interprets the evidence not as an institutional reform but a deliberate differentiation of senior clerks, *scribae*, from those exercising lower tasks, *librarii*.
[208] *lex Urson.* 62. 12–13.
[209] Cic. *leg.* 3. 46: *Legum custodiam nullam habemus, itaque eae leges sunt quas apparitores nostri uolunt. A librariis petimus, publicis litteris consignatam memoriam publicam nullam habemus.* Cf. also Ascon. *Mil.* test. 19, who speaks of *codices librariorum* with regard to Clodius' funeral in 52 BC.
[210] Varro *rust.* 3. 2. 14. Perhaps as late as during Varro's proquaestorship of 49 BC in Spain under Pompey, cf. Broughton (1951–1952) II 269.
[211] *Tab. Heracl.* 80.
[212] See for example Fronto's private *librarius*, Fronto *Aur.* 5. 41.

at a fourth of the pay of the top-earning *scribae*.[213] In addition, the *scribae* were subject to an oath of due diligence in order to be allowed to manage the public money and write the *rationes*. The *librarii*, in turn, were not, which suggests that their clerical responsibilities might have been markedly different.[214] It is plausible that, at least in principle, these regulations were modelled on the state. By design, the Republican order provided the *scribae* with a monopolistic position with regard to the *tabulae publicae*. Besides the magistrates, they were the only officials allowed to wield authority over the sensitive documents. As such it would have made sense that they were subject to an oath. We know, after all, that the *scribae* were, together with the censors and the other magistrates, anointed at the censorial *lustrum*.[215] Whether this also applied to the *scribae librarii* is not known. At any rate, the legal and social status of holders of the two apparitorial posts might reflect the distinction made in the colonial law. While *scribae* were, as a rule, freeborn citizens, the post of *scriba librarius* was usually held by individuals with a libertine background.[216] The new apparitorial charge was evidently oriented towards the basic conditions of its model, the private, unfree *librarius*. What this meant for the daily business of *scribae* and *scribae librarii* is difficult to say as we lack informative evidence of the two charges working side by side. Drawing on the origins of the newly created apparitorial charge, we might be tempted to associate *scribae librarii* with the more mechanical task of copying rather than the composition of documents, which had traditionally been a responsibility of the *scribae* tout court. Yet, already the example of Varro's *vilicus* M. Seius may advise us to be cautious. It was certainly no coincidence that the person carrying out the financial and administrative management of Varro's estates was a former *scriba librarius*. In fact, we might envision both charges working the same documents as senior and junior clerks. Fulvius Priscus' titles at least suggest a differentiation along hierarchical lines rather than by technical department. According to Festus it was also the *scribae librarii*, '*qui rationes publicas scribunt in tabulis*'[217] – a task that had been at the heart of the professional activities of the Republican *scriba*. The difference between *scribae* and *scribae librarii* might, ultimately, have been one of authority

---

[213] *lex Urson*. 62. 32–35. Cf. Table 3.1.
[214] The *ius iurandum* attested for the *scribae* of the *duumviri* of Urso, *lex Urson*. 81. 17–29; also in the *lex Flavia municipalis, lex Irn*. 73. 31 47.
[215] Varro *ling*. 6. 87.
[216] See Chapter 5 and the known *scribae librarii* in the appendix. Freedmen and their offspring abound.
[217] Fest. 446.26–29 (333M).

and responsibilities, not so much one of function and skills; a difference determined by legal and social status.

Scriptum Facere

The *tabulae publicae* and *scribae* (including the *scribae librarii*) were two elements of an equation. It is the *scribae* who are strongly associated with the repository of public knowledge; it is to their integrity (*fides*) that, in Cicero's words, the '*tabulae publicae periculaque magistratuum*' were committed.[218] Cicero's statement perfectly sums up the activities of the *scribae*. Not only were they responsible for and occupied with the *tabulae publicae*, but they were also tasked, in the first place, with the making of the magistrates' records (*pericula*) that were later incorporated into the public repository. As apparitors they were designated to serve and assist specific magistrates; as professional scribes they took care of clerical duties in the staff of these office holders; *scriptum facere* in technical terms.[219] As a result, we encounter *scribae* busy at work wherever their respective superiors are found. The Capitoline Hill with the *aerarium*, the political and administrative centre of the Republic, is perhaps the most obvious place of scribal activity.[220] In general, any place in and outside the city of Rome could serve as workplace for the *scribae*. The *Tabula Heracleensis* explicitly marks out '*loca publica porticusve publicae*', i.e. public places and porticoes, for the utilisation of *scribae (librarii)* who were attending magistrates.[221] The *senatus consultum* concerning the endowment of the *curatores aquarum* provides the assistance of clerical *apparitores* both in and outside the city of Rome.[222] Magistrates fulfilling their duty in the provinces, above all the *quaestores*, customarily brought their *scribae* and *scribae librarii* along with them.

The provisions in the *Tabula Heracleensis* regarding the *scribae* suggest that documenting the daily dealings of a magistrate may have been an effortful and bulky business. The legal provisions state that *scribae* attending to magistrates were exempt from the general ban on occupying and obstructing public space.[223] A look at depictions of working *scribae* and scribes in general illustrates why. While writing on small wax tablets was certainly feasible in a standing position and without further equipment,

---

[218] Cic. *Verr.* 2.3.183.
[219] Gell. 7.9.2–3 (Piso *frg.* F29 (FRH)), Liv. 9.46.2–3 (Macer *frg.* F24 (FRH)), Suet. *vita Hor.* 24.
[220] Cic. *Phil.* 2.16; Cic. *Pis.* 61.
[221] *Tab. Heracl.* 68–80.
[222] Frontin. *Aq.* 2.100.
[223] *Tab. Heracl.* 68–80.

minuting on large-format wooden tablets or papyrus was done seated, ideally at a table. The *scriba* recording the *census* on the bas-relief of the so-called altar of Domitius Ahenobarbus handles his large-format tablets seated, resting them on his knees. Additional tablets are stacked at his feet (see Fig. 2.3). The depiction resembles the one on the 'Ara degli Scribi', where the enormous wax tablets are stashed on a low table and the *scribae* are seated next to them (see Fig. 2.1). Typically, sophisticated clerical work entailed furnishings in the form of chairs and, additionally, tables.[224] It is evident that it might not have been feasible for a *scriba* to bring along a *sella* to all of his apparitorial performances, let alone an unwieldy table. Yet, circumstances and locality permitting, we may envision *scribae* making themselves at home in public spaces by means of a kind of mobile scriptorium, warranting their legal privileges named in the *Tabula Heracleensis*. Roman *scribae* sitting in the midst of an array of differently sized wax tablets (and possibly also papyrus sheets), equipped with various other writing utensils,[225] documenting Roman political life, must have made for a marvellous display of literate practice in action. The Roman *scriba*-ship was no secretive trade when it came to its outward appearance. Roman *scribae* must have been easily recognisable by their conspicuous writing tablets alone and were, thus, commonly associated with them. Quite typically, when Cn. Flavius stood for election as *aedilis curulis*, he demonstratively put down his writing tablets to make clear that he had given up his post as a *scriba*.[226]

The Roman *scriba* and his writing tablets were at home in the documentary culture I have laid out in the previous sections. As a result, writing was at the centre of his daily business. Yet, what made a *scriba* was much more. Documenting Roman political life included not only making records but also keeping and using them. Roman *scribae* were not only scribes but also documentary specialists and archivists.

The primary association of the *scribae* was with financial documentation. We have seen that in Livy's retrospection, the Etruscan '*scriba*' was occupied with financial registers. And it is this trait of Roman documentary practice that was set to have a defining impact on the Roman *scriba*-ship. Although the *scribae*, as I will try to show, were involved with all the various areas

---

[224] See exemplarily a bas-relief from Ostia depicting scribes recording the speech of an orator seated at low tables writing on large-format tablets, Museo Ostiense, inv. nr. 130, ICCD E49915; and one from Portus, showing the unloading of a ship with a scribe seated at a table registering the goods on tablets, Museo Torlonia, ICCD E36853, E36854; cf. Houston (2014) 201f.
[225] An overview in Božič and Feugère (2004).
[226] The term is *tabulas ponere*, Piso *frg.* F29 (FRH) (Gell. 7. 9. 1–6); Liv. 9. 46. 2.

Figure 2.3 Relief of the so-called altar of Domitius Ahenobarbus, left side, detail. Roman *scriba* documenting *census* on large-format *tabulae ceratae*. Campus Martius, temple of Neptune, Rome. Late 2. c. BC. (Marie-Lan Nguyen)

of Roman documentary culture discussed above, it was financial administration that they were perceived to have a close relationship with. Festus, as I have shown, defined *scribae* solely by their handling of *rationes*.[227] Already Cicero had highlighted this connection.[228] And indeed, financial documentation ranks first in our sources on *scribae*. It seems to have been the most prestigious, i.e. most responsible, of activities for these clerical apparitors. As a result, the quaestorian *scribae* came first in social mobility and status among their scribal colleagues (see Chapter 5) and, at the same time, were those most prone to be compromised in cases of embezzlement and mismanagement (see Chapter 4).

We are fortunate enough to be able to gain insight into the responsibilities of a quaestorian *scriba* through Cicero's correspondence during his proconsulate in Cilicia of the years 51/50 BC. A certain M. Tullius (A.178) had been one of the two *scribae quaestorii* assigned to Cicero's governorship for the year 51 BC together with the *quaestor* L. Mescinius

---

[227] FEST. 333.19–22.
[228] Exemplarily CIC. *dom*. 74: *scribae, qui nobiscum in rationibus monumentisque publicis versantur.*

Rufus.[229] We first meet him on his way to the province, when he caught up with Cicero in *Beneventum*.[230] In Athens, both were later joined by the *quaestor* himself.[231] From the moment when Cicero entered his province and arrived at Laodicea, we are fairly well informed about his activities, which he is keen on communicating to his correspondents. However, M. Tullius, the *scriba*, and the *quaestor* Mescinius Rufus make no further appearance when it comes to daily duties. We must assume that they were at Cicero's side while he toured his province to adjudicate, settle financial dues and campaign.[232] It is only at the very end of Cicero's governorship that both come into focus. In July of 50 BC, Cicero was intent on leaving his province and the undesirable duties behind and heading back to Rome. However, new regulations regarding provincial financial administration, instated by C. Iulius Caesar in 59 BC (the *lex Iulia de repetundis*), compelled governors to deposit copies of the *rationes* of their gubernatorial period in two cities of the province before heading back to Rome to submit the accounts to the *aerarium*. What once had been done upon return to Rome, namely the settling of the accounts, now had to be finished while still in the province. However, Cicero had been in great haste and decided to leave behind his *quaestor* Mescinius to deposit the *rationes* as prescribed.[233] Yet, the latter was not happy with the arrangement. He especially disapproved of the settling of the accounts. As we learn from a letter of Cicero to his *quaestor*, written when he arrived back at Rome at the beginning of January 49 BC, the accounts were usually the joint work of the governor and his financial officer. But Cicero's great haste had made it impossible to settle the accounts face to face, which obviously led to misunderstandings as to how the final accounts should look. Cicero countered his *quaestor*'s reproaches by reminding him of the procedure they had agreed upon. In his stead, Cicero had chosen the *scriba quaestorius* M. Tullius to draw up the *rationes* together with Mescinius. Once finished, the accounts were referred back to Cicero by the *scriba* for approval and were subsequently deposited by Mescinius. In his eyes, Cicero had given his *quaestor* free rein, doing 'nothing whatever beyond reading' the

---

[229] On the identification of M. Tullius as a proper *scriba quaestorius* rather than an (ex-)slave of Cicero see Shackleton Bailey (1965–1970) III 96f.; Shackleton Bailey (1965) 50. Cf. Chapter 3.
[230] CIC. *Att.* 5. 4. 1.
[231] CIC. *Att.* 5. 11. 4.
[232] See Cicero's respective letters of his time as governor, Treggiari (1996). Pliny the Younger, when he was *legatus Augusti* of Trajan in the province of *Bithynia* some 150 years later, saw it as his duty to control the books of account of provincial cities, PLIN. *ep.* 10. 7b. 2, 10. 48. 1.
[233] CIC. *Att.* 6. 6. 2.

rationes.²³⁴ As a result, Cicero ended up defending not himself but the *scriba quaestorius* Tullius, whose intentions and actions had become suspicious to Mescinius.

At the heart of the dispute lies the fact that the *scriba* in practice wielded much more authority than was provided for in theory. Even a magistrate as considerate as Cicero effectively devolved financial administration to the *scriba*. When it came to details and technicalities in the *rationes*, the *scriba* was the expert to go by.

> Ad ea, quae scripsisti [scil. Mescinius], commodius equidem possem de singulis ad te rebus scribere, si M. Tullius, scriba meus, adesset ... Ego tamen, cum Tullius rure redierit, mittam eum ad te, si quid ad rem putabis pertinere.²³⁵

Cicero, at least, was unable to discuss anything but the big picture without the aid of M. Tullius, so much so that he promised to send the *scriba* to Mescinius as soon as he could get hold of him – again in the role of his knowledgeable deputy. The fact that magistrates tended to outsource technicalities to members of their entourage must certainly not surprise us. Mescinius, too, had delegated the work on the *rationes* to his cousin M. Mindius, who apparently had been part of his quaestorian staff.²³⁶ Yet, in the Republican framework of financial administration, the *scribae quaestorii* were no mere delegates. They were the pivotal element. Not only were they the ones documenting provincial finances and drafting *rationes*. When it came to registering these accounts with the *aerarium* it was again the *scribae* who represented the interface between magistrates and the public repository. Registration by transcription into the *tabulae publicae* by the hands of a *scriba* was the usual procedure (see above). The finances of the Republican state passed through the hands of the *scribae*. And they stayed there. The *scribae* were not only assigned to *scribere* but also to *ordinare*²³⁷ and *concustodire*.²³⁸

This active, or rather proactive, role of the *scribae* in public accounting comes to life in a recently surfaced relief depiction of a local *scriba* of early imperial times (see Fig. 2.4). The scene depicted on a partially broken marble slab, which was found spoliated in the vicinity of the ancient

---

[234] The procedure in Cɪᴄ. *fam.* 5. 20. 1–2: *Rationes confectae me absente sunt tecum; ad quas ego nihil adhibui praeter lectionem*, transl. E. S. Shuckburgh.
[235] Cɪᴄ. *fam.* 5. 20. 1–9: '*It would be easier for me to reply to your letter in detail if my Secretary, M. Tullius, were here ... All the same, if you think it would be of any use, I'll send Tullius over to you, when he gets back from the country.*' Transl. W. G. Williams.
[236] Cɪᴄ. *fam.* 5. 20. 2.
[237] *lex Irn.* 73. 30–31.
[238] *lex Urson.* 81. 20.

Figure 2.4 Marble plaque. Funerary inscription for [Ca]murtius [Se]verus (A.242) with relief depiction showing the *scriba* registering money to the public coffers. Attached to the outer wall of the estate 'Seliano' (Capaccio, Italy), c. 2 km north of Paestum. Early 1. c. AD.
(Umberto Soldovieri)

colonia of Paestum, shows a certain [Ca]murtius [Se]verus (A.242), who is identified by the accompanying inscription as *scriba*, very likely of the *colonia Paestanorum*.[239] The *scriba*, wearing a *toga*, is shown sitting on a chair or bench, in his left hand an open *tabula cerata* – at the same time working tool and identification. With his raised right hand, thumb and index finger extended, the *scriba* indicates the amount of a deposit made by a *togatus* standing to his left, who is handing over a small bag. This individual is assisted, to his left, by an aide clad in a *tunica*, who seems to be reaching down to fetch another bag of some sort of container (the

---

[239] In general Mello (2012). While the reading of the *nomen gentile* as Camurtius is beyond reasonable doubt – the *gens* is well attested in *Paestum* – the reading of the *cognomen* is uncertain. The *ordinatio* of the inscription suggests letters missing at the beginning of the line. The *cognomen* of the *scriba* might thus have been [Se]verus rather than Verus.

relief breaks off here) as he becomes aware of the *scriba*'s gesture.[240] The bag changing hands is accepted by an assistant clad in *tunica* standing to the right of the *scriba*, who stores the bag in a semi-globular container (*cista*). Undoubtedly, the transaction is to be understood as monetary, as is symbolised by the table in front of the *scriba*, which is covered with coins.[241] The fragmentary condition of the relief makes it impossible to establish the exact context of the transaction. We might be dealing with a magistrate depositing money or a citizen making a payment (e.g. taxes). Still, what remains of the depiction makes it clear that what was considered typical work for a *scriba* (in this specific case a *scriba* of the local *duumviri*) was registering money to the public coffers or, in general, administering the public accounts. In this, he did not merely act as a subsidiary but rather played the leading and most important part. He administered and controlled the register, he transacted and oversaw the financial operations.

The strong connection between *scriba* and public finances, which is evident in our written sources and which is visualised in [Se]verus' funerary monument, seems to have been a common theme. A mid-second-century funerary inscription from the Phrygian city of Hierapolis exemplifies the connection in a remarkable way. It sanctions unauthorised co-use of the appertaining tomb with a heavy fine of a thousand *denarii* and stipulates that the sum would have been due in equal parts to the city as well as to the state, i.e. the emperor and the provincial governor, respectively. While the city is represented by the γερουσία, its council, the state is represented by the σκρίβα, meaning the governor's *scriba quaestorius*.[242] As we have seen with Cicero's *scriba quaestorius* M. Tullius, the *scriba* of the governor's *quaestor* was at the heart of provincial financial affairs and *rationes* – so much so that he evidently became the embodiment of provincial financial matters.

---

[240] The sign corresponds to 900 (right hand for hundreds; little finger, ring finger and middle finger touching the palm) of an unknown unit, certainly monetary, most likely *denarii*; on Roman finger counting and computation cf. B. P. Williams and R. S. Williams (1995). Mello (2012) 106 argues that the sign represents the number two to coincide with the two bags visible in the scene. However, there seem to be more than two bags involved in the scene. In any case, I would argue that an accountant, besides being used to counting on fingers, would rather have calculated in specific monetary units rather than unspecified bags of money.

[241] The motif is common in depictions of Roman bankers and the like, cf. D. Jones (2006) pl. 6, 26, 27.

[242] Guizzi, De Martino, and Ritti (2012) no. 14 (*AE* 2013, 1557): Ἡ σορὸς Θεογενίδος Ἀττάλου τοῦ Σόλωνος τοῦ Μηνοδό/του ἐν ᾗ κεκήδευται Φλαβιανὸς θρεμάτιν αὐτῆς κηδευ-θήσεται αὐ/τὴ ἡ Θεογενὶς καὶ ὁ ἀνὴρ αὐτῆς Γλύκων Ἀντιόχου / τοῦ Γλύκωνος Ἑρμογένης οὐκ ἐξέσται οὐ'δενὶ ἑτέρῳ κηδευ/θῆναι ἢ ὁ ἀψιδήσας ἀποτίσι τῇ γερουσίᾳ ✗ Φ' καὶ τῷ σκρίβᾳ ✗ Φ' / ἢ τὰ γράμματα ἐξχαράξι.

In addition to financial administration, the *scribae* were also involved in the procedural and legal documentation of a magistrate's term of office. As I have discussed above, the *commentarii*, Cicero's *pericula*, had become an essential part of public documentation during the Republic. These magisterial daybooks were mainly concerned with questions arising from the day-to-day business of the magistrate. An inscription dated to the 18th of March AD 69 cites passages '*ex codice ansato*' of the proconsul of the province Sardinia of the same year, L. Helvius Agrippa.[243] The inscription reproduces the decision reached by Agrippa five days earlier in a long-standing boundary dispute between the Patulcenses Campani and the Galillenses. The *codex ansatus*, which contained Agrippa's sentence and which served as a template for the inscribed text, was brought forward by the *scriba quaestorius* Cn. Egnatius Fuscus (A.65). It is certainly no coincidence that it was the *scriba* who acted as the record-keeper. The procedure described in the inscription suggests that the connection between the *scriba* and the *codex ansatus* of the proconsul was a natural one. The *scriba* had been responsible for writing the *codex* and he had been entrusted with its subsequent custody.[244] A similar testimony from the city of Caere, although in a local context, confirms this procedure. The *scriba* of the Caerites, a certain T. Rustius Lysiponus (A.282), is ordered to bring forward the *commentarium cottidianum* of the city, likewise to draw up a certified copy of a decree of the local senate.[245] Again, it is the *scriba* who is responsible for the official documentation. A closer look at what was copied from the documents in both cases reveals that this lasting connection between *scriba* and document had, above all, practical reasons. The *scriba*, writing and administering these documents, brought the knowledge and familiarity needed to expertly and expeditiously navigate and utilise the documents. The passages cited in the Caeritan inscription were dispersed over different tablets and even different *codices* (see above). Keeping track of subjects in the *commentarii* would have been exceedingly difficult for anyone not acquainted with the workings and contents of the documentation. The Sardinian example, in turn, illustrates the complex genesis of Agrippa's judgment and makes a case for the involvement of documentary specialists. The text makes reference to a late second-century BC verdict of the then proconsul M. Caecilius Metellus, to two more recent sentences by the *procurator Augusti* M. Iuventius Rixa and to one decision by Caecilius

---

[243] *CIL* 10, 7852; cf. PIR² H 64.
[244] See also PLIN. *ep.* 6. 22. 4: access to *commentarii* was possible through bribery of the *scriba*.
[245] *CIL* 11, 3614, 4347; AD 113.

Simplex, most probably the predecessor of Agrippa.[246] While they are not cited verbatim, it becomes clear that Agrippa must have been in the know about these previous rulings in order to be able to formulate his own. The experts involved with the collection and the retrieval of these documents from the available repositories as part of the preparation of the case were bound to be *scribae* – both in the staff of the *proconsul* as well as in the respective archives.

A Roman *scriba* functioned at the centre of a magistrate's daily business, which was dominated by political, financial and jurisdictional questions. Depending on the respective magistrate's area of responsibility, a *scriba* could thus be found keeping accounts,[247] recording people and property,[248] minuting in court,[249] registering documents at an archive,[250] producing authorised copies,[251] or reading in an assembly,[252] among other things. As far as it touched on a magistrate's official documentation that was destined to enter the *tabulae publicae* we may expect that a *scriba* was involved through his professional, secretarial capacity. It was, thus, in the nature of things that a *scriba* was in a position to gain expertise in various fields of administrative practice. It would certainly not surprise us that a quaestorian *scriba librarius* would say of himself that he had 'lived for lawsuits while himself having been free of lawsuits' (A.118).[253] A *scriba* of the curule aediles even boasted to have been *iuris prudens*, i.e. a jurist proper (A.203).[254]

What emerges from our sources is a Roman documentary system that was dominated by *scribae* who were veritable specialists in writing, keeping and using the documents. Many a Roman magistrate must have shared Cato the Younger's frustration at these knowledgeable permanent residents of the Roman archives. Cicero certainly did, as he complained bitterly about the Romans' lack of an institutionalised guardianship of law.

---

[246] The most thorough analysis of the inscription still Mommsen (1867); corrections in Mommsen (1887) I 349 n. 2.
[247] Liv. 26. 36. 11; Liv. 27. 16. 8; Cic. *Verr.* 2. 1. 150.
[248] Cic. *Phil.* 2. 16.
[249] V. Max. 5. 7. ext. 2.
[250] Cic. *Sul.* 44; Cic. *Pis.* 61; *CIL* 11, 1421.
[251] Cic. *nat. deor.* 3. 74; Cic. *leg.* 3. 46; *CIL* 8, 270.
[252] Cic. *Verr.* 2. 3. 26; App. *BC* 1. 1. 11–12; Plut. *Cat. Mi.* 28. 1 and Dio 37. 43. 2.
[253] *CIL* 6, 1819: *vixi iudicio sine iudice*, L. Naevius L. libertus Urbanus.
[254] *CIL* 6, 1853, his name is lost; cf. Liebs (1980) 161f., I.15; Liebs (1993) 21. Maybe another jurist in C. Aelius Domitianus Gaurus (A.4), *scriba librarius quaestorius* and *scriba aedilium curulium*, *AE* 1888, 125, possibly identical with the Gaurus mentioned in Dig. 8. 2. 10. Cf. Düll (1943); more cautious Kunkel and Wittmann (1995) 118, 111 n. 28.

Legum custodiam nullam habemus, itaque eae leges sunt quas apparitores nostri uolunt. A librariis petimus, publicis litteris consignatam memoriam publicam nullam habemus.[255]

In Cicero's eyes, the public knowledge was hid away in the public repository. Retrieval was only possible at the hands of the apparitorial personnel in charge, the *(scribae) librarii*. In fact, our sources suggest that it was the *scribae* themselves who were authorised to write out certified copies of the *tabulae publicae* they managed. The signature (*chirographum*) of the *sex primi*, the senior *scribae quaestorii*, was considered a sign of authenticity (cf. Chapter 3).[256] The *senatus consultum de nundinis saltus Beguensis*, resolved in Rome early in the year AD 138 and set in stone some months later in the North African city of Casae, had travelled across the Mediterranean by means of a diptych of wax tablets. The copy, transcribed from an archived *liber sententiarum*, had been signed and authenticated, in the first place, by two *scribae*. The *scribae* had registered and archived the *senatus consultum* in the *aerarium* and they were the ones to subsequently retrieve and copy it.[257]

All that said, it is evident that we have to take Cicero's grievance *cum grano salis*. The *scribae* certainly did not constitute a deep state; they were no all-powerful and devious archivists, jealously guarding and even fabricating the laws and arcana of the state. What is at the heart of Cicero's statement is the fact that the *scribae*, by means of their official position and their professional knowledge, were intimately connected with the public knowledge they helped produce and maintain. As such, they acted as intermediaries between this knowledge and the public. It is symptomatic that Republican tradition has it that it was a *scriba*, Cn. Flavius, who had published the *ius civile* and the *legis actiones*. And it might not surprise us that, equally fabled, it was another *scriba*, L. Petilius (A.130), in whose garden the books of the legendary second king Numa Pompilius had purportedly been found.[258]

---

[255] CIC. *leg.* 3. 46, the same statement in CIC. *leg.* 3. 48: 'We have no guardianship of the laws, and therefore they are whatever our clerks want them to be; we get them from the State copyists, but have no official records.' Transl. C. W. Keyes.
[256] CIC. *nat. deor.* 3. 74.
[257] *CIL* 8, 270, 11451, 23246 (A.75, A.93). Cf. Haensch (1996) 460, who suggests that the *scribae* did not produce an authoritative copy but rather unofficially did the senator, who addressed the petition, a favour. The fact that we are dealing with a document witnessed and sealed by seven individuals, i.e. the proper procedure for legal documents, strongly suggests an authoritative character, however.
[258] The older tradition in PLIN. *nat.* 13. 84 (CASS. HEM. *frg.* F35 (FRH)), the younger in LIV. 40. 29. 3–14. Cf. Rosen (1985).

The nexus between public documents and *scribae* becomes most apparent when we look at public appearances of the latter. For a *scriba*, to act in public in most cases meant reading, more precisely reading aloud in front of a crowd, be that in court or in an assembly. Cicero, again, is our most valuable source. In his forensic speeches, he is keen on presenting documentary evidence to make his case, having the pieces read out loud to the jury. We learn from a passage in his second oration against Verres that these readers, who are usually unspecified, must be identified with *scribae*. While making a case against Verres' regulations of corn lease, he orders to have them read '*ex tabulis*': '*Da, quaeso, scribae, recitet ex codice professionem. Recita*'.[259] The *scriba* is ordered to recite from the *tabulae publicae*. We might imagine that Cicero could have read the edict himself, quite possibly to greater effect. However, reading from the *tabulae publicae* seems to have been inextricably linked with *scribae*. We know of several episodes of the late Republic in which tribunes of the plebs quarrelled about bills in front of public assemblies.[260] Every episode culminates in a tribune ordering the bill to be recited from the *tabulae publicae*. Again, in all these cases it is a *scriba* who comes forward to read. It is only in the emergency situation in which the *scriba* is silenced by the opposing party that the tribunes end up reading their own bills. One of these episodes is particularly informative, as it deviates from this normal procedure. A commentary on Cicero's lost oration *pro Cornelio de maiestate* by Asconius reads:

> Is [scil. P. Servilius Globulus, *trib. plebis*], ubi legis ferundae dies venit et praeco subiciente scriba verba legis recitare populo coepit, et scribam subicere et praeconem pronuntiare passus non est. Tum Cornelius ipse codicem recitavit.[261]

Even though we now encounter a *praeco* who, according to his official function, heralds, it is not he but the *scriba* who is reading from the wax tablets. The *scriba* is prompting the *praeco*. We know of the same procedure from a passage by Valerius Maximus in which a *scriba* prompts the *carmen* for the ritual of the *Suovetaurilia* '*ex publicis tabulis*' to the *censor*.[262]

---

[259] Cic. *Verr.* 2. 3. 26: 'Kindly hand this to the clerk, and ask him to read aloud from the volume the passage about the returns to be made. – Read it, please.' Transl. L. H. G. Greenwood.
[260] Ascon. *Corn.* 58; Plut. *Cat. Mi.* 28. 1; Dio 37. 43. 2; App. *BC* 1. 1. 11–12.
[261] Ascon. *Corn.* 58: 'This man, when the day came for passing the law and the herald, as the *scriba* prompted him the text, began to enunciate it to the people, refused to allow either the *scriba* to prompt the text, or the herald to enunciate it. Then Cornelius himself recited the codex.' Transl. R. G. Lewis (adapted).
[262] V. Max. 4. 1. 10a: *qui censor, cum lustrum conderet inque solitaurilium sacrificio scriba ex publicis tabulis sollemne ei precationis carmen praeiret* ....

Scriptum Facere 59

It is evident that the explanation for this scribal priority in reading cannot lie with the fact that the *scriba* was literate while the other protagonists were not. While we may argue that the *praeco*, in fact, might have been illiterate, the magistrates certainly were not. I have already shown that the *scribae* must have been those most familiar with the form, functioning and content of *tabulae publicae*. Official documents, loaded with a great number of technical particularities – material, typographic and content-related – must have been fairly cryptic to the uninitiated.[263] Thus, practical considerations suggested that their navigation was best left to the scribal specialist.

Yet, the connection between *scriba* and *tabulae publicae* was not a mere product of professional practice. It entailed more. The *scribae* were literally *entrusted* with the care of the public documents. Cicero had used the concept of *fides* to qualify the relationship between the *scribae* and the *tabulae publicae*. It was diligence and conscientiousness that was expected from the *scribae*. In Cicero's eyes, *scribae* worthy of the title were '*patres familias, viri boni atque honesti*'.[264] Their righteousness and honour guaranteed the legitimacy and validity of the documents they made, kept and used. That is why they swore an oath of due diligence when they took office. They swore, as we can read in the *lex Flavia municipalis*, to write the *tabulae* 'bona fide', neither writing anything false nor omitting anything.[265] It is easy to see why Cicero and the other officials would call on *scribae* to recite from the public repository rather than act as intermediaries themselves. In legal and ritual practice, exact and correct wording was pivotal to guaranteeing due process and conveying authority.[266] 'Since a

---

[263] Apart from the peculiarities of the physical medium discussed above, the texts themselves might have contained typographic specialties and abbreviations (shortand, *notae*); cf. on the different character of literary and documentary writing Haines-Eitzen (2000) 62–4. Unfortunately, we do not possess direct evidence of shorthand writing related to *scribae* or *tabulae publicae*, not least because sophisticated shorthand writing did not come into use until the Late Republic; on shorthand writing still fundamental Boge (1973). It is as late as AD 411 that the minutes of the Conference of Carthage, a congress held to settle the ecclesiastical dispute between Catholics and Donatists, describe a situation similar to our Late Republican *scribae* reading aloud. The assembled clergymen quarrel about the legitimacy of the transcripts of the conference, as there existed two forms: one protocol in shorthand (*codex notarum*), produced simultaneously to the proceedings, as well as a fair copy (*scheda*), produced later on the basis of the protocol. Except for the specialists (the *notarii* and *exceptores*), the attendees were not able to read *in codicibus*, that is the minutes written in shorthand; *Gesta Conl. Carth.* 2. 43; the context in Teitler (1985) 9–13. Thus, one of the shorthand writers (*exceptor*) was needed to interpret the *notae* and read aloud from the protocol in shorthand – obviously a point of contention for the opposing party that feared partisan bias.
[264] Cic. *Verr.* 2. 3. 183. Cf. Chapter 4.
[265] *lex Irn.* 73 37–40: *se tabulas communes municipum suorum fide bona scripturum, neque se [scientem] d(olo) m(alo) falsum in eas tabulas relaturum, doloue malo, quod in eas referri oporteat, praetermissurum.*
[266] Ogilvie (2000) 34f., 50f.

tablet was final and authoritative, and since reading from it was in itself final and authoritative, its recitation compelled, or was expected to compel, respect and silence, belief and obedience.'[267] By definition, the *scribae* guaranteed these authoritative characteristics of the *tabulae*, the validity of the documents and the veracity of their content. They represented the official and impartial voice of the *tabulae publicae*.

The Roman *scribae* had become the embodiment of the Republic's documentary culture. In a community that gradually learned to embrace and utilise written procedure to govern, those trusted with literate administrative practice were bound to eventually find themselves at the very centre of it. When written knowledge had eventually come to mean power, the *scribae* ceased to be mere clerks. Instead, they became guardians of the public repository of knowledge – both in a functional and a symbolic way. The quasi-monopoly of the *scribae* in making, keeping and using official documentation led to their being fully conversant with its contents, to the extent that their knowledge had, in the eyes of the political elite, become exclusive and possibly dangerous. This development had furthered a strong connection between individual and materiality: *scribae* and *tabulae publicae* had become two sides of an equation, inseparable from each other. The *scribae* had become a human archive.

Knowing how to read, write and reckon obviously played a key role in the making of the Roman *scriba*. The image of the working *scriba* that is manifest in our primarily late Republican evidence is based upon their literate expertise. Becoming and being a *scriba* entailed, to use Bourdieu's term, embodied cultural capital. It was personal skill that made the Republican *scriba* in the first place. This cultural capital in itself provided its owner with a prestigious position. The close connection and interaction with the *tabulae publicae* and what they entailed had eventually come to distinguish the holders of the scribal posts. Measuring this prestige is nearly impossible, however. What might have been more important was the fact that the cultural capital of the *scribae* opened up new possibilities. In the case of the *scribae* their literate skills put them, by way of access to the apparitorial office, in close proximity to the elite and in control of authoritative documents. Exploiting these systematics of the apparitorial system could result in social and financial gain.

[267] E. A. Meyer (2004) 88.

CHAPTER 3

The Attendant

Or, le scribe est rarement un fonctionnaire ou un employé du groupe: sa science s'accompagne de puissance.

Claude Lévi-Strauss, *Triste Tropiques*

Roman Civil Servants

It is a truism that the Roman Republican government was lean. Even when Rome had acquired an empire spanning the entire Mediterranean, the principles geared towards governing a city state were retained. What had worked for the city of Rome was eventually extended to the provinces. Aristocrats in turn assumed one of the few yearly offices. To fulfil their official duties, these magistrates were expected to mobilise private financial and personnel resources. Being a magistrate meant fulfilling a duty towards the *res publica*. Holding office was part of an honourable and meritorious political career (*cursus honorum*). What the state contributed to its government in civic resources was minimal. What we might call the Roman civil service was confined to the essentials.[1] It consisted of a few positions of so-called *apparitores*, skilled supporting staff who were supposed to be at the magistrates' disposal (*apparere*) during their terms of office in the city and the provinces. The post of *scriba* was one of them.[2]

Despite the limited nature of Roman civil service, *apparitores* were seen as an essential part of what made the Roman republican state. Evidently, as I have already discussed with regard to the *scribae* (see Chapter 2), *apparitores* fulfilled practical tasks in the staff of an office holder. Yet, the assignment of apparitors to magistrates was also of symbolic value.

---

[1] The designation in A. H. M. Jones (1949); cf. Yakobson and Horstkotte (1997) 247f.; contra Eich (2005) 62f.
[2] In general Mommsen (1887) I 332–71; A. H. M. Jones (1949) and Purcell (1983); Kunkel and Wittmann (1995) 110–30.

In general, apparitors were seen as a sign of power, and their number distinguished the holder of office and his authority.[3] Thus, even as late as the third century AD, when Republican customs had long become a fossilised tradition, a depiction of an entourage of *apparitores* on a sarcophagus still indubitably marked out the successful senatorial holder of office.[4] The apparitors were not merely professionals in their respective fields – even if charges such as those of interpreter (*interpres*), architect (*architectus*) or surveyor (*finitor*) clearly required specialised expertise. Rather, many of these posts held additional political or sacral ceremonial value. The *lictores*, who carried the *fasces* in front of the magistrates, not only made way for the magistrate and carried out corporal punishments, but were a sign of official authority (*imperium*) per se; the *pullarii* and *haruspices* not only performed auspices and extispicy but also stood for a ritually proper discharge of one's office; *viatores* (summoners), *praecones* (heralds) and *accensi* (assistants) exercised practical functions, yet, at the same time, their presence stood for the legitimate authority of the Roman magistrate.[5] I have argued along the same lines with respect to the *scribae*. The duties they exercised were of a practical nature, but their association with official authority and their position as guardians of the public repository of the Republican state provided them with symbolic value and authority (Chapter 2).

Much of the history of the Roman *apparitores* remains dubious or unknown. The Republican annalistic tradition offers only small glimpses into the world of the Roman civil service. It is as late as the time of Sulla that we gain a first detailed insight into an undoubtedly evolving system via the epigraphically attested *lex de XX quaestoribus*. Our understanding of the apparitorial system thus stems mainly from its last phase before it was eventually incorporated into the framework of the Empire. Consequently, most of the office holders are known from imperial times thanks to our rich epigraphic tradition. The basic principles of the apparitorial system as a whole are reasonably clear to us, however. Entry into the system was open to free citizens, who joined an apparitorial *decuria*, which served as the internal organising principle. It was this decurial affiliation that set the members of the Roman civil service apart from other members of Roman society. It was from these *decuriae* that *apparitores* were chosen to serve

---

[3] Cic. *leg. agr.* 2. 32 speaks of *apparitores* as '*insignia potestatis*'. See e.g. the *lictores*, the carriers of the bundles of rods (*fasces*), whose number was determined by the rank of the magistrate; Kunkel and Wittmann (1995) 119.
[4] Wrede (2001) 19.
[5] Kunkel and Wittmann (1995) 119–29.

the magistrates for their term of office.[6] Doing service in a *decuria* meant drawing a salary as well as enjoying other benefits of corporate membership, such as having reserved seats in theatre.[7]

At this point, it is neither possible nor useful to delve deeper into the difficult and only incompletely known intricacies of the different apparitorial charges and their functional and organisational systematics. In what follows, I will focus on the *scribae* alone. It will suffice to note that the *scriba*-ship was the best paid, most prestigious and arguably the most powerful of all the apparitorial charges.[8] As such, the phenomena and constellations brought about by the systematics and workings of the apparitorial system as a whole become particularly manifest with the *scribae*. A closer look at organisational aspects of the foremost *apparitores* will thus reveal the influence of social relations and personal patronage in the workings of the Roman civil service. It will highlight the social capital of the *scribae*.

Origins

The dearth of reliable sources shrouds much of early Republican history in legend. As a result, the origins of the Roman apparitors and the *scribae* are far from clear. I have already discussed above that the Roman annalistic tradition took the view that the political institution of the *apparitores* was of Etruscan origin.[9] Such generalisations in retrospect are, for obvious reasons, highly problematic; even more so when late Republican historiography had the general tendency to equate 'ancient' with 'Etruscan'.[10] We are luckily in a position to make recourse to actual Etruscan evidence. Our earliest non-Roman testimony of Etruscan '*scribae*' stems from the Etruscan city of Clevsins (Clusium, now Chiusi). A bas-relief on a funerary monument, which belongs to the first half of the fifth century BC, depicts a scribe beside other apparitorial personnel attending to two magistrates, who are overseeing games (see Fig. 3.1).[11] In a similar fashion, later Etruscan relief depictions regularly show magistrates accompanied by apparitors, among

---

[6] Purcell (1983) 127f.
[7] Tac. *ann.* 16.12.1.
[8] The salary hierarchy in *lex Urson.* 62–63; cf. Table 3.1.
[9] Liv. 1.8.3.
[10] Cornell (1995) 169.
[11] Colonna (1976) 187–9 w. Fig. 1. Note the intriguing coincidence of locality between the finding place of the funerary monument and Livy's story of Lars Porsenna's '*scriba*' (see Chapter 2). Lars Porsenna had been king of Clevsins.

Figure 3.1 Etruscan funerary monument, bas-relief. Etruscan scribe (centre left) together with other apparitorial attendants in a tribunal scene, attending to two magistrates overseeing games. Clevsins (Chiusi). First half 5. c. BC. (Museo Archeologico *Antonino Salinas*)

them scribes, who are identified by their writing material, most often *tabulae*. It is generally striking that the Etruscan apparitorial classes are very much akin to what we know of their Roman counterparts.[12]

As a result, we have no reason to doubt the close connection between Etruscan and Roman *apparitores*. The traditional view of the origins of the Roman apparitorial personnel reported by Livy might hold true – at least in the sense that their apparent similarities must have been a product of mutual cultural influence. Delving deeper into this relationship with regard to the genesis of the Roman *scriba*-ship is more difficult, however. While Etruscan evidence for apparitorial scribes is, as discussed, early, reliable evidence on Roman Republican *scribae* is comparatively late. In accordance with the 'Etruscan view' on Roman *apparitores*, late Republican and early imperial historiography naturally projects the existence of Roman *scribae* to the very beginning of the Roman Republic. Dionysius of Halicarnassus, for example, has a *scriba* read out the letters that implicated two of the sons of L. Iunius Brutus, the legendary founder of the Republic, in treasonous activities.[13] This is not the only case in which Dionysius lets *scribae* read in public. In the year 447 BC, a *scriba* had allegedly been ordered to read out a decree in the senate.[14] It is easy to dismiss Dionysius' account as a

---

[12] Lambrechts (1959) 193f.
[13] D.H. *ant.* 5. 8. 2; 5. 9. 1.
[14] D.H. *ant.* 11. 21. 6.

projected construction.¹⁵ Not only do we know that *scribae* had not been present in the senate until the Later Roman Empire (see Chapter 6). It is also obvious that Dionysius' narrative catered to an early imperial audience that was acquainted with the concept of the reading *scriba* (see Chapter 2). This is not necessarily to say that the early Republic had not known *scribae*. On the contrary: from what I have laid out, we should be wary of dismissing the Etruscan evidence lightly. However, our late sources unfortunately do not allow for a ready reconstruction of early conditions.

We know that *apparitores* were seen as a common feature of Roman magistrates by the late Republic at the latest. And indeed, as will become clear in the following, *scribae* were assigned to most magistrates by that time. The allotment of auxiliary personnel was neither uniform nor random, however. Rather, the types and number of *apparitores* given to specific magistrates were a matter of debate. As Cicero argued when he spoke out against the proposed staffing of the members of P. Servilius Rullus' agrarian commission of 63 BC, *apparitores* were a sign of authority, their assignment thus no trivial detail.¹⁶ Depending on the type of *apparitor*, practical considerations were even more important. When, in 11 BC, the office of the *curator aquarum* was created, it was, among others, staffed with one or more *scribae librarii* who were to assist the *curatores* in the discharge of their duties. The resolution of the senate informing us about these provisions, which is recorded by Sex. Iulius Frontinus, who had himself been *curator* under Nerva and had hence written a treatise on the aqueducts of the city, tellingly budgets the supply of writing material as part of the apparitorial staffing. Writing tasks were an integral part of the daily routine of the water commissioners; it was what had warranted their staffing with *scribae* in the first place. Ironically enough, Frontinus subsequently informs his readers that, by his time, the *apparitores* had, due to the incompetency of his predecessors, ceased to assist the *curatores* in the field, even though they were still registered at and paid for by the *aerarium* according to the provisions made by the *senatus consultum*.¹⁷

The constraints that had initially persuaded the Romans to allocate scribal professionals to their magistrates must have been, above all, functional. The magistrates occupied with the repartition and distribution of public land, water and grain – Rullus' *decemviri agris dandis adsignandis*, the *curatores aquarum* and their institutional model mentioned in the senate's resolution of 11 BC, the *praefecti frumenti dandi* – are telling cases. All three

---

¹⁵ Cf. Mommsen (1887) I 349 n. 3.
¹⁶ Cic. *leg. agr.* 2. 32.
¹⁷ Frontin. *Aq.* 2. 100–101.

posts naturally involved a great deal of paperwork and were created in a phase when Roman documentary culture was already well developed. The assignment of documentary specialists ensured the functioning of these offices. This had most likely been true for earlier times and other magistrates as well. It is true that in times when documentation had neither been a functional facilitation nor a political necessity of government, many a magistrate may simply not have been in need of documentary specialists. However, as soon as documentation had become a substantial factor we would expect that experts proficient in a comparatively rare skill were employed and indeed much sought after. The gradual evolution of an apparitorial system initially grounded in functional practice is thus the most plausible scenario.

What had stood at the beginnings of apparitorial scribal activity remains, nevertheless, a matter of conjecture. Livy, as we have seen, linked early Etruscan scribal activity with accounting.[18] This might not surprise us. Financial administration had, after all, been the most obvious occupation of *scribae* in Livy's time. Following a functional argument, we could reason that *scribae* would have become a necessity after the establishment of the *aerarium* sometime in the second half of the fifth century BC, coinciding with the introduction of the quaestorship.[19] However, we are in no position to know for certain whether the early *quaestores* of the city were already assisted by *scribae*. The earliest hard evidence for quaestorian *scribae* remains the Sullan *lex de XX quaestoribus* of the late eighties of the first century BC.[20] Evidence referencing earlier appearances of quaestorian *scribae* since the end of the third century BC is of a later date and thus possibly retrojects more recent conditions.[21] The situation is very similar for *scribae* of the other major Roman magistrates. Evidence for early Republican times is poor, even nonexistent. It is true that the censorship, which had allegedly been created in 443 BC, is purported to have been tasked with the oversight of the *tabulae publicae* and the '*ministerium scribarum*' upon its inception, thus suggesting the existence of *scribae* very early on.[22] Yet, Livy's singular testimony is without a doubt to be taken with a grain of salt. We might argue that Early Republican fiscal policy must have made some degree of documentation a necessity. Rome's main revenue, the *tributum*, a loan

---

[18] Liv. 2. 12. 1–16.
[19] The traditionally purported date of 447 BC in Tac. *ann.* 11. 22. 4; cf. Latte (1936) 31–3, Kunkel and Wittmann (1995) 511–13.
[20] *CIL* I², 587.
[21] Liv. 26. 36. 11; Flor. *epit.* 1. 22. 23–25 (Jord. *Rom.* 192) on 210 BC; cf. Cic. *Phil.* 2. 16; Liv. 27. 16. 8; Plut. *Fab.* 22. 5 on 209 BC; App. *Pun.* 9. 66 on 201 BC; Liv. 38. 55. 5 on 187 BC.
[22] Liv. 4. 8. 4.

made by citizens to finance its expensive wars, was based on the *census*.²³ The administration of the *census* and *tributum*, together with Rome's other revenues (*vectigalia*), will likely have demanded professional bookkeeping at the treasury. However, we lack any hard evidence for the extent of financial documentation in this early period. When we meet the elaborate practice of fiscal documentation of the Late Republic with the *scribae quaestorii* at its centre, Rome's fiscality had long undergone a major shift, abandoning the levying of *tributum* in favour of tax farming in the provinces.²⁴

What we might gather from our sparse sources is the notion that early *scribae* seem to have been associated with written procedures in sacral contexts. We learn from Festus that the person presiding over a public funeral was not only assigned *lictores* and *accensi* in the style of a magistrate, but was also provided with a *scriba* when he held *ludi publici* in honour of the deceased.²⁵ Most intriguingly, what we have observed on the bas-relief from the Etruscan city of Clevsins (Fig. 3.1) fits Festus' description perfectly. Holding games in a cultic context obviously required the presence of an apparitorial scribe, most likely to 'keep records of competitors and prizewinners'.²⁶ What Festus described in the second century AD could supposedly have been a Roman reality as early as the fifth century BC. Another hint at the early association of *scribae* with the sacred might be seen in the tale of Cn. Flavius' cunning publication of the Roman legal calendar, which had been kept under wraps by the *pontifices*. We learn from Livy that the position that had eventually become known as *pontifex minor* had, prior to the second century BC, gone by the name of *scriba pontificius*.²⁷ Flavius is thus commonly identified as a *scriba pontificius*, who had gone from assisting the pontiffs in the codification of the calendar, which had been underway since the middle of the fifth century BC, to eventually making it public.²⁸

All in all, the evidence on the early centuries of the Roman *scriba*-ship seems highly accidental. The foregoing deliberations are thus provisional at best. It is only once we enter the final stages of the Republic that our sources become more abundant and we get a clearer idea of the systematics of the

---

[23] On the *tributum* and Rome's early fiscality in general Nicolet (2000) 71–7; cf. Tan (2015) 211.
[24] Tan (2015) 214; on tax farming Badian (1972) esp. 67–81; on the Hieronic model in Sicily, on which the Romans built, Scramuzza (1937) 237–9; on the system's implications for literate practice cf. Levi (1988) 82; Butler (2002) 38.
[25] FEST. 272.5–15 (237M); cf. CIC. *leg.* 2. 61 62.
[26] Purcell (2001) 663.
[27] LIV. 22. 57. 3. On the date of the change Rüpke (2005) 20; cf. Ryan (2002) 72.
[28] Rüpke (2011) 44; Rüpke (2005) 986 no. 1657; Ryan (2002) 68f.; cf. DIOM. 484 (Heil), *publici annales, quos pontifices scribaeque conficiunt*, Frier (1979) 194f.

Roman *scriba*-ship. The introduction of a second scribal charge besides the *scribae* around the middle of the first century BC – the *scribae librarii* – which I have argued was the result of the increasing demands of Roman documentary culture (see Chapter 2), is a case in point. At the same time it may serve as a cautionary tale about what we might have missed of the early history of *scribae* due to our fragmentary body of source material.

Association

With the exception of the higher magistrates, all Republican magistrates were eventually equipped with *scribae* (see below). Of all these, the figureheads were the *scribae quaestorii*. As discussed in the previous chapter, it was their association with the principal archival and financial centre of the *aerarium* that gave them prestige and put them above their scribal peers and, as a consequence, all the other apparitorial classes. It is thanks to this prominence that they have left a comparatively big footprint in our sources. As a result, it is with the *scribae quaestorii* that we begin to understand the organisational aspects of Roman *scriba*-ship.

Both the *quaestores* assigned to oversee the *aerarium* in the capital and the *quaestores* who accompanied provincial governors overseas were attended by *scribae*. Provincial *quaestores* were, as a rule, assigned two *scribae*. This is the number indicated by our late Republican sources.[29] We might expect that this number was retained throughout the imperial period for the *quaestores* of the senatorial provinces. However, our sparse evidence points rather to a quantitative reduction of *scribae quaestorii* assigned to provincial office holders. When (and if at all) we encounter provincial *scribae quaestorii* during the Empire, we meet them acting alone, usually occupied with the *commentarii* of the provincial governor.[30] What is more, a fragmentary second-century AD inscription, which is usually identified as a list of members of the *consilium* of an unknown *proconsul* of Africa, lists the names of two *scribae librarii* but only one *scriba quaestorius*.[31]

---

[29] CIC. *Verr.* 2. 3. 182: L. Mamilius (A.110) and L. Sergius (A.160) with Cicero in Sicily in 75 BC; SALL. *hist.* 3. 83. 1 (= SERV. *Aen.* 1. 698): Maecenas (A.107) and Versius (A.189) with Q. Sertorius in Spain in 73 BC; LIV. 38. 55. 4–5: two unnamed *scribae* with C. Furius Aculeo under L. Cornelius Scipio Asiagenes in 190 BC; later PLUT. *Cat. Mi.* 34. 3: Cato the Younger was assigned two *scribae* for his quaestorship in Sicily in 58 BC.

[30] *CIL* 10, 7852; PLIN. *ep.* 6. 22. 4.

[31] *ILAfr* 592 names the *scriba quaestorius* L. Marius Perpetuus (A.114) and the *scribae librarii* L. Pomponius Carisianus (A.139) and P. Papienus Salutaris (A.124). The identification of the list as members of the *consilium* of the *proconsul Africae* by Birley (1997) 2696; cf. Haensch (1997) 712 n. 20.

Admittedly, the evidence available is neither exhaustive nor unambiguous. Nevertheless, we might imagine that the introduction of the additional apparitorial charge of the *scriba librarius* caused a reform of the apparitorial systematics. The replacement of one of the senior *scribae quaestorii* with two junior *scribae librarii quaestorii* could have been a consequence.

Trying to determine the number of *scribae* assigned to the two *quaestores urbani* who presided over the *aerarium* in Rome brings us to the depths of a system of which we have only very limited knowledge. In the complete absence of any clear evidence, we might argue that the administration of the Republic's main financial and legal archive would, out of practical necessity, have tied up additional scribal resources. At least that is what is suggested by Plutarch's account of Cato the Younger's *quaestor*-ship, in which he successfully brought into line what seemed to be a host of *scribae* occupied at the *aerarium*.[32] The exact number of *scribae quaestorii* employed at the *aerarium* is unrecorded, however. What we know for certain is that the *scribae quaestorii* of the *aerarium* were organised in *decuriae*. In fact, decurial organisation was a feature of Roman apparitorial organisation in general; it was membership of one of the *decuriae urbis Romae* that was seen as prestigious as it bestowed privileges on its holder. According to the *lex coloniae Genetivae Iuliae*, apparitors were exempt from military recruitment and service.[33] We still find the affirmation of these privileges for members of the *decuriae urbis Romae* in the fourth and fifth century AD (cf. Chapter 6).[34]

What it meant to hold a place in a quaestorian *decuria* is first attested by Sulla's *lex de XX quaestoribus* of 81 BC.[35] Sulla's legislation not only raised the number of *quaestores* to twenty, it also detailed the workings of the quaestorian *decuriae* with respect to the new demands made by the increased number of office holders. Unfortunately, what survives of the statute is only the eighth tablet, which just happens to start at the very end of the paragraphs concerning the quaestorian *scribae*. What we are left with are the provisions for the quaestorian *viatores* and *praecones*. The fact that *viatores* and *praecones* were treated as a unit and separate from the *scribae* might make us wary of simply extrapolating the findings to the missing parts on the *scribae*.[36] Nevertheless, the surviving regulations may

---

[32] PLUT. *Cat. Mi.* 16. 2–3.
[33] *lex Urson.* 62. 24–31.
[34] Con. *Theod.* 14. 1; cf. Purcell (1983) 134.
[35] *CIL* I², 587. Roman Statutes no. 14 w. literature and commentary; cf. Gabba (1983); Purcell (2001) 650–4.
[36] Gabba (1983) 489.

give us an idea of how apparitorial *decuriae* could be organised and what membership in them implied. As the Sullan legislation modified current use, the law naturally addresses the status quo ante. We learn that the quaestorian *viatores* and *praecones* used to be assigned to *decuriae* by the *quaestores* ('*legere sublegere*') three years in advance (II.7–14). The *quaestores* in office had, as a result, designated three *viatores* and *praecones* to each yearly *decuria*. The magistrates were then to adopt ('*sumere*') apparitors to serve ('*quaestoribus ad aerarium apparere*', I.31) from the *decuria* of their respective year of office, which started on the fifth of December (II.18–24). What the new Sullan legislation introduced to these systematics was an increase in *apparitores* appointed by the *quaestores* to the yearly *decuriae* from three to four, with the provision that the missing *viatores* and *praecones* for the coming three years were to be extraordinarily appointed to the *decuriae* by the *consules* (I.7–II.1). The *apparitores* eligible to be voted into the *decuriae* were those deemed to be '*eo ordine digni*' (I.32–33); admission to a *decuria* thus must have implied entry into the respective *ordo*. Once admitted to a *decuria*, the name of the *apparitor* was to be recorded on the inner enclosing wall of the *aedes Saturni* (II.40–41). Decurial *viatores* and *praecones* were entitled to a wage ('*merces*', II.31–73) and had the option to provide a substitute to take their place in the *decuria* ('*vicarium dare*', II.24–30).

As detailed as the clauses of the *lex de XX quaestoribus* are, much about the basic workings of the apparitorial *decuriae* still remains unknown. While it seems clear enough that the *decuriae* functioned as yearly pools of *apparitores* from which the acting *quaestores* could draw their staff, we do not know how large and personally stable or iterative these pools were. At first sight, it seems obvious that three or alternatively four *decuriales* per year could not possibly have been enough to staff the mass of *quaestores*. It would mean assuming *viatores* and *praecones* only for the two *quaestores urbani*, another particular *quaestor* (perhaps the one overseeing the *provincia aquaria*)[37] as well as one additional quaestorship, which must have been newly introduced by the *lex*; it would mean that the *viatores* and *accensi* assigned to the provincial quaestors[38] must have had their own *decuriae* and were not affected by the regulations of the *lex* – a highly unlikely arrangement since the *lex* explicitly includes '*pro magistratus*' (II.32).[39]

---

[37] Harris (1976) 102.
[38] They are not well attested, but attested nevertheless; Cic. *Verr.* 2.3.183; cf. Kunkel and Wittmann (1995) 124.
[39] Contra Roman Statutes I 300, according to which this wording 'may have been inserted unthinkingly'.

Even stretching the reading of the regulations and assuming that every yearly pair of *quaestores urbani* would assign *decuriales* for the following three years, thus tripling their numbers, would have left the magistrates understaffed. As a possible solution to the problem, I would propose that membership in a *decuria* was permanent and that the triennial *lectio* of a limited amount of new *decuriales* was to counteract fluctuations caused by abandonment or death rather than to fully staff the *decuriae*. Such a long-term arrangement would also help to explain the explicit possibility of selling decurial places and provide a substitute for the actual exercise of the office. Yet, inconsistencies remain. There is the strong notion that only *apparitores* actually administering their office in a given year were considered members of the *decuria*. A certain L. Fabius Eutychus (A.257), himself *scriba* and *librarius* in *Ostia* and father of a *scriba* of the *aediles curules*, C. Domitius Fabius Hermogenes (A.63), founded a charity upon the untimely death of his son, which paid out annual dividends to the *decuriones* as well as the *decuriales* of the *scribae cerarii*, the *librarii* and the *lictores*.⁴⁰ Michael Swan has related the sums donated to the *decuriae* to the numbers of their members by comparing them with the numbers provided by the *lex Ursonensis* (see Table 3.1 below). He found that the relative numbers of *scribae* (six), *lictores* (four) and *librarii* (two) that were in office with the *duumviri* and *aediles* each year according to the *lex* is in proportion to the sums provided by Eutychus to each. The members of the different *decuriae* thus might all have received the same amount per capita (25 HS).⁴¹ If this calculation is correct, we might infer that the actual *decuria* was made up of only those apparitors who were in office at the time. Applied to the *lex de XX quaestoribus*, this would mean that even a complementary *lectio* of the decurial members would have had to be highly flexible in order to appoint the exact amount of missing *decuriales*. Evidently, such workings are at odds with the statute's explicit definition of a fixed number of decurial candidates. Granted, Eutychus' charity was set up some 200 years after Sulla's legislation. We might, after all, misguidedly be trying to find rigid and fixed rules in a system that was, in reality, flexible and evolving. However, with an institution like the *decuriae* I am inclined to count on Roman conservatism rather than innovation.

Our sources on the *scribae quaestorii* hint at a rather stable and static decurial organisation. I have already mentioned the notion found in Cato the Younger's case that the *aerarium* was buzzing with *scribae*, who had

---

⁴⁰ *CIL* 14, 353; 4642. Cf. Chapter 5.
⁴¹ Swan (1970).

obviously been administering the *tabulae publicae* for a long time. It is exactly Plutarch's argument that the *scribae* were not, in contrast to the *quaestores*, renewed annually. In fact, Cato's efforts to oust one notorious *scriba* was only temporarily successful, as the *scriba*, even though Cato refused to employ him, could be picked up again by the next year's *quaestores*. In other words, he could not be dismissed from the *decuria*.[42] Posts of *scribae* were generally seen as permanent holdings. Already in Cicero's time it had been common practice to buy into a *decuria* ('*decuriam emere*'), most probably via the provision of the vicariate.[43] It was none other than the famous Augustan poet Horace (A.88) who later purportedly '*scriptum quaestorium comparavit*'.[44] And if we are to believe Frontinus, the scribal posts attached to the *curatores aquarum* had finally become de facto sinecures in his time. The posts were still paid for by the state, yet they ceased to do any work for the *curatores*, who had themselves become negligent.[45] It is difficult, however, to discern to what extent the scribal posts associated with the main magistrates were affected by this development. As a matter of fact, beginning in the first century AD, we encounter the phenomenon that some holders of the title of *scriba* were keen on highlighting that they were, in fact, working officials. The most striking example is a certain C. Allius Niger (A.13), who referred to himself as '*scriba librarius ex III decuriis quaestoriis decuriae II honore usus*', thus strongly emphasising his membership in an officiating *decuria*.[46] Other known expressions are '*honore functus*'[47] and '*(et) munere functus*'.[48] As a result, it is highly likely that the *decuriae* became overmanned in imperial times as the *princeps*' own administration gradually claimed most of the empire's administrative duties and, as a consequence, significantly reduced the functional necessity for *scribae*. Yet, once granted, the privileges enjoyed

---

[42] PLUT. *Cat. Mi.* 16. 3–6.
[43] CIC. *Verr.* 2. 3. 184.
[44] SUET. *vita Hor.* 24; in Porphyrio's commentary '*hoc loco significat se Horatius decuriam habuisse*', PORPH. *Hor. sat.* 2. 6. 36.
[45] FRONTIN. *Aq.* 2. 101.
[46] *CIL* 6, 37146 (*ILS* 9036, Langford Wilson (1909) no. 1). Other *honore usi*: Atinius Paternus, A.25; M. Pontius, A.141; T. Flavius, A.78. Cf. for the interpretation of the expression *CIL* 11, 3805 (*ILS* 6579), a decision of the *centumviri* of Veii to bestow upon a certain C. Iulius Gelos, freedman of the emperor Augustus, the rights of an *Augustalis* including the right to sit among the acting *Augustales* at spectacles as if he was actually executing the office ('*ac si eo honore usus sit*'). Cf. Purcell (1983) 131, who, on the contrary, interprets these designations as denoting honorary posts.
[47] Natronius Rusticus, A.120.
[48] Papirius Maximus, A.127; Servilius Draco, A.58; Fabius Largus, A.111; *scribae quaestorii* honouring their patron, *CIL* 9, 2454 (*ILS* 1033); *scribae aedilium curulium* in a very fragmentary inscription, *CIL* 6, 1854, 32268; cf. DIG. 50. 4. 18. 17 (Arcadius Charisius): *scribae magistratus personali muneri serviunt*.

by the holders of a decurial place were hard to rescind, even more so when that place had become permanent and sellable.

We might very well imagine that the scribal *decuriae* were renewed on a regular basis on the model of the *lex de XX quaestoribus*. The places in the *decuriae* seem to have gradually stabilised, however, inasmuch as the *lectio* must have become a mere formality. Once a member of a *decuria*, always a member of a *decuria*. Cicero lets us know that, in 68 BC, he had defended a certain D. Matrinius, a *scriba aedilicius* (A.115), who had been demoted to the status of *aerarius* by the censors on grounds not known to us.[49] The point at issue was that the curule *aediles* had, in consequence of his demotion, refused to designate Matrinius once more to the *decuria* ('*legere*'). Needless to say, Cicero managed to clear Matrinius. Only a tremendous transgression, such as L. Cantilius' (A.36) fornication with the vestal virgin Floronia in 216 BC, would lead to the ousting of a *scriba*.[50]

It was possible to drop out of a *decuria* – albeit mostly voluntarily. Selling one's place to a *vicarius* was the most obvious case. For many others, the office of *scriba* was not the final and lasting station of their career.[51] Once dropped out of a *decuria*, one did not cease to be a *scriba*, however. We have seen in the *lex de XX quaestoribus* that a successful *lectio* into a *decuria* entailed suitability for being a member of the *ordo*.[52] Cicero characterised the *ordo scribarum* as a whole as '*honestus*'; the *scribae* could be entrusted with the *tabulae publicae*; they were '*digni illo ordine*'.[53] Entry into a *decuria* was thus an assertion of a specific status. Whoever was chosen to enter a *decuria* became a member of the respective *ordo*, which functioned as a normative status-group.[54] Holding the title of a *scriba* was meaningful and exclusive. It is the reason we know of so many *scribae* in the first place. People were proud to show it off on their tombstones.

Being a member of the *ordo scribarum* must have been a very prestigious matter indeed. Cicero goes to great lengths to paint Verres' *scribae* as the immoral antithesis and exception to the usual, honourable member of the *ordo*, so as not to alienate the whole group while accusing certain members

---

[49] CIC. *Cluent.* 126.
[50] LIV. 22. 57. 3. The *scriba pontificius* was flogged to death. Cf. the unnamed *scriba quaestorius* who was exiled by Claudius for a petty personal offence; SUET. *Claud.* 38. 2.
[51] Cf. C. Stertinius Orpex (A.169), who moved to *Ephesos* and is denoted as '*quondam scriba librarius*' on his tombstone; *I. Ephesos* 4123 (*IK* 59, 24, *AE* 1935, 169).
[52] Cf. *CIL* 6, 40702 mentions an '*ordo decuriae nomenclatorum*'.
[53] CIC. *Verr.* 2. 3. 183: '*Ordo est honestus*' Quis negat, aut quid ea res ad hanc rem pertinet? Est vero honestus, quod eorum hominum fidei tabulae publicae periculaque magistratuum committuntur. Itaque ex his scribis qui digni sunt illo ordine, patribus familias, viris bonis atque honestis.
[54] Cohen (1984) 23.

of misdemeanour in office.⁵⁵ In fact, the *ordo scribarum* as a corporate body is known to have represented its members' interests.⁵⁶ Cicero himself seems to have had first-hand experience with this slippery slope when he was forced to pass sentence on a *scriba* and subsequently clashed with the whole *ordo*.⁵⁷ If we are to believe the famous orator, the *scribae* even constituted the fourth most important *ordo* of the Roman body politic, right after the *senatores*, *equites* and *publicani* as well as *tribuni aerarii*, respectively.⁵⁸ This certainly did not mean that the *ordo scribarum* had a say on the big political stage. Yet, they were the highest ranking officials of the Roman state who were, as a whole, neither formally senators nor knights; their position of responsibility as guardians of the *tabulae publicae* warranted their prestige. And as the case of Cicero shows, the *ordo scribarum* was certainly something to be taken into account.

As far as we can discern, there was only one *ordo scribarum* incorporating all the *scribae*. A certain Cluvius Formica (A.51), who had been a *scriba* of the quaestors, aediles and the tribunes of the plebs, also acted as *procurator* of the *ordo* in the first century AD. Even the junior *scribae librarii* might have been part of this same association. M. Ulpius Celsianus (A.181), a second-century AD *scriba librarius*, was honoured '*ex decreto ordini[s]*'.⁵⁹ We eventually encounter the '*ordo decuriarum scribarum librariorum*' as a privileged group as late as the fifth century AD (see Chapter 6).⁶⁰

Besides forming an *ordo*, the decurial *scribae* also united collegiately.⁶¹ In contrast to the one *ordo*, there were different *collegia*, however. Yet, we do not know for certain how the *decuriae* and *collegia* were linked; or put more precisely, we do not know whether the *decuriae* were carried over as organising principle for corresponding *collegia*.⁶² Our evidence suggests that collegiate associations did not necessarily run along decurial lines. All the different decurial *scribae librarii* had, for example, most likely formed one single *collegium scribarum librariorum* at the end of the Republic. P. Pompeius Pylades (A.138) held the honorary post of '*magister collegii scribarum librariorum quinquennalis*' while himself being a *scriba librarius* of the tribunes of the plebs (*tribunicius*).⁶³ Interestingly enough, we also

---

⁵⁵ Cic. *Verr.* 2. 3. 182–184.
⁵⁶ Cic. *Catil.* 4. 15; Hor. *sat.* 2. 6. 35.
⁵⁷ Cic. *Mur.* 42: *scriba damnatus, ordo totus alienus*.
⁵⁸ Cic. *dom.* 74; Cic. *Catil.* 4. 15.
⁵⁹ *CIL* 6, 32282, the text on a '*basis parva marmorea*', originally likely including a statue.
⁶⁰ Cod. *Theod.* 8. 9. 1, an edict of the emperor Constantine of AD 335.
⁶¹ Cf. Mart. 8. 38. 1–16, who mentions the commemoration of the dead as a function of such a collegiate association of *scribae*.
⁶² Cf. Ausbüttel (1982) 38.
⁶³ *ILLRP-S* 37 (*AE* 1991, 114).

know of a freedman of the *collegium* of the '*(scribae) librarii quaestorii*'.⁶⁴ What is more, we find the *scribae librarii* of the curule aediles specifically associated with the *praecones* of the same magistrates throughout imperial times.⁶⁵ Their *schola* was prominently situated between the temple of Saturn and the Rostra on the Forum.⁶⁶ The *scribae quaestorii*, in addition, shared a common *patronus*, whom they honoured together.⁶⁷ And we know of a *collegium sex primorum*, an association of the highest ranking *scribae quaestorii*.⁶⁸

Furthermore, a few of the attested *scribae* refer to themselves as '*princeps*'. They might be identified as heads of their respective *collegia*.⁶⁹ What we do not know is whether their scribal title given alongside their honorary position also designates the relevant *collegium*. To be sure, these denominations happen to run very much along decurial lines; they do not contradict any collegiate combination we know otherwise, however.⁷⁰

Hierarchy

The *scribae quaestorii* were divided into three *decuriae ab aerario*. These must have been regarded as *maiores* after the introduction of three additional *decuriae minores ab aerario* made up of junior *scribae librarii*

---

⁶⁴ *CIL* 6, 1826 (*ILS* 1897): '*L(ucius) Quaestorius / Cinyra / lib(ertus) librar(iorum) quaestor(iorum)*'.
⁶⁵ *CIL* 6, 103 (*CIL* 6, 30692 = *ILS* 1879); cf. Huelsen (1888); inscriptions on remains of a marble *epistylium* mention the building and rebuilding of the *schola* of the '*collegium scribarum librariorum et praeconum aedilium curulium*' by a certain Bebryx Drusianus, freedman of an emperor – most likely Julio-Claudian – and Fabius Xanthus, two *curatores* of the association, as well as by C. Avillius Licinius Trosius (A.30), himself *scriba librarius aedilium curulium* and curator of the *collegium*, who is otherwise known from a dedicatory inscription to Caracalla of AD 214, *CIL* 6, 1068 (*ILS* 1880).
⁶⁶ Chioffi (1999) 257.
⁶⁷ *CIL* 9, 2454 (*ILS* 1033), L. Neratius Priscus, PIR² N 59; cf. Camodeca (2007).
⁶⁸ *Frg. Vat.* 124. Cf. *CIL* 6, 37145 (*AE* 1901, 134), which mentions *VI primi curatores* as members of most likely the *album* of a *collegium* of the quaestorian *scribae*; see below. We know of four different *magistri scribarum*, who could possibly have held honorary positions in scribal *collegia*. The only one whose title is undisputed is Cornelius Surus, a *magister scribarum poetarum*, Andreae (1957) 235f. no. 20 (*AE* 1959, 147, Panciera (1986) 35, Jory (1968) 125), who was no *scriba* himself and thus was most likely *magister* of the *collegium scribarum poetarum* mentioned by FEST. 446.26–29 (333M), cf. Chapter 2. The late Republican M. Claudius (A.216) might be identified as '*scr(ibarum) mag(ister) q(aestoriorum) et aed(iliciorum) cur(ulium)*'; *AE* 1939, 153, Giovagnoli (2012b). The abbreviations of the inscription might more plausibly be expanded to '*scr(iba) mag(istratuum) q(uaestorum) et aed(iliorum) cur(ulium)*', Badian (1989) 597. T. Perperna Quadra, *CIL* 6, 37148 (*CIL* 1, 1356 = *ILS* 9040 = *ILLRP* 773 = *AE* 1908, 110), might be identified as '*mag(ister) scr(ibarum)*' of an unknown *collegium*. The same goes for a certain L. Romilius; Gregori (2007). Both could also be identified as '*mag(istri) scr(ipturae)*', i.e. accountants of a *societas publicanorum*; Bücheler (1908), Badian (1989) 597.
⁶⁹ Q. CIC. *pet.* 30; cf. Ausbüttel (1982) 85.
⁷⁰ M. Antonius Rufus, a '*scriba quaestorius princeps*' (A.19); Q. Petronius Melior, a '*scriba quaestorius VI primus princeps*' (A.132); [M.] Iunius Menander, a '*scriba librarius aedilium curulium princeps*' (A.104); Sorilius Bassus, a '*scriba princeps*' (A.164).

quaestorii.⁷¹ As laid out above, we cannot know the precise number of members of these *decuriae*. Since the Sullan reform, the *decuriae* had to supply at least up to twenty – for a short period under Caesar forty – *quaestores*.⁷² We may assume that the tripartite division lent itself to workings similar to those we have found in the *lex de XX quaestoribus* for the *viatores* and *praecones*. The *decuriae* of the quaestorian *scribae* most likely rotated in a three-year cycle, while only one of the *decuriae* was active for any given year. This must have been the only feasible systematics for the quaestorian *apparitores*, as it would not have been possible to accompany a quaestor to the province and be back at Rome in time to head off to another *provincia* with another quaestor in the following year. The example of M. Tullius (A.178), who was *scriba* of Cicero's quaestor L. Mescinius Rufus during the former's governorship in Cilicia and whose itinerary and activities after his year of duty we know, is a case in point (see Chapter 2).

At the head of the *decuriae* of the *scribae quaestorii* were the so-called *sex primi curatorum*.⁷³ They were themselves *scribae quaestorii*, but occupied a more privileged position than their decurial colleagues. We find them unified in a separate *collegium* as they shared the privilege of being exempt from having to assume *tutela*.⁷⁴ Their superior position is manifest in the fact that the *sex primi* had the authority to authenticate copies made from the *tabulae publicae*.⁷⁵ We might expect them to have acted as the de facto deputies to the senatorial head of the *aerarium*.

Since their publication by Theodor Mommsen in 1891, fragments of *fasti* found in the vicinity of the temple of Saturn have gone by the name of '*fasti sex primorum ab aerario*' or '*fasti scribarum quaestoriarum sex primorum*'

---

71 The earliest attestation of a *scriba quaestorius ab aerario trium decuriarum* with L. Herennius (A.87) from the first century BC in *CIL* 6, 1816; for the minor decuries see L. Naevius Urbanus (A.118), a *scriba librarius quaestorius ex tribus decuriis minoribus ab aerario, CIL* 6, 1819. Cf. Kunkel and Wittmann (1995) 116 n. 44; Purcell (2001) 642.
72 Mommsen (1887) I 338, 351 postulated, in applying his reading of the regulations concerning the *viatores* and *praecones* in the *lex de XX quaestoribus* to the *scribae quaestorii*, the number of thirty-six members per *decuria*, of whom twenty-two were assigned to eleven provincial *quaestores* and the remaining fourteen worked at the *aerarium*. Gabba (1983) 491 rightly criticised Mommsen's problematic assumption, but refrained from proposing a number himself.
73 The full title for an anonymous *scriba* (A.205). Other known holders of the position: M. Natronius Rusticus (A.120), P. Septumius (A.159), T. Sabidius Maximus (A.150), Cluvius Formica (A.51), Q. Papirius Maximus (A.127), Q. Petronius Melior (A.132), P. Aelius Agathoclianus (A.2), M'. Valerius Bassus (A.185), L. Pontius Martialis (A.142).
74 *Frg. Vat.* 124.
75 Cic. *nat. deor.* 3. 74: *Qui transscripserit tabulas publicas: id quoque L. Alenus fecit, cum chirographum sex primorum imitatus est*.

respectively.⁷⁶ Mommsen interpreted these lists, which cover the years from AD 12 to 16, 18 to 20, 26 to 28, as well as 81 and 82, as yearly registers of the main officials of the *aerarium*. Divided by year, the *fasti* list the names of *praetores* – in the latest fragment *praefecti aerarii* – charged with the supervision of the *aerarium*. Additionally, three individuals are mentioned per year under the header of '*cur(atores)*'.⁷⁷ Mommsen naturally identified these *curatores* with the *sex primi curatorum*, postulating a second column of names of *curatores* where the inscription had broken off.⁷⁸ This possibility has, however, been invalidated by the coming to light of another, more complete fragment, which affirmed the number of only three *curatores* per year.⁷⁹ Trying to uphold the identification of the *fasti*'s *curatores* with the *sex primi curatorum* of the *scribae quaestorii* thus poses a problem. We would assume that every quaestorian *decuria* had six *curatores*. At least this is what is suggested by the analogous organisation of the scribal *decuria* of the *aediles curules*, which knew *sex primi* as well.⁸⁰ At the same time, as already discussed with regard to the archival functions of the *aerarium* (see Chapter 2), we happen to know other *curatores* employed at the main archive, who would neatly fit the evidence of the *fasti*.⁸¹ According to Cassius Dio, in AD 16 Tiberius instated three *curatores tabularum publicarum* to put in order the *tabulae publicae* of the *aerarium*.⁸² These *curatores* were possibly former *praetores* or *praefecti aerarii*, certainly senatorial in rank. C. Ummidius Quadratus, who appears in the *fasti* as *praetor aerarii* for AD 18, is known to have been *curator tabularum publicarum* in the course of his career.⁸³ Unfortunately, his name is not attested as *curator* for the few years covered by the *fasti*. At the same time, we are not able to identify any of the *curatores* named in the *fasti* with any known *scribae quaestorii* or senators.⁸⁴ I would, nevertheless, tend to identify the *curatores*

---

76 Mommsen (1891), originally discussing the fragments CIL 6, 1495 (CIL 6, 32271) and CIL 6, 1496 (CIL 6, 32270, 37141); later added CIL 6, 37144; the ensemble in InscrIt 13-01, 27. Cf. Corbier (1974) 34f.
77 On the officials of the *aerarium* in general Millar (1964).
78 Mommsen (1891) 161.
79 Huelsen (1902) 47 (CIL 6, 37144); already CIL 6, 1495 (CIL 6, 32271) shows that the text of the *fasti* was centred on the word '*cur(atores)*'.
80 The single *decuria* of the curule aediles in CIL 8, 8936. Statius Optatus (A.167) and Apusulenus Secundus (A.22) were both *sex primi* of the *scribae aedilium curulium*. Attilio Degrassi's unsubstantiated workaround that only three of the *sex primi curatorum* were in office each year must remain hypothetical at best; InscrIt 13-01, 27.
81 In the same vein Purcell (2001) 662 n. 123; contra Hammond (1938) 130f.
82 Dio 57. 16. 2, with reference to AD 16.
83 Corbier (1974) 44–50 no. 10 assumes his office as *curator* for the following year AD 19.
84 Langford Wilson (1909) 64, associated C. Allius Niger (A.13) with the fragmentarily known Niger (figm. I/II, col. I, v. 6). Such an identification seems unjustified, however, as *scribae librarii* never advanced to this post exclusively held by *scribae* tout court.

of the *fasti* with the *curatores tabularum publicarum* rather than with the *sex primi curatorum*, even if it meant challenging Cassius Dio's dating of the institution of the *curatores*.[85]

Mommsen also associated another fragmentary inscription, which was likewise found close to the temple of Saturn on the Capitoline Hill, with the alleged *fasti scribarum quaestoriorum sex primorum*.[86] Because of the mention of a certain L. Aelius (A.1), who, according to the fragmentary text, had been a *sex primus curatorum*, Mommsen took the marble tablet to be the header of the aforementioned *fasti*. He subsequently interpreted the fragmentary *senatus consultum* recorded on the tablet as a resolution regarding the publication of the names of the *aerarium*'s officials according to the way he found them on the *fasti*.[87] Needless to say, his argument is highly circular and most certainly erroneous. It is true that the *senatus consultum* in one way or another concerned the heads of the *aerarium* and was thus naturally posted at the temple of Saturn. That the senatorial decree dealt with the *lectio* of *scribae quaestorii*, as Mommsen imagined, can be ruled out according to a recent review of the inscription, however.[88] Besides, it is not easily understandable why the *fasti* should start with a *sex primi curatorum* rather than with the consular date we find on the other fragments, breaking with regular form. In fact, the cymatium moulding at the bottom of the stone tablet suggests a much more mundane solution to the problem. As discussed, the *sex primi curatorum* had the privilege and authority to authenticate certified copies made from the *tabulae publicae*.[89] The *senatus consultum* in question is one such certified copy that bears the name of the *sex primus* L. Aelius (A.1) (and, space permitting, perhaps of a second *curator*, now lost) as a sign of authenticity at its end.

---

[85] On the other hand, Cassius Dio reports the appointment of three ex-consuls to oversee finances for AD 6; Dio 55. 25. 6. The tradition of *curatores* associated with the *aerarium* might very well have been older than his purported date of AD 16.

[86] *CIL* 6, 32272 (*CIL* 6, 10621, 37142); Mommsen (1891) 157f.

[87] Mommsen (1891) 157 amended as follows: '[*ut ad aerarium nomina eorum, qui secundum id] decretum [creati erunt, eius anni consulibus et pra]et(oribus) aerario praescr[iptis publice proponantur, itemque ibidem proponatur] sei quit de le[gendis scribis quaestoriis Cn. Pis]o L. Se[n]tius co(n)s(ulibus) a(lter) (ambo)ve, si ei[s videbitur, dum ne quid] (contra) l(eges) tulerin[t, alive qui magistratus deind]e ferent. Cens(uere). I(n) s(enatu) f(uerunt) CCCCV[- - -]. L(ucius) Aeliu[s - - - se]x prim(us) c[uratorum - - -]*'.

[88] A 1994 autopsy by the late Géza Alföldy, available at the Epigraphische Datenbank Heidelberg (edh-www.adw.uni-heidelberg.de/edh/foto/F029955), gives an improved reading of the inscription. The traces of the letters at the beginning of v. 3 do not allow for Mommsen's reading of the term *lectio*. '[- - -]VIRI[- - -]DAMRE[- - -] / decretum [- - -]ei aerario praesun[t - - -] / sei quit de le[/[- - - Cn(aeus) Pis]o L(ucius) Seitius (!) co(n)s(ules) a(lter) a(mbo)ve si EI[- - -] / (contra) l(eges) tulerin[t - - -]I ferent cens(uere) i(n) s(enatu) f(uerunt) CCCCV[- - -] 5/ L(ucius) Aeliu[s - - - se]x prim(us) c[ur(atorum) - - -]*'.

[89] Cic. *nat. deor.* 3. 74.

Figure 3.2 Marble tablet, 27 × 14.5 × 3.5 cm. Fragment of an *album* of the *scribae quaestorii* (*CIL* 6, 37145). Found behind the Rostra on the Forum Romanum. (Parco Archeologico del Colosseo)

Despite these negative results, Mommsen was certainly right in assuming that the names of the members of the *scribae* would eventually have ended up in inscribed lists. It is the procedure the *lex de XX quaestoribus* provided for the *decuriae*, after all (II.40–41). And we may certainly expect that the scribal *collegia* kept lists of their members. Nine years after Mommsen's deliberations on the alleged *fasti scribarum quaestoriorum sex primorum*, archaeologists unearthed the fragment of another marble tablet just behind the Rostra, again in the area of the ancient temple of Saturn (see Fig. 3.2).[90]

[90] Dante Vaglieri (1900) 20; Huelsen (1902) 271 no. 60; *CIL* 6, 37145. A more recent and improved autopsy by Géza Alföldy, available at the Epigraphische Datenbank Heidelberg (edh-www.adw.uni-heidelberg.de/edh/foto/F029810), on which the following reading is based: '[- - -]L [- - -] / [- - -] Petronius [- - -] / [- - ·]Q(intus) Fabius N(umeri) [f(ilius)? - - -] / 1(itus) Varronius C(ai) [f(ilius)? - - -] ⁵/ [- - -] Cassienius [- - -] / ⟦[- - - ⟨⟨VI pr(imus) cur(atorum)⟩⟩ - - - ⟧/ ⟦[- - - ⟨⟨Q(intus) Iunius Amit[- - -]⟩⟩ - - -⟧/ ⟦[- - - ⟨⟨VS VI pr(imus) cur(atorum)⟩⟩ - - -⟧/ [- - -]ammius N(umerii) [f(ilius) —] ¹⁰/ [- - -]usius Q(uinti) f(ilius) [- - -] / [- - -]ius A(uli) f(ilius) [- - -] / [- - -] A(uli) f(ilius) [- - -]'.

What is left of the inscription fits our expectations on *fasti* or an *album*, respectively: a list of names, neatly arranged one underneath the other. The organising principle is, however, not easily recognisable due to the very fragmentary nature of the inscription. Two of the persons are defined more precisely by the abbreviation '*VI pr(imus) cur(atorum)*'. Evidently, the list contains the names of *scribae quaestorii*; it is only in this context that the honorary title of *sex primus* makes sense. A detailed inspection shows that the list had been tampered with, however. The middle part of the fragment shows clear signs of erasure, over which new names had been inscribed in a very conspicuous fashion. While the letter forms are virtually indistinguishable from those of the original inscription, the added letters are much bigger and disregard the original arrangement of lines. The regular nature of the lines above and below the erasure shows that the original inscription must have had two other names in place of the new ones. The addition of the title of *sex primus* to an existing name alone might not have warranted such a radical reworking. Two of the *scribae quaestorii* must have dropped out of the association and their names were replaced by the two *sex primi*. That said, our identification of the list as an *album* of *scribae quaestorii* is not invalidated by these findings – rather, the heavy-handed reworking of the list has made the identification possible in the first place. Determining the association to which the *album* pertained is difficult, however. The find place of the inscription in the vicinity of the temple of Saturn and thus of the *aerarium* would suggest the identification with the decurial lists mentioned in the Sullan statute. We have seen, however, that at least one of the scribal *collegia* had its *schola* in the area between the Rostra and the *aedes Saturni*. Hypothetically speaking, the little that is left of the headline of the inscription – L· – could have belonged to the abbreviation of the term *coll(egium)*, thus making the fragmentary *album* a register of members of a *collegium* of quaestorian *scribae*.

Diversity

The main Republican and imperial types of *scribae* were the quaestorian, aedilician and tribunician. At least they are the ones that feature most prominently in our body of evidence. The three different aedilician magistrates – *curules*, *plebis* and *ceriales* – were assigned *scribae* and eventually *scribae librarii*.[91] They were organised in single *decuriae*, which were

---

[91] Only one *scriba* of the *aediles ceriales* is attested: Q. Papirius Maximus (A.127).

differentiated into *maiores* (*scribae*) and *minores* (*scribae librarii*); at least the one of the *scribae aedilium curulium* was headed by *sex primi*.⁹² Very similarly, the *scribae* of the tribunes of the plebs were likely sorted into single *decuriae* for both the major *scribae* and the minor *scribae librarii*.⁹³

The higher magistrates were not formally equipped with *scribae*. Neither the *praetores* nor the *consules* (and the respective promagistrates) had their own scribal *decuriae*. The same is true for the non-permanent magistrates, the *dictator* and the *censores*. The reason for this is neither obvious nor documented. I have already emphasised functional aspects. Magistrates with a responsibility for financial and legal administration were permanently staffed with *scribae*.⁹⁴ Yet, to argue that the *consules*, the *praetores* and even more so the *censores* were exempt from documenting their official acts would demonstrably miss the point. In fact, we find *scribae* in the proximity of these higher magistrates. A certain Faberius (A.68) had allegedly been C. Iulius Caesar's *scriba* during his dictatorship. The *censores* were entrusted with the oversight of the *tabulae publicae* and the *scribae* as a whole, and their exercise of office naturally involved the aid of *scribae*.⁹⁵ At times, *scribae* show up in the proximity of consuls.⁹⁶ And while we do not find *scribae* with the *praetores* themselves, they are well attested for the courts, the *quaestiones*.⁹⁷ That said, we are not informed about the systematics of the assignment of *scribae* to these higher magistrates. It seems natural that many of the *scribae* who show up in the proximity of the higher magistrates were in fact *scribae* formally assigned to the subordinate magistrates of these higher office holders, i.e. mainly the *quaestores*. We may certainly expect the higher magistrates in the provinces to have made use of the apparitorial personnel of their assistant magistrates.⁹⁸ At least this is what is suggested

---

⁹² The single decuria in *CIL* 8, 8936; *CIL* 6, 1848 (*CIL* 6, 2176 = 32267). Both C. Iulius Iustus (A.94) and Q. Modius Proculus (A.219) were members of a *decuria aedilicia maior*; cf. Purcell (2001) 643. The two known *sex primi* are Statius Optatus (A.167) and Apusulenus Secundus (A.22).
⁹³ P. Aelius Agathoclianus (A.2) and M. Aurelius Hermogenes (A.28) are attested as *scriba tribunicius maior*.
⁹⁴ Cf. Kunkel and Wittmann (1995) 111.
⁹⁵ Censorial supervision in Liv. 4. 8. 4; *scribae* together with *censores* at the *lustrum*, Varro *ling*. 6. 86–87, V. Max. 4. 1. 10; the censors concluding their census at the *tabularium* in the *aerarium*, Liv. 43. 16. 13.
⁹⁶ Registering spoils at the side of Q. Fabius Maximus Verucosus Cunctator after the sack of *Tarentum* in 209 BC, Liv. 27. 16. 8; assisting a consul in a *convivium*, Plut. *quaes. conv.* 1. 3. 10; in the entourage of the *proconsul* Pompeius in 63/62 BC, V. Max. 5. 7. ext. 2; C. Cicereius (A.40) is said to have been the *scriba* of P. Scipio Africanus, V. Max. 4. 5. 3; C. Septimius (A.157) the one of M. Bibulus in 59 BC, Cic. *Att*. 2. 24. 2.
⁹⁷ As common constituents of a *quaestio* in Cic. *Cluent*. 147; Cic. *Verr*. 2. 3. 26; Cic. *ad Brut*. 290; cf. Mantovani (2000) 661–8.
⁹⁸ In this vein already Mommsen (1887) I 348; mainly followed by Badian (1989) 598f.; A. H. M. Jones (1949) 40 w. n. 25 argues that one *scriba quaestorius* was officially assigned to the provincial

by Cicero's characterisation of Verres' praetorship in Sicily as well as his own handling of his quaestor's *scriba* during his governorship in *Cilicia*.[99] Both *censores* and *iudices quaestionum* might have drawn on the *aerarium* for their scribal assistants. Unfortunately, we lack further details.

What we know about *scribae* of other Roman magistrates is exemplary for the volatility of our body of evidence: many types of *scribae* are attested only once. Thus, we know of *scribae* for the *viginti(sex)viri* in general[100] and the *triumviri mensarii*[101] as well as the *decemviri stlitibus iudicandis*[102] in particular. Furthermore, *scribae* are attested for the *decemviri agris dandis adsignandis*,[103] the *curatores aquarum* and the *praefecti frumenti dandi*.[104] All of them were most likely organised in their own *decuriae*.[105] We might expect that many other apparitorial *scribae* simply have not found their way into our body of sources.[106]

The principate brought about a new quasi-Republican magistrate: the *princeps* himself. As his position grew out of Republican magisterial power – in fact the new form of government was officially the *res publica restituta* – the emperor was assigned *apparitores* in the style of a Republican magistrate.[107] We have already encountered Albinovanus Celsus (A.10), who is described by Horace in 20 BC as '*comes scribaque*' of the eventual emperor Tiberius.[108]

---

quaestor, the other to the provincial governor; cf. Kunkel and Wittmann (1995) 117 w. n. 50 and 51; Purcell (2001) 648f. assumes a system of former *scribae* of the lower magistrates who were, later in their career, picked up to attend to the higher magistrates.

[99] Verres' close connection with the whole provincial staff, Cic. Verr. 2. 2. 27, 2, 3, 181–187. For Cicero's governorship see Chapter 2.
[100] A certain [- - -]lius Clemens, A.201.
[101] Liv. 26. 36. 11, Flor. epit. 1. 22. 23–25 (Jord. Rom. 192); perhaps referencing *scribae quaestorii*.
[102] A certain L. Cornelius Terentianus, A.55.
[103] Cic. leg. agr. 2. 32.
[104] Frontin. Aq. 2. 100.
[105] See e.g. the *viatores*, of which we know a *decuria Xviralis*, CIL 6, 32294.
[106] Purcell (1983) 155f., following Mommsen (1887) I 368 n. 5, has argued for the existence of *scribae armamentarii*, i.e. *scribae* assigned to the *curator* of the arsenal of the capital. The argument is based mainly on CIL 6, 999 (CIL 6, 31221, ILS 333), an honorary inscription to Antoninus Pius of the year AD 138, consisting of Pius' title and ending in two lines '*scribae / armamentari*'. We otherwise know that the *armamentarii* had their own *decuria* and were, thus, counted among the *apparitores*; CIL 10, 4832 ('*armamentarius decuria(lis)q(ue)*' (?)), CIL 5, 1883 ('*ex decuria [a]rmamentaria*'). A joint honour to Pius by two apparitorial charges, the *scribae* and the *armamentarii*, might thus be more plausible. Cf. CECapitol 4, a votive inscription by veterans of the Praetorian Guard, allegedly mentioning a '*scr(iba armamentarius)*', a certain Valerius (A.386), might rather be read as '*scr(iniarius)*' as *scriniarii praefecti praetorii* are otherwise attested; Todisco (1999) 74f.
[107] Suet. Dom. 14. 3; cf. Millar (1977) 66–9.
[108] Hor. epist. 1. 8. 1–2.

A recent epigraphic find in the Spanish city of *Segobriga* attests to a '*Caesaris Augusti scriba*', i.e. a *scriba* of Augustus himself.¹⁰⁹

M. Porcius (A.144) had most likely accompanied Augustus to Spain in the years 15–13 BC, where he was honoured as patron by the Segobrigenses with an equestrian statue.¹¹⁰ I would argue that the staffing of the *principes* with *scribae* was a transient affair in a phase when the traditional political system and its institutions were renegotiated. Augustus is said to have offered to the poet Horace, himself a quaestorian *scriba*, the *officium epistularum*.¹¹¹ The post later became known as the office *ab epistulis*, one of several secretarial and documentary posts newly created for the administrative needs of the emperor.¹¹² While it is possible that the post of *scriba* of the *princeps* lived on as a sinecure, it is certain that these new clerical offices of the imperial household obviated the need for apparitorial *scribae* of the emperor.¹¹³

In the same vein, the newly created imperial branch of government, independent of the Republican one, which it paralleled and eventually superseded, did not draw on the *scribae* for its documentary needs – just as it, in general, did not make use of *apparitores* apart from *lictores*.¹¹⁴ A recent epigraphic discovery from the Lycian city of Patara, which attests to a *scriba* of a *legatus Augusti*, is challenging our received understanding of these systematics, however.¹¹⁵ C. Iulius Augustalis (A.91) is referred to as *scriba* of the *legatus Augusti pro praetore* M. Flavius Aper, who governed the province of *Lycia et Pamphylia* in c. AD 124–6.¹¹⁶ Yet, the testimony is doubly unique. Not only is it the first and only testimony of a *scriba* of an Augustan legate (and of any provincial governor, for that matter).

---

¹⁰⁹ Alföldy, Abascal, and Cebrián (2003) no. 10 (*AE* 2003, 986). Cf. similar denominations for other *apparitores* assigned to the *principes*; *CIL* 6, 32294 ('*lictor III [decuriar]um qui Caesari et [magist]ratibus apparent*'), *CIL* 9, 4057 ('*lictor Augusti Caesaris*'), *CIL* 6, 1945 ('*praeco ex tribus decuri(i)s qui co(n)s(ulibus) cens(oribus) pr(aetoribus) apparere solent apparuit Caesari Augusto*').
¹¹⁰ Alföldy, Abascal, and Cebrián (2003) 273f. They suggest that Porcius might have been involved in the foundation of Segobriga as a colony to warrant his extraordinary position.
¹¹¹ SUET. *vita Hor.* 24.
¹¹² Hirschfeld (1905) 318f.; Ausbüttel (1998) 12f.
¹¹³ Cf. Sex. Caecilius Epagathus (A.34), a most likely second-century AD *scriba librarius* with a rich apparitorial career, is called *apparitor Caesarum*; T. Iulius Saturninus (A.99), a *scriba tribunicius*, was *apparitor Caesaris* with Antoninus Pius; the designation is otherwise only attested for Nero's famous freedman Epaphroditus (*ILS* 9505, plausibly supplemented). Which apparitorial posts the title incorporated is not clear, however.
¹¹⁴ A general characterisation of the system by Eich (2005) 180–4; cf. Palme (1999) 92–5; on the *apparitores* of the *legati Augusti* Haensch (1997) 711–13.
¹¹⁵ Bönisch and Lepke (2013) no. 6: '*[Dis Manibus] / C(ai) Iuli(i) Augustalis / scrib(ae) Flavi Apri / leg(ati) Aug(usti) Marcia / Pia (vac.) coniunxs (!) ⁵/ f(aciendum) c(uravit).* / Θεοῖς καταχθ(ονίοις) / Γ(αίου) Ἰουλίου Αὐγοσ/ταλίου σκρίβ(α) / Φλαουίου Ἄπρου ¹⁰/ πρεσβ(ευτοῦ) Μαρκία / Πία σύνβιος / ἀνέθ(ηκεν)'.
¹¹⁶ PIR² F 208; Eck (1983) 160.

It is also the only *scriba* mentioning his affiliation not with a magisterial office but rather in direct terms ('*scriba Flavi Apri*'), a style that is otherwise known for *lictores* assigned to provincial governors.[117] While this testimony may certainly be evidence that Augustan legates were allowed to draw on the apparitorial *decuriae* other than for *lictores*, the unique wording of the inscription suggests that we should treat its historical value with due care until further evidence comes to light. Hypothetically, Augustalis could have been a private secretary of Aper, whereas his employment was later stylised in official terminology by his wife, who was responsible for his funerary inscription. Another possibility could be that Augustalis had held the office of a *scriba quaestorius* while Aper had been *quaestor*. When Augustalis eventually died and the inscription was erected, Aper had become Augustan legate, of all places of the province Augustalis had lived in, which is why Augustalis' wife chose to connect her husband with the well known legate.

Model

The city of Rome and its empire provided a model for other organisational units within the state. The concept of the *scriba* can thus be found with other cities and municipalities, corporations and associations as well as the Roman navy.

Roman municipal laws were modelled on the example of Rome itself. As a result, apparitorial officials were a common feature of communities under Roman law. Thanks to two extant municipal charters, the Caesarian statute for the *colonia Iulia Genetiva* (Urso) as well as the Flavian *lex municipalis* (Irni, Malaga and Salpensa), we are well informed about the *scribae* of cities. The *lex Ursonensis* provides us with a clear hierarchical overview over the *apparitores* of a Roman colony (see Table 3.1).[118] It highlights the eminent position of the *scribae*, which is, for one thing, reflected in their superior pay relative to the other apparitorial officials. Then again, they are the only apparitors whose duties are treated in detail by the *lex*.[119] As I have already discussed, they needed to be approved by the *decuriones*, sworn in publicly and take an oath of due diligence in order to have their name entered into the public records and be allowed to perform their duty. Only

---

[117] Bönisch and Lepke (2013) 515.
[118] Cf. for similar regulations in *municipia lex Irn.* 18.34, Lebek (1994) for the number of *scribae* of the *duoviri*; *lex Irn.* 73. 43–47 for their conditions of pay, which were to be determined by the *decuriones*.
[119] Cf. Rodríguez Neila (2008) 69.

Table 3.1. *Hierarchy of* apparitores *of the* colonia Iulia Genetiva *(Urso) according to annual wages, with number of yearly assignments to municipal officials (lex Urson. 62)*

	duumviri		aediles	
	no.	wage (HS)	no.	wage (HS)
scriba	2	1200	1	800
accensus	1	700	—	
lictor	2	600	—	
haruspex	1	500	1	100
viator	2	400	—	
praeco	1	300	1	300
librarius	1	300	—	
tibicen	1	n/a	1	300

then were they entrusted with the administration of the city's financial records and *tabulae publicae*.[120] It was this responsibility for the public repository that added to their eminent position. In fact, the *scribae* held the second rank after the *decuriones*.[121] Some communities even seem to have equated the prerequisites for the office of *scriba* with those of membership of the council of *decuriones*. A letter of the second-century AD orator Fronto on behalf of a certain Volumnius Serenus (A.298), who was *scriba* and *decurio* of the colony of Concordia and whose legitimate membership in the town council had become contested, takes the interconnection between the two municipal institutions for granted.[122] Fronto suggests that it had been common practice in Concordia that candidates for the position of *scriba* had to be fit to be a *decurio*. As a result, holders of the *scriba*-ship usually became members of the town council once their term of office had concluded.[123] Judging by the small number of *decuriones* among our attested municipal *scribae*, the practice described by Fronto may have been an ideal conception rather than reality, however.[124]

---

[120] *lex Urson.* 81; *lex Irn.* 73. In Tibur we find two *scribae* as executive powers, most likely assisting the *curator aquarum*; T. Sabidius Victor (A.284) and D. Rupilius Menander (A.281), the *scribae rei publicae*, on a *fistula*, *CIL* 14, 3699 (*CIL* 15, 7892, *InscrIt* 04-01, 625), cf. Eck (1995) 208.

[121] *CIL* 8, 9052; *CIL* 10, 4643 (*EAOR* 08, 6).

[122] FRONTO *amic.* 2.7; cf. Kleijwegt (1994).

[123] FRONTO *amic.* 2.7. 4–6: *estne lege coloniae Concordiensium cautum, ne quis scribam faxit nisi eum quem decurionem quoque recte facere possit? Fueruntne omnes et sunt ad hoc locorum, quibus unquam scriptus publicus Concordiae datus est, decuriones? Factusne est Volumnius decreto ordinis scriba et decurio?*

[124] Four of the known municipal *scribae* were also *decuriones* (A.232, A.243, A.262, A.300); two were honoured with the *ornamenta decurionalia* (A.237, A.267), making it clear that at least in these communities this was not automatic.

As far as we understand, municipal *scribae* were also organised in *decuriae*, from which they were assigned to the local magistrates for a yearly tenure.[125] At least in *coloniae*, we also find the division into senior and junior *scribae*. In the case of Urso these were the *scribae* and *librarii*, in Ostia they went by the names of *scribae cerarii* (emphasising their work with wax tablets) and *(scribae) librarii*, respectively.[126] Municipal chief magistrates were usually staffed with two *scribae* and a further *librarius*, warranting their supervision of the local *aerarium*.[127] Other magistrates had to make do with fewer clerical staff.

According to the legal status and the varying magistrates of a community, we find a variety of different designations of municipal *scribae*. Besides the two basic titles of *scriba*[128] and *(scriba) librarius*[129] we know of *scribae* of the *duoviri*,[130] the *quattuorviri*,[131] the *aediles iure dicundo*,[132] the *quaestores*[133] and the *quinquennales*.[134] Frequent is the association with the legal status of the settlement, such as *scriba civitatis*,[135] *coloniae*,[136] *municipii*[137] or *rei publicae*.[138] However, these are optional variants to the basic title of *scriba*, which is otherwise often followed by a toponym. Alternative versions of these designations are *scriba publicus*,[139] *scriba publicus aedilicius*[140] and *scriba publicus rei publicae*.[141] The title of *scriba aerarii*[142]

---

[125] Attested for *Ostia*, *CIL* 14, 353 (*ILS* 6148); *CIL* 14, 409 (*ILS* 6146, *IPOstia*-B, 339, *EAOR* 04, 39); scribal *decuriales* M. Licinius Privatus (A.267), A. Egrilius Secundus Threptianus (A.255), A. Egrilius Plarianus (A.254) and P. Cornelius Victorinus (A.251).
[126] *CIL* 14, 409 (*ILS* 6146, *IPOstia*-B, 339, *EAOR* 04, 39).
[127] These were commonly the *duoviri iure dicundo* or *quattuorviri iure dicundo*, Liebenam (1900) 255f.; Abbott and Johnson (1926) 59; H. Galsterer (1976) 121–7; the *duoviri* of *Irni* with the supervision of the *tabulae communes*, *lex Irn.* 73. 31–36; a *scriba* of an *aedilis iure dicundo* and *praefectus aerarii* who brings forward documents in Caere, *CIL* 11, 3614 (*CIL* 11, 4347, *ILS* 5918a).
[128] A.269 (*Aesernia*); A.288 (*Asculum*); A.291 (*Atella*); A.268 (*Augusta Taurinorum*); A.258 (*Auximum*); A.282 (*Caere*); A.243 (*Cularo*); A.235 (*Luna*); A.246 (*Mediolanum*); A.247 (*Mursella*); A.242 (*Paestum*); A.295, A.273, A.286, A.265 (*Puteoli*); A.252, A.256 (*Salona*); A.270 (*Sulmo*); A.264 (*Tolosa*); A.294, A.248, A.280, A.241 (*Tropaeum Traiani*); A.238 (*Uselis*); A.296 (*Venafrum*).
[129] A.257, A.267, A.251 (*Ostia*).
[130] A.236, A.250 (*Capua*).
[131] A.277 (*Aquae Sextiae*).
[132] A.261 (*Beneventum*), contra Kleijwegt (1994) 116.
[133] A.236 (*Capua*).
[134] A.275 (*Asculum*).
[135] A.263 (*Aquincum*).
[136] A.239 (*Napoca*); A.259 (*Sarmizegetusa*).
[137] A.232 (*Aquae Balissae*); A.278 (*Siscia*); A.292 (*Mogetiana*); A.240 (*Potaissa*).
[138] A.245 (*Antium*); A.260 (*Cubulteria*); A.293 (*Forum Novum*); A.274 (*Potentia*); A.271 (*Sulmo*); A.284, A.281 (*Tibur*).
[139] A.237 (*Comum*); A.298 (*Concordia*); A.233 (*Delminium*); A.262 (*Mediolanum*); A.234 (*Messana*); A.287 (*Sentinum*).
[140] A.276 (*Neapolis*).
[141] A.297 (*Capena*).
[142] A.285 (*Cularo*).

seems to have been a local peculiarity of Cularo as was of *scriba cerarius* in Ostia.¹⁴³

Roman associations were modelled on the civic organisation of the Roman *res publica*. As such, these *collegia*¹⁴⁴ were organised internally along hierarchical lines. Magistrates held offices on behalf of the ordinary members of the association (*plebs*), who were divided into several divisions (*decuriae*). The *scribae* constituted one element of the magisterial level, often in a minor position and in varying numbers.¹⁴⁵ Still, we lack any precise information about the duties and functions of the *scribae* within these associations. We might assume that they were occupied with the association's finances and documentary needs – the *collegia* functioned very much along the lines of other civic bodies we have discussed, after all. We find *scribae* in civic, religious, professional and military associations as well as in *collegia* of the *familia Caesaris*.¹⁴⁶

The Roman military had a highly developed documentary culture with a sophisticated staff of writing personnel.¹⁴⁷ Yet, only the Roman fleet made use of the title *scriba* for its clerks.¹⁴⁸ Naval *scribae* were assigned per ship, i.e. per *triere*, *quadriere* or *liburna*, where they carried out their duty.¹⁴⁹ The exact nature of their tasks is unknown, however. Interestingly enough, the *scribae* are believed to have constituted the lowest grade of naval scribes.¹⁵⁰ Work on a ship was regarded as highly dangerous, which is why Festus attributed to the naval *scriba* the lowest dignity of the whole '*genus scribarum*'.¹⁵¹

---

¹⁴³ A.257, A.255, A.254, A.266, A.272 (*Ostia*). There is no reason to question P. Aelius Aelianus' (A.232) perfectly plausible *cursus* of *scriba*, *decurio* and finally *IIIIvir* of the *municipium Aquae Balissae* to propose an exotic reading such as *scriba dec(urionis)*, Gallego Franco (2001) 118, or even *scriba dec(urionibus) IIIIvir(is)* [sic!], Cîrjan (2010) 186.
¹⁴⁴ On the terminology of Roman associations Ausbüttel (1982) 17.
¹⁴⁵ The internal organisation of associations in Royden (1988) 13–17.
¹⁴⁶ See App. A.3.
¹⁴⁷ In general Stauner (2004), on the diverse clerical personnel 113–48.
¹⁴⁸ Roger Tomlin's recent identification of a *scriba* of a *tribunus militum* in an address on a wax tablet from Londinium, *WT* 18, remains hypothetical, not least because it is based on an alternative reading of Cn. Ricinius Persa's (A.148) career, who had most likely been *scr(iba)* and *tr(ibunus) mil(itum)*, rather than *scr(iba) tr(ibuni) mil(itum)*; cf. Devijver R 7; Demougin (1992) 162f. no. 178. The Roman army knew *librarii*, yet not as a minor grade of *scribae* but as an independent office. Interestingly enough, the *librarii* were occupied with the *rationes* of the soldiers; Veg. *mil.* 2. 7, cf. Stauner (2004) 133.
¹⁴⁹ See app. A.4 for the designations. Cf. Fest. 168.8–9 (169M): *Navalis scriba, qui in nave apparebat*.
¹⁵⁰ Stauner (2004) 146; Reddé (1986) 538f.
¹⁵¹ Fest. 168.10–11 (169M); cf. Plaut. *frg. inc.* 17.1.

Human Relations

The nomination and appointment of apparitorial *scribae* were no mere administrative and technical acts. Instead, they were highly politicised. Personal patronage, a key structual feature of Roman social relations, pervaded the Roman civil service.[152] Evidently, having a confidant occupy a post as *scriba* not only meant access to and control of key documentary resources. It could also mean being able to draw on your own client for your term of office or position him as a factor of influence in a political opponent's tenure.[153] The former is particularly well attested, as it features prominently in late Republican cases of magisterial malpractice and embezzlement. *Scribae* had become important partners in crime of their senatorial superiors (see Chapter 4). For its holder, a place in a *decuria* meant access to the important figures of Roman society. A *scriba* had knowledge and access to it to offer; he was in for the social contacts and the possibilities they entailed.

In principle, the Roman *scriba*-ship had been conceived as an apolitical institution. Theoretically, the *scribae* were subordinate auxiliary personnel with no autonomous power. As I have argued above, the main prerequisite for a place in a *decuria* was, apart from the obvious technical skills, moral integrity – the trait needed to resist partisan corruption. It is the characteristic highlighted by Cicero in his bitter complaint about Verres' scribal auxiliaries.[154] The Romans were not naive, however. The weaknesses and pitfalls of the apparitorial system were well known. External influence on and manipulation of its workings were taken for granted. Not by chance is the earliest annalistic episode featuring a *scriba* a tale about the abuse of position and the political importance of social relations. Cn. Flavius (A.73) had betrayed his moral integrity by publishing the calendar on behalf of his political patron App. Claudius Caecus (see Chapter 1). Cicero made a case against Verres in highlighting that his partner in crime, Maevius (A.109), had not only been a *scriba* in his entourage during his time as *propraetor* in Sicily in 73–71 BC, but also when Verres had held the office of legatus in

---

[152] I understand Roman patronage as an enduring relationship between unequals that entailed dissimilar, but reciprocal benefits for both parties; see Saller (1982) 1. I include not only voluntary but also partly involuntary, legal relationships, such as the link between patron and freedman; cf. Garnsey (2010) 37–9. Brunt (1988) 382–442, esp. 441, still very influential, has negated the importance of patronage especially for the late Republic. His deliberations mainly concern a macro level. My own remarks relate to the micro level.
[153] Cf. MacMullen (1988) 125f.
[154] Cic. *Verr.* 2. 3. 184.

Cilicia in 80 BC and during his time as *praetor urbanus* in 74 BC.¹⁵⁵ Maevius, in his capacity as *scriba quaestorius*, probably met Verres for the first time in Cilicia, where the latter had been promoted from his post as legate to *legatus pro quaestore* upon the *quaestor* C. Publicius Malleolus' untimely death.¹⁵⁶ If we are to believe Cicero, Verres had hence been able to influence the assignment of the *scriba* in his favour for years to come.

The scribal apparitorial system I have laid out above was, at least partially, designed to prevent such partisan influence and exploitation. The quaestorian *scribae* used to be assigned to the quaestors and provinces, respectively, by lot. Cicero, when he was headed to the senate to deliver his fourth and final invective against Catilina on the fifth of December 63 BC, came upon the assembled *scribae* at the *aerarium*. They had gathered there '*ab expectatione sortis*'.¹⁵⁷ The drawing of lots was officially still the standard procedure to assign quaestorian *scribae* to their superiors more than a century and a half later.¹⁵⁸ Nevertheless, Maevius' case shows that, despite these basic principles, certain individuals left nothing to chance. The assignment of *scribae* must have been as political as any personnel issue in times of intense political struggle; so much so that quaestorian *scribae* were used as political pawns. When, in 58 BC, Cato the Younger had been chosen as *quaestor pro praetore* to annex Cyprus, the request, made by his adversary P. Clodius Pulcher, was entirely political. To add to Cato's removal from the politics of the capital, Clodius is said to have influenced the assignment of the two *scribae* due to Cato. Subsequently, he ended up with a thief and a client of Clodius himself.¹⁵⁹ A more constructive utilisation of scribal connections was also possible. One of Cicero's *scribae* during his quaestorship in Sicily in 75 BC was named L. Sergius (A.160). It is certainly not by mere chance that this *scriba quaestorius* bears the same name as L. Sergius Catilina, the later conspirator, with whom Cicero had cultivated contacts at that time.¹⁶⁰

The crucial element of the system prone to partisan influence was, I would suggest, entry into a *decuria*. The *lectio* into one of the scribal *decuriae* was dependent upon the magistrates themselves. Yet, the fact that

---

¹⁵⁵ CIC. *Verr.* 2.3.187.
¹⁵⁶ Broughton (1951–1952) II 80f.
¹⁵⁷ CIC. *Catil.* 4.15; cf. SCHOL. *Cic. Bob.* 87 St. on Cicero's *In Clodium et Curionem*: *Aput aerarium sortiri provincias et quaestores solebant et scribae, ut pro certo appareret, in quam provinciam vel cum quo praeside proficiscerentur.*
¹⁵⁸ PLIN. *ep.* 4.12.2.
¹⁵⁹ PLUT. *Cat. Mi.* 34.3–4: δύο γραμματεῖς μόνον, ὧν ὁ μὲν κλέπτης καὶ παμπόνηρος, ἅτερος δὲ Κλωδίου πελάτης.
¹⁶⁰ Badian (1989) 584 no. 8, 589f.

the places in the *decuriae* were filled in advance must have constituted only a small impediment. As membership in the *decuriae* was permanent, placing one's confidant would, thus, likely become useful in the years to come, anyway. What is more, when selling one's place in a *decuria* had become a custom, placing one's familiar must have become even easier. It is thus hardly surprising that, according to our evidence, placing confidants in scribal *decuriae* to further one's own goals seems to have been common practice during the late Republic. In a seemingly odd conjecture, Livy found it natural to amend the name of Cn. Terentius (A.130), the *scriba* traditionally associated with the finding of the books of the legendary Etruscan king Numa in 181 BC, to L. Petilius. In Livy's retrojection it made perfect sense that the *scriba* had been a client of the then *praetor urbanus* Q. Petilius Spurinna, who had been involved in the finding of the books and who, allegedly, had chosen his client for a scribal *decuria* when he had been *quaestor urbanus* some years before.[161] It is peculiar that our late Republican sources on *scribae* know other such obvious patron–client pairings. A certain Q. Cornelius (A.54) was *scriba* of L. Cornelius Sulla, the dictator;[162] Sex. Clodius (Cloelius) (A.49) was *scriba* of the infamous tribune of the plebs P. Clodius Pulcher;[163] last but not least, a certain M. Tullius (A.178) was *scriba* of M. Tullius Cicero's *quaestor* during his governorship in *Cilicia*.[164] Once placed in a *decuria*, influential patrons seem to have been willing to defend their clients' position by all available means. When Cato the Younger, as he famously cleared up the *aerarium* during his term as *quaestor urbanus* in 65 BC, expelled and tried one of the *scribae quaestorii*, the *censor* Q. Lutatius Catulus came to the defence of his client. Even the fact that Lutatius, in his official capacity, was overseeing the adherence to justice and piety did not prevent him from resorting to dubious tactics to accomplish the acquittal of the incriminated *scriba*.[165] Even Cicero had obviously found it in his interest to defend a *scriba*, a certain D. Matrinius (A.115), whom he successfully helped restore to his decurial place.[166]

---

[161] LIV. 40. 29. 3–14; in the same vein Badian (1989) 599; on the tradition of the episode Rosen (1985) 66–9; on the *scriba*'s alleged identification as *scriba pontificius* Ryan (2002) 71; Rüpke (2005) 1315 n. 6.
[162] Badian (1989) 584 no. 6, 586–9; cf. Ryan (2002) 81f.
[163] On the name of Clodius, who is also know as Cloelius, Shackleton Bailey (1960); contra Flambard (1978); on his close connection to Pulcher Benner (1987) 156f.; Damon (1992).
[164] Cf. Chapter 2.
[165] PLUT. *Cat. Mi.* 16. 4–10.
[166] CIC. *Cluent.* 126.

Our late Republican sources abound with examples of *scribae* who ranked prominently in the entourage of their senatorial patrons. In the first quarter of the second century BC, C. Cicereius (A.40) had been the *scriba* of Scipio Africanus. He seems to have remained loyal to the family. He later became a textbook example of moderation as he had ceded the post of *praetor* to Africanus' son when they both stood as candidates for the office.[167] Two of the closest confidants of Q. Sertorius, the anti-Sullan partisan in Spain of the seventies of the first century BC, were his two *scribae quaestorii*, Maecenas (A.107) and Versius (A.189).[168] Sulla himself seems to have supported the career of a *scriba*, Q. Cornelius (A.54), who eventually managed to become *quaestor urbanus* under Caesar.[169] L. Papirius Potamo (A.125) had not only been the *scriba quaestorius* of Verres' quaestor Q. Caecilius Niger in Sicily, he was also his '*familiaris*'.[170] He subsequently stayed with his *amicus* Verres in Sicily after his term with Niger.[171] A certain Faberius (A.68) had been a *scriba* of C. Iulius Caesar and stayed loyal to M. Antonius after the *dicator*'s assassination; in the same vein, the *scriba* M. Flavius (A.74), who had assisted Caesar in his reform of the calendar,[172] must have been a familiar of his. Granted, these examples represent only a very small number of *scribae* who held the post during the Roman Republic. Yet, interestingly enough, we find these influential *scribae* with the most prominent senatorial office holders of their age. And indeed, when Ernst Badian surveyed the familial connections of the known Republican *scribae*, he found that the great majority of them bore the names of senatorial families of their time.[173] Cicero must have been painfully aware of the hypocrisy of his words when he accused Verres of the fact that

> comites illi tui delecti manus erant tuae; praefecti, scribae, accensi, medici, haruspices, praecones manus erant tuae; ut quisque te maxime cognatione adfinitate necessitudine aliqua attingebat, ita maxime manus tua putabatur.[174]

---

[167] V. Max. 4. 5. 3. Cf. Badian (1989) 584 no. 5; Chapter 5.
[168] Badian (1989) 584 no. 9, 590, 584 no. 10. Interestingly enough, it is still disputed whether the two *scribae* were involved in the plot which eventually murdered Sertorius; pro Konrad (1994) 211, contra Schulten (1926) 135.
[169] Badian (1989) 586–9 no. 6; cf. Chapter 5.
[170] CIC. *div. in Caec.* 29; cf. Badian (1989) 584 no. 12, 603.
[171] CIC. *Verr.* 2. 4. 44; contra David (2007) 36f., 46, who thinks that Potamo was further employed as *librarius* after his term.
[172] Cf. Rüpke (2005) 986 n. 1655, who counts him thus as a *scriba pontificius*; contra Ryan (2002) 72f.
[173] Badian (1989) 599; cf. on similar political roles of senatorial *liberti* Treggiari (1969) 177–92.
[174] CIC. *Verr.* 2. 2. 27: 'The members of your select retinue were your hands; your managers, secretaries, orderlies, doctors, soothsayers, and criers were your hands; the more closely a man was connected with you by any tie of blood, marriage, or friendship, the more he was reckoned one of your hands', transl. L. H. G. Greenwood.

Influencing the workings of the decurial system in one's own favour and surrounding oneself with loyal and familiar *scribae* must, to a great extent, have been accepted practice.

Keeping track of such particular relations of patronage during the Empire is much more difficult as our evidence is much less explicit in pointing out partisan usurpation of the scribal *decuriae*. Even when many scribal apparitorial posts had probably become sinecures, a place in a *decuria* most certainly remained prestigious and profitable. Yet, these positions likely became much less politically contested as senatorial advancement now largely depended upon one's relation to the emperor rather than the intricacies of partisan politics.[175] The post of *scriba* had become politically uncontentious. What we can still trace, however, are relations of known *scribae* with senatorial families. As a matter of fact, influential senators continued to place their protégés in scribal *decuriae*. A prime example is the family of the Volusii Saturnini, a consular dynasty of the first century AD.[176] Among the many members of the *familia*, five freedmen and their sons are known to have been *scribae librarii*. Interestingly enough, they all belong to Augustan times.[177] In addition, many a *scriba* of imperial times can be linked with a senatorial patron.[178] We also find freedmen of emperors

---

[175] Cf. Treggiari (1969) 192.

[176] On the Volusii Saturnini Eck (1972); the reconstruction of the now dispersed corpus of inscriptions of the *columbarium* the Volusii Saturnini maintained for their freedmen and slaves at the via Appia in Buonocore (1984a).

[177] L. Volusius Himerus (A.196), L. Volusius Plocamus Maior (A.197), L. Volusius Primanus (A.198) and his son L. Volusius Hermes (A.195) were freedmen of L. Volusius Saturninus, *consul suffectus* of 12 BC; PIR¹ V 660. Another freedman of the *familia*, whose name is lost (A.194), was freed by the *consul* of AD 3; PIR¹ V 661.

[178] Sex. Caecilius Epagathus (A.34) and his son Sex. Caecilius Birronianus (A.33) perhaps members of the African senatorial family of the Sexti Caecilii; PIR² C 17, 18, 37, 87. – Ti. Claudius Helvius Secundus (A.43) most likely promoted by the *consul* Q. Pomponius Rufus, cf. Jarrett (1963) 212. – C. Domitius Fabius Hermogenes (A.63) likely protégé of C. Domitius Dexter, *consul* AD 196; PIR² D 144; Meiggs (1973) 211; d'Arms (1976) 401. – Q. Fabius Cytisus (A.69) freedman of Q. Fabius Africanus, *consul* of 10 BC; PIR² F 43. – C. Fonteius Claudianus (A.79) perhaps son of a senatorial freedman; Eck (1978) 43 n. 24. – T. Iunius Achilles (A.198) connected to T. Iunius Severus, *consul suffectus* in AD 154; PIR² I 820; cf. Le Roux (1982) 460. – A. Iunius Pastor (A.105) most likely connected to A. Iunius Pastor, *consul* of AD 163; PIR² I 796. – L. Marius Doryphorus (A.113) probably a freedman of the family of the Marii Perpetui, presumably of L. Marius Maximus, the consular historian. The founder of the family, another Marius Perpetuus, had been *scriba quaestorius* himself (A.114); Birley (1997) 2702; Purcell (1983) 184. – C. Stertinius Orpex (A.169) freedman of C. Stertinius Maximus, *consul suffectus* of AD 23; PIR¹ S 661. – Stertinius Maximus Eutyches (A.168) probably a descendant of Stertinius Orpex, sponsored by Attidius Tuscus, *legatus pro praetore* of *Asia* in the second century AD; PIR² A 1345. – P. Sufenas Myro (A.170) and P. Sufenas Severus Sempronianus (A.171) sons of Sufenas Hermes, a freedman of P. Sufenas Verus, *consul suffectus* AD 132/133; Demougin (1978) 623. – M'. Suillius Celsus (A.172) perhaps was a member of the family of P. Suillius Rufus, *proconsul* of Asia in AD 53/54; PIR¹ S 700. – T. Tettienus Felix (A.176) connected to T. Tettienus Serenus, *pontifex* from c. AD 80-115; he had been his *calator*; Eck

and their descendants among the occupants of decurial places, albeit in much smaller numbers.¹⁷⁹ The particulars of the relationship between these *scribae* and their senatorial patrons remain elusive, however, as we lack further evidence on the lives of these *scribae*.

The Roman *scribae* were to be found at the centre of the Roman Republican polity. As the most senior of the *apparitores*, they were part of the backbone of the Roman Republican administration; they belonged to what we might call the Roman civil service. Becoming a *scriba* thus meant entering a highly systematised and hierarchised organisation, which was designed to cater to the needs of the slim governing body of the Republican state. Entry into one of the scribal *decuriae* entailed financial and other privileges as well as collegiate representation. In the previous chapter, I have stressed the close relationship of the *scribae* with the written arcana of the Roman state as an important factor for their position within the Roman polity. It was this position at the heart of Roman documentary culture that made the *scriba*-ship interesting for the political elite. In principle designed to withstand partisan influence, the scribal apparitorial system eventually became politicised. Access to the *decuriae* was only partially dependent on one's scribal skills. Social and monetary patronage was equally, arguably even more important. At least in the late Republic it was common practice for the ruling aristocracy to place their clients and familiars in a scribal *decuria* as a means of political leverage and influence. In such a constellation, the *scribae* themselves could become profiteers. Having a place in a scribal *decuria* meant direct and personal access to the ruling and societal elite, which more often than not resulted in close and lasting relationships. It was this social capital that was the basis for many a *scriba*'s financial and social advancement, which I will discuss in the following chapters.

(1978) 48 n. 23. – D. Valerius Propolus (A.187) *libertus* of one of the senatorial Valerii Asiatici, either the *consul* of AD 46; PIR¹ V 25; or the *consul designatus* of AD 69; PIR¹ V 26.
¹⁷⁹ Ti. Claudius Secundus Philippianus (A.46) a freedman of Claudius; cf. Chantraine (1967) 328 no. *265. – C. Octavius Auctus (A.173) a freedman of Octavia minor. – T. Statilius Messalinianus (A.165) perhaps a descendant of a freedman of Statilia Messalina, Nero's third wife; Purcell (1983) 158; contra Kajanto (1982) 194. – Tyrannus (A.179) a freedman of Acte, the freedwoman of Claudius and lover of Nero; cf. Mastino and Ruggeri (1995). – M. Ulpius Callistus (A.180) a freedman of Hadrian.

CHAPTER 4

The Profiteer

A scribe at whatever post in town,
He will not suffer in it;
As he fills another's need,
He will not lack rewards.

Ancient Egyptian saying,
'The Satire of the Trades'

Thieves and Opportunities

One of the many merits accredited to the Romans by Polybius, the second-century BC Greek historiographer and admirer of the Roman *res publica*, was that their system was virtually free of political corruption.[1] While the Greeks, in comparison, would to go to great lengths to make sure that officials handling public money were monitored and controlled at every step, only to betray the community's trust at the first possible opportunity, the Romans could be trusted with public money without detailed precautionary measures. What kept Romans honest was, according to Polybius, their faithfulness to the oath they had sworn.[2] More than a century later, another attentive political observer drew a fundamentally different picture of the Roman polity. C. Sallustius Crispus, much influenced by the unfulfilled hopes he had invested in Caesar and the ensuing atrocities committed by the triumvirs, depicted an antithesis to Polybius' favourable characterisation.[3] In his eyes, the Romans had forsaken their faithfulness

---

[1] I have adopted the categories of corruption established by Rosillo-López (2010a). 'Political corruption', which is distinguished from 'electoral' and 'judicial corruption', includes accusations *de peculatu* and *de repetundis*, i.e. embezzlement of public money and extortion of provinces and provincials. Both cases eventually affected *scribae*.
[2] Plb. 6. 56. 13–15.
[3] On the impact of contemporary events on Sallust's narrative of decline and decadence Perl (1969) 201.

shortly after the Third Punic War and the final destruction of Carthage in 146 BC, an event Polybius had himself witnessed and in fact ended his histories with. After the loss of any external enemy, the Romans quickly became corrupt and, in the words of Sallust, 'every man took, pillaged, and plundered for himself'.[4]

It is obvious that both accounts are oversimplifying historical reality in favour of their own narrative. Yet, evidence suggests that political corruption had indeed become an escalating problem during the late Republic. At least it was perceived as such, judging by the legislation passed in relation to the two *crimina de peculatu* and *de repetundis*. Both the accusation of embezzlement of public money and of abuse and extortion of provincials and their belongings were certainly far from unknown before the late Republic, both being publicly prosecuted by the *comitia* in a *iudicium populi*.[5] It is only in the late Republican period, however, that these two legal subject areas became intensely regulated and institutionalised in permanent tribunals, so-called *quaestiones perpetuae*. While the embezzlement of public money was already a punishable crime by the time of the Law of the Twelve Tables, its punishment was eventually institutionalised by a new *lex* in the last century BC, probably before Sulla. It was renewed by a *lex Iulia peculatus* under Caesar or Augustus.[6] The *crimen de repetundis* was subject to even more legislatorial fervour. A *lex Calpurnia* of 149 BC for the first time established permanent tribunals, to which wronged provincials could appeal, making it easier to initiate a process against a Roman magistrate, which had been a thorny endeavour in the decades before.[7] It was followed by a series of *leges de repetundis*, which culminated in Caesar's *lex Iulia* of 59 BC.[8] Among other precautionary measures, this reinstated and reinforced the long-standing regulation that senators were barred from engaging in large-scale commerce, an obvious source of magisterial conflicts of interest.[9] Regulating and controlling the behaviour of magistrates had become an

---

[4] SALL. *Iug.* 41. 1–5: *sibi quisque ducere, trahere, rapere*, transl. J. C. Rolfe.

[5] Rosillo-López (2010a) 90–4, 98–105, on the *iudicium populi* 115; on the *crimen de repetundis* in particular Lintott (1981) 165f. w. app.

[6] See in general Gnoli (1979); on the dating of the first *quaestio perpetua* before Sullan times Gnoli (1975); the *lex Iulia peculatus* in DIG. 48. 13. 1.

[7] See the practice of *recuperatores* used before in Lintott (1981) 169–71; Richardson (1987) has argued that the *lex Calpurnia* of 149 BC was designed to protect the economic interests of Roman citizens in the provinces against the abuse of Roman office holders rather than to constitute an instrument for provincials against Roman magistrates. Only the later Gracchan legislation created adequate resources for provincials.

[8] The evolution of the legislation in Rosillo-López (2010a) 119–23; Lintott (1981) 172–207; cf. DIG. 48. 11. 6. 2; 48. 11. 27. pr.

[9] DIG. 50. 5. 3 (Scaevola), making reference to the so-called *plebiscitum Claudianum* of 218 BC; LIV. 21. 63. 3.

apparent need of late Republican politics – not only for the gain of the *res publica* but also for partisan, political reasons.[10]

Closely related to political corruption was the falsification and forgery of public documents. In an age when written documentation had gained an important position in how the Republican state functioned, covering up one's criminal energy involved covering one's written tracks. If we are to believe Cicero, Verres had carried out his deceptions by tampering with documents.

> Hoc modo iste [scil. Verres] sibi et saluti suae prospicere didicit referendo in tabulas et privatas et publicas quod gestum non esset, tollendo quod esset, et semper aliquid demendo, mutando, interpolando.[11]

Verres obviously did not flinch from retroactively altering in his favour documents that were part of the *tabulae publicae*.

Verres, like anyone who dared to tamper with the public repository, walked a fine line. The nature and materiality of the documentation was double-edged. The wooden tablets that were used to accommodate the public documentation – large wooden sheets hollowed out and filled with wax to produce a writing surface – were a variety of the common *tabula cerata* (see Chapter 2). It is true that, thanks to their wax surface, their main convenience was, once inscribed, ease of modification and even complete reusability.[12] Yet, at the same time, emendations (*liturae*) of a text left conspicuous marks in the wax writing surface. This is how Cicero convicted Verres: he followed his traces, which he had 'left clear and fresh in the official documents'.[13] A perfect and inconspicuous forgery of a wax tablet must have demanded the utmost effort. The tell-tale nature of a pristine wax surface, disturbed only by the minute and precise carvings of the letters, was regarded as a feature of these documents.[14]

---

[10] Cf. Lintott (1981) 207.
[11] Cic. *Verr.* 2.1.158: 'This is the kind of precaution that Verres has learnt to take for himself and his own safety: he takes records, private and official, inserts what never happened and erases what did, and is always scratching out or altering or interpolating something', transl. L. H. G. Greenwood.
[12] See e.g. Quint. *inst.* 10.3.31: *scribi optime ceris, in quibus facillima est ratio delendi.*
[13] Cic. *Verr.* 2.2.105: *tuis vestigiis persequamur, quae tu in tabulis publicis expressa ac recentia reliquisti*, transl. C. D. Yonge (adapted). Cic. *Verr.* 2.1.92 on the case of Malleolus; Cic. *Verr.* 2.2.101; 2,2,104; 2,3,41 on the case of Sthenius; Cic. *Verr.* 2.2.187; 2,2,189; 2,2,191 on the case of Carpinatius / C. Verrucius.
[14] Cf. Suet. *Claud.* 16.1, when Claudius assumed the censorship and removed a *nota censoria* from the record of a knight he remarked that the *litura* would nevertheless stand out. On the falsification of documents in general Erman (1905), for the particularities of *tabulae ceratae* 122–4; cf. E. A. Meyer (2004) 34; for the different kinds of forgeries cf. Andreau (2007) 89.

As an additional layer of security, documents could be sealed in order to prevent their content being accessible in the first place. As a matter of fact, this was almost exclusively the case only with documents that travelled.[15] Documents that stayed within the administration remained unsealed and were at best subscribed by the office holder in charge or his delegates. We have already seen that entry into the *tabulae publicae* meant that the text was copied into the tablets and verified.[16] It was usually the supervisor of the archive who controlled the authenticity of these documents. Cato the Younger, portrayed by Plutarch as the responsible and diligent head of the *aerarium*, is known to have refrained from entering *senatus consulta* into the *tabulae publicae* without further confirmation of their validity by the *consules*.[17] The *scribae*, or more precisely the heads of the decurial *scribae*, the *sex primi*, in one way or another were likewise authorised to authenticate official documents.[18] These measures of precautions were deemed sufficient.

This notion that the public archival of a document in general meant that it was safe from negative influence was characteristic of Roman documentary practice.[19] This does not mean that the Romans were not sensitive to the possibility of falsification and forgery – far from it. But I would argue that they did not seek a remedy for this problem in the documents and the writing material itself, i.e. in advancing sealing techniques and other characteristics immanent in the materiality of the documents.[20] Rather they sought to control and regulate the individuals who handled the documents.[21] In this respect, Polybius had been right: what decided between the performance of one's duty and corruption was the individual's trustworthiness, his *fides*. As Polybius had observed correctly, officials entrusted with public documents swore an oath (*ius iurandum*) to refrain from tampering with documents consigned to their care; their personal integrity guaranteed the integrity of the *tabulae publicae* (see below). It was, in a way, an internalisation of the materiality of

---

[15] In general Haensch (1996) 449–62, 474.
[16] Cf. Chapter 2.
[17] PLUT. *Cat. Mi.* 17. 3–4.
[18] CIC. *nat. deor.* 3. 74 mentions the '*chirographum sex primorum*'; cf. Chapter 3.
[19] CIC. *Flacc.* 21, in characterising the standard procedure for the safe transfer of a document, emphasises its public custody as a safeguard against forgery.
[20] The only known measure taken to enhance the security of sealed deeds was a piece of legislature initiated by Nero, the so-called *senatus consultum Neronianum* of AD 61, which commanded that the seal cord should be fixed through a newly required perforation in the tablets rather than the groove at the border of the tablets, as had been common practice before. SUET. *Nero* 17. 1 qualifies the measure with the words '*tunc primum repertum*'; cf. PAUL. *sent.* 5. 25. 6; for the date Camodeca (1993). Similar measures concerning publicly archived documents are not known.
[21] Cf. Scheid (2016) 90.

the *tabulae publicae*. It is thus not surprising that accusations of forgery were often used to taint an opponent's character, regardless of the factual evidence. This should, however, not take away from Cicero's observation that forgery of public documents had become widespread in his lifetime.[22] If Roman legislation may once again be an indicator, Cicero's sentiments were shared by his peers in the senate. The falsification of documents in general and *tabulae publicae* in particular had already been regulated extensively by Sulla. It was punishable by confiscation of one's property and deportation.[23] What we find with Cicero is the connection between the wilful modification of public documents and the *crimen de peculatu*. Cicero makes this link explicitly in his indictment of Verres.[24] With the *lex Iulia peculatus* at the latest, the *crimen falsi* finally became part of the legislation concerning embezzlement.[25] A later senatorial decree eventually regulated access to the *tabulae publicae*, in that nobody was allowed to either inspect or transcribe *tabulae publicae* without the consent of the magistrate in charge.[26] Tampering with the public repository carried a heavy penalty. Since the last decades of the first century BC at the latest it could even fall into the category of high treason – harsh measures to protect the 'authoritative finality' of the *tabulae publicae*.[27]

A Matter of Trust

In any given polity, political corruption is minimised by holding officials both accountable and responsible for their actions. Ideally, legal control of an office holder is met with an equal portion of identification with and responsibility for the health of the state by the magistrate himself.[28] It was the loss of this personal responsibility that Sallust lamented. The oath, a solemn pledge to the gods, had become simple lip-service. The quasi-utopic order praised by Polybius, free of the need for control and

---

[22] Culham (1996) 181f.; cf. for example CIC. *leg. agr.* 2.37; CIC. *Phil.* 5.4; CIC. *nat. deor.* 3.74.
[23] The *lex Cornelia de falsis* in DIG. 48.10; on the falsification of *tabulae publicae* DIG. 48.10.16.2 (Paulus): *Sed et ceteros, qui in rationibus tabulis litteris publicis aliaue qua re sine consignatione falsum fecerunt uel, ut uerum non appareat, quid celauerunt subripuerunt deleuerunt subiecerunt resignauerunt, eadem poena adfici solere dubium non esse*; cf. DIG. 48.10.1.4. The penalties in DIG. 48.10.1.13.
[24] CIC. *Verr.* 2.3.83.
[25] DIG. 48.13.12. pr. (Marcianus); DIG. 48.13.10.1 (Venuleius Saturninus); cf. Gnoli (1979) 150f.
[26] DIG. 48.13.11.5 (Paulus): *Senatus iussit lege peculatus teneri eos, qui iniussu eius, qui ei rei praeerit, tabularum publicarum inspiciendarum describendarumque potestatem fecerint*.
[27] On the *lex Iulia maiestatis* DIG. 48.4.2.1 (Ulpianus); cf. Williamson (2016) 339f. On the perception of *tabulae publicae* E. A. Meyer (2004) 33.
[28] Seibel (2016) 78f.

coercion, had necessarily made way for the imposition of accountability. It is a characteristic of the late Republic that the solemn oath of office was joined by extended 'profane' measures of control. I have outlined these legal sanctions above. Magistrates were eventually forced to document their actions in written form (see Chapter 2) as well as to provide financial security in case they happened to take their oath lightly and embezzle public money and extort provincials.[29]

In this framework of accountability, the *scribae* constituted an essential piece. Crucial to the late Republican concept of accountability was written proof, public documentation. Consequently, the *scribae*, in their role as experts in documentary practice and guardians of the *tabulae publicae*, were bound to become the linchpin in this framework. Cato the Younger's clash with the *scribae* of the *aerarium* during his quaestorship is, again, our most vivid example. It exemplifies the discrepancy between idealised standards and the sobering reality of the workings of the *scriba*-ship in the last phase of the Republic. In Plutarch's rendering, Cato left the *aerarium* 'inaccessible to public informers and free from their taint, but full of money'.[30] This description corresponds with the ideal conception of Roman *scriba*-ship. The *scribae* were intended to be non-partisan and independent, concerned solely with the trustworthy management of the public documentation, upholding the sanctity of the *tabulae publicae* and their content. In this sense it is both logical and ironic that Cato, in order to achieve this pristine state of the *aerarium*, had to take action against the *scribae*, of all people. As his prosecution of individual *scribae* shows, they had been dedicated to upholding neither the impeccability of the *tabulae* nor their impartiality and non-partisanship. Rather, they chose to take advantage of their monopoly for the benefit of themselves and their senatorial patrons. Cato managed to expel one individual for forgery and tried another one for embezzlement. Nevertheless, the latter was eventually acquitted thanks to the active support of his powerful patron, the *censor* Q. Lutatius Catulus – ironically enough the holder of the office that was charged with the oversight of the *scribae* and the *tabulae publicae*.[31] The increased importance of written documentation must inevitably have empowered those closest to the matter. Powerful protectors further enabled the shameless abuse of this scribal monopoly for their own ends.

---

[29] Rosillo-López (2010a) 107–14.
[30] Plut. *Cat. Mi.* 18. 2: ἐπιδεικνύμενος δὲ τὸ ταμιεῖον ἄβατόν τε καὶ καθαρὸν συκοφαντῶν, πλῆρες δὲ χρημάτων, transl. B. Perrin.
[31] Plut. *Cat. Mi.* 16. 4–10; cf. Chapter 3. On the censorial oversight Liv. 4. 8. 4.

What was expected to keep the *scribae* on the right track was their sworn responsibility towards the Roman republican state. In analogy to their magisterial superiors, *scribae* were obliged to take an oath of due diligence prior to assuming office. This *ius iurandum* had been a long-standing tradition during the Republic as a part of the *mos maiorum*, the traditional mores.[32] And even when legislative measures were tightened in the last phase of the Roman Republic, as I have outlined above, the oath was retained. We might even argue that its symbolic value was all the more important in times when traditions were challenged. Judging by our sources, the solemn *ius iurandum* was a pivotal part of the conception of the *scriba*-ship. We find it featured prominently in the extant city laws. The Caesarian colonial and the Flavian municipal laws stipulate a solemn oath to Iupiter and the Penates (the latter naturally includes the deified emperors as well as the *numen* of the current ruler).[33] It is the same oath the magistrates swore upon taking office.[34] In this regard, the *scribae* occupied a truly extraordinary position in the Roman polity. They were not elected magistrates and were not regarded as having any governmental authority, but rather were paid subaltern personnel. Yet, their position at the heart of Roman financial and legal documentation warranted their solemn assurance to refrain from abusing the trust they had been bestowed with. The *scribae*, as the *lex Ursonensis* states, were to take

> in contione palam luci nundinis in forum ius iurandum ... per Iovem deosque Penates sese pecuniam publicam eius colon(iae) concustoditurum rationesque veras habiturum esse u(ti) q(uod) r(ecte) f(actum) e(sse) v(olet) s(ine) d(olo) m(alo) neque se fraudem per litteras facturum esse sc(ientem) d(olo) m(alo).[35]

What the *scribae* were required to vow they would not do was what we eventually find penalised by the *lex de falsis* and, consequently, by the legislation against embezzlement. Malignantly tampering with the *tabulae publicae* naturally amounted to forgery and peculation.

These strict legal regulations were a surprisingly late development, however. What had made only slow headway with regard to regular magistrates took even longer to be applied to the *scribae*. For much of the Roman

---

[32] Freyburger (1986) 206–12.
[33] *lex Urson.* 81; *lex Irn.* 73.
[34] See e.g. in the late second century BC *lex latina tabulae Bantinae*, Roman Statutes no. 7 ll. 14–22.
[35] *lex Urson.* 81.17–23: 'an oath, ... in a *contio*, openly, before the light of day, on a market day, (facing) the forum, by Jupiter and the ancestral gods, that they will guard the public money of that colony and keep true accounts, as they shall deem it proper, without wrongful deceit, and that they will not falsify records knowingly with wrongful deceit', transl. M. H. Crawford; cf. the very similar wording in *lex Irn.* 73. 39–42.

Republic, the *scribae*, in their function as *apparitores*, had been primarily accountable to their direct superiors. They must have been treated similarly to the *comites*, the magistrate's entourage of friends, who were generally exempt from criminal prosecution.[36] Although we find *scribae* implicated in corruption trials of their superiors as early as 187 BC,[37] it is doubtful whether they had initially been included in the tightened legislation of the first decades of the first century BC regarding the *crimen de peculatu*. Our earliest reliable source is Cicero, who reports that *scribae* were tried *de peculatu* in the late 60s.[38] This is the time when Cato the Younger prosecuted one of the blameable *scribae* of the treasury, likely under this same legal proposition.[39] In 55 BC, the consuls Cn. Pompeius Magnus and M. Licinius Crassus tried without success to broaden the legislation *de repetundis* to cover the *comites* of the magistrates, which would have included the *scribae*. Although, according to Cicero, the measure would have been much needed after an escalation of such delicts, Pompey's and Crassus' plan was not implemented until the *lex Iulia peculatus*. It is telling that the proposed measures were opposed by the senators themselves.[40] Being able to do business by proxy was too lucrative an opportunity to give up lightly; members of the *ordo senatorius* had been forbidden to engage in large-scale commerce since the *plebiscitum Claudianum* of 218 BC, after all.[41] Consequently, a Clodian law – likely by the infamous P. Clodius Pulcher, tribune of the plebs in 58 BC[42] – extended this ban to the *scribae quaestorii*. Its implementation does not seem to have come to fruition, however. It was common for *scribae* who were dispatched to the provinces to make a profit, so much so that Domitian felt compelled to pardon some *scribae quaestorii* for past offences.[43]

Consequently, for most of the period of the Republic, the parameters of the discharge of the office of the *scribae* were determined mainly by the solemn *ius iurandum*. The *scribae* were expected to act out of personal responsibility towards the *res publica*. From a modern perspective and in

---

[36] Rosillo-López (2010a) 131. Cf. Cicero's characterisation of Verres' delinquent *cohors*, which included the *scribae*; CIC. *Verr.* 2. 2. 27.
[37] LIV. 38. 55. 4–5, the famous case against L. Cornelius Scipio Asiagenes, who had allegedly been bribed by the Seleucid king Antiochos the Great.
[38] CIC. *Mur.* 42.
[39] PLUT. *Cat. Mi.* 16. 3; the term used by Plutarch is ῥᾳδιουργία, fraud. Cf. Rosillo-López (2010a) 128f.
[40] CIC. *Rab. Post.* 13.
[41] LIV. 21. 63. 3.
[42] Thommen (1989) 89f.
[43] SUET. *Dom.* 9. 3. Similar regulations existed in Roman municipalities. Neither magistrates nor their *scribae* were allowed to take part in the purchase or rent of public property; *lex Irn.* 48.

hindsight given what we know about the developments in the late Republic, we might deem the trust the Romans put in their office holders naive or even careless. Yet, subjecting their magistrates to an oath of due diligence seems to have worked well enough. We may not expect it to have been foolproof in preventing abuse of office and corruption altogether; we know from late Republican times that it was not. But it seems to have worked acceptably well.[44] It certainly left a lasting impression on Polybius. After all, the oath of office was not without consequences. What the *ius iurandum* premised was the fidelity – *fides* – of the oath taker. It was a quality originally rooted in religious practice ('true faith'), which came to characterise an individual's social credit.[45] A person with his *fides* intact and protected by the gods was considered to be righteous and honourable. A breach of this *fides* meant the loss of honour and standing.[46]

Cicero's emphatic characterisation of the *ordo scribarum* and its members in his denunciation of Verres is based on this concept and shows that, at least in public perception, the *scribae* were closely linked to the idea of *fides*. It was to their *fides* that the *tabulae publicae* were entrusted; and it was the observance of this fidelity that distinguished the *scribae*:

> 'Ordo [scil. scribarum] est honestus.' Quis negat, aut quid ea res ad hanc rem pertinet? Est vero honestus, quod eorum hominum fidei tabulae publicae periculaque magistratuum committuntur.[47]

Cicero provides an idealised picture of the prototypical, honourable Roman *scriba* as an antithesis to the *scriba* of Verres, Maevius (A.109), who had wilfully broken his pledge of *fides*. The revered *scribae* of olden times were '*sanctissimi homines atque innocentissimi*',[48] those still worthy of the *ordo* in Cicero's day '*patres familias, viri boni atque honesti*',[49] who themselves strongly disapproved of Maevius' conduct. In Cicero's eyes, the latter belonged to a group of *scribae* by name only, who did not possess the characteristics sanctioned by sworn fidelity but rather had gained the position

---

[44] Cf. Freyburger (1986) 212.
[45] See Cicero's definition in Cic. *off.* 3.104: *Est enim ius iurandum affirmatio religiosa; quod autem affirmate quasi deo teste promiseris, id tenendum est. Iam enim non ad iram deorum, quae nulla est, sed ad iustitiam et ad fidem pertinet*. Cf. in general Morgan (2015), who argues that *fides* was 'everywhere understood as a basic buliding block of societies, emerging from the need of individual and groups to make and maintain relationships', 75.
[46] Freyburger (1986) 206–8.
[47] Cic. *Verr.* 2.3.183: '"The clerk's profession" you tell us "has a high standing." Who denies that? And what has it to do with the matter in hand? It has, in fact, a high standing because its members are entrusted with the public accounts and the records of our magistrates.' Transl. L. H. G. Greenwood (adapted).
[48] Cic. *Verr.* 2.3.182.
[49] Cic. *Verr.* 2.3.183. Cicero's own two *scribae* are characterised as *frugalissimi*, Cic. *Verr.* 2.3.182.

by corrupt practices.⁵⁰ Cicero's characterisation is necessarily hyperbolical, his words carefully chosen so as not to alienate the *ordo* by bringing charges against some of its members.⁵¹ Yet, as it catered to a realistic ideal, Cicero's characterisation of the diligence and integrity of the *scribae* must have hit home, not only with the *scribae* themselves but also with the broader (reading) audience of the oration. Cicero puts forward a positive narrative of Roman *scriba*-ship based on the *fides* sworn to the state and its citizens. It may ultimately have been grounded in Cicero's own conviction that a functioning *res publica* was an undertaking of honourable and responsible citizens. It was a view in line with the *mos maiorum* and as such likely carried considerable weight. It was what contributed to the generally high esteem in which the *scribae* were held. It was part of what made the Roman *scriba*.

At the same time, Cicero's characterisation shows another side of *scriba*-ship. Only thinly veiled, Cicero's words expose the susceptibility of the *scribae* to corruption and mismanagement. It is another, less favourable narrative: one of abuse of trust and power for personal gain. This narrative, too, was part of what made the Roman *scriba*.

Under Suspicion

Nicholas Purcell has aptly characterised the *scribae* depicted by Middle and Late Republican historiography as 'paragons of the problematic'.⁵² Indeed, the cultural and social capital of the *scribae*, i.e. their professional expertise, their position of trust and their social and political affiliations, made for potentially conflict-laden constellations. We find the most conspicuous example of this phenomenon in the narrative tradition of the life and deeds of our scribal hero Cn. Flavius (A.109; see Chapter 1). While the historical nucleus of Flavius' biography is hard to come by, later actualisations of his life in late Republican literature have been prolific.⁵³ According to the annalistic tradition in the wake of L. Calpurnius Piso, Flavius' skills and position as *scriba* as well as his patronage by the popular champion App. Claudius Caecus, which led to the infamous publication of the *fasti* and

---

⁵⁰ Maevius belonged to the ones *qui nummulis corrogatis de nepotum donis ac de scaenicorum corollaris, cum decuriam emerunt, ex primo ordine explosorum in secundum ordinem civitatis se venisse dicunt*, Cɪᴄ. *Verr.* 2.3.184.
⁵¹ Cicero later remarks that the prosecution of a *scriba* would alienate the whole *ordo*, Cɪᴄ. *Mur.* 42: *scriba damnatus, ordo totus alienus*.
⁵² Purcell (2001) 638.
⁵³ The genesis of the tradition on Cn. Flavius in Wolf (1980).

the *legis actiones*, were crucial features of the stereotypical Roman *scriba*.[54] Obviously, the intricate social and institutional relations of power and their potentially problematic implications surrounding the *scribae* of his time could not possibly have escaped a figure like Piso, the ideological father of the *lex Calpurnia de repetundis* of 149 BC. And even historiographers across the political divide identified Flavius' professional skills, the opportunities afforded by his subsequent apparitorial position and his association with a mighty patron as the crucial and powerful elements of *scriba*-ship.[55] It is doubtful whether these characterisations did justice to the historical Flavius. What they represented without any doubt was a mirror image of the current perception of *scribae*.

In his indictment of Verres' *scriba* Maevius (A.109), Cicero made every effort to stick to a positive narrative of *scriba*-ship and to stress that Verres' malevolent consorts had been an exception to the righteous norm. As far as we know, Cicero's careful approach was based on personal interest, as he seems to have cultivated contact with members of the *ordo scribarum*.[56] Nevertheless, even Cicero presents Maevius' abuse of his position of trust as Verres' bookkeeper as a highly realistic scenario. He has no difficulty whatsoever in making the constellations and mechanics involved believable – as deplorable as they were, they were plausible. Cicero himself at this point seems to have drawn on an existing, negative narrative of *scriba*-ship for his own argument. Using the example of Verres, he himself highlights that the easiest access to a magistrate was through his *apparitores* in general and his *scribae* in particular. They were the ones to bribe and intimidate.[57] It is for a reason that Cicero stresses the trustworthiness and fidelity of the *scribae* he himself had been provided with for his quaestorian post in Sicily in 75 BC. L. Mamilius (A.110) and L. Sergius (A.160) are '*frugalissimi*', allegedly complete strangers to corruption and peculation.[58]

The notion of scribal complicity in dubious dealings involving the written documentation of the Roman magistrates was neither a novelty of Cicero's times nor was it to vanish into thin air in the following years. Already in 202 BC, *scribae* of the *aediles curules* had been found guilty of abusing their position and embezzling money from the *aerarium* together

---

[54] Wolf (1980) 25f.
[55] Wolf (1980) 26.
[56] Cicero successfully defended a *scriba aedilicius*, D. Matrinius (A.115), only two years later, in 68 BC; CIC. *Cluent.* 126. In 63 BC he eventually alluded to the difficulties in walking this fine line between different interests; CIC. *Mur.* 42.
[57] CIC. *Verr.* 2.3.155–157.
[58] CIC. *Verr.* 2.3.182.

with the *viatores*.⁵⁹ In 187 BC, when L. Cornelius Scipio Asiagenes was accused of having accepted a bribe by the Seleucid king Antiochos the Great and of having embezzled money due to the public treasury, his *quaestor* and the *scribae quaestorii* were implicated as well. Even though they were eventually acquitted, the nature of their posts suggested that they likely were complicit.⁶⁰ Some three hundred years later, the scribal staff of a magistrate was still thought to be the leverage point for corruption and the forgery of public documents.⁶¹ What distinguished the late Republican period from earlier and later times was the fact that the grey area of what was accepted magisterial behaviour had been substantially extended. The goalposts of politics were moved – a development the extensive legislation against corruption, not only political but also electoral and judicial, could barely keep track of.⁶² The *scribae*, through their professional expertise, their institutional position and their social relations, found themselves in the midst of it. As accomplices of powerful patrons, as I have outlined above (Chapter 3), they often ceased to be the non-partisan, selfless civil servants of Cicero's ideal conception. In the late Republic, the *scribae* had come under general suspicion of malpractice and corruption. Negligent and corrupt *scribae* in the *aerarium* supplied an ideal backdrop for Plutarch's rendering of Cato the Younger, a model of Republican rectitude.⁶³ And Cicero saw no problem in characterising the *scribae librarii* as manipulative and corrupt when he complained about their firm grip on public documentation and the lack of independent guardianship of Roman law.⁶⁴ Such portrayals are a far cry from his praise of scribal fidelity. They were no mere narrative, however. As far as we can discern, the new bad repute was likely justified. Maevius was not the only *scriba* gone astray. Cicero gives us further cases of corrupt *scribae* for the late 70s and 60s. A certain Cornificius (A.56) had been an accomplice of Verres' alleged embezzlement during his urban praetorship in 74 BC.⁶⁵ D. Matrinius (A.115) had been defended by Cicero himself.⁶⁶ And at least one more case *de peculatu* was brought against another *scriba* in the late 60s.⁶⁷ It is possible that Cicero's reference is to the

---

⁵⁹ Liv. 30. 39. 7.
⁶⁰ Liv. 38. 55. 4–5.
⁶¹ Plin. *ep.* 6. 22. 4. Cf. a funerary inscription from *Hierapolis* in Phrygia from the second century AD, which references the *scriba quaestorius* as the main contact in provincial financial matters; Guizzi, De Martino, and Ritti, 2012, no. 14 (*AE* 2013, 1557).
⁶² Rosillo-López (2010a).
⁶³ Plut. *Cat. Mi.* 16–18.
⁶⁴ Cic. *leg.* 3. 46.
⁶⁵ Cic. *Verr.* 2. 1. 150.
⁶⁶ Cic. *Cluent.* 126.
⁶⁷ Cic. *Mur.* 42.

prosecution initiated by Cato the Younger in these years.[68] It was only a few years after these incidents that Pompey and Crassus saw the need to try and extend the criminal prosecution *de repetundis* to the *scribae* of magistrates.[69]

Making a Living

The post of *scriba* gave good returns – even for those refraining from corrupt practices. As a rule, apparitorial posts were salaried. And we might expect that the payment of an adequate salary was seen as one possible way of keeping *scribae* from exploiting their position and laying hands on the treasury. Cicero insinuates as much in his denunciation of Verres' *scriba* Maevius (A.109): he who was paid a '*merces tanta*' for his duties had the audacity to illegally mend his allegedly 'small wage'![70] To what exact figure the salary of a *scriba* of the state amounted, we unfortunately do not know. The only concrete listing of apparitorial pay survives in the town charter of the Caesarian colony of Urso. The *lex coloniae Genetivae* provides us with a pay scale of their *apparitores* (see Table 3.1). The *scribae* are the high flyers by a big margin, nearly doubling the earnings of the post directly below theirs, with what is supposed to be an annual salary of 1,200 sesterces.[71] Interestingly enough, in absolute numbers, this figure only amounted to what an ordinary workman would have earned at that time.[72] Leonard Curchin has thus advanced the possibility that these municipal posts were not exercised full time but rather on demand.[73] In this way, a place in a municipal *decuria* would have constituted a stable additional income to an individual's regular living. This might very well have been true for the lower grades of the *apparitores*, such as flautists and the like, whose services were needed on very specific occasions only. Local *scribae* were in all likelihood kept busy during the tenure of the magistrates they were assigned to, however. The mismatch of Cicero's assessment with the data from Urso should not trouble us. After all, our evidence shows a big discrepancy in the lucrativeness of these different scribal posts. The post of a city *scriba* might have assured a comfortable livelihood. Yet, there is

---

[68] Brennan (2000) 806 n. 304.
[69] Cic. *Rab. Post.* 13.
[70] Cic. *Verr.* 2. 3. 182–183. Cicero's labelling of the *scriba*'s wage as '*parva merces*' must be read as ironic exaggeration in his rhetoric questioning concerning Maevius' demand for money.
[71] *lex Urson.* 62.
[72] Curchin (1986) 185; cf. Speidel (1992) 88, who shows that a legionary foot soldier would have earned three-quarters of the annual salary of a *scriba* in Urso.
[73] Curchin (1986) 185.

no evidence that individuals with careers as local *scribae* were in one way or another able to amass riches. Access to the city council of the local *decuriones* seems to have been the highest possible advancement and only for a few individuals at that.⁷⁴ In contrast, the *scriba*-ship on the state level was truly lucrative. Not for nothing was the purchase of a position in a scribal *decuria* considered to be profitable.⁷⁵ Even though we do not know the exact sums paid for a vicariate, the initial investment must have paid off many times over. The Augustan poet Horace (A.88) is said to have made his way back to a livelihood worthy of a Roman knight by buying a post as *scriba quaestorius*.⁷⁶ Although he considered it a tedious business that kept him from writing, he eventually put 'virtue after money'.⁷⁷

Formal membership in a scribal *decuria* alone might already have yielded a sizeable profit. It was money earned effortlessly when some of these posts had eventually become sinecures (see Chapter 3). Yet, it was the actual exercise of the office which entailed the full benefits of the position.⁷⁸ In dealing with the important political figures and their documentary needs, the *scriba* attained what Ivan di Stefano Manzella has labelled 'collateral power'.⁷⁹ As I have laid out above, 'virtue was not the hallmark of Roman administration in the provinces',⁸⁰ neither in Republican times nor during the Empire.⁸¹ This is not to say that all Roman magistrates were cut from the same cloth as the C. Verres of Cicero's portrayal.⁸² But it is well established that magistrates in general streamlined their provincial tenure for maximum financial gain, most of it within the grey area of legality, exploiting the authority invested in them by the state. Administering a province was considered to be a lucrative endeavour.⁸³ In this, *scribae* not uncommonly became close confidants of their superiors. Shady business involving public funds necessarily required the connivance of the bookkeeper.⁸⁴ In addition we know that, despite the fact that it had been outlawed since the middle

---

74 Only four of the known municipal *scribae* were also *decuriones*, A.232, A.243, A.262, A.300; two were honoured with the *ornamenta decurionalia*, A.237, A.267. Cf. Chapter 3.
75 Cf. the usual practice of buying into a governmental position in the Later Roman Empire (the so-called *suffragium*), Palme (1999) 113.
76 SUET. *vita Hor.* 24; cf. Armstrong (2010) 18.
77 HOR. *sat.* 2. 6 on the inconvenient duties of the city; HOR. *epist.* 1. 1. 54: '*virtus post nummos*', on the social importance of money.
78 Cf. Purcell (1983) 130.
79 Stefano Manzella (2000).
80 Tan (2017) 89.
81 Cf. MacMullen (1988) 135.
82 On Cicero's narrative of illegality Steel (2007).
83 In general Tan (2017) ch. 3; cf. Rosillo-López (2010b).
84 See e.g. Maevius' (A.262) role in Verres' transactions regarding interest on public money, CIC. *Verr.* 2. 3. 168–169; and the purchase of public corn, CIC. *Verr.* 2. 3. 171–176; cf. the role of Cicero's *scriba* M. Tullius (A.178) during his governorship in Cilicia, Chapter 2.

of the first century BC, the *scribae quaestorii* sent to the provinces had continued to engage in trade endeavours that benefited them heavily. The emperor Domitian's blanket pardon of '*scribae quaestorii negotiantes*' was an acknowledgement of common, yet illegal practice.[85] Trade was only one side of the coin, however.

The case of Verres' *scriba* Maevius (A.109) illustrates that there was money to earn with the peculiarities of a *scriba*'s core business. What Cicero took exception to with regard to Maevius' discharge of office was the so-called '*cerarium*'. Maevius allegedly used to syphon off public money as a fee for his services – the very services he was salaried to provide by the state in the first place. He was mainly involved in the purchase of grain from local farmers. Thereby, he used to reduce the money due to them by deducting his 'wax tax', which amounted to two-fiftieths of any transaction value.[86] Needless to say, as a result, Maevius' apparitorial work in the province made him filthy rich. His Sicilian *cerarium* was worth 1.3 million sesterces, more than three times the amount the census required from a Roman knight.[87] Cicero makes the case that such fees were as illegal as they were unprecedented. In his eyes, they were a sign of a corrupt regime, perfectly fitting Verres' governorship.[88] Yet, Maevius' deductions seem to have been the norm rather than the exception. They seem to have been common enough to find their way into Verres' official *rationes*. Without doubt, Cicero's imagery of a Republican administration devoid of corruption and bribery was a rhetorical recourse to an ideal world, which existed only in the abstract notion of the *mos maiorum*. Bribes and fees are a symptom of any administrative body that lacks effective oversight. In this way, the Republican *scribae* were the precursors of the *officiales* of the Later Roman Empire, the larger part of whose income was based on additional fees, the *sportulae*.[89] Fees for services rendered – corrupt practices, in Cicero's rhetoric – had thus likely been a source of income even for those 'most frugal' *scribae* who happened to serve under Cicero's own authority.[90] In fact, two *scribae* whom Cicero praises as '*primi homines atque honestissimi*', C. Antistius (A.17) and P. Servilius (A.162), were also *magistri* of a Sicilian publican society (*societas publicanorum*), which farmed public taxes in the provinces and which, allegedly, had been robbed by deductions made by

---

[85] SUET. *Dom.* 9.3.
[86] CIC. *Verr.* 2.3.181: *Scribae nomine de tota pecunia binae quinauaegesimae detrahebantur*.
[87] CIC. *Verr.* 2.3.184.
[88] CIC. *Verr.* 2.3.182–184.
[89] Palme (1999) 113; cf. COD. *Theod.* 8.9.1, the AD 335 renewal of privileges granted to the *scribae librarii* to act in civil cases and issue *libelli*, which involved money.
[90] CIC. *Verr.* 2.3.182.

Maevius. Ironically enough, Cicero failed to see any conflict of interest in the highly problematic double engagement of the two *scribae* as long as it suited his argument against Verres.[91] We may assume that the position of the *scribae* facilitated profiteering – even more so when they were otherwise involved in the state's financial activities in the provinces.

Maevius' profitable time as *scriba quaestorius* in Sicily not only allowed him to amass a fortune, but, as a direct result, also to climb socially. Maevius now easily reached the census of 400,000 sesterces required to advance to the order of the *equites*. Consequently, he was gifted the *anulus aureus*, the golden ring of the knights, by Verres at the conclusion of his tenure.[92] It comes as no surprise that Cicero objected to this ennoblement of a *scriba* he had on another occasion characterised as belonging to a group of contemptible upstarts, lowly individuals who had bought into a *decuria* with money obtained by disreputable means; absurd caricatures of those dignified *scribae* worthy of the *ordo*. As much as Cicero despised such individuals, even he could not deny that entry into the *ordo scribarum* brought them close to the '*secundus ordo civitatis*', the *ordo equester* – if not ideally then certainly financially.[93] This is not to say that membership of the *ordo scribarum* automatically meant becoming a Roman knight. A look at our sources suggests that it was only a fraction of the *scribae* who could aspire to make the jump to the second class of Roman society. Approximately one-third of the known *scribae quaestorii* eventually became *equites*. For the *scribae aedilicii* the ratio is close to one in four (cf. Chapter 5). The posts of quaestorian and aedilician *scriba* were not regarded as the most prestigious ones by chance. After all, they were the ones most closely connected to the management of the *aerarium* (see Chapter 2). Similar to their quaestorian counterparts, aedilician magistrates met competences that involved big sums of money and could easily be monetised. Policing the city, distributing grain and overseeing the organisation of games will likely have included an element of 'wax tax'.[94]

---

[91] Cic. *Verr.* 2.3.167–168; cf. Badian (1972) 72 w. n. 27, 165.
[92] Cic. *Verr.* 2.3.185–187. On the prerequisites of membership in the *ordo equester* Demougin (1988) 39–52; Demougin (1993) 236; cf. Plin. *nat.* 33.32–33.
[93] Cic. *Verr.* 2.3.184: *Ad eos me scribas [scil. qui digni sunt illo ordine, patribus familias, viris bonis atque honestis] revoca, si placet, noli hos colligere, qui nummulis corrogatis de nepotum donis ac de scaenicorum corollariis cum decuriam emerunt, ex primo ordine explosorum in secundum ordinem civitatis se venisse dicunt.* Cf. Cic. *dom.* 74.
[94] See e.g. Ganymedes' complaint in Petronius' *Satyrica* about the manipulation of the price of corn and collusive behaviour by the *aediles*; Petron. 44. Cf. the harsh measures decreed against corrupt *scribae* employed in the *annona* in the Later Roman Empire; Cod. *Theod.* 14.17.6 (AD 370).

As the sole guardians of the *tabulae publicae*, the Roman *scribae* played a central role in the Republican framework of accountability. It was to the fidelity of the Roman *scribae* that the public repository was entrusted. Confirmed by an oath (*ius iurandum*), the *fides* of the *scribae* was believed to be pivotal in preventing corrupt practices and embezzlement of public money. This position of responsibility and the association of the *scribae* with integrity was a source of high esteem. At the same time, the system's susceptibility to social relations and the lack of effective oversight was a recipe for abuse and profiteering. Roman *scribae* naturally shared in the dubious practices of their superiors and were (even) able to abuse their position on their own behalf. Their eventual inclusion in late Republican legislation against forgery and corruption did not do much to make these posts less lucrative. Keeping the magistrates' books and handling financial operations gave ample room for profiteering and emoluments. The *scribae*'s newly acquired financial capital in most cases translated directly into social advancement.

CHAPTER 5

The Parvenu

Theirs was the affectation of respectability – if indeed there be an affectation so honorable.

Edgar Allan Poe, *The Man of the Crowd*

An *Ordo* of *Scribae*

de re communi scribae magna atque nova te
orabant hodie meminisse, Quinte, reverti.[1]

Horace (A.88) preferred the otiose life in the countryside to the noisy and busy life in the *urbs*. On his country estate he could pass the hours in sweet idleness, with his books or sleeping. The city commanded his attention, being in Rome meant work. In the countryside he was a man of letters. In the city he was compelled to meet social obligations.[2] Not only was he the client of Octavian's powerful confidant Maecenas. He had also bought into a *decuria* and had thus become a *scriba*. Consequently, when in Rome, Horace had to do the bidding of his patron. At the same time, he belonged to the *ordo scribarum*, he was involved with their '*res communis*'.

Horace's dislike for the busy hours in Rome might have been more than just poetic hyperbole. Earning a living by working was certainly not his preferred and practised lifestyle. Yet, after ending up on the loser's side of the battle of Philippi in 42 BC, there was no denying that these new social relations were the basis of his way back to a life befitting his rank as Roman knight. Deprived of his father's comfortable heritage in his home town of Venusia, membership in a scribal *decuria* became his lifeline. To be sure,

---

[1] HOR. *sat.* 2. 6. 36–37: '"The clerks beg you, Quintus, to be sure to return to-day on some fresh and important business of common interest"', transl. H. R. Fairclough.
[2] See his emphatic juxtaposition of rural and city life in HOR. *sat.* 2. 6.

his later inclusion in Maecenas' circle proved to be a tremendous boon. Yet, what had initially kept him afloat was his post as *scriba quaestorius*.[3]

There was not only money on the line. Despite being the son of a freedman from a Samnite town,[4] Horace had been educated together with the offspring of the Roman elite, which earned him the equestrian post of *tribunus militum* in Brutus' army. Money, education and consequent social connections made for impressive social climbing. But the prestige gained was on the line when money was suddenly lacking and his acquaintances became proscribed. Obtaining the post of a *scriba quaestorius* was a way to compensate for these shortcomings. As I have outlined in the preceding chapters, a place in a scribal *decuria*, let alone in a quaestorian one, was not only financially but also socially profitable. Besides becoming a confidant of powerful magistrates through his work as *scriba*, Horace profited socially from being a member of the *ordo scribarum*.

The association of *scribae* was no mere occupational and administrative union. As the use of the term *ordo* suggests, the *scribae* were a recognised status-group within Roman society. Similar to other *ordines*, membership entailed an honorific grade of citizenship (*gradus dignitatis*). The members of an *ordo* were '*digni*'.[5] As such, membership in the *ordo* entailed significant social capital. Cicero characterised the *ordo scribarum* as a whole as '*honestus*', mainly because of the role of the *scribae* as guardians of the *tabulae publicae*. Those worthy of membership were *patres familias*, virtuous (*boni*) and honourable (*honesti*) men.[6] Consequently, he ranked the *scribae* high in his stratification of Roman society. He effectively subsumed the *ordo scribarum* under the second order, that of the *equites*.[7]

Cicero's characterisation of the *ordo scribarum* was obviously grounded in an idealising idea of Roman *scriba*-ship, rather than its realities. Membership in the *ordo equester* had never been a requirement to hold the post of *scriba*, neither in Cicero's lifetime nor before or after. And it was only some of the *scribae* who would formally find entrance into the equestrian *order* (see below). Yet, Cicero's assessment gives us a valuable outside view on the social standing of the *scribae* as a whole. At least in Cicero's time, the common *scriba* was seen as an individual held in high social esteem. And if our epigraphic evidence is anything to go by, this

---

3 On Horace's life see in general Nisbet (2007).
4 Most plausibly, Horace's father had been a native of the region who had been enslaved during the Social War, G. Williams (1995); Nisbet (2007) 7.
5 The wording '*eo ordine digni*' in the *lex de XX quaestoribus*, *Roman Statutes* no. 14 ll. 32–33; '*digni illo . . . ordine*' in Cic. *Verr.* 2. 3. 183; cf. Chapter 3. In general Cohen (1984) 49.
6 Cic. *Verr.* 2. 3. 183.
7 Cic. *Verr.* 2. 3. 184; Cic. *dom.* 74.

notion of the Roman *scriba*-ship as a worthwhile and respected occupation was carried over into imperial times. Holders of these posts confidently identified (or were proudly characterised by friends and family) as *scribae* on honorific monuments and their tombstones – even if they had made a distinguished career since holding the office. Being a *scriba* was seen as an honour.

Needless to say, in reality, there was no such thing as a 'common *scriba*'. Despite their identification as an *ordo*, the *scribae* were no socially homogenous group. What they all shared was the fact that they held the post of *scriba* and with it the rights, duties and opportunities that the office entailed. Viewed from a social perspective, they were a mixed bag, however. Granted, as I will try and show, there are certain traits that had become somewhat characteristic of scribal careers. While *scribae* were required to be freeborn citizens, they tended to stem from otherwise ordinary circumstances. It was the combination of these lowly origins with the financial and social opportunities opened up by the office of a *scriba* that could result in high social mobility. Our evidence does not allow us to deal in absolutes, however. Our sources do not stand up to statistical analysis. The Republican literary tradition is notoriously scarce, difficult and biased; the mainly imperial epigraphic sources, even though numerous, are fragmentary and selective; and to make things worse, we have to assume that most individuals who happened to have been Roman *scribae* did not even make it into what is left of the ancient tradition. It is certainly true that the rise of an 'epigraphic habit' with the onset of the Empire under Augustus brings us copious new evidence.[8] And while our mainly literary Republican sources are biased towards the extraordinary, the epigraphic medium was undoubtedly more democratic and did not shy away from the ordinary. As a result, with the advent of the Empire, a broader cross-section of *scribae* comes into view; we are able to grasp a more complete picture of the social conditions of the Roman *scribae*. Yet, the coincidence of this new and abundant evidence with regime change advises caution in its assessment. Does the new epigraphic evidence indeed allow us to finally apprehend the logical continuation of what we might call the phenomenon of the Republican *scriba*-ship? Or is the sudden increase and diversification in evidence rather a manifestation of a qualitative change in the social structure of the apparitoral scribal organisation, induced by its incorporation into the new imperial order?

[8] Cf. MacMullen (1982) and Alföldy (1991).

In what follows I will try to outline peculiarities and tendencies in our evidence on the social standing of the Roman *scribae*. It is only in this way that we may answer the methodological questions and arrive at a picture – necessarily a collage – of the position of the *scribae* in Roman society at various times.

Humble Beginnings

249 P. Claudius Ap. f. C. n. Pulcher, L. Iunius C. f. L. n. Pullus
    M. Claudius C. f. Glicia, qui scriba fuerat, dictator coact(us) abd(icavit) sine mag(istro) eq(itum). In eius locum factus est
    A. Atilius A. f. C. n. Caiatinus dict(ator) rei ger(undae) caussa
    L. Caecilius L. f. C. n. Metellus mag(ister) eq(uitum)[9]

M. Claudius Glicia's (A.42) spot in the limelight of Republican politics was as fleeting as it was extraordinary. The Augustan *fasti consulares*, the authoritative list of the Republic's yearly chief magistrates, sparing with words by nature, are unusually verbose for the year 249 BC. We learn that, in the year when P. Claudius Pulcher and L. Iunius Pullus were *consules*, Glicia was named *dictator*. Yet, even before he was able to appoint his deputy, he was forced to abdicate. In lieu of an explanation for this unprecedented procedure we find the laconic '*scriba fuerat*' – 'he had been a *scriba*'. His scribal occupation had been the source of the fleetingness as well as the extraordinariness of his short term. To be sure, from a legalistic standpoint, promoting a *scriba* to become *dictator* does not seem to have been out of bounds. In fact, despite his forced abdication, Glicia nevertheless continued to formally belong to the group of ex-dictators. He is said to have attended games clad in the *toga praetexta*, which identified curulic magistrates and priests, even after his abdication.[10] Yet, from an ideological perspective, creating a *scriba dictator* went against the *mos maiorum*, meant breaking all social norms. Dictators were customarily chosen from the ranks of the senate. Exercising the power otherwise reserved for only the most deserved of the *patres* was deemed an utterly improbable career step for anyone usually serving senatorial magistrates as a paid scribal *apparitor*. Glicia's name among the ranks of the aristocracy must have been an affront to the *ordo senatorius*.

In fact, Glicia's designation as *dictator* was intended to offend. The *scriba* had been designated by P. Claudius Pulcher, one of the *consules*

---

[9] *FCap cons.* 249 (*InscrIt* 13-01, 1ab, *AE* 1927, 101, *AE* 1940, 59, *AE* 1940, 60).
[10] Liv. *perioch.* 19.

of the year 249 BC, who had just lost an entire Roman fleet to the Carthaginians in a failed attack on the harbour of the Sicilian city of Drepana.[11] Pulcher, who unlike his consular colleague Pullus escaped with his life, was subsequently charged with treason before the senate, even more so as his catastrophic loss seemed to have involved contempt for the religious auspices. Late Republican tradition has it that when the sacred chickens had failed to eat and thus refused to provide a good omen for the imminent battle, Pulcher had them drowned in the sea, so that 'they should drink when they would not eat'.[12] Pulcher was forced to step down and, as his last official act, designate a *dictator*. In protest, his calculated choice fell on the least feasible person at hand, the one with the lowest social rank. Glicia, in his capacity as *scriba*, had been a '*sortis ultimae homo*'.[13]

It is worth noting that Pulcher's and Glicia's negative portrayal was likely not an accident. The late Republican annalistic tradition was heavily biased against the Claudii. Pulcher's great-grandfather,[14] App. Claudius Caecus, was infamous for having sided with the *plebs* and having scandalously allowed sons of freedmen to enter the senate during his term as *censor*.[15] That Glicia's name suggests libertine ancestry might thus not be entirely coincidental. His *cognomen* was of Greek origin[16] and his *gens* the same as the *consul*'s. Any ancient reader would naturally have made the link to Pulcher's great-grandfather. It was a staple of late Republican historiography that Caecus himself had sided with a *scriba*, Cn. Flavius (A.73), who likewise happened to be of libertine ancestry and had entered the senate as a protégé of the *censor*.[17] All in all, it might be more than a happy coincidence that we find Pulcher continuing his ancestor's tradition. This is not to say that the persona of Glicia was a mere narrative tool and invention of late Republican

---

[11] PLB. 1. 49–52; D.S. 24. 1. 5.
[12] CIC. *nat. deor.* 2. 7; cf. LIV. *perioch.* 19; SUET. *Tib.* 2. 2.
[13] LIV. *perioch.* 19.
[14] Walbank (1957–1979) I 113.
[15] Humm (2005) 77–97, esp. 80.
[16] SUET. *Tib.* 2. 2 has the Greek form Glycias.
[17] Flavius' precise alliance with App. Claudius is not known. Pliny the Elder makes Flavius the *scriba* of Claudius; PLIN. *nat.* 33. 17: *ipse scriba Appi Caeci*; in this tradition DIG. 1. 2. 2. 7. Flavius could not possibly have been the *scriba* of a *censor*, however. Wolf (1980) 29, who has analysed the annalistic tradition of Flavius' life, writes off any qualification of his scribal office, including Livy's characterisation as *scriba aedilicius*, as tendentious historiographic additions. Flavius might very well have been Claudius' *scriba* in one of his earlier magisterial functions. Rüpke (1995b) 246 identifies Flavius as a *scriba pontificius* due to the fact that he had access to the pontifical calendars. In the same vein Ryan (2002) 68f.; cf. DIOM. 484 (Heil), '*publici annales, quos pontifices scribaeque conficiunt*', Frier (1979) 194f.; see Chapter 3.

historiography.[18] Yet, it goes to show that the link between low birth and the post of *scriba* was a well-established notion.

Being a *scriba* was, in fact, tantamount to being of low social origin. The Roman *apparitores* as a whole were commonly associated with servile or quasi-servile origin. They also went by the name of *Bruttiani*, so called from the Italic Bruttii, who had defected to Hannibal during the Second Punic War and were subsequently punished by the Romans with the '*officia servilia magistratibus*', i.e. with having to serve as *apparitores*.[19] Even though the *scribae* occupied the highest rank of the apparitorial class by a margin, the denomination nevertheless implied humble beginnings. In the late third century AD still, being a *scriba* was equated with being of low birth. The father of the emperor Diocletian is said to have been of such obscure social origin as to have been either a freedman or the son of a *scriba*.[20]

Scrutinising this notion and tracking the social origins of the known Republican *scribae* is a difficult endeavour. Our mainly literary evidence is only rarely detailed enough to provide firm ground for a sound analysis. The little we can infer, however, points to the humble beginnings purported by the Republican historiographic tradition. With the analytical tools of prosopography, Ernst Badian has linked more than two-thirds of the Republican *scribae* with senatorial (or equestrian) families of their time.[21]

---

[18] Polybius, the source closest to the events at Drepana, fails to make mention of Glicia as well as of any incident that would point to sacrilegious behaviour on the part of P. Claudius Pulcher. Polybius provides his second-century BC audience with a very detailed account of the catastrophic naval battle and its context; PLB. 1. 49–51. He even recounts Pulcher's fall from grace due to his personal failure and details his subsequent severe prosecution in Rome; PLB. 1. 52. 2–3. Yet, his account bears no similarity whatsoever to the Late Republican version of the episode discussed above. This is not necessarily to say that Cicero or anyone before him invented a tall tale about P. Claudius Pulcher. While Polybius is fully aware of the function of religious sanctioning and explaining in Roman history and society, he might just not have been interested in this kind of explanation for the failure of the Roman efforts at Drepana; PLB. 6. 56. 6–12. In fact, he provides his readers with a more rational version in the vein of his 'pragmatic historiography' based on his knowledge of the harbour at Drepana and the navigation of ships. Nevertheless, doubts remain. Is it plausible that a keen observer of Rome's political system such as Polybius would have failed to mention the most extraordinary political event of a low-born citizen attaining the dictatorship? Taking the Augustan *fasti* as reliable historiographic evidence is at least problematic; Rüpke (1995a).

[19] FEST. 28.19–21 (31M); cf. STRAB. 5. 4. 13.

[20] EUTR. 9. 19: *virum obscurissime natum, adeo ut a plerisque scribae filius, a nonnullis Anullini senatoris libertinus fuisse credatur*.

[21] Badian (1989) 599 identified as belonging to a senatorial family C. Antistius (A.17), Aufidius Luscus (A.27), M. Claudius Glicia (A.42), Q. Cornelius (A.54), N. Decumius Vaarus (A.61), Cn. Flavius (A.73), L. Herennius (A.87), L. Mamilius (A.110), L. Nigidius Sors (A.121), L. Papirius Potamo (A.125), L. Petilius (A.130), D. Saufeius (A.153), C. Septimius (A.157), P. Septumius (A.159), L. Sergius (A.160), P. Servilius (A.162), M. Tullius (A.178); Sex. Cloelius / Clodius (A.49) may be added to this list, cf. Benner (1987) 156f.; belonging to an equestrian family Maecenas (A.107), Sarmentus (A.152).

Humble Beginnings

I have already discussed the close connections between the Republican *scribae* and their senatorial patrons (Chapter 3). Often, these connections extended beyond the acquainted to the familial. The historiographic topos of the freedman's son become *scriba* might thus very well have had its roots in reality.

We are on a more solid footing with the onset of the Empire. Fortunately enough, exhibiting the social status and relations of an individual was a key purpose of honorary and funerary inscriptions. What we can gather from our imperial epigraphic evidence thus confirms what we have found for Republican times. The connection of the *scribae* with low social origins and recent citizenship is prominent in our sources. Our most picturesque example of imperial *scriba*-ship, the so-called Ara degli Scribi, a lavish funerary altar for two *scribae aedilicii* of the first half of the first century AD, corroborates the Republican narrative (Fig. 5.1).[22] According to the main inscription on the altar, the monument was set up to honour the *memoria* of Q. Fulvius Priscus (A.82), a *scriba* of the *aediles curules*, who had died at the young age of 27.

> Dis Manibus
> Q(uinto) Fulvio Q(uinti) f(ilio) Qui(rina) Prisco
> scr(ibae) aed(ilium) cur(ulium) vixit an(nos) XXVII
> Q(uintus) Fulvius Eunus pater
> fecit.

Tragically enough, the family of the Fulvii was not spared further grief. Supposedly only some years after one son's death, the parents had to carry a second son to his grave. Faustus (A.81), at the age of 32, rejoined his brother in the necropolis at the *via Appia*, not far from the *porta Capena*.[23] An attachment was made to the altar at its top to record the life of Faustus, who had been *scriba librarius* and *scriba* of the curule aediles.

> Dis Manibus
> Q(uinto) Fulvio Q(uinti) f(ilio) Qui(rina tribu)
> Fausto scribae et
> scribae librario aedilium
> curulium vix(it) an(nis) XXXII.

It was the father of the two scribal brothers who took the responsibility to immortalise his sons with this extraordinary monument. While his two sons bore perfectly Roman *tria nomina* including the mention of their voting district (*tribus*), his own name hints at a former, different social status. He

---

[22] On the archaeological context Rotondi (2010); an epigraphic edition and art-historical placement Zevi and Friggeri (2012).
[23] The altar was found at 'vigna Casali', just opposite the *sepulcrum Scipionum*; Rotondi (2010).

Figure 5.1 So-called Ara degli Scribi, front view. Richly decorated funerary altar for Q. Fulvius Priscus and his brother Q. Fulvius Faustus. Via Appia, 'vigna Casali', Porta S. Sebastiano, Rome. Early 1. c. AD. (Museo Nazionale Romano, Terme di Diocleziano)

shared the privilege of Roman citizenship with his sons and in fact passed on his forename and family name to his offspring. Yet, his *cognomen*, Eunus, suggests a Greek background. As such, Eunus was most likely a freedman, his sons the family's first generation of freeborn Roman citizens.

Many of the other *scribae* whom we know from the imperial period shared a social background similar to that of the Fulvii. Approximately one-fifth of all the imperial *scribae* demonstrably came from families that had only recently acquired Roman citizenship. Many still bore non-Roman, mainly Greek, *cognomina*.[24] The other *scribae* without any recognisable

[24] Roman *scribae* with libertine background: *scribae*: P. Mercusenus Theodotus (A.116) Greek, cf. Adak and Şahin (2004) 98. – A. Perperna Fronto (A.129) *Spuri filius*. — *scribae quaestorii*: P. Aelius Agathoclianus (A.2) non-Roman ancestry. – Sex. Aelius Victor (A.5) non-Roman ancestry. –

Humble Beginnings 119

connection to freedman ancestry generally make an appearance as ordinary citizens in the sense that we are not able to further determine their social status. Nearly half of them are attested in Italian and, to a lesser degree, provincial towns (see below). A look at the social background of the junior *scribae librarii* reveals an even closer proximity to the milieu of the freedman. The *scribae librarii* were, with few exceptions, either sons of freedmen[25] or, even more commonly, freedmen themselves.[26] Only a few *scribae librarii* can reliably be identified as freeborn. Very much in contrast to the majority of their freedmen peers, who are mainly attested in Rome, these freeborn *scribae librarii* are mainly found in Italian and western provincial towns.[27] Both scribal charges, the major *scribae* and minor *scribae librarii*, were evidently recruited from similar milieus. As such, career

M. Aurelius Hermogenes (A.28) freedman father / grandfather. – Ti. Claudius Hispanus (A.44) non-Roman ancestry. – Flavius Liberalis (A.77). – L. Maelius Flaccus (A.108) freedman father. – P. Scrasius Naeolus (A.154) Greek. — *scribae aedilicii*: Q. Apusulenus Secundus (A.22) married to a freedwoman. – P. Curtius Tutus (A.59) freedman father / grandfather. – C. Domitius Fabius Hermogenes (A.63) freedman father. – C. Fonteius Claudianus (A.79) freedman father, cf. Eck (1978) 43 n. 24. – Q. Iulius Agathocles (A.89) non-Roman ancestry. – L. Iulius Alexander (A.90) probably son of freedman. – Marius Doryphorus (A.113) freedman, former *scriba librarius*. – P. Sufenas Myro (A.170) freedman father, cf. Demougin (1978) 622f. – P. Sufenas Severus Sempronianus (A.171) freedman father, cf. Demougin (1978) 622f. — *scribae tribunicii*: L. Faenius Alexander (A.71) non-Roman ancestry, former *(scriba) librarius*.

[25] Sons of freedmen, *scribae librarii*: L. Granius Eutyches (A.85). – A. Iunius Pastor (A.105) possibly freedman. – Q. Lucretius Quintianus (A.106) possibly freedman. – A. Pompeius Aemilianus (A.134). – A. Popillius Helenus (A.143). – T. Tettienus Felix (A.176), cf. Eck (1978) 48 n. 23. – M. Ulpius Celsianus (A.181) possibly freedman. — *scribae librarii quaestorii*: P. Aelius Andri [- - -] (A.3). – Aemilianus (A.6). – Avidius Charito (A.29). – Q. Caecilius Amandus (A.32). – Sex. Caecilius Birronianus (A.33). – Sex. Caecilius Epagathus (A.34). – M'. Cutius Amemptus (A.60). – T. Iunius Achilles (A.100), cf. Le Roux (1982) 460. – M. Servilius Eunicus (A.161), cf. Ramsay (1967) 61. – Stertinius Maximus Eutyches (A.168). – C. Sulpicius Olympus (A.173). – M. Valerius Hedymeles (A.186). — *scribae librarii aedilicii*: Clodius Fortunatus (A.48). – L. Iunius Lyco (A.103). – L. Pituanius Eros (A.133).

[26] Freedmen *scribae librarii*: Ti. Claudius Secundus Philippianus (A.46). – D. Cloelius Hermio (A.50). – T. Fulvius Eros Modestus (A.80). – M. Iunius Auctus (A.102). – C. Octavius Auctus (A.123). – L. Pulfennius Phileors (A.147). – M. Seius (A.156). – M. [- - -]cius (A.200). – C. Stertinius Orpex (A.169). – Tyrannus (A.179). – L. Volusius Hermes (A.195). — *scribae librarii quaestorii*: C. Allius Niger (A.13). – Q. Fabius Cytisus (A.69). – [M.] Iunius Menander (A.104). – L. Naevius Urbanus (A.118). – L. Numpidius Philomelus (A.122). – C. Telegennus Anthus (A.175). – Valerianus (A.182). – D. Valerius Propolus (A.187). – M. Ulpius Callistus (A.180). – [Volusius] (A.194). – L. Volusius Himerus (A.196). – L. Volusius Plocamus Maior (A.197). – L. Volusius Primanus (A.198). — *scribae librarii tribunicii*: T. Veturius Crescens (A.190). — *scribae librarii aedilicii*: L. Atiedius Dorus (A.24). – M. Porcius Pollio (A.145). – L. Volusius Volusianus P[- - -]anus (A.199).

[27] Freeborn *scribae librarii*: C. Aletius Lupus (A.12) *Aeclanum*. – C. Annius Priscus (A.15) *Eporedia*. – C. Aufidius (A.26) *Aquileia*. – P. Papienus Salutaris (A.124) unknown. – L. Peducaeus Saturninus (A.128) *Albanum*. — L. Pomponius Carisianus (A.139) unknown. – C. Statius Celsus (A.166) *Ad Mercurium*. — *scribae librarii quaestorii*: P. Annius Protectus (A.16) *Roma*. – Apidius Valerus (A.21) *Lugdunum*. – A. Pompeius Carpus (A.136) *Roma*. — *scribae librarii aedilicii*: C. Avillius Licinius Trosius (A.30) *Roma*. – P. Tettius Certus (A.177) *Nepet*.

mobility was a natural possibility. We have already met Q. Fulvius Faustus, who had begun his career as a *scriba librarius* of the *aediles curules* and advanced to become a *scriba* of the same magistrates. Three other *scribae librarii* made the same career step.[28] Their small number suggests that the advancement from *scriba librarius* to *scriba* proper was not the regular one. If *scribae librarii* pursued a further civil career (most are attested with the post of *scriba librarius* as their only one), they customarily occupied other apparitorial posts below the rank of *scriba*.[29] Yet in principle, career paths were open upwards, giving *scribae librarii* the chance to pursue even an equestrian career (see below).

Contested Mobility

> Ceterum Flavium dixerat aedilem forensis factio, Ap. Claudi censura vires nacta, qui senatum primus libertinorum filiis lectis inquinaverat et, posteaquam eam lectionem nemo ratam habuit nec in curia adeptus erat quas petierat opes, urbanis humilibus per omnes tribus divisis forum et campum corrupit. Tantumque Flavi comitia indignitatis habuerunt, ut plerique nobilium anulos aureos et phaleras deponerent.[30]

The advancement of a freedman's son to the upmost order of Roman society, to become a Roman senator, was an incredible, even scandalous feat. Although Roman Republican society allowed for a high degree of social mobility, tales of such grandeur were nevertheless extraordinary and rare. Unsurprisingly, their narrative power made them good fodder for Republican historiography. I have already discussed the difficulties

---

[28] C. Aelius Domitianus Gaurus (A.4). – L. Marius Doryphorus (A.113). – M. Pon[tius] (A.141).

[29] Apparitorial careers of *scribae librarii*: Sex. Caecilius Epagathus (A.34) *scriba librarius tribunicius, scriba librarius quaestorius, scriba librarius aedilium curulium, apparitor Caesarum, viator IIIvirum et IIIIvirum.* – Ti. Claudius Secundus Philippianus (A.46) *scriba librarius, accensus velatus, viator.* – Q. Fabius Cytisus (A.69) *scriba librarius tribunicius, scriba librarius quaestorius, viator quaestorius.* – [M.] Iunius Menander (A.104) *scriba librarius aedilium curulium, scriba librarius quaestorius.* – L. Peducaeus Saturninus (A.128) *scriba librarius, praeco consularis.* – M. Porcius Pollio (A.145) *scriba librarius aedilium curulium, lictor curiatius.* – C. Telegennus Anthus (A.175) *scriba librarius quaestorius, viator quaestorius.* – T. Tettienus Felix (A.176) *scriba librarius aedilium curulium, viator quaestorius, viator plebis, accensus consulis, calator pontificum.* – L. Volusius Primanus (A.198) *scriba librarius quaestorius, lictor.*

[30] Liv. 9. 46. 10–12: 'Now Flavius had been elected aedile by the faction of the market-place, which had become powerful in consequence of the censorship of Appius Claudius. Claudius had been the first to debase the senate by the appointment of the sons of freedmen, and afterwards, when no one allowed the validity of his selection, and he had failed to gain the influence in the senate-house which had been his object, he had distributed the humble denizens of the City amongst all the tribes, and had thus corrupted the Forum and the Campus Martius. And so great was the indignation over the election of Flavius that many of the nobles laid aside their golden rings and medals', transl. B. O. Foster.

surrounding the life of Cn. Flavius (A.73). Different narratives focused either on his skills as *scriba* and his infamous publication of the *fasti* and *legis actiones*, or on his relationship to the powerful *censor* App. Claudius. The main theme of the competing narratives was a shared one, however: social mobility. This social mobility was, by nature, extensive and, as such, controversial. Nicholas Purcell has convincingly demonstrated that, in the eyes of a Middle to Late Republican beholder, 'scribes were just the sort of people to make the protagonist of a story about contested upward social mobility'.[31] The notion of their humble origins I have described above, combined with their embodied cultural capital in their scribal skills as well as the social capital inherent in their close occupational connection to the powerful, bore the potential for an upward trajectory of great extent. As a result, Roman Republican tradition knows various examples of extraordinary social mobility of *scribae*. Even so, it is a characteristic of these Republican careers that they were contested and, as a result, more often than not, precarious. Flavius, our foremost example, had a hard time justifying his meteoric rise. He was despised by his new colleagues in the senate for being a petty upstart, the son of a freedman enabled by the '*forensis factio*'.[32] In the eyes of the nobility he had obtained his new place by abusing his position as *scriba*, by betraying the very group of people he was bound to join, by overstepping the boundaries of his designated place in society. It did not befit a *scriba* – the epitome of low social standing – to rise this high. Flavius is an extraordinary example insofar as the nobility did not succeed in limiting the damage, despite their protest note of depositing the insignia that marked their social standing. Flavius was stigmatised, a fact that the annalist Piso illustrated with a story about Flavius being mistreated by young noblemen as he made a sick-bed visit to a colleague. Flavius, requesting that his curule chair be brought from the senate house, found a way to shame the harassers into submission.[33] Flavius had been able to defend his newly acquired status; in App. Claudius he had found a potent supporter.

I have outlined above that Claudius Glicia (A.42) had been less fortunate in asserting his newly obtained status. He had obviously not been backed up by a powerful patron as had been the case with Flavius. Rather, he had been a political pawn, likely chosen with Flavius' example in mind to embarrass the nobility. His social climbing had been too abrupt to be successful. The fall of his patron spelled his own doom. As a result he was forced to abdicate.

---

[31] Purcell (2001) 637.
[32] Cf. V. Max. 2. 5. 2: *cum ingenti nobilitatis indignatione factus aedilis curulis*.
[33] Piso *frg.* F29 (FRH) = Gell. 7. 9. 5–6.

A third example of a *scriba* reaching the senatorial *ordo*, the case of C. Cicereius (A.40), underlines the importance of social connections in the advancement of Republican *scribae*. The *fasti triumphales* inform us that Cicereius had been *praetor* in Sardinia and as such had triumphed over the Corsi in 172 BC – the only former *scriba* to have celebrated a triumph.[34] His advancement to the Roman senate had not been regarded as inconspicuous, however. The *fasti* are careful to point out – in a fashion similar to the case of Claudius Glicia – that Cicereius had been a *scriba*. It might have been symptomatic of his position as a scribal parvenu that the senate had refused to grant him an official triumph over the Corsi. He eventually held an unofficial triumphal procession on the *mons Albanus* as had become common practice for those rejected by the senate.[35] His footing in the senate might not have been the most secure after all. The temple to Moneta, which he had vowed during his campaign against the Corsi, was eventually dedicated on the Alban Mount rather than in Rome.[36] Nevertheless, Cicereius had successfully managed to advance from *scriba* to the highest order of Roman society, and remain there. As far as we can discern, close relations to the most powerful family of the time had been key to his success. Cicereius had been *scriba* under P. Cornelius Scipio Africanus the Elder[37] and it is evident that Cicereius owed his social and political advancement to the subsequent protection of Africanus. We finally find Cicereius standing as candidate to the praetorship of 174 BC together with Africanus' son. He eventually decided to forego his candidacy for the benefit of his protector's son, which brought him lasting fame as a prime example of moderation and might have helped his candidacy for the following year.[38] Cicereius' association with the Cornelii Scipiones was as long-lasting as it was productive. In 167 BC, Cicereius was part of a legation of the senate to assist in the reordering of Macedonia.[39] The *proconsul* charged with the task had not by chance been L. Aemilius Paullus, Africanus' brother-in-law.

The last *scriba* to reach the ranks of the Roman senate became *quaestor urbanus* under Caesar's dictatorship in 44 BC. Ernst Badian has plausibly reconstructed his life and career, of which nevertheless much remains

---

[34] *FCap triumph.* 172 (*CIL* 1, p. 459); cf. *CIL* 9, 5564 (triumphal *fasti* of Urbs Salvia): *C(aius) Cicereius qui scr(iba) fuer(at) pro pr(aetore) ex Cors(ica) in mont(e) Alb(ano) K(alendis) Octo(bribus)*.
[35] LIV. 42. 7. 1–2, 42. 21. 6–7. On the lower prestige of the *triumphus in monte Albano* as opposed to the regular triumph in Rome see Rosenberger (2009), on Cicereius 33.
[36] LIV. 45. 15. 10.
[37] V. MAX. 3. 5. 1. The exact office of Africanus in which Cicereius met him as *scriba* is unknown.
[38] V. MAX. 4. 5. 3.
[39] LIV. 45. 17. 4.

uncertain.⁴⁰ Q. Cornelius (A.54), as his name suggests, must have had his roots in a freedman family either of the Cornelii Scipiones or of Cornelius Sulla himself. He had been *scriba* during Sulla's dictatorship.⁴¹ It is very likely that he went on to become *pontifex minor*, a post that historically shared a close relationship with the *scriba*-ship (see Chapter 3).⁴² It was there that he must have made contact with C. Iulius Caesar, who was co-opted to the pontifical college in 74/3 BC. Q. Cornelius was eventually rewarded by Caesar late in life, in his late fifties or even sixties. Cicero identifies it as an obvious case of nepotism and as such condemns it strongly. For him, Q. Cornelius represented a link between Sulla and Caesar and their respective civil wars.⁴³ Q. Cornelius' advancement to the senate was clearly out of the ordinary.

The lives of Cn. Flavius, Claudius Glicia, C. Cicereius and Q. Cornelius do not represent what we might call the 'ordinary' career of a Republican *scriba*. Clearly, they were exceptions to the norm, anomalous to the lives of the mass of *scribae*. As such, they showcase what had been possible in extreme cases, in which the benefits that came with the post had come to full fruition. The factors that made a *scriba* and were responsible for his advancement, namely his professional expertise, thus his access to important social relations and to financial resources, must have been amplified in times of crisis and instability. Trying to establish the ordinary career of the average Republican *scriba* is, as a result, exceedingly difficult. Our sources are only ample enough for the last century BC, a period of Republican history that might not be regarded as ordinary in any sense of the word. It might thus come as no surprise that the picture painted by our sources of the late Republican *scriba* very much resembles that of our four extraordinary cases, even though its colours are less bright. I have already discussed the fact that most late Republican *scribae* can be linked to senatorial families or powerful patrons. In most cases, our knowledge barely extends beyond this basic observation of possible social protection, however.

It is primarily Cicero who gives us a broader idea of the social standing and mobility of the *scribae* of his time. His characterisation of Verres' *scriba* Maevius (A.109) reads like the lives of the four *scribae* become senators in a

---

⁴⁰ Badian (1989) no. 6, 586–9.
⁴¹ Cɪᴄ. *off*. 2. 29.
⁴² Cɪᴄ. *har. resp.* 12.
⁴³ Cɪᴄ. *off*. 2. 29: *alter [scil. Q. Cornelius] autem, qui in illa dictatura [scil. Sulla's] scriba fuerat, in hac [scil. Caesar's] fuit quaestor urbanus. Ex quo debet intellegi talibus praemiis propositis numquam defutura bella civilia.*

nutshell. Maevius must have started from humble beginnings when he met Verres on the job. In the years that followed, he accompanied Verres during his subsequent magisterial tenures and associated closely with his superior. Thus protected, Maevius was able to profit financially from his scribal skills and position. The logical conclusion of Maevius' advancement was his entry into the equestrian order, a move furthered by his financial gains and promoted by his longtime patron.[44] It is obvious that Cicero tried to single out Maevius as an extraordinary case that diverged from the norm. Interestingly enough, what Cicero objected to was not Maevius' social mobility per se, but rather the semi-legal manner in which he had amassed a fortune and the selfish way that Verres had promoted him. In Cicero's eyes it was not out of the ordinary that a *scriba* – in this case a *scriba quaestorius* – would enter the *ordo equester*. On the contrary, he accepted it as a given that entry into a scribal *decuria* would entail access to 'the second order of Roman society'.[45] According to Cicero, the Roman *scribae* were, some unworthy subjects such as Maevius notwithstanding, respectable and honourable members of Roman society, after all.[46] It is true that Cicero was a master of the subtle overstatement. And we should, therefore, exercise caution in taking his statement too literally, in particular when exaggeration helped his case. Yet, I would nevertheless hesitate to dismiss Cicero's characterisation of the social standing and mobility of the late Republican *scribae* too easily. He described a paradigm that matches the general tendency of our Republican evidence – even if this paradigm most likely only touched upon the tip of the iceberg. Some thirty years after Cicero's statement, Horace's early career should demonstrate the close adjacency of the two *ordines* – granted, in even more troubled times and as a sign rather of social decline than advancement.

Imperial Careers

Distinguished careers were still a possibility for *scribae* during the Empire. However, our imperial evidence lacks extraordinary tales of Republican proportions. Scribal careers seem to have moved along more orderly courses in imperial times compared to what Republican evidence suggests. While imperial *scriba*-ship is still characterised by upward social mobility, the post had most certainly become less contentious. Not only was the Republican

---

[44] Cic. *Verr.* 2. 3. 181–187.
[45] Cic. *Verr.* 2. 3. 184.
[46] Cic. *Verr.* 2. 3. 183–184.

apparitorial system overshadowed by the administrative apparatus of the emperor and eventually rendered obsolete. The key factor in exceptional scribal advancement during the Republic, the formidable power of senatorial patrons, was also reined in by the monopolisation of power by the *princeps*. As a result, the limit of scribal advancement was now the equestrian order. It had to be left to subsequent generations to make it to the senate. We can trace back two senatorial families of the late second and early third century AD to holders of scribal posts. Marius Perpetuus (A.114), whom we find as *scriba quaestorius* in the staff of the *proconsul* of *Africa proconsularis*,[47] had most likely been the father of a man with the same name, who made a successful procuratorial career under Marcus Aurelius.[48] The latter's sons and grandsons reached the consulate, among them Marius Maximus Perpetuus Aurelianus, commonly identified with the historian of this name.[49] We might assume that Marius Perpetuus had reached the equestrian order after holding his scribal post, thus laying the foundation for his family's rise. Q. Petronius Melior (A.132), who had held the highest scribal honours as *scriba quaestorius VI primus princeps*, had himself passed through a military and procuratorial career which culminated in his appointment as *procurator annonae*, stationed in Ostia, where we find him honoured in the year AD 184.[50] His grandson of the same name eventually entered the senate in c. AD 231. He was *consul suffectus* in AD 244/5.[51]

Holding a post as *scriba* during the Empire entailed a strong probability of advancement to the equestrian order. By the end of the Civil Wars, monetary means had become the predominant selection criterion for access to the *ordo equester*. It was a development that had been in the making for some time; I have already discussed Cicero's complaints about the venality of scribal posts, their scandalous profits and the subsequent rise of the scribal nouveaux riches to the *ordo equester* (see Chapter 4). As a result, the equestrian order had become increasingly accessible to subjacent status groups such as the *apparitores*.[52] It might come as no surprise that it was most notably the *scribae* who were able to profit from this opportunity.[53]

---

[47] *ILAfr* 592 (*ILPBardo* 370, *AE* 1921, 39).
[48] Among other procuratorial posts *proc. prov. Lugd. et Aquit.*, *CIL* 13, 1810; cf. Pflaum, I, no. 168.
[49] The stemma of the family in Pflaum I 411; for Perpetuus Aurelianus, who was *consul* in AD 198/199 and 223, see Birley (1997).
[50] *CIL* 14, 172 (*ILS* 1429); cf. *CIL* 14, 5345. Cf. Pflaum no. 201.
[51] PIR² P 290; Dietz (1980) 198; Hächler (2019) no. 215.
[52] Demougin (1988) 34–44, 706–9; cf. Duncan-Jones (2016) 89–93.
[53] Purcell (1983) 148–52 lists three *lictores*, one *praeco* and two *viatores* who made it to the equestrian order. These apparitorial charges apart from *scribae* gained access to the equestrian order only from the Flavian dynasty onwards, Demougin (1988) 709.

We know of thirty-five *scribae* to have made it to the second order of Roman society; about every third *scriba* and every tenth *scriba librarius*.[54] Of these, ninteen had demonstrably held one or more military posts (the others identified simply as either '*eques Romanus*' or '*equo publico*').[55] Quaestorial *scribae* were those with the highest success rate in making it into the *ordo equester*. They seem to have enjoyed the highest prestige and most opportunities of all the *scribae*.[56] Interestingly enough, once member of a *decuria*, the *scriba*'s social background does not seem to have played a defining role in his further advancement to the equestrian order.[57] From the

---

[54] We might expect our evidence to be skewed in favour of more successful careers. Equestrian careers of *scribae* are thus most certainly over-represented.

[55] Roman imperial *scribae* with membership in the *ordo equester*, highest military post given: *scribae*: Cn. Ricinius Persa (A.148) *tribunus militum*; Devijver R 7. — *scribae quaestorii*: L. Aemilius Rectus (A.9) also *scriba aedilicius, equo publico ab imperatore* (Hadrian). – Sex. Atellius Paetus (A.23) *tribunus militum*; Devijver A 174. – M. Aurelius Hermogenes (A.28) also *scriba tribunicius, praefectus alae*, procuratorial career; Devijver A 230. – Ti. Claudius Helvius Secundus (A.43) also *scriba aedilicius, praefectus alae bis, adlectus in quinque decuriis*; Devijver C 143. – Ti. Claudius Hispanus (A.44) *tribunus militum*; Devijver C 145. – P. Curius Servilius Draco (A.58) *equo publico*. – Gavius Capito Maximianus (A.84), also *scriba tribunicius* and *aedilicius, tribunus militum*; Devijver G 8bis. – L. Mamius Fabius Largus (A.111) *eques Romanus equo publico, militiis equestribus ornatus*. – Q. Papirius Maximus (A.127) also *scriba aedilicius, tribunus militum*; Devijver P 13. – Q. Petronius Melior (A.132) *tribunus militum*, procuratorial career; Devijver P 25. – P. Scrasius Naeolus (A.154) *equo publico*. – D. Severius Severus (A.163) *praefectus praesidiorum et montis Berenicidis*; Devijver 739f., 2237; Lesquier (1918) 153. – C. Valerius (A.184) *equo publico ab imperatore* (unknown). – M'. Valerius Bassus (A.185) *tribunus militum*; Devijver V 4. – C. Vibius Publilianus (A.191) *tribunus militum bis*; Devijver V 104. – An anonymous individual (A.204) *eques Romanus*. — *scribae tribunicii*: T. Iulius Saturninus (A.99) *tribunus militum*, procuratorial career; Devijver I 120. — *scribae aedilicii*: C. Aelius Domitianus Gaurus (A.4) also *scriba librarius quaestorius, tribunus militum, equo publico ab imperatore* (Antoninus Pius); Devijver A 31. – A. Atinius Paternus (A.25) *praefectus alae, equo publico ab imperatore* (Trajan?); Devijver A 182. – Claudius Paulus (A.45) *tribunus militum*; Devijver C 163. – C. Domitius Fabius Hermogenes (A.63) *equo publico*. – L. Fabricius Caesennius Gallus (A.70) *eques Romanus*. – T. Flavius R[ufin]ianus (A.78) *tribunus militum*; Devijver F 66. – C. Iulius Iustus (A.94) *eques Romanus*. – Marius Doryphorus (A.113) '*anulos aureos consecutus a divo Commodo*'; cf. Duncan-Jones (2016) 123f. – M. Pontius (A.141) also *scriba librarius aedilicius, tribunus militum*; Devijver P 86. – T. Statilius Messalinianus (A.165) also *scriba tribunicius, praefectus cohortis*; Devijver S 68. – P. Sufenas Myro (A.170) *eques Romanus*. — *scribae librarii*: A. Iunius Pastor (A.105) *eques Romanus*. – M. Servilius Eunicus (A.161) *praefectus cohortis*; Devijver S 41. – C. Statius Celsus (A.166) *eques Romanus*. – Stertinius Maximus Eutyches (A.168) ἱππικὸς Ῥωμαίων. – L. Volusius Volusianus P[- - -]anus (A.199) *equo publico*. – [- - -i]us (A.202) *equo publico*.

[56] Approximately one-third of *scribae quaestorii* (fifteen out of forty-six) were Roman knights, of whom two-thirds had held no other scribal post. More than a quarter of the *scribae aedilicii* became *equites* (fifteen out of fifty-three), yet about half of them had held at least another scribal post. More than half of the known *scribae tribunicii* advanced to the equestrian order (five out of nine). Only one had held the tribunician post exclusively, however.

[57] The ratio of freeborn to sons of freedmen to freedmen is not significantly different from the entire pool of known *scribae*. Even a freedman, Marius Doryphorus (A.113), was awarded '*anulos aureos*' by Commodus after having passed through a successful apparitorial and scribal career. Cf. Duncan-Jones, 2016 123f., who argues that the imperial grant technically did not imply equestrian status.

middle of the second century AD onwards, even the post of *scriba librarius* offered direct access to the equestrian charges.

Despite the rather impressive extent of this social mobility, the scribal parvenus constituted, as Ségolène Demougin has observed, the lowest social group within the *ordo equester*.[58] Equestrian careers of *scribae*, especially in the first century AD, usually peaked in one or several posts of the equestrian *militiae*.[59] We find the most successful equestrian careers from Trajanic times onwards. Ti. Claudius Helvius Secundus (A.43), hailing from North African Caesarea, completed the *tres militiae* twice. His career had profited from the protection of a powerful consular patron as well as imperial support from Nerva and Trajan.[60] Another holder of the *tres militiae* and former *scriba* of the curule aediles, A. Atinius Paternus (A.25), was honoured with *dona militaria* by Trajan for his merits in the Parthian War. After his military career he acted as *curator kalendarii* in Fabrateria Nova.[61] It was as late as the middle of the second century AD that *scribae* came to occupy procuratorial posts, exclusively lower ones (*sexagenarii* and *centenarii*) at that. The first to attain an elevated position in the imperial administration was Titus Iulius Saturninus (A.99), a *scriba tribunicius*. He reached the post of *praefectus vehiculorum* under Antoninus Pius and eventually became *procurator* of Marcus Aurelius and Lucius Verus as well as of Faustina the Younger. Some years later, Q. Petronius Melior (A.132), having been *scriba quaestorius*, made it to the post of *procurator annonae*. And finally a century later, M. Aurelius Hermogenes (A.28), a *scriba tribunicius* and *quaestorius*,

---

[58] Demougin (1988) 712.
[59] They belonged to the biggest and lowermost group of equestrians; Duncan-Jones (2016) 106, 110–12.
[60] AE 1925, 44 [Caesarea]: *Ti(berio) Claudio L(uci) f(ilio) / Helvio Secundo / praef(ecto) fabr(um) Romae adlecto / a divo Nerva in quinque decuriis ⁵/ praef(ecto) coh(ortis) equitatae II Bracar(orum) / Augustanorum iterum pr[ae]f(ecto) coh(ortis) I / Flaviae c(ivium) R(omanorum) equitatae trib(uno) leg(ionis) IIII / Scythicae iterum trib(uno) leg(ionis) XII / Fulminatae praef(ecto) eq(uitum) alae Phrygum ¹⁰/ iterum praef(ecto) alae II Gallorum / scribae decuriarum quaestoriae / et aedilium curulium / Caesariensis / quem absentem cives sui ¹⁵/ omnibus magistrat[u]um / honoribus publico decreto / exornaverunt / Caesarienses / d(ecreto) d(ecurionum)*. Jarrett (1963) 212 postulated that Secundus had been appointed *praefectus fabrum* by the *consul* Q. Pomponius Rufus in AD 95. The same was governor of *Moesia inferior* in AD 98/99, where Secundus held his first military post.
[61] CIL 6,1838 (CIL 3, 263.2*, ILS 2727): *D(is) M(anibus) / A(ulo) Atinio A(uli) f(ilio) Pal(atina) / Paterno / scrib(ae) aedil(ium) cur(ulium) ⁵/ hon(ore) usus ab Imp(eratore) / equo publ(ico) honor(e) / praef(ecto) coh(ortis) II Bracar(um) / Augustan(orum) trib(uno) mil(itum) / leg(ionis) X Fretens(is) a divo ¹⁰/ Traiano in expedition(e) / Parthica donis donat(o) / praef(ecto) alae VII Phryg(um) cur(atori) / kal(endarii) Fabraternor(um) Novor(um) / Atinia A(uli) f(ilia) Faustina patri ¹⁵/ optimo fecit*; Devijver A 182. For other *curatores* of cities see an anonymous *scriba quaestorius sex primus* (A.205), who had been *curator* in Cora; Duthoy, 1979, p. 178; Q. Petronius Melior (A.132), *curator* in Saena; Duthoy (1979) 189; and Claudius Paulus (A.45), *curator* in Circeii; Duthoy (1979) 178.

came to hold the post of *procurator a studiis*.⁶² The success of the three *scribae* become *procuratores* was, in comparison to their scribal predecessors in the equestrian order, unprecedented. The career of Saturninus was likely jump-started by the fact that his family were well-to-do as the Iulii had held the lucrative *portorium* of Illyricum and Thracia. What must have been a special relationship with Antoninus Pius earned him the post of *apparitor Caesaris*. Through the apparent protection of the emperor and by way of a place in a tribunician scribal *decuria*, Saturninus eventually started an equestrian career, which peaked under Pius' successors.⁶³ Melior's remarkable advancement must have ultimately resulted from his standing in his hometown of Faesulae and the family's footing in the region around Florentia. In Faesulae he had been *quattuorvir quinquennalis*. In addition, he had held the post of *pontifex Faesulis et Florentiae*. It comprised the region where his family would remain influential. His consular grandson eventually came to be buried in Florentia. Even though we do not know all the circumstances, Melior must have been one of the most important notables of the region when he decided to bid for a spot in a scribal *decuria* in the capital and thus set up his subsequent equestrian career, which, not by chance, brought him back to the region as *curator* of the nearby Etrurian city of Saena.⁶⁴ Hermogenes' family already belonged to the equestrian order when he had started his career. His father as well as his father-in-law had both been equestrians of the second-highest level of *perfectissimus*. Hermogenes himself had nevertheless initiated his own equestrian career with two scribal posts. He successfully completed the *tres militiae* to become *procurator a studiis*.⁶⁵

A spot in a scribal *decuria* could in many cases function as a gateway to an equestrian career. And it seems that its relative success depended on an individual's level of entry into the system. The three *scribae* become *procuratores* had a headstart when they decided to undertake an equestrian

---

⁶² Cf. Purcell (1983) 159. A possible fourth *scriba* with a procuratorial career, T. Flavius R[ufin]ianus (A.78), who had been *scriba* of the *aediles curules*, held the post of *curator viarum Ostiensis et Campanae*. It is unclear whether the post was identical with the nearly homonymous one of *procurator Augusti viarum Ostiensis et Campanae*; cf. Pflaum no. 553; Eck (1979) 54, 86. *CIL* 6, 1648, a very fragmentary honorary inscription for an equestrian *procurator*, occasionally attributed to a former '[scriba] aedil(ium) cur(ulium)', is to be disregarded; Pflaum no. 279.

⁶³ PIR² I 548; Pflaum no. 174; Devijver I 120; Thomasson 260 no. 52; cf. on his post as *conductor* Bounegru (1981–1982); as *praefectus vehiculorum* Kolb (2000) 163.

⁶⁴ PIR² P 291; Pflaum no. 201; Devijver P 25; cf. on his various posts Camodeca (1980) 514–17; Saulnier (1984) 528 no. 40; Jacques (1983) 278–80; Scheid and Granino Cecere (1999) 156 no. 4; Rüpke (2005) 1199 no. 2662.

⁶⁵ Pflaum no. 352; Devijver A 230; cf. Christol (1981).

career, so that they likely already envisaged a procuratorial career when starting out. Those less privileged could increase their odds by passing through true scribal careers, accumulating different scribal *decuriae*. We find a few individuals who pursued such an apparitorial career, as it were, and managed to accumulate several scribal posts, frequently in sequence with other apparitorial charges. Those mainly garnering charges at the level of *scriba* in most cases went on to pursue an equestrian career.[66] For most of the *scribae*, coming from socially humble backgrounds, just making it into the *ordo equester* must have been a tremendous achievement. As a matter of fact, for the majority of the imperial *scribae*, such an accomplishment was out of bounds.[67] Three out of four *scribae* and *scribae librarii* held one single scribal post during their lifetime. It was the highlight of their state career; it was as far as they would make it in the imperial administration. Obviously, such a career paled in comparison to the advancement of the newly knighted. Still, for most of the *scribae*, having a place in a *decuria* was no small achievement, particularly as their frame of reference was not so much the global Empire, but rather their local, mostly Italian communities, in which they eventually settled and played a part.

---

[66] Apparitorial careers: M. Aurelius Hermogenes (A.28) *eques, scriba quaestorius, scriba tribunicius maior*. – [Clu]vius Formica (A.51) *scriba aedilium curulium, scriba quaestorius sex primus, scriba tribunorum plebis*. – L. Cornelius Terentianus (A.55) *scriba Xvirum litibus iudicandis, scriba aedilium curulium*. – Gavius Capito Maximianus (A.84) *eques, scriba aedilium curulium, scriba quaestorius, scriba tribunicius, tribunus militum*. – T. Iulius Saturninus (A.99) *eques, apparitor Caesaris, scriba tribunicius*. – Q. Papirius Maximus (A.127) *eques, scriba aedilium plebis cerialium, scriba aedilium plebis, scriba aedilium curulium, scriba quaestorius VI primus, tribunus militum*. – Sex. Pompeius Baebianus (A.135) *scriba aedilicius, scriba quaestorius*. – T. Statilius Messalinianus (A.165) *eques, scriba aedilicius, scriba tribunicius*. For others, passing through lower apparitorial posts could mean eventually getting hold of a prestigious place in a scribal *decuria*: P. Aelius Agathoclianus (A.2) *accensus velatus, pullarius maior, scriba aedilium curulium, scriba quaestorius sex primus, scriba tribunicius maior*. – Sex. Caecilius Epagathus (A.34) *scriba librarius aedilium curulium, viator IIIvirum et IIIIvirum, scriba librarius quaestorius, apparitor Caesarum, scriba librarius tribunicius*. – Ti. Claudius Secundus Philippianus (A.46) *viator, scriba librarius, accensus velatus*. – Q. Fabius Cytisus (A.69) *scriba librarius quaestorius, scriba librarius tribunicius, viator quaestorius*. – T. Marius Clementianus (A.112) *lictor curiatius, scriba aedilium curulium*. – M. Porcius Pollio (A.145) *lictor curiatius, scriba librarius aedilium curulium*. – L. Varronius Capito (A.188) *accensus velatus, scriba aedilicius*. – [Volu]ntilius Macer (A.193) *viator XVvirum sacris faciundis, viator IIIvirum et IIIIvirum, scriba aedilium curulium*. – Anonymus (A.211) *accensus, scriba aedilicius, scriba tribunicius*. The most extensive and prominent example is L. Marius Doryphorus (A.113), a freedman, who had begun his apparitorial career as *lictor curiatius* and went on to become *sacerdotalis viator augurum, praeco quaestorius, praeco consulis, scriba librarius aedilium curulium* and finally *scriba tribunicius* as well as *scriba aedilicius*. He was eventually honoured with the *anuli aurei*, the insignia of the *equites*, by the emperor Commodus; cf. Duncan-Jones (2016) 123f.

[67] On the achievability of equestrian status during the Empire Armstrong (2012) 62–8.

Local Notables

> Fundos Aufidio Lusco praetore libenter
> linquimus, insani ridentes praemia scribae,
> praetextam et latum clavum prunaeque vatillum.[68]

Aufidius Luscus (A.27) had seemingly lost his mind. When Horace met his scribal colleague in his hometown of Fundi, Luscus had given rise to much wonder and ridicule. He, who in Rome had been equipped with writing tablets and a stylus, at home showed himself in the pomp of a Roman magistrate, donning the dress of a curule office holder and high priest, caught in the act of performing a cultic ritual, so much so that he now appeared as the veritable '*praetor*' of the small town in Latium.

Horace's vignette of the '*insanus scriba*', in its obvious exaggeration, served a satirical purpose. We can be certain that Luscus was no fraud. Indeed, he had likely been a local magistrate in Fundi, presumably one of the three *aediles* who governed the *municipium*.[69] Horace's portrait of the *scriba* become magistrate plays on the discrepancy of reference that was inherent in the life of Luscus. Horace, himself a member of a scribal *decuria*, must have been well aware of the clashing social identities that could arise from being a public servant on the global stage and acting the part of a political and social notable at the local level. It becomes blatantly obvious in the context of the satire. Horace's travelling party was on its way to the Gulf of Taranto to help forge a compact between Octavian and Marcus Antonius, which would become the Treaty of Tarentum of 37 BC.[70] Luscus thus serves as a satirical allusion to the big politicians and the gravity of the matter at hand. Luscus, oblivious to the bigger picture, cannot help but lose himself in the seeming importance of his local position. For an informed observer, the antics of the *scriba* must clearly have been out of place.

Our evidence suggests that Horace's exaggerated portrait of the pompous Luscus was based on a real-world paradigm of scribal careers. It is the story of men of inconspicuous social backgrounds getting hold of a prized place in a scribal *decuria* in the capital with the prospect of money and social

---

[68] HOR. *sat.* 1. 5. 34–36: 'Fundi, with its "praetor" Aufidius Luscus, we quit with delight, laughing at the crazy clerk's gewgaws, his bordered robe, broad stripe, and pan of charcoal', transl. H. R. Fairclough. Cf. PORPH. *Hor. sat.* 1. 5. 35.

[69] For the mention of the magistrates see the building inscription of the north gate of the city, *CIL* 10, 6239; cf. *CIL* 10, 6238.

[70] Horace's fifth poem of his first book of satires, an unexpectedly apolitical and profane rendering of Horace's journey down the via Appia as part of Octavian's delegation to negotiate with Marcus Antonius in Tarentum in 37 BC, has left generations of philologists puzzled and intrigued. Its interpretation and significance remains disputed. For a discussion of the main points see Tennant (1991). The only allusion to the serious political subject matter HOR. *sat.* 1. 5. 27–29.

Local Notables 131

relations, eventually returning to the periphery and making their newly gained assets count. While they had been mere public servants in Rome, in their local communities they now were eminent personalities. 'Briefly, men of parochial concerns became more cosmopolitan. They acquired a knowledge of how the status-game was played at Rome, and continued to play it at home, bringing their new resources to bear.'[71]

Luscus was certainly no exceptional case. The first attestation of a Roman *scriba* getting involved in local public life is M. Anicius (A.14), whom we find as *praetor* in Praeneste in the year 216 BC.[72] From the first century BC onwards, epigraphic evidence gives us a clearer picture. A certain M. Papirius (A.126), who had been *scriba quaestorius* in Rome and had subsequently become *praetor* in Cumae, was involved in the building of a temple on the acropolis of the city sometime during the seventies and sixties.[73] Clemens (A.201), whose family name is unfortunately lost, had been *scriba* of the *XXVIviri* before assuming the mayoral office of *IIvir iure dicundo* in Carsulae. He boasts that he had been able to pay for lavish gladiatorial games, a first for the city. This Republican paradigm lived on throughout the imperial period. Many a *scriba* assumed a public role in an Italian, more rarely in a provincial community.[74] Some, such as T. Sabidius Maximus (A.150) in Tibur, to great success.[75] The *scriba quaestorius sex primus* of the late first century AD must have been one of the city's most important honoraries. He had begun his local career with the cultic functions of

---

[71] Purcell (1983) 162f.
[72] Liv. 23.19.17–18.
[73] Camodeca (2010) 58.
[74] Other *scribae* with local careers, not discussed in detail: C. Aelius Domitianus Gaurus (A.4) *scriba librarius quaestorius, scriba aedilium curulium* and *decurio adlectus* in Puteoli. – C. Aufidius (A.26) *scriba librarius* and *quaestor* in Aquileia. – Ti. Claudius Helvius Secundus (A.43) *scriba aedilium curulium*, quaestura and *omnibus magistratuum honoribus (functus)* in Caesarea (MAUR. CAES.). – Ti. Claudius Hispanus (A.44) *scriba* and *flamen perpetuus* in Madauros (NUM.). – C. Domitius Fabius Hermogenes (A.63) *scriba aedilium curulium* and *flamen divi Hadriani* as well as *aedilis* and *decurio adlectus* in Ostia. – M. Ennius Vicetinus (A.67) *scriba aedilium curulium* and *aedilis* in Suessa Aurunca as well as *decurio* in Rufrae and Vicetia. – L. Fabricius Caesennius Gallus A.70) *scriba aedilicius* and *omnibus honoribus functus* in Ostia. – C. Furius Tiro (A.83) *scriba quaestorius* and *pontifex* as well as three times *quattuorvir quinquennalis* in Carsulae. – M. Licinius Privatus (A.267) *scriba librarius* and *decurio adlectus* in Ostia. – C. Septimius Libo (A.158) *scriba aedilium curulium* and *aedilis* in Puteoli. – D. Severius Severus (A.163) *scriba quaestorius* and *aedilis* as well as *quattuorvir iure dicundo* in Sulmo. – P. Sufenas Myro (A.170) *scriba aedilium curulium* and *quattuorvir* as well as *decurio* in Bovillae. – P. Sufenas Severus Sempronianus (A.171), *scriba aedilium curulium* and *sacerdos Apollinis* as well as *decurio* in Bovillae.
[75] CIL 14, 3674 (InscrIt 04-01, 197, ILS 1889) [*Tibur*]: T(ito) Sabidio T(iti) f(ilio) Pal(atina) / Maximo / scribae q(uaestorio) sex / prim(o) bis praef(ecto) ⁵/ fabrum pontifici / salio curatori / fani Herculis V(ictoris) / tribuno aquarum / q(uin)q(uennali) patrono ¹⁰/ municipii locus / sepulturae datus / voluntate populi / decreto senatus / Tiburtium.

pontifex Salius and *curator* of the *fanum* for Hercules Victor. He then became *curator aquarum* of the town. His extensive activities in water engineering are attested by inscriptions of members of his *familia*, most likely his freedmen, on *fistulae* from Tibur and the nearby Trebula Suffenas.[76] Interestingly enough, another freedman of his, T. Sabidius Victor (A.284), had become a local *scriba* of the *res publica* of Tibur, most likely during his patron's tenure as water commissioner. His name is found on a waterpipe he had laid together with his scribal colleague, D. Rupilius Menander (A.281), most likely on behalf of Maximus.[77] Maximus went on to become *quinquennalis* and finally *patron* of the *municipium*, which honoured his service to the community with a grant of public land for his burial place. T. Sabidius Maximus was the first of a series of *scribae* of the second century AD to advance to become *patronus* of their city, often to remarkable enrichment for the community.[78] Sex. Caecilius Birronianus (A.33), son of a *scriba librarius* with a rich apparitorial career and *scriba librarius quaestorius* himself,[79] had held the prestigious office of *quinquennalis* in the Latin *colonia* of Sinuessa. He had the funds necessary to add a podium to the city's amphitheatre at his own expense.[80] Another beneficent scribal patron, P. Aelius Agathoclianus (A.2), adorned the public baths of Forum Clodii with marble and columns and celebrated his munificence with additional gifts of money to the local nobility. He had passed through a successful apparitorial and scribal career – he had been *scriba aedilicius, quaestorius sex primus* and *tribunicius maior* – and was headed to enter the *ordo equester* at the time he showed his gratitude towards the Etrurian city.[81]

---

[76] '*P(ublius) Sabidius Dionysius fec(it)*', *CIL* 14, 3532 (*CIL* 14, 3705a-b, *CIL* 15, 7904,1), found in *Tibur* as well as in a *balneum* of the nearby *Trebula Sufenas*, Marino (2014) 101; '*T(itus) Sabidius Helico fec(it)*', *CIL* 14, 3706a (*CIL* 15, 7905,2), and '*Publius Sabidius Hermes fec(it)*', *CIL* 14, 3707 (*CIL* 15, 7907a).

[77] *CIL* 14, 3699 (*CIL* 15, 7892, *InscrIt* 04-01, 625) [*Tibur*]: *T(ito) Sabidio Victore et D(ecimo) Rupilio Me/nandro scrib(is) r(ei) p(ublicae)*; cf. Eck, 1995, p. 208.

[78] Roman *scribae* who had become *patronus*, not discussed in detail: M. Aurelius Hermogenes (A.28) *scriba quaestorius, scriba tribunicius* and *sacerdos Genii coloniae* in Ostia. – Ti. Claudius Armiger (A.41) *scriba aedilicius* and *duumvir* in Sinuessa. – L. Varronius Capito (A.188) *scriba aedilicius* and *duumvir quinquennalis* as well as *curator aquarum* in Formiae.

[79] Sex. Caecilius Epagathus (A.34) had been *scriba librarius aedilium curulium, viator IIIvirum et IIIIvirum, scriba librarius quaestorius, apparitor Caesarum* and *scriba librarius tribunicius*.

[80] *CIL* 10, 4737 (*ILS* 1898a, *EAOR* 08, 37) [*Sinuessa*]: *Sex(tus) Caecilius Sex(ti) f(ilius) Quir(ina) Birronianus scriba librar(ius) / quaest(orius) III decuriarum quinquen(nalis) p(atronus) c(oloniae) Sinues(sanorum) / gratissimis podium amphitheatri a solo fecit*.

[81] *CIL* 11, 7555 (*ILS* 1886, *AE* 1889, 99) [*Forum Clodii*]: *P(ublio) Aelio P(ubli) f(ilio) Pal(atina) / Agathocliano / pontif(ici) praetori Laurenti/um Lavinatium scrib(ae) tribuni⁵/cio maior(i) scrib(ae) q(uaestorio) sexs(!) primo / scrib(ae) aedil(ium) curulium de/curial(i) pullario maiori / praef(ecto) fabr(um) III accens(o) velat(o) / Foroclodienses ex decr(eto)* ¹⁰ / *decur(ionum) patrono ob meri/ta eius et quod primus / ad thermas publicas / marmora et columnas / [de]derit cuius ob dedicati*¹⁵/*[onem] sportulas decu[ri]o/[nibus et IIIIII]viris [- - -]*.

The most extraordinary case of them all was a former *scriba aedilicius* and *quaestorius*, who did not settle in an Italian town but in the province of Hispania Tarraconensis. L. Aemilius Rectus (A.9) was a globetrotter. He allegedly was '*domo Roma*', but when we finally find him in Carthago Nova on the eastern coast of the Spanish peninsula, he had amassed a variety of honorary citizenships in southern Greece as well as eastern Spain. He had become a citizen of Lacedaemon and Argos in the province of Achaia as well as of Carthago Nova, Sicelli, Asso and Basti in the province of Hispania Tarraconensis.[82] It is quite possible that Rectus had earned his honours in Greece during a stint in the senatorial province as *scriba quaestorius*.[83] He must have moved to Spain for other reasons.[84] We can only imagine the enormous financial and social efforts that had earned him all these honorary citizenships. In Carthago Nova he was '*civis adlectus ob honorem aedilitatis*'; in Asso he had become the city's *patronus*. Rectus certainly was an influential figure. He was eventually bestowed with the *equus publicus* by Hadrian. And when he died, he could afford to have sizeable monuments

---

[82] Rectus' career is documented in four inscriptions, *CIL* 2, 3423 (*CartNova* 59) [Carthago Nova]: L(ucius) Aemilius M(arci) f(ilius) M(arci) nep(os) Quir(ina) Rectus domo Roma / qui et Carthaginensis et Sicellitan(us) et Assotan(us) et Lacedaemon(ius) / et Argivus et Bastetanus scrib(a) quaestorius scrib(a) aedilicius civis / adlectus ob honorem aedilitatis hoc opus testamento suo fieri iussit; *CIL* 2, 3424 (*ILS* 6953, *CartNova* 60) [Carthago Nova]: L(ucius) Aemilius M(arci) f(ilius) M(arci) nepos Quir(ina) Rectus / domo Roma qui et Carthag(inensis) et Sicellitanus / et [A]ss[o]tan(us) et Laced[ae]monius et Argi(v)us et Ba[s]titanus / et scriba quaestorius scriba aedilicius civis / adlectus ob honorem aedilitatis concordiae / decurionum testamento suo fieri iussit ⁵/ L(ucius) Aemilius Senex heres sine deductione / XX vel tributorum ex CCL libris argenti fecit; *CIL* 2, 5941 (*ILS* 6954) [Asso]: L(ucius) Aemil(ius) M(arci) f(ilius) M(arci) nep(os) Quirina Rectus domo Roma qui et Karth(aginensis) / et Sicellitanus et Assotanus et Lacedaemonius et Bastetanus / et Argius scriba quaestorius scriba aedilicius donatus equo publ(ico) / ab Imp(eratore) Caesare Traiano Hadriano Aug(usto) aedilis coloniae Karthagi(nensis) ⁵/ patronus rei publicae Assotanor(um) testamento suo / rei pub(licae) Assotan(orum) fieri iussit epulo annuo adiecto; *CIL* 2, 5942 [Asso] fragmentary.

[83] In this vein Daguet-Gagey, 2015, p. 217, n. 78.

[84] He could not possibly have been posted there as *scriba quaestorius* as Hispania Tarraconensis had been an imperial province; contra Abascal Palazón and Ramallo Asensio in *CartNova* 59. Rectus might have had familial ties with Aemilii Recti who provided *praefecti Aegypti* under Tiberius and Claudius; cf. Aemilius Rectus (father), PIR² A 394; L. Aemilius Rectus (son), PIR² A 395. Kavanagh (2001) 379f., 383 has suggested that, due to an error in the literary tradition, an otherwise unknown son of the older Aemilius Rectus is to be identified with a certain Aemilius Regulus, friend of the Stoic philosopher and co-conspirator against Caligula, Iulius Canus. This would mean that this new-found Aemilius Rectus was, on the one hand, related to the family of the philosopher Seneca through his aunt on his mother's side, on the other hand a native of Corduba in the province Baetica. The ties of the scribal Aemilius Rectus to Spain would make sense at last; cf. Purcell (1983) 160, who thinks that he was of provincial origin; on the discussion of his *tribus* and his origin see Abascal Palazón and Ramallo Asensio in *CartNova* 59, 216, n. 609. Rectus' declaration '*domo Roma*' could be explained by the Aemilii Recti's involvement in Roman politics. It is not hard to imagine that a sideline of the Aemilii Recti were domiciled in Rome as the family obviously played a significant part in the politics of the capital – while one son of Aemilius Rectus (the alleged Regulus) was put to death for conspiring against Caligula immediately before the latter's assasination, the other became *praefectus Aegypti* immediately after the accession of Claudius.

built as a memento of his social standing, the one in Carthago Nova adorned with an honorary statue made from 250 pounds of silver, the one in Asso accompanied by the donation of an annual banquet. Two massive inscribed marble blocks of approximately four metres in length, which presumably served as lintels for the buildings, are the impressive remnants of Rectus' post-scribal career as a local notable.[85]

There is a certain romantic value to interpreting the involvement of *scribae* in local communities as a return to their hometowns: sons of Italian cities setting out to make it big (or at least bigger) in Rome and eventually finding their way back, to their own and their native town's benefit. Alas, such a linear explanation faces methodological problems. Most of our evidence is epigraphic. As such, we are usually well informed about the findspot of the monument and, consequently, about the point of reference for a given individual at a certain point in his life. However, a reconstruction of an individual's origin is usually difficult, more often than not impossible. Parameters to narrow down the provenance of an individual, such as the *tribus* of the *scriba* matching the city's assigned voting tribe or his name suggesting possible familial connections to *familiae* traditionally located in certain areas or cities, provide clues at best. And in fact, there are only a few instances in which our evidence provides us with direct information about the origin of the individuals involved. C. Annius Priscus (A.15), who, according to his funerary monument had died in Rome, is marked as a native of the cisalpine colony of Eporedia (he also bore the city's *tribus*). L. Aemilius Rectus (A.9), whom we have seen to be active in communities of the Hispania Tarraconesis, is referred to as '*domo Roma*'. P. Petilius Colonus (A.131) hailed '*ex provincia Baetica*', from the city of Tucci. And Ti. Claudius Helvius Secundus (A.43) was honoured in absentia as '*Caesariensis*' by the citizens of the North African city of Caesarea. We might argue that these cases show that specifying one's place of origin was only relevant in cases of displacement. Often, this might very well have held true. We might, nevertheless, be wary of taking this reasoning as a given.

Connections of *scribae* to local communities could indeed be multifaceted. M. Ennius Vicetinus (A.67), as his *cognomen* suggests, must have been a native of the Venetian city of Vicetia.[86] He was inscribed in the

---

[85] See *CartNova* 59.
[86] *CIL* 10, 4832 [*Rufrae*]: *M(arcus) Ennius M(ani) f(ilius) / Men(enia) Vicetinus / scr(iba) aed(ilium) curulium / armamentarius decuria(lis)q(ue)* [5] */ decurio Vicetiae / dec(urio) colonia Saturnia / aedilis colonia Iulia / Felici classica Suessa / C(aius) Satilius C(ai) l(ibertus) Pileros* [10] */ apparitor tr(ibuni) pl(ebis) / Satilia uxor.*

city's *tribus*[87] and had been a *decurio* there. In addition, he had also been *decurio* in the Umbrian city of Saturnia, some four hundred kilometres south. He eventually assumed responsibility as *aedilis* of Sinuessa in Latium. This is not where we finally meet him, however. He was buried in Rufrae, some forty kilometres east of Sinuessa; this is where his tombstone was found. We might imagine that his career as *scriba* of the curule aediles led him to the greater Rome area. The exact circumstances of Vicetinus' career elude us, however. Due to the matter-of-fact nature of our epigraphic evidence, explaining the attestation of a *scriba* in any given city is mostly guesswork; even more so as most cases are far less detailed and informative than Vicetinus' dossier. Determining the origin of the attested Roman *scribae* and with it the areas of recruitment of the scribal *apparitores* is, thus, a near impossibility. Even though nearly half of the *scribae* and a quarter of the *scribae librarii* are attested outside of Rome, sticking pins in a map would not do to accurately assess the phenomenon. Such a map would rather measure the activity of *scribae*[88] and show that, besides Rome, *scribae* mainly settled and got involved in local communities in central Italy, i.e. in proximity to the capital – an insight that might not surprise us, after all. We might imagine that the system of rotating scribal duty and the possibility of renting out one's place in a *decuria* (see Chapter 3) must have made it feasible for *scribae* to settle in the broader vicinity of Rome, thus having easy access to the capital when needed while being able to pursue other activities and live the best of both worlds, the global and the local. It is the way of life we find with M. Tullius (A.178), who had been on duty in Cilicia with Cicero and, upon returning from the province, would be found '*rure*' rather than in Rome.[89]

That said, I would venture to postulate that Italians must naturally have made up a fair share of the pool of *scribae*.[90] The basic prerequisite for entry into a scribal *decuria* was Roman citizenship, while relations to a sympathetic patron most certainly came a close second. As such, the Italian Peninsula and proximity to the political centre had been the predestined area of recruitment for most of the period investigated. The traditional notion that *apparitores* were '*Bruttiani*', i.e. former Italics relegated to fill lower posts in the state, might have held some truth. Horace was certainly

---

[87] Bertolazzi and Lamonaca (2010) 282.
[88] In particular, the bulk of inscriptions for *scribae* found in Rome might not accurately represent the actual share of *scribae* recruited from the *plebs* of the capital as the inscriptions' findspot was necessarily the usual place of residence of active *scribae*.
[89] Cic. *fam.* 5. 20. 6; cf. Chapter 2.
[90] Cf. Purcell (1983) 160f.

not the only one to agree that the amenities of *scriba*-ship were attractive to ambitious Italians of an ordinary social background. Only four *scribae* can, with some certainty, be identified as hailing from outside of the Apennine Peninsula. It may be telling that their social backgrounds show very close ties with Roman magisterial representatives.[91] The prerequisites to becoming a *scriba* were undoubtedly unequally distributed – geographical origin was likely not the sole factor.[92]

The Tale of a *Scriba*

The twentieth of July was a special day in the life of the late second-century AD city of Ostia. It was the day when L. Fabius Eutychus and his wife Artoria would go to the forum of the city to honour the *memoria* of their beloved son. They would position themselves in front of the equestrian statue of their deceased offspring to greet the city's *decuriones* as well as the *decuriae* of *scribae cerarii*, *librarii* and *lictores* in order to present them with a gift of money. It had been their late son's birthday.

Some years earlier, a visitor to the city would have witnessed a very similar procession, that time one in overt mourning rather than in solemn remembrance. C. Domitius Fabius Hermogenes (A.63) had been honoured with a *funus publicum*, a public funeral.[93] Eutychus and Artoria, the grieving parents, would have been seen heading the procession of *decuriones* and apparitorial *decuriae* escorting the body through the city to the forum, where Eutychus would have held the funeral oration, seeking solace in his son's virtues and his successful career while promising a charity worth 50,000 sesterces to honour the memory of Hermogenes. The city, in turn, resolved to honour the deceased with an equestrian statue and extraordinary

---

[91] Ti. Claudius Helvius Secundus (A.43) was likely the grandson of a veteran settled in the North African colony of Caesarea; H. G. Pflaum (1968) 156. M. Servilius Eunicus (A.161), whom we find in the Lydian city of Nysa, was a descendant of a native, who was granted Roman citizenship by P. Servilius Isauricus, *proconsul* of Asia 46–44 BC; Zucca (2010) 33; contra Ramsay (1967) 61. Stertinius Maximus Eutyches (A.168) in Ephesos most certainly was the son of another *scriba librarius* attested in the city, C. Stertinius Orpex (A.169), who had been a freedman of the *consul suffectus* of the year AD 23, C. Stertinius Maximus; Eck (1999) 15. P. Petilius Colonus (A.131) was a native of the Baetican city of Tucci. The circumstances of his recruitment are not known.

[92] A difficult passage in the Theodosian Code from the year AD 389 mentions *decuriales*, who used to be recruited in pairs from the most important city of every province; '*decuriales, quos binos esse ex singulis quibusque urbibus omnium provinciarum veneranda decrevit antiquitas*', COD. THEOD. 14. 1. 3. The reference is not clear, however. Mommsen (1887) I 370 and Purcell (1983) 170 interpret the passage as a reference to *scribae* and their provincial recruitment. This identification is hypothetical, however.

[93] On the *funus publicum* and its elements see Wesch-Klein (1993) 85; cf. Toynbee (1971) 55f.

The Tale of a Scriba

Figure 5.2 The remains of the tomb of C. Domitius Fabius Hermogenes at the via Ostiense (on the right in between the cypress trees) as seen through the remains of the Porta Romana (front) in Ostia sometime after AD 1915. (Luciano Morpurgo)

admission to the *ordo decurionum*, owing to his devotion and commitment for the city. The procession would then have proceeded to the necropolis at the *via Ostiense*, where Hermogenes was put to rest in a richly decorated sarcophagus, sepulchred in a stately tomb at the most privileged spot right next to the *Porta Romana* (see Fig. 5.2).[94] It is the place where Hermogenes' funerary inscription was found.

> C(aio) Domitio L(uci) fil(io) Pal(atina) F[abio]
> Hermogeni
> e[quiti] Romano scribae aedil(ium) curul(ium) dec(urioni) adle[ct(o)]
> fl[am(ini)] divi H]ad[ria]ni in cuius sacerdotio solus ac primus lud[os]
> 5 [scaenic]os sua p[e]cunia fecit aedili hunc splendissimus ordo decur[ion(um)]
> [fun(ere) publ]ico hon[o]ravit eique statuam equestrem subscriptione ob amor[em et]
> [industr]iam o[mne]m in foro ponendam pecunia publica decre[v]it
> [in l]oc[um e]ius [ae]dil(em) substituendum non putavit in solacium Fab[i pa]tris
> [qu]i ob honores [ei h]a[bi]t[o]s HS L m(ilia) n(ummum) rei publicae dedit ex quorum usuris quincun[ci]bus

---

[94] The circumstances of finding the tomb and the fragment of the sarcophagus, decorated with scenes from the life of Achilles in Dante Vaglieri (1910) 12–14, 17–18 w. Fig. 4. On the type of its decoration G. Koch and Sichtermann (1982) 127–31, who date it to around AD 200; cf. Giuliani (1989); on the sepulchral monument Heinzelmann (2000) 127f.

10 [qu]odannis XIII K[al(endas)] Aug(ustas) die natali eius decurionib(us) ✶ DL
      praesentibus in foro ante [statuas]
      [divi]dantur dec[u]rialibus scribis ceraris ✶ XXXVII s(emissem) libraris ✶ XII
      s(emissem) item lictoribus ✶ [XXV]
      L(ucius) Fabius Sp(uri) f(ilius) Eutychus lictor curiatius scrib[a c]er[arius]
      et librarius q(uin)q(uennalis) collegi(i) fabr(orum) tignuar(ium) Ostiens(ium) et
      Artoria eius par[entes].[95]

Nobody would have foreseen Hermogenes' extraordinary honours. His father, Eutychus, had been a freedman[96] and carpenter in Ostia. He had married Artoria, a member of a local family of craftsmen.[97] These were humble origins for a future Roman *eques*, indeed. Eutychus must, however, soon have moved on from carpentry and sought an apparitorial career in the city. He got hold of a place in the scribal *decuriae* of Ostia to become *librarius* and *scriba cerarius* (A.257). Eutychus' apparitorial career eventually culminated in a post as *lictor curiatius* in Rome.[98] It must have been his father's success as an *apparitor* which primed the young Hermogenes for a career in the *decuriae* of the capital. Following in the footsteps of his father, he aspired to become a *scriba* of the *aediles curules*. For Hermogenes, holding a place in a scribal *decuria* must have entailed substantial social advancement. When we eventually find him back in his home town, he had become a local notable. He was now *flamen* of the cult of the deified emperor Hadrian and had been 'the first to stage and pay for theatrical performances' for the benefit of the city. The scribal post in the service of the Roman people brought him not only sizeable financial assets, but also new and eminent social relations. Hermogenes had obviously made an impression on a powerful senatorial patron, most likely while he had been in his service as *scriba*. He now bore the name of the consular C. Domitius Dexter, the future confidant of the emperor Septimius Severus.[99] Most likely as a result of this new-found fortune,

---

[95] *CIL* 14, 4642; lacunae supplemented by the nearly identical honorary inscription found on the forum on a basis for an equestrian statue, *CIL* 14, 353 (*ILS* 6148).

[96] L. Fabius Eutychus was a *Spuri filius*. The filiation, together with his Greek *cognomen*, hints at his unfree background. Hermogenes, who most likely inherited the voting district from his birth father (the *tribus* of his possible adoptive father is unknown; PIR² D 144), was registered in the Palatina, the *tribus* of the freedmen of Ostia; cf. Mouritsen (2011) 127.

[97] Besides other Artorii (*CIL* 14, 617a; 618), a L. Artorius Hilarianus is known from the *fasti* of the corporation of boatsmen; *CIL* 14, 251 (Commodus).

[98] On the enigmatic nature of the *lictores curiatii* see Scheid and Granino Cecere (1999) 92f. It is possible that Ostia also had *lictores curiatii*. The fact that Eutychus gives this post as his most prestigious, above his post as *scriba*, suggests an employment in the capital, however.

[99] Dexter had been *consul suffectus* in the last years of Marcus Aurelius' reign. He became *praefectus urbi* in AD 193 and *consul ordinarius* in AD 196; PIR² D 144; cf. Meiggs (1973) 211; d'Arms (1976) 401.

The Tale of a Scriba

C. Domitius Fabius Hermogenes, as he was named after his adoption, became *eques Romanus* and entered the second order of Roman society.[100] Hermogenes' massive career upswing was abruptly halted when death suddenly overtook him as he was in office as *aedilis* in his home town. It ended an auspicious career and prompted the extraordinary measures taken by the city for its successful and generous son.

The story of Hermogenes' life, condensed into two nearly identical inscriptions – one at his tomb, another on a base for an equestrian statue found on the forum[101] – exhibits perfectly the characteristics of Roman *scriba*-ship I have identified in the preceding chapters. Humble beginnings made an apparitorial career as *scriba* a worthwhile career trajectory. The opportunities of the post were bound to further his social advancement. His place in a scribal *decuria* provided him with financial benefits as well as eminent social connections, which helped catapult him to the *ordo equester* and to a prestigious local career. We can only guess at the possible career paths his premature death prevented.

The social history of the Roman *scribae* is marked by outstanding social mobility. The Republican stereotype portrayed the *scriba* as a man of low social origins, poised to seize the social and financial opportunities of the office and make his way to the higher echelons of the social pyramid. Rapid and far reaching social advancement made the *scriba* of the Republican historiographic tradition a contentious figure. This combination of humble social beginnings with opportunities for social advancement furthered by the apparitorial post is substantiated by the imperial epigraphic tradition. Mainly recruited from the lower strata of Roman society, *scribae* could indeed aspire to climb to the equestrian order and pursue a military or even procuratorial career. The benefits offered by the scribal position in the *decuriae* of the capital often led *scribae* to assume magisterial responsibility and find eminent standing in local communities.

---

[100] Salomies (1992) 26–30, type E nomenclature; cf. Lindsay (2009) 87–96.
[101] The funerary inscription, found at his tomb, *CIL* 14, 4642, with fragments from the epistyle, *CIL* 14, 4643. The nearly identical, but fragmentary honorary inscription on a basis for an equestrian statue, found on the forum, *CIL* 14, 353 (*ILS* 6148), cf. Marchese (2003) 319 for a possible fragment of Hermogenes' equestrian statue.

CHAPTER 6

The Roman Scriba *Reimagined*

A Classical Model

Ab scribendo autem scriba nomen accepit, officium exprimens vocabuli qualitate.[1]

Throughout antiquity, the Roman *scribae* were defined by their primary activity: writing. Still in the early seventh century AD, Isidore, who had been bishop of Hispalis in southern Spain and had compiled and edited the knowledge of classical antiquity in his *Etymologiae*, attested to the congruity of denomination, activity and function of a Roman *scriba*. Writing, or more precisely the ability to write, was what had defined the *scribae* since the early Republic, earned them their title and set them apart from other members of Roman society. The Roman *scribae*, in their role as *apparitores* of the Republican magistrates, were experts hired to cater to the documentary needs of the lean Republican state. It was 'writing' in a broader sense – literacy as well as numeracy in the service of the state – that enabled and even empowered the Roman *scribae*. Their cultural capital was a prerequisite for the entry into the *decuriae* of the scribal *apparitores* of the Roman magistrates. A place among the apparitorial *scribae*, in turn, was bound to open up new financial and social possibilities, which in most cases lead to social advancement.

The Roman *scribae* acted as the administrators and guardians of the public repository of legal and financial documentation, which was stored on wooden wax tablets, the so-called *tabulae publicae*. As the importance of literate administrative practice increased steadily in the course of the middle and late Republic, the Roman *scribae* were bound to gain in importance, influence and esteem. Their expertise in literacy and numeracy and their handling of the *tabulae publicae* – be it in the staff of a magistrate or

---

[1] IsID. *orig.* 6.14.2: 'The *scriba* got his name from writing, expressing his function by the character of his title'. Transl. S. A. Barney et al. (adapted).

at the archive in the *aerarium* at Rome – resulted in a monopolisation of administrative literate practice. The *scribae* had eventually become the authority on the public repository, not only with regard to its content but also concerning its form and function. The Roman *scribae* came to stand for the *tabulae publicae*, which they swore to diligently make, use and keep. They had become their symbolical representatives. It was to their personal fidelity (*fides*) that the public repository was entrusted. The Roman magistrates were still expected to supervise the Roman *scribae* and the *tabulae publicae*. Effective oversight was difficult however, even more so when the knowledge lay with those to be supervised. The *fides* of the *scribae* and eventually also corresponding legislation were expected to keep the *scriba*-ship and Roman administration free from corrupt practices. The systematics of the Roman *decuriae* of *apparitores*, however, furthered nepotism and profiteering as the aristocratic elite themselves were able to influence the composition of the pools of *scribae* to their own and their scribal protégés' benefit. The history of the Roman *scribae* is, thus, not least a history of social relations. It was often what decided between honest performance of one's duties and the potential abuse of power.

A post as *scriba* was lucrative. Despite the fact that their apparitorial position bore the stigma of paid labour, the *scribae* were held in high esteem. Their position of trust at the heart of public documentary practice, handling the state's written arcana, entailed significant prestige and brought with it social and financial benefits. Close proximity to senatorial office holders was a recipe for profit, even more so as the *scribae* were responsible for their superiors' bookkeeping. Protection by a powerful senatorial patron could easily result in profiteering and even complicity in corrupt and illegal practices. The lucre of the office usually translated directly into social mobility. It belonged to the stereotypical characterisation of the Roman *scriba* that he was of low and obscure social origins, of libertine ancestry even. As a result, the social advancement of holders of the post was usually outstanding, their ascent steep. As such, their social success was controversial, especially if the scribal upstart managed extraordinarily to rise as high as the senatorial *ordo*. Social advancement was a constant in the history of the Roman *scribae*. Their adjacency to the equestrian order, alleged for the Republic, can be substantiated for the imperial period. The cultural, financial and social benefits of the *scriba*-ship facilitated upward mobility, which for a significant proportion of *scribae* resulted in eminence in local communities or even equestrian careers in the imperial military or administration.

Remnants and Revivals

As a relic of the Roman Republican state, the apparitorial *scribae* already played a marginalised part in the literate administrative practice of the Empire. In the government of the Later Roman Empire, they finally ceased to have a dedicated, functional place. The administration of the newly organised state since Diocletian was built on the administrative facilities of the emperors, which were continually expanded and complexified. Compared with Republican times, the civil service was now a personnel-hungry apparatus, pervaded by writing and documentation. What *scribae* had been responsible for in personal union now kept a host of *officiales* busy – evidently in an unprecedented quantity and quality.[2] Since the third century, administrative posts had increasingly been staffed with military personnel, to the disadvantage of the civil *apparitores*.[3] As a result, the *scribae* found no entry into the tightly hierarchised, permanent imperial bureaus, the *scrinia*. The fully fledged administrative system of the Later Roman Empire, as becomes apparent in the *Notitia Dignitatum*, the late fourth-century state handbook, does not know *scribae*.[4]

Testimonies of Roman *scribae* become scarce in the course of the third century. Already M. Aurelius Hermogenes (A.28), who had been *scriba* of the quaestors and tribunes sometime around the middle of the century and advanced to become *procurator* under Valerian and Gallienus, was a singular occurrence (see Chapter 5). C. Statius Celsus (A.166), a *scriba librarius* and *eques Romanus*, is the last known Roman *scriba*, attested immediately before Diocletian's remodelling of the state. A fragment of a pictorial senatorial sarcophagus made in a workshop of the capital but found in the African town of Ad Mercurium, reworked to fit Celsus' equestrian status, can be dated to the seventies of the third century.[5] What we find subsequently are but remnants of the old *scriba*-ship. The *decuriae* of the capital seem to have survived, albeit only rudimentarily. Their members seem to have struggled to secure their privileges. A rescript by the emperor Constantine of the year AD 335 mentions *ordines decuriarum scribarum librariorum et lictoriae consularis* and ascertains their traditional right to 'perform the formalities of the office staffs in civil cases and in the

---

[2] On the civil service in general A. H. M. Jones (1964) I 563–606; cf. the schematic outline in Delmaire (1995); on the *officia* of the governors Palme (1999).
[3] Palme (1999) 101.
[4] Cf. A. H. M. Jones (1964) I 601, who has argued that the *quaestor* mentioned in the *officium* of the *proconsul Achaiae*, Not. dig. Or. 21. 9, was in fact a *scriba quaestorius*. There is no substantiating evidence, however.
[5] Himmelmann (1973) 4f.; Wrede (2001) 72 w. Taf. 16,2.

issuance of petitions'.⁶ It must have been, above all, a financial privilege, independent of any specific governmental function. We meet the *decuriae urbis Romae* in further legislation of the fourth century. In AD 357/60, we find mention of an *ordo* that encompassed *decuriae 'librariorum vel fiscalium sive censualium'*.⁷ Whether the *librarii* mentioned were direct successors of the *scribae librarii* of old is at least doubtful, however. Constantine had reorganised the senatorial chancery under a *magister census* as the *officium censuale*, which seems to have absorbed and reorganised the old *decuriae*.⁸ Later legal propositions simply name *decuriales* and *decuriae*, respectively, leaving us in the dark about their internal organisation and actual affiliation to the original *scriba*-ship.⁹ The title of *scriba* seems to have continued to be used in these newly organised *decuriae*, however. We eventually find *scribae* active in the senate.

During the Republic and the Empire, the senate had been exclusive to senators – not only in terms of membership but also in terms of physical attendance.¹⁰ The written versions of *senatus consulta* were attended to by the senators themselves. And when Caesar had introduced the writing of *acta senatus*, it had been senators rather than clerical staff who were responsible.¹¹ The post had eventually become institutionalised in the senatorial *ab actis senatus*.¹² Our fourth- and fifth-century sources now attest to two non-senatorial *scribae senatus*, who likely fulfilled these same tasks. A tombstone found in Rome marks the death of Laurentius (A.76), *scriba senatus*, for the year AD 451.¹³ We find the same Laurentius in the preface of the Theodosian Code where he assumes responsibility for the composition of the acts of the senate in his role as '*exceptor amplissimi senatus*'.¹⁴ Another *scriba senatus*, Aemilius Eucharpus (A.7), is attested on

---

⁶ COD. *Theod*. 8.9.1: *Ordines decuriarum scribarum librariorum et lictoriae consularis oblatis precibus meruerunt, ut in civilibus causis et editionibus libellorum officiorum sollemnitate fungantur, ita ut vetusta aetate servatum est*, transl. C. Pharr.
⁷ COD. *Theod*. 14.1.1.
⁸ Chastagnol (1960) 76f.; cf. Mommsen (1887) I 370f.
⁹ COD. *Theod*. 14.1.2 (AD 386); COD. *Theod*. 14.1.3 (AD 389); COD. *Theod*. 14.1.4 (AD 404); COD. *Theod*. 14.1.5 (AD 407); COD. *Theod*. 14.1.6 (AD 410).
¹⁰ Talbert (1984) 195f.
¹¹ Caesar's introduction of the *acta* in 59 BC; SUET. *Iul*. 20; Coudry (1994) 79f. Cf. Cicero, who, during his consulate of 63 BC, had witness statements against Catilina recorded by senators; CIC. *Sul*. 41–43.
¹² The first holder of the office we know by name was Iunius Rusticus in AD 29; TAC. *ann*. 5.4.1. On the later holders of the post and its evolution Coudry (1994) 87f.; cf. Talbert (1984) 310–13.
¹³ CIL 6, 33721 (*ICUR*-08, 23064; *ILS* 1958; *ILCV* 705): *Hic quiescit in pace Laurentius / [s]criba senatus dep(ositus) die IIII Iduum Mart(ium) / Adelfio v(iro) c(larissimo) cons(ule)*.
¹⁴ COD. *Theod*. gesta. 8: *Fl(avius) Laurentius exceptor amplissimi senatus edidi sub d(ie) VIII k(alendas) Ian(uarias)*.

a sarcophagus dated to the fourth century.[15] The introduction of *scribae* to the senate seems to have been a result of Constantine's reorganisation of the senatorial chancery. The newly appointed *magister census* with his *censuales* was put in charge of matters concerning the senate, including the administration of the senate's resolutions and its archive.[16] We meet these *censuales* together with *scribae* in an episode related in the *Historia Augusta*.[17] The author's attribution of the episode to the reign of Maximinus Thrax and his appeal to an obviously fake authority cannot conceal the fact that the account evidently referred to his own times of the late fourth century.[18] According to Iulius Capitolinus, everyone else except the senators had to leave the building during a so-called *senatus consultum tacitum*. In this extraordinary situation, the senators themselves 'minuted (*exciperent*) and fulfilled the tasks of the *censuales* and *scribae*'. The clerical staff usually present at senate meetings were likely the same *censuales* and *(scribae) librarii* we find as part of the newly organised *decuriae*.

The post of *scriba* lived on in the Later Roman Empire. It was a life in new contexts, however. The designation of *scriba* turns up in new environments, seemingly revived to describe functions that bore similarities to the role filled by classical *scriba*-ship. The author of the vita of Probus in the *Historia Augusta* mentions '*regesta* of the *scribae* of the *porticus porphyretica*' among sources he had consulted.[19] The *porticus porphyretica* is commonly identified with the *porticus Purpuretica* of the *forum Traiani*.[20] Whether the scribal association of the *porticus porphyretica* was the successor organisation to the former *scribae* of the state or an association of different scribes is impossible to say, however. Their archive in the portico seems to have housed documentation of public importance as it is mentioned in the same breath as the collections of the libraries of Tiberius and Hadrian as well as

[15] *CIL* 6, 37098 (*ILS* 9041; *AE* 1907, 132): *D(is) M(anibus) / Aemilio Eucharpo eq(uiti) R(omano) / scribae senatus / qui vixit annis LVI (h)or(is) VIIII* [5]/ *filia et heres huius / patri suo bene merenti // Eusebi // Eusebi.* On the date of the richly decorated sarcophagus Gatti (1906) 303.
[16] Chastagnol (1960) 76f.; cf. Mommsen (1887) I 370f.
[17] Hist. Aug. *Gord.* 12. 3–4: *Hunc autem morem apud veteres necessitates publicae reppererunt, ut, si forte aliqua vis ab hostibus immineret, quae cogeret vel humilia captare consilia vel aliqua constituere, quae non prius oporteret dici quam effici, vel si nollent ad amicos aliqua permanare, senatus consultum tacitum fieret, ita ut non scribae, non servi publici, non censuales illis actibus interessent, senatores exciperent, senatores omnium officia censualium scribarumque conplerent, ne quid forte proderetur. Factum est ergo senatus consultum tacitum, ne res ad Maximinum perveniret.*
[18] On the fictitious authority Iunius Cordus see Syme (1983); Lippold (1991) 84–93.
[19] Hist. Aug. *Prob.* 2. 1: *Usus autem sum, ne in aliquo fallam carissimam mihi familiaritatem tuam, praecipue libris ex bibliotheca Ulpia, aetate mea thermis Diocletianis, et item ex domo Tiberiana, usus etiam [ex] regestis scribarum porticus porphyreticae, actis etiam senatus ac populi.*
[20] The *porticus* is attested on a slave collar of the fourth century, *CIL* 15, 7191; cf. Platner (1965); Papi (1995).

the archives of the senate and the people. The *cura annona*, newly organised in the early thirties of the fourth century, likely employed subaltern clerks with the title of *scriba*, thus making reference to the Republican foundations of the office. An imperial rescript of AD 370 makes reference to a *scriba* working in the offices of the *praefectus annonae*.[21] Another *scriba* subordinate to the *praefectus urbi* is attested for the meat supply.[22] In AD 411, we unexpectedly meet *scribae* at the Conference of Carthage, convened to settle the lingering dispute between Donatists and Catholics. The acts of the convention mention a certain Nampius (A.119), *scriba* of the *officium* of the legate of Carthage, and Rufinianus (A.149), *scriba* of the *curator* of Carthage.[23] It is the only and exceptional mention of *scribae* in any provincial *officium* of the Later Roman Empire.[24] Listed above the *exceptores* and *notarii*, they clearly constituted a distinct charge, a fact that is reflected in their duties.[25] While the *exceptores* and *notarii* are mainly found minuting,[26] the *scribae* were no mere recorders and copyists, but seem rather to have performed higher secretarial tasks. Echoing the duties performed by their classical eponyms, they played the role of consultants and antiquary specialists, managing public documents.[27]

In Constantinople, Constantine established two *praetores*, one of which, the *praetor tutelarius*, was assigned a *scriba*.[28] We do not know about this office holder's scribal duties and functions, however. John the Lydian relates a representative function as an attendant of the consul, in whose entourage the *scriba* carried and symbolically showcased writing tablets[29] – a performance very reminiscent of the Republican apparitorial roots of the *scriba*-ship.

---

[21] COD. *Theod.* 14. 17. 6. On the reforms of the *cura annonae* Chastagnol (1960) 52, 62; Pavis d'Escurac (1976) 43f., 289.
[22] *CIL* 6, 1770 (*CIL* 6, 31927; *AE* 1980, 42) in AD 362/3; cf. Chastagnol (1953) 13f.
[23] *Gesta Conl. Carth.* 1. 1; 2. 1; 3. 1.
[24] The almost contemporary *Notitia Dignitatum* fails to make mention of *scribae* while the other charges of the *officium* present at the conference are listed; NOT. *dig. Occ.* 18. 2–14.
[25] Teitler (1985) 294 n. 188.
[26] For the *exceptores* see A. H. M. Jones (1964) I 587f.; Teitler (1985) 73–85.
[27] Rufinianus intervenes much more often than Nampius. During the first day he reads out loud the *mandatum* as well as the list of the Donatists; *Gesta Conl. Carth.* 1. 148; 1. 149; 1. 157; 1. 163; 1. 176. He also gives the numbers of the Catholic and Donatist priests; *Gesta Conl. Carth.* 1. 207; 1. 213; 1. 214; asserts Marcellinus, the chairman, about the correct constitution of the delegations according to the edict; *Gesta Conl. Carth.* 1. 218; and gives the time of day; *Gesta Conl. Carth.* 1. 219. During the third meeting he specifies the date of archival documents; *Gesta Conl. Carth.* 3. 172; 3. 173. Nampius relates the date of an edict; *Gesta Conl. Carth.* 1. 27; and gives the number of Catholic bishops; *Gesta Conl. Carth.* 1. 216. Cf. Lancel (1972–1991) 343 n. 1.
[28] LYD. *mag.* 2. 30. 4.
[29] LYD. *mens.* 1. 28.

Unlike in the central imperial administration, in the cities of the empire, the scribal tradition seems to have been uninterrupted. Municipal *scribae* still seem to have played their part in the Later Roman Empire – or were at least expected to do so. In AD 341, the emperor Constantius II decreed that local *scribae*, besides *tabularii* as well as *decuriones* and their sons, were not allowed to 'perform imperial service on any office staff'. Rather, they should be constrained to their duties in their own communities.[30] As the burden on local officals went unabated, the appeal of imperial service must have remained great for local *scribae* throughout the third century AD. The emperors Gratian, Valentinian II and Theodosius felt the need to reiterate and reinforce the regulations in AD 380.[31] Municipal *scribae* are finally attested in the year AD 409 as part of the public staff, customarily involved in the literate administrative practice of their communities.[32]

The Legacy of an Idea

The legacy of the Roman *scriba*-ship reached far. Despite the fact that the classical tradition of the post had come to an end with the Constantinian reforms at the latest, the idea of Roman *scriba*-ship survived. It is as late as the thirties of the sixth century AD that we find a *scriba* in what was arguably the last polity to identify heavily with Roman structures and tradition.[33] Cassiodorus, praetorian prefect of the Ostrogothic Kingdom during the years AD 533–7, appointed a certain Deusdedit (A.253) to the post of *scriba Ravennas*, i.e. *scriba* in Ravenna, the capital of the *regnum Italiae*.[34] That the praetorian prefect chose to designate Deusdedit's new position with the term *scriba* is highly remarkable. The *scriba* last known to serve in the civil service had been a *scriba senatus* in the middle of the fifth century. Attestations for municipal *scribae* break off at the beginning of the fourth century. Thus, while we know of several individuals from the ranks of Ravenna's court and municipal administration of the period with the name of Deusdedit, evidently, none bears the title of *scriba*. What we find are individuals known as *exceptor* or *forensis*, titles common at that time for holders of clerical and notarial positions. Further identification

---

[30] COD. *Theod.* 8. 2. 1 (12. 1. 31; COD. *Iust.* 10. 71. 1); transl. C. Pharr.
[31] COD. *Theod.* 8. 2. 3.
[32] COD. *Theod.* 11. 8. 3 (COD. *Iust.* 1. 55. 9).
[33] Maier (2005); cf. O'Donnell (1979) 65.
[34] CASSIOD. *Var.* 12. 21.

The Legacy of an Idea

of Deusdedit is, thus, not possible; his institutional association remains unknown.[35]

At the time of writing, Cassiodorus had been responsible for the coordination and administration of a slowly deteriorating kingdom, which faced increasing hostility from the East and emperor Justinian, who would eventually gain the upper hand and take Ravenna in AD 540. Cassiodorus' efforts to rally the resources and manpower of the Ostrogothic Kingdom are evident in his letter to Deusdedit, which was, in fact, only one of a series of similar communications with other office holders in the kingdom.[36] Cassiodorus' central message was to close ranks in the face of imminent war. As a result and indeed fortunately for us, he goes to great lengths to remind Deusdedit of his duties and responsibilities, giving us an outline and appraisal of the post of '*scriba*' in the Ostrogothic Kingdom. What we find shows that Cassiodorus' denomination for Deusdedit, as peculiar and antiquarian as it must have seemed already at that time (and even more so for the modern observer), was without a doubt highly intentional. His admonitions to Deusdedit and his outline of the latter's duties and responsibilities could pass for a – somewhat inflated – description of the classical *scriba*-ship I have outlined in the course of this study.

> Deusdedit scribae Ravennati Senator praefectus praetorio
> Scribarum officium securitas solet esse cunctorum, quando ius omnium eius sollicitudine custoditur. Alios enim depopulantur incendia, alios nudat furtiva subreptio, nonnullis neglegentia perit quod diligens auctor adquirit; sed de fide publica robustissime reparatur quicquid a privatis amittitur. Diligentior est in alienis quam potest esse cura de propriis: non admonitus facit quod vix rogatus impleret et requisitus non potest negare quod is cuius interest se fatetur amisisse. Armarium ipsius fortuna cunctorum est et merito refugium omnium dicitur, ubi universorum securitas invenitur. Ad paterna transit officia si incorrupte sit veritas custodita. Nam sicut diligens genitor servat quod otiosus successor inveniat, sic arbiter partium nullum patitur propria utilitate fraudari. Et ideo tantae rei iugiter praecipimus esse custodem ut qui hactenus de integritate placuisti nulla debeas varietate fuscari. Vide quid tibi committitur: antiqua fides et cotidiana diligentia. Dirimis iurgantium litem: apud cunctos praesules de tua cura litigatur et tu potius iudicas, qui causarum vincla dissolvis. Hoc honorabile decus, indisputabile testimonium: vox antiqua chartarum cum de tuis adytis incorrupta processerit, cognitores reverenter excipiunt; litigantes quamvis improbi coacti tamen oboediunt. Et cum fas sit promulgatam sententiam suspendi, tibi non licet obviari. Quocirca non habeat venale propositum. Tinea documentorum est oblatio maligna

---

[35] On the possibilities of identification of Deusdedit see the elaborate commentary by Giardina et al., (2014–2015) comm. on 12. 21. 1. They argue for an identification as *exceptor curia civitatis*, i.e. the municipal office holder rather than the official of the court. Deusdedit's appointment by the praetorian prefect might make a case for the office's localisation at the royal court, however.
[36] The other office holders in Castritius (1982) 230 n. 30.

redimentis, dum quaerunt consumere quod se cognoverint impedire. Pascat te editio decora veritatis, facultas tua habeatur integritas. Da petentibus quae olim facta sunt. Translator esto, non conditor antiquorum gestorum. Exemplar velut anulum ceris imprime, ut sicut vultus expressa non possunt signa refugere ita manus tua ab authentico nequeat discrepare. Quod si te aliquis iniqua subreptione traduxerit, quemadmodum in alia causa tibi adquiescat credi, quem scit potuisse corrumpi? Inpugnat te fraude sua et facile convincit, quem in una parte deceperit. Ama iustitiam, de qua nemo queritur, ut etiam iratus testimonium salubre possit dicere qui te in cassum voluit deviare. Publicum est omne quod feceris, dum aut laudatus gratiam aut accusatus invenire possis offensam.[37]

Cassiodorus' characterisation of the *scriba* portrays Deusdedit at the centre of administrative literate practice. We find him amongst archival material, making, keeping and using the documents entrusted to his care. He has a monopoly on reading and copying the pieces of writing, is designated and, in fact, vital to giving an account of their content. He is a knowledgeable and indispensable archivist.

The central and most remarkable passage of the letter to the *scriba* is Cassiodorus' memento to Deusdedit that, as a result of his monopoly position, he is expected to exhibit not only due diligence on a daily basis but also to observe the '*antiqua fides*'. It was in fact the very *fides* that had been expected from the *scribae* of old as a result of their authority over the *tabulae publicae*. Cassiodorus' plea revolves around this loyalty and dutifulness of the *scriba* to resist any abuse of power and venality in his daily dealings with making,

---

[37] CASSIOD. *Var.* 12. 21. 1–5. Cf. the useful yet neither always complete nor literal translation by T. Hodgkin: 'Senator, Praetorian Praefect, to Deusdedit, a Scribe of Ravenna. The Scribe's office is the great safeguard of the rights of all men. The evidence of ownership may be destroyed by fire or purloined by dishonest men, but the State by making use of the Scribe's labours is able to make good the loss so sustained. The Scribe is more diligent in other men's business than they are in their own. His muniment-chest is the refuge of all the oppressed, and the repository of the fortunes of all men. In testimony of your past integrity, and in the hope that no change will mar this fair picture, we appoint you to this honourable office. Remember that ancient Truth is committed to your keeping, and that it often really rests with you, rather than with the Judge, to decide the disputes of litigants. When your indisputable testimony is given, and when the ancient voice of charters proceeds from your sanctum, Advocates receive it with reverence, and suitors, even evil-intentioned men, are constrained into obedience. Banish, therefore, all thoughts of venality from your mind. The worst moth that gets into papers and destroys them is the gold of the dishonest litigant, who bribes the Scribes to make away with evidence which he knows to be hostile. Thus, then, be ready always to produce to suitors genuine old documents; and, on the other hand, transcribe only, do not compose ancient proceedings. Let the copy correspond to the original as the wax to the signet-ring, that as the face is the index of the emotions so your handwriting may not err from the authentic original in anything. If a claimant succeed in enticing you even once from the paths of honesty, vainly will you in any subsequent case seek to obtain his credence for any document that you may produce; for he will always believe that the trick which has been played once may be played again. Keep to the line of justice, and even his angry exclamations at the impossibility of inducing you to deviate therefrom, will be your highest testimonial. Your whole career is public, and the favour or disgrace which awaits you must be public also'.

keeping and using the public documents. It is exactly the issue addressed by Cicero six centuries earlier. The constellation of an expert in literacy and literate practice, who occupies a pivotal position as a guardian of documents of public interest and importance, which Cassiodorus describes in his letter, invokes the image of the *scriba* we find in our Late Republican sources. The *scriba* is to faithfully maintain and reliably consult the public repository for the benefit of the community. His 'solicitude' – to use the emphatic wording of Cassiodorus – 'protects the rights of everybody', 'his duty means security for all'. Deusdedit is described as the veritable, impartial voice of the documents he administered. Cassiodorus, a man of letters and classical learning, certainly knew his Cicero. Not by chance did he address Deusdedit with the title of *scriba*, even more so at a time when the Roman *scriba* must have been an office of times long past. He thus knowingly made reference to an ancient ideal.

The idea of *scriba*-ship had weathered the centuries. It was the idea of a diligent and faithful keeper of the written public repository, the embodiment of trustworthiness and incorruptibility, the voice of ancient truth. It was the idea of a human archive, the guardian of the written. It was a noble idea, even if its faithful realisation had been subject to change.

Appendix
The Roman Scribae

The following list includes persons known to have occupied the office of *scriba*. Only persons clearly identifiable as *scribae* are included. The names are given in alphabetical order (by family name), followed by the scribal denomination found in the sources. Individuals for whom identification as *scriba* is uncertain but can be deduced by contextual evidence are categorised as *incerti*.

A.1 Roman State

1. **L. Aelius**
   scriba quaestorius sex primus curatorum. — *CIL* 6, 32272 (*CIL* 6, 10621; 37142).

2. **P. Aelius** *P. filius Palatina (tribu)* **Agathoclianus**
   scriba tribunicius maior. scriba aedilium curulium. scriba quaestorius sex primus. — *CIL* 11, 7555 (*ILS* 1886. *AE* 1889, 99).

3. **P. Aelius Andri[- - -]**
   scriba librarius quaestorius III decuriarum. — *CIL* 6, 1802 (*CIL* 6, 30428.2).

4. **C. Aelius** *P. filius Claudia (tribu) Quirina (tribu)* **Domitianus Gaurus**
   scriba librarius quaestorius trium decuriarum. scriba aedilium curulium. — *AE* 1888, 125 (*ILS* 2748. *EE* 8, 368).

5. **Sex. Aelius Victor**
   scriba quaestorius. — *CIL* 6, 1803.

6. *A. filius Pupinia (tribu)* **Aemilianus**
   scriba librarius quaestorius III decuriarum. — *CIL* 6, 1807 (*CIL* 6, 1830. *CIL* 6, 32274).

7. **Aemilius Eucharpus**
   scriba senatus. — *CIL* 6, 37098 (*ILS* 9041. *AE* 1907, 132).

8. **Aemilius Proculus**
   scriba quaestorius. — Bloch (1953) no. 36.

9 **L. Aemilius** *M. filius M. nepos Quirina (tribu)* **Rectus**
scriba aedilicius. scriba quaestorius. — CIL 2, 3423 (CIL 8, 33.4*. CartNova 59). CIL 2, 3424 (ILS 6953. CartNova 60). CIL 2, 5941 (ILS 6954). CIL 2, 5942.

10 **Albinovanus Celsus**
scriba (Ti. Claudii) Neronis. — HOR. epist. 1. 8. 2.

11 **L. Albius** *L. filius Fabia (tribu)* **Rufus**
scriba aedilicius. — CIL 14, 2108.

12 **C. Aletius** *P. filius* **Lupus**
scriba librarius. — CIL 9, 1193.

13 **C. Allius** *C. libertus* **Niger**
scriba librarius ex III decuriis quaestoriis. — Langford Wilson (1909) no. 1 (CIL 6, 37146. ILS 9036. AE 1907, 131. AE 1909, 91).

14 **M. Anicius**
scriba. — LIV. 23. 19. 17–18.

15 **C. Annius** *C. filius Pollia (tribu)* **Priscus**
scriba librarius. — CIL 6, 1858.

16 **P. Annius Protectus**
scriba librarius quaestorius III decuriarum. — CIL 6, 1804.

17 **C. Antistius**
scriba. — CIC. Verr. 2. 3. 167–168.

18 **M. Antistius Maximus**
scriba decuriae aediliciae. — CIL 6, 1836 (CIL 10, 1088.33*).

19 **M. Antonius** *M. filius Collina (tribu)* **Rufus**
scriba quaestorius princeps. — CIL 6, 1805 (ILS 1890).

20 **C. Apidius Proculus**
scriba aedilium curulium. — CIL 6, 1837.

21 **Apidius Valerus**
scriba librarius trium decuriarum quaestoriarum. — CIL 13, 1815.

22 **Q. Apusulenus Secundus**
scriba aedilium curulium sex primus. — CIL 6, 32276 (ILS 1881).

23 **Sex. Atellius** *Sex. filius Pupinia (tribu)* **Paetus**
scriba quaestorius. — CIL 6, 1806 (CIL 6, 32265).

24 **L. Atiedius** *L. libertus* **Dorus**
scriba librarius aedilium plebis. — CIL 6, 1855.

25 **A. Atinius** *A. filius Palatina (tribu)* **Paternus**
scriba aedilium curulium. — CIL 6, 1838 (CIL 3, 263.2*. ILS 2727).

26 **C. Aufidius** *C. filius*
    scriba librarius. — Petraccia Lucernoni (1988) no. 396 (*AE* 1990, 385. *InscrAqu* 01, 43. *CIL* 1, 3421).

27 **Aufidius Luscus**
    scriba. — Hor. *sat.* 1. 5. 35. Porph. *Hor. sat.* 1. 5. 35.

28 **M. Aurelius Hermogenes**
    scriba tribunicius maior. scriba quaestorius. — *CIL* 14, 5340.

29 **Avidius Charito**
    scriba librarius quaestorius ab aerario. — *CIL* 6, 3871 (*CIL* 6, 32273. *IG* 14, 1607. *IGUR* 03, 1216).

30 **C. Avillius Licinius Trosius**
    scriba librarius aedilium curulium. — *CIL* 6, 1068 (*ILS* 1880). *CIL* 6, 103 (*CIL* 6, 30692. *ILS* 1879).

31 **Bellicus**
    scriba quaestorius. — *CIL* 11, 3618.

32 **Q. Caecilius Amandus**
    scriba librarius quaestorius III decuriarum. — *CIL* 11, 7764 (*AE* 1913, 37).

33 **Sex. Caecilius** *Sex. filius Quirina (tribu)* **Birronianus**
    scriba librarius quaestorius III decuriarum. — *EAOR* 08, 37 (*CIL* 10, 4737. *ILS* 1898a). *CIL* 6, 1808 (*ILS* 1898).

34 **Sex. Caecilius** *Quirina (tribu)* **Epagathus**
    scriba librarius tribunicius. scriba librarius aedilium curulium. scriba librarius quaestorius III decuriarium. — *CIL* 6, 1808 (*ILS* 1898).

35 **C. Caecilius Proculus**
    scriba aedilium curulium. — F. Barbieri (1975) no. 2 (*AE* 1975, 376).

36 **L. Cantilius**
    scriba pontificius. — Liv. 22. 57. 3.

37 **Canuleius** *Collina (tribu)* **Cilo**
    scriba. — Gasperini (2009) (*AE* 2009, 336).

38 **Cassienius**
    scriba quaestorius VI primus curatorum. — *CIL* 6, 37154.

39 **L. Cassius Priscus**
    scriba aedilium curulium. — *CIL* 6, 1837.

40 **C. Cicereius**
    scriba. — *FCap triumph.* 172 (*CIL* 1, p. 459). *CIL* 9, 5564 (*InscrIt* 13-01, 35, *AE* 1926, 121). Liv. 42. 1. 5; 42. 7. 1–2; 42. 21. 6–7; 45. 15. 10; 45. 17. 4. V. Max. 3. 5. 1; 4. 5. 3.

41 Ti. Claudius *Ti. filius Claudia (tribu)* Armiger
   scriba aedilicius. — Pagano (1990) 27.

42 M. Claudius Glicia
   scriba. — *FCap cons.* 249 (*InscrIt* 13-01, 1ab). LIV. *perioch.* 19. SUET. *Tib.* 2. 2.

43 Ti. Claudius *L. filius* Helvius Secundus
   scriba decuriae aedilium curulium. scriba decuriae quaestoriae. — *AE* 1925, 44.

44 Ti. Claudius *Ti. filius Quirina (tribu)* Hispanus
   scriba. — *AE* 1920, 19 (*ILAlg*-01, 2194).

45 Claudius *Ti. filius Palatina (tribu)* Paulus
   scriba aedilium curulium. — *CIL* 14, 3625 (*InscrIt* 04-01, 156. *IDRE*-01, 115).

46 Ti. Claudius *Aug. libertus* Secundus Philippianus
   scriba librarius. — *CIL* 6, 1859. *CIL* 6, 1860.

47 A. Clodius *M. filius Palatina (tribu)*
   scriba. — *CIL* 10, 1074 (*ILS* 5053).

48 (Clodius) Fortunatus
   scriba librarius decuriae aedilium curulium. — *CIL* 6, 1839.

49 Sex. Cloelius
   scriba. — ASCON. *Mil. test.* 19.

50 D. Cloelius *D. libertus* Hermio
   scriba librarius. — *CIL* 6, 1861.

51 [Clu]vius *P. filius Pupinia (tribu)* Formica
   scriba tribunorum plebis. scriba aedilium curulium. scriba quaestorius sex primus. — *CIL* 6, 1810.

52 Cn. Cor[- - -] Auguri[- - -]
   scriba aedilicius. — *CIL* 6, 32277.

53 Cn. Cornelius
   scriba aedilicius. — *CIL* 6, 29752 (*CIL* 6, 32277).

54 Q. Cornelius
   scriba. — CIC. *har. resp.* 12. CIC. *off.* 2. 29. SALL. *hist.* 1. 55. 17. J. *AJ* 14. 219.

55 L. Cornelius *L. filius Palatina (tribu)* Terentianus
   scriba Xvirum (litibus iudicandis). scriba aedilium curulium. — *CIL* 6, 1840 (*ILS* 1900).

56 Cornificius
   scriba. — CIC. *Verr.* 2. 1. 150.

57 T. Culciscius *T. filius Voltinia (tribu)*
   scriba aedilium curulium. — *CIL* 6, 1841.

58   P. Curius *P. filius Quirina (tribu)* Servilius Draco
scriba quaestorius trium decuriarum. — CIL 8, 11033 (*ILTun* 15).

59   P. Curtius *P. filius* Tutus
scriba aedilicius. — CIL 6, 1842 (CIL 11, 205a*).

60   M'. Cutius Amemptus
scriba librarius quaestorius III decuriarum. — CIL 6, 1811.

61   N. Decumius *N. filius Collina (tribu)* Vaarus
scriba. — CIL 6, 1862 (CIL 1, 1299. ILLRP 811. ILLRP.Imagines 307).

62   Domatius Sabinus
scriba quaestorius. — CIL 6, 1813.

63   C. Domitius *L. filius Palatina (tribu)* Fabius Hermogenes
scriba aedilium curulium. — CIL 14, 353 (*ILS* 6148). CIL 14, 4642 (*AE* 1910, 181). CIL 14, 4643.

64   Q. Durius *Q. filius Pupinia (tribu)*
scriba. — CIL 10, 6326.

65   Cn. Egnatius Fuscus
scriba quaestorius. — CIL 10, 7852 (*ILS* 5947. *AE* 1983, 447. 1989, 353. 1993, 836a–b).

66   C. Ennius *C. filius Teretina (tribu)*
scriba quaestorius. — CIL 6, 1814.

67   M. Ennius *M'. filius Menenia (tribu)* Vicetinus
scriba aedilium curulium. — CIL 10, 4832.

68   Faberius
scriba. γραμματεύς. — Vitr. 7. 9. 2. App. *BC* 3. 1. 5.

69   Q. Fabius *Africani libertus* Cytisus
scriba librarius tribunicius. scriba librarius quaestorius trium decuriarum. — CIL 6, 1815 (CIL 6, 32266. *ILS* 1926).

70   L. Fabricius *L. filius Palatina (tribu)* Caesennius Gallus
scriba aedilicius. — CIL 14, 354 (*IPOstia*-A, 50a. *ISIS* 5).

71   L. Faenius Alexander
scriba tribunicius. (scriba) librarius. — Mingazzini (1923) no. 5 (*AE* 1926, 43).

72   C. Flaminius *C. filius Pollia (tribu)* Severus
scriba. — CIL 3, 257 (*GLIA* 01, 180).

73   Cn. Flavius *A. filius*
scriba. — Piso *frg.* F29 (FRH) = Gell. 7. 9. 1–6. D.S. 20. 36. 6. Cic. *Mur.* 25. Cic. *de orat.* 1. 186. Cic. *Att.* 6. 1. 8. Liv. 9. 46. 1–12 = Macer *frg.* F24 (FRH). Liv. *perioch.* 9. V. Max. 2. 5. 2; 9. 3. 3. Plin. *nat.* 33. 17–19. Dig. 1. 2. 2. 7. Macr. 1. 15. 9.

74 M. Flavius
    scriba. — MACR. 1. 14. 2.

75 T. Flavius Cominus
    scriba quaestorius (sex primus curatorum?). — *CIL* 8, 270 (*CIL* 8, 11451. 23246. *ILPBardo* 26. *ILTun* 396. *AE* 1907, 17).

76 Flavius Laurentius
    scriba senatus. — COD. Theod. gesta. 8. *CIL* 6, 33721 (*ILS* 1958. *ICUR*-08, 23064. *ILCV* 705).

77 Flavius Liberalis
    scriba quaestorius. — SUET. *Vesp.* 3.

78 T. Flavius R[ufin]ianus
    scriba aedilium curulium. — *CIL* 6, 1610.

79 C. Fonteius *C. filius Collina (tribu)* Claudianus
    scriba aedilium curulium. — *CIL* 6, 32278.

80 T. Fulvius *TT. libertus* Eros Modestus
    scriba librarius. — *CIL* 6, 1863.

81 Q. Fulvius *Q. filius Quirina (tribu)* Faustus
    scriba librarius aedilium curulium. scriba aedilium curulium. — Zevi and Friggeri (2012).

82 Q. Fulvius *Q. filius Quirina (tribu)* Priscus
    scriba aedilium curulium. — Zevi and Friggeri (2012).

83 C. Furius *C. filius Clustumina (tribu)* Tiro
    scriba quaestorius. — *CIL* 11, 4572 (*Acquasparta* 3).

84 Gavius Capito Maximianus
    scriba tribunicius. scriba aedilium curulium. scriba quaestorius. — F. Barbieri (1975) no. 1 (*AE* 1975, 375).

85 L. Granius [Eut]yches
    scriba librarius. — *CIL* 6, 19082 (*CIL* 6, 32283).

86 Cn. Hellenius *Cn. filius Collina (tribu)* Rufus
    scriba. — *CIL* 6, 1864.

87 L. Herennius *L. filius Stellatina (tribu)*
    scriba quaestorius ab aerario III decuriarum. — *CIL* 6, 1816 (*CIL* 1, 1313. *ILLRP* 812. *ILS* 1895).

88 Q. Horatius Flaccus
    scriba quaestorius. — HOR. *sat.* 2. 6. 36. PORPH. *Hor. sat.* 2. 6. 36. SUET. *vita Hor.* 24.

89 Q. Iulius Agathocles
    scriba aedilium curulium. — *AE* 1964, 73.

90   L. Iulius *C. filius* Alexander
scriba aedilium curulium. — *CIL* 10, 1723.

91   C. Iulius Augustalis
scriba legati Augusti (pro praetore). — Bönisch and Lepke (2013) no. 6.

92   Iulius Florus
scriba. — Porph. *Hor. ep.* 1. 3. 1.

93   C. Iulius Fortunatus
scriba quaestorius (sex primus curatorum?). — *CIL* 8, 270 (*CIL* 8, 11451. 23246. *ILPBardo* 26. *ILTun* 396. *AE* 1907, 17).

94   C. Iulius Iustus
scriba decuriae aediliciae maioris. — *CIL* 6, 1843 (*ILS* 1883).

95   Iulius *C. filius* Martialis
scriba decurialis decuriae aediliciae. — *CIL* 8, 8936.

96   Sex. Iulius Paulinus
scriba aedilium curulium. — *CIL* 6, 1844.

97   C. Iulius *C. filius Quirina (tribu)* Priscus
scriba quaestorius. — *CIL* 6, 1817.

98   C. Iulius *C. filius Aemilia (tribu)* Receptus
scriba decuriae aedilium curulium. — *CIL* 6, 1845 (*ILSanMichele* 11. *GLISwedish* 4).

99   T. Iulius *T. filius Fabia (tribu)* Saturninus
scriba tribunicius. — *AE* 1928, 153 (*ILBulg* 246). Florescu (1927–1932) 504–7 no. 6 (*AE* 1934, 107. *IScM*-05, 10). *CIL* 3, 1568 (*IDR* 03-01, 60. *AE* 1960, 344. 2010, 1385). *CIL* 3, p. 958 (*IDR* 01, 54). *CIL* 13, 1864. *CIL* 13, 1750 (*ILS* 1384). *CIL* 13, 3636 (*ILS* 1382. *AE* 1994, 1238. *CSIR*-D 04-03, 26). *CIL* 6, 559 (*ILS* 1383). *IDR* 03-01, 35 (*AE* 1960, 343). *ILJug*-02, 920 (*AE* 1940, 101. *CIMRM* 02, 1847). *CIL* 3, 4720. *CIL* 3, 12363 (*ILBulg* 336. *AE* 1895, 45). *CIL* 5, 5079 (*SIRIS* 638. *RICIS*-02, 515/1401). *CIL* 5, 5080 (*ILS* 1859. *SIRIS* 639. *RICIS*-02, 515/1402).

100   T. Iunius *Galeria (tribu)* Achilles
scriba librarius quaestorius trium decuriarum. — *CIL* 2, 3596 (*IRPAlicante* 50).

101   Q. Iunius Ami[- - -]
scriba quaestorius VI primus curatorum. — *CIL* 6, 37154.

102   M. Iunius *M. libertus* Auctus
scriba librarius. — *CIL* 6, 37147 (*AE* 1913, 113).

103   L. Iunius Lyco
scriba librarius aedilium curulium. — *CIL* 6, 296.

104   [M.] Iunius *M. libertus* Menander
scriba librarius aedilium curulium princeps. scriba librarius quaestorius. — *CIL* 6, 32279 (*ILS* 1882).

105   A. Iunius Pastor
scriba librarius. — *AE* 2004, 1521 (*IK* 61, 409).

106   Q. Lucretius Quintianus
scriba librarius. — *CIL* 6, 1865.

107   Maecenas
scriba. — Sall. *hist.* 3. 83. 1 (Serv. *Aen.* 1. 698).

108   L. Maelius *L. filius Aniensi (tribu)* Flaccus
scriba aedilium curulium. scriba quaestorius. — *CIL* 6, 1818.

109   Maevius
scriba. — Cic. *Verr.* 2. 1. 157; 2, 3, 171–187.

110   L. Mamilius
scriba. — Cic. *Verr.* 2. 3. 182.

111   L. Mamius *Palatina (tribu)* Fabius Largus
scriba quaestorius. σκρείβας κουεστώριος. — Lehmler and Wörrle (2002) 573–5 no. 2, Abb. 2 (*SEG*-52, 1251. *AE* 2002, 1393).

112   T. Marius *T. filius Palatina (tribu)* Clementianus
scriba aedilium curulium. — Ferrua (1958) 132 (*AE* 1961, 114. *CIL* 6, 1846. 1888a2. 32289b. 37140a).

113   [L.] Marius *L. libertus* Doryphorus
scriba librarius aedilium curulium. scriba tribunicius. scriba aedilicius. — *CIL* 6, 1847 (*ILS* 1899).

114   L. Marius Perpetuus
scriba quaestorius. — *ILAfr* 592 (*ILPBardo* 370. *AE* 1921, 39).

115   D. Matrinius
scriba aedilicius. — Cic. *Cluent.* 126.

116   P. Mercusenus Theodotus
scriba. σκρείβας. — Adak and Şahin (2004) no. 12 (*SEG*-54, 1453. *AE* 2005, 1518).

117   Sex. Mutilius *Sex. filius Collina (tribu)* Primus
scriba aedilium curulium. scriba quaestorius. — *CIL* 14, 3949.

118   L. Naevius *L. libertus* Urbanus
scriba librarius quaestorius ex tribus decuriis minoribus ab aerario. — *CIL* 6, 1819 (*ILS* 1896).

119 **Nampius**
scriba officii viri clarissimi legati almae Karthaginis. — *Gesta Conl. Carth.* 1. 1; 1. 27; 1. 216; 2. 1; 3. 1.

120 **M. Natronius** *C. filius Pupinia (tribu)* **Rusticus**
scriba quaestorius sex primus curatorum. — *CIL* 6, 1820 (*ILS* 1891).

121 **L. Nigidius** *L. filius* **Sors**
scriba aedilium curulium. — *CIL* 1, 2640 (*ILLRP* 814d. *AE* 1927, 112).

122 **L. Numpidius** *L. libertus* **Philomelus**
scriba librarius quaestorius trium decuriarum. — *CIL* 6, 1821.

123 **C. Octavius** *Octaviae Augusti sororis libertus* **Auctus**
scriba librarius. — *CIL* 6, 8881 (*ILS* 1877).

124 **P. Papienus Salutaris**
scriba librarius. — *ILAfr* 592 (*ILPBardo* 370. *AE* 1921, 39).

125 **L. Papirius Potamo**
scriba. — Cic. *div. in Caec.* 29. Cic. *Verr.* 2. 3. 137; 2, 3, 154.

126 **M. Papirius** *M. filius*
scriba quaestorius. — Camodeca (2010) 57–9 (*AE* 2010, 305).

127 **Q. Papirius** *Q. filius Pupinia (tribu)* **Maximus**
scriba aedilium plebis cerialium. scriba aedilium plebis. scriba aedilium curulium. scriba quaestorius VI primus. — *CIL* 6, 1822 (*ILS* 1893).

128 **L. Peducaeus Saturninus**
decurialis decuriae scribarum librariorum. — *CIL* 14, 2265 (*ILS* 1935).

129 **A. Perperna** *Sp. filius* **Fronto**
scriba. — *CIL* 14, 3714 (*CIL* 14, 3715. *InscrIt* 04-01, 253).

130 **L. Petilius (Cn. Terentius)**
scriba. — Plin. *nat.* 13. 84 = Cass. Hem. *frg.* F35 (FRH). Liv. 40. 29. 3–14. Liv. *perioch.* 40. V. Max. 1. 1. 12. Lact. *inst.* 1. 22.

131 **P. Petilius** *Q. filius Galeria (tribu)* **Colonus**
scriba aedilium curulium. — F. Barbieri (1975) 149 (*AE* 1975, 19).

132 **Q. Petronius** *Q. filius* **Melior**
scriba quaestorius VI primus princeps. — *CIL* 14, 172 (*ILS* 1429). *CIL* 14, 5345.

133 **L. Pituanius Eros**
scriba librarius aedilicius. — *AE* 1975, 44.

134 **A. Pompeius** *A. filius* **Aemilianus**
scriba librarius. — *CIL* 6, 1866.

135 Sex. Pompeius *Sex. filius Colina (tribu)* Baebianus
scriba aedilicius. scriba quaestorius. — *CIL* 14, 2839.

136 A. Pompeius Carpus
scriba librarius quaestorius III decuriarum. — *CIL* 6, 1824 (*CIL* 10, 948.29*. *ILS* 1894).

137 M. Pompeius *M. filius* Mai[- - -]
scriba quaestorius. — *CIL* 6, 1823.

138 P. Pompeius *P. libertus* Pylades
scriba librarius tribunicius. — *ILLRP-S* 37 (*AE* 1991, 114).

139 L. Pomponius Carisianus
scriba librarius. — *ILAfr* 592 (*ILPBardo* 370. *AE* 1921, 39).

140 L. Pomponius Niger
scriba quaestorius. — Ramsay (1916) 90, no. 1 (*AE* 1920, 75).

141 M. Pon[tius]
scriba librarius aedilium curulium. scriba aedilium curulium. — *CIL* 11, 3101.

142 L. Pontius *L. filius Palatina (tribu)* Martialis
scriba quaestorius sex primus. — *CIL* 6, 1825 (*CIL* 10, 1089.173*. *ILS* 1888. *IMCCatania* 379).

143 A. Popillius Helenus
scriba librarius. — *AE* 1976, 138 (*LMentana* 47).

144 M. Porcius *M. filius Pupinia (tribu)*
scriba Caesaris Augusti. — Alföldy, Abascal and Cebrián 2003 no. 10 (*AE* 2003, 986).

145 M. Porcius *M. libertus* Pollio
scriba librarius aedilium curulium. — *CIL* 6, 1852.

146 Prastina Fronto
scriba aedilicius. — *CIL* 11, 3259 (*ILS* 1884).

147 L. Pulfennius *L. libertus* Phileros
scriba librarius. — *CIL* 6, 1867.

148 Cn. Ricinius *Cn. filius Pupinia (tribu)* Persa
scriba. — *CIL* 14, 2108.

149 Rufinianus
scriba viri clarissimi curatoris celsae Karthaginis. — *Gesta Conl. Carth.* 1. 1; 1. 148; 1. 157; 1. 163; 1. 176; 1. 207; 1. 213; 1. 218; 2. 1; 3. 1; 3. 171.

150 T. Sabidius *T. filius Palatina (tribu)* Maximus
scriba quaestorius sex primus. — *CIL* 14, 3674 (*InscrIt* 04-01, 197. *ILS* 1889).

151 Sallustius *T. filius Pupinia (tribu)* Virgula
scriba aedilium curulium. — *CIL* 6, 3872 (*CIL* 6, 32280. *CIL* 11, 4358).

152 **Sarmentus**
scriba quaestorius. — Hor. *sat.* 1.5.51–70. Porph. *Hor. sat.* 1.5.66. Iuv. 5.3. Schol. *Iuv.* 5.3.

153 **D. Saufeius**
scriba. — Plin. *nat.* 7.183.

154 **P. Scrasius Naeolus**
scriba quaestorius. — *CIL* 3, 12690.

155 **Cn. Seius**
scriba. — Gell. 3.9.2–6.

156 **M. Seius** *M. libertus*
scriba librarius. — Varro *rust.* 3.2.14.

157 **C. Septimius**
scriba. — Cic. *Att.* 2.24.2.

158 **C. Septimius** *C. filius* **Libo**
scriba aedilium curulium. — *CIL* 10, 1725 (*CIL* 6, 1849).

159 **P. Septumius** *P. filius Collina (tribu)*
scriba quaestorius de sex primis. — *CIL* 14, 3645 (*CIL* 1, 1490. 1827. 3646. *InscrIt* 04-01, 30 = *ILLRP* 813).

160 **L. Sergius**
scriba. — Cic. *Verr.* 2.3.182.

161 **M. Servilius** *P. filius Palatina (tribu)* **Eunicus**
σκρείβας κουαιστώριος λιβράριος. — Zucca (2010) (*AE* 2010, 1601. Ramsay (1883) 275 no. 17. *ILS* 8859. *SEG*-60, 1131).

162 **P. Servilius**
scriba. — Cic. *Verr.* 2.3.167–168.

163 **D. Severius** *D. filius Palatina (tribu)* **Severus**
scriba quaestorius. — *CIL* 9, 3083 (*ILS* 2699).

164 **Sorilius** *C. filius Pupinia (tribu)* **Bassus**
scriba princeps. — Kockel (1993) 167f., K2. w. im. Taf. 80d, 81a, 84a–b (Bordenache Battaglia and Sgubini Moretti (1975) w. im. TAV. 78, 5. *AE* 1983, 409).

165 **T. Statilius Messalinianus**
scriba tribunicius. scriba aedilicius. — *CIL* 6, 1850 (*ILS* 1885).

166 **C. Statius Celsus**
scriba librarius. — *ILPBardo* 188 (*AE* 1913, 20. *ILAfr* 325).

167 **P. Statius** *Q. filius Aniensi (tribu)* **Optatus**
scriba aedilium curulium sex primus. — *SupIt*-06-CI, 3 (*AE* 1990, 312).

168 Stertinius Maximus Eutyches
σκρείβας λιβράριος κουαιστώριος. — Wood (1877) App. 3, no. 14 (*I. Ephesos* 1540. *ILS* 8833).

169 C. Stertinius *C. libertus* Orpex
scriba librarius. — *I. Ephesos* 4123 (*AE* 1935, 169. *IK* 59, 24). *I. Ephesos* 411. *I. Ephesos* 720.

170 P. Sufenas *P. filius Palatina (tribu)* Myro
decurialis scribarum aedilium curulium. — *CIL* 6, 1851 (*ILS* 6188).

171 P. Sufenas *P. filius Palatina (tribu)* Severus Sempronianus
decurialis scribarum aedilium curulium. — *CIL* 6, 1851 (*ILS* 6188).

172 M'. Suillius *M'. filius Collina (tribu)* Celsus
scriba. — *CIL* 6, 33910.

173 C. Sulpicius Olympus
scriba librarius quaestorius. — *CIL* 6, 1822a (*CIL* 6, 5722).

174 L. Tarquitius *L. filius Pomptina (tribu)* Etruscus Sulpicianus
scriba quaestorius. — *CIL* 6, 1828 (*CIL* 10, 64*. *ILS* 1887).

175 C. Telegennus *Optati libertus* Anthus
scriba librarius quaestorius trium decuriarum. — *CIL* 6, 1829.

176 T. Tettienus *T. filius* Felix
scriba librarius aedilium curulium. — *CIL* 10, 531 (*AE* 1998, 349. *InscrIt* 01-01, 11. *ILS* 359). *CIL* 6, 32455a (*CIL* 6, 2184. *ILS* 4971). *CIL* 6, 31034 (*CIL* 6, 2185).

177 P. Tettius Certus
scriba librarius aedilium plebis. — *CIL* 11, 7541.

178 M. Tullius
scriba. — Cic. *Att.* 5. 4. 1. Cic. *fam.* 5. 20. 1–6.

179 *Actes libertus* Tyrannus
scriba librarius. — *CIL* 6, 1867a (*CIL* 6, 32269).

180 M. Ulpius *Aug. libertus* Callistus
scriba librarius quaestorius. — *CIL* 6, 1809.

181 M. Ulpius Celsianus
scriba librarius. — *CIL* 6, 32282 (*CIL* 6, 37143. *ILS* 1878).

182 *A. libertus* Valerianus
scriba librarius quaestorius III decuriarum. — *CIL* 6, 1807 (*CIL* 6, 1830. *CIL* 6, 32274).

183 Valerius
scriba aedilium curulium. — *AE* 1975, 71.

184   C. Valerius
      scriba quaestorius. — *CIL* 6, 1832.

185   M'. Valerius *M'. filius Quirina (tribu)* Bassus
      scriba quaestorius VI primus. — *CIL* 6, 2165 (*ILS* 4951a).

186   M. Valerius Hedymeles
      scriba librarius quaestorius III decuriarum. — *CIL* 6, 1831 (*AE* 1990, 111).

187   D. Valerius *Asiatici libertus* Propolus
      scriba librarius quaestorius. — *AE* 1974, 224.

188   L. Varronius *L. filius Palatina (tribu)* Capito
      scriba aedilicius. — *CIL* 10, 6094 (*ILS* 6283. *AE* 1927, 125).

189   Versius
      scriba. — Sall. *hist.* 3. 83. 1 (Serv. *Aen.* 1. 698).

190   T. Veturius *T. libertus* Crescens
      scriba librarius tribunicius. — *CIL* 6, 1856.

191   C. Vibius *C. filius Velina (tribu)* Publilianus
      scriba quaestorius. — *CIL* 14, 3548 (*ILS* 2706. *InscrIt* 04-01, 47).

192   C. Vivius Iulianus
      scriba quaestorius. — Granino Cecere (2012) (*CIL* 14, 4250. *ILS* 1391. *InscrIt* 04-01, 148).

193   [Volu]ntilius *C. filius* Macer
      scriba aedilium curulium. — *CIL* 14, 2940 (*ILS* 1931).

194   [L.] [Volusius] *[Sat]urnini libertus* [- - -]us
      scriba librarius quaestorius III decuriarum. — *CIL* 6, 1834 (*CIL* 6, 33251. Schiavi 8. Franchetti 7).

195   L. Volusius Hermes
      scriba librarius. — *CIL* 6, 1868 (Schiavi 34).

196   L. Volusius Himerus
      scriba librarius quaestorius III decuriarum. — *CIL* 6, 1833a (*AE* 1983, 23. Schiavi 6).

197   L. Volusius Plocamus Maior
      scriba librarius quaestorius III decurionatuum. — *CIL* 6, 1833b (*AE* 1999, 199. Schiavi 55).

198   L. Volusius Primanus
      scriba librarius quaestorius III decuriarum. — *CIL* 6, 1833c (Schiavi 56).

199   L. Volusius Volusianus P[- - -]anus
      scriba librarius aedilicius. — Pensabene (2008) (*AE* 2008, 239).

200   M. [- - -]cius *M. libertus*
      scriba librarius. — *CIL* 6, 33421.

201 [- - -]lius *T. filius Pupinia (tribu)* Clemens
scriba XXVIvirum. — *CIL* 11, 4575 (*ILS* 1901. *EAOR* 02, 12. Acquasparta 5).

202 [- - - i]us *A. filius*
scriba aedilium curulium. — Giovagnoli (2013) (*AE* 2013, 211).

203 [- - -]nus
scriba aedilium curulium. — *CIL* 6, 1853.

204 Anonymus
scriba quaestorius. — PLIN. *nat.* 26. 3.

205 Anonymus
scriba quaestorius sex primus curatorum. — *CIL* 6, 32275a (*ILS* 1892).

206 Anonymus
scriba quaestorius. — *CIL* 6, 1812.

207 Anonymus
σκρείβας κουαιστώριος λιβράριος. *scriba librarius quaestorius.* — Ramsay (1967) 59f. no. 41).

208 Anonymus
scriba quaestorius. — *CEACelio* 22 (*AE* 2001, 239).

209 Anonymus
scriba librarius quaestorius ab aerario. — *CIL* 6, 1835 (*IG* 14, 2171).

210 Anonymus
scriba librarius quaestoriarum decuriarum. — *AE* 1975, 189.

211 Anonymus
scriba tribunicius. scriba aedilicius. — Fusco (2008–2009) 475–83, no. 2 (*AE* 2008, 528).

212 Anonymus
scriba aedilicius. — *EURom* 87.

213 Anonymus
scriba librarius. — *CIL* 6, 1861a.

Incerti

214 Alexandros
ὑπογραμματεύς. — PLUT. *Aem.* 37. 4.

215 Eumolpus
scriba quaestorius. — PETRON. 85.

216 M. Claudius *M. filius*
scriba quaestorius. scriba aedilicius. — *AE* 1939, 153 (Giovagnoli (2012b)).

217 Fabius *A. filius*
scriba quaestorius. — *CIL* 6, 37154.

218 [F]ulviu[s]
scriba quaestorius ab aerario III decuriarum. — *ILLRP-S* 38 (*AE* 1991, 115).

219 Q. Modius *Q. filius* Proculus
scriba decuriae aediliciae maioris. — *CIL* 6, 1848 (*CIL* 6, 2176; 32267. *CECapitol* 328; 331).

220 Petronius
scriba quaestorius. — *CIL* 6, 37154.

221 Salonius
ὑπογραμματεύς. — Plut. *Cat. Ma.* 24. 2.

222 Valerius
scriba aedilium curulium. — F. Barbieri (1975) no. 2 (*AE* 1975, 376).

223 Varronius *C. filius*
scriba quaestorius. — *CIL* 6, 37145.

224 [- - -]ammius *N. filius*
scriba quaestorius. — *CIL* 6, 37145.

225 [- - -]anius Rufus
scriba librarius. — *GLIA* 01, 181 (*IAnkara* 50. *AE* 2006, 1481).

226 [- - -]ius *A. filius*
scriba quaestorius. — *CIL* 6, 37145.

227 [- - -]usius *Q. filius*
scriba quaestorius. — *CIL* 6, 37145.

228 *A. filius*
scriba quaestorius. — *CIL* 6, 37145.

229 Anonymus
scriba quaestorius de sex primis. — *ILLRP-S* 39 (*AE* 1991, 116).

230 Anonymus
scriba librarius tribunicius. — *CIL* 6, 32281.

231 Anonymus
scriba librarius. — *CIL* 6, 33252.

A.2   Cities and Communities

232 P. Aelius *P. filius* Aelianus   [*Aquae Balissae* - Pan. sup.]
scriba municipii. — Alföldy (1964) 96 (*AE* 1964, 11. *ILJug*-02, 1132).

233 P. Aelius Quintus   [*Delminium* - Dal.]
scriba publicus. — Škegro (1994) no. 3 (*AE* 1994, 1364).

234 M. Aemilius Felicianus   [*Messana* - reg. i]
scriba publicus. — *CIL* 10, 6979 (*IGLMessina* 60g).

235 Q. Albatius Verna   [*Luna* - reg. vii]
scriba. — *CIL* 11, 1355a (*ILS* 7227).

236 Q. Alfius *Q. filius Falerna (tribu)* Iustus   [*Capua* - reg. i]
scriba quaestorius. scriba IIviralis. — *CIL* 10, 3906 (*ILS* 6316. *CECasapulla* 27).

237 [Am]erimnus   [*Comum* - reg. xi]
scriba publicus. — *CIL* 5, 5314 (*IRComo* 3).

238 C. Antistius Vetus   [*Uselis* - Sard.]
scriba. — *CIL* 10, 7845 (*ILS* 6107. *AE* 1998, 668).

239 Aurelius Marcianus   [*Napoca* - Dac.]
scriba coloniae. — *AE* 2000, 1243 (*ILD* 566).

240 Aurelius Viator   [*Potaissa* - Dac.]
scriba municipii. — *AE* 1974, 550 (*ILD* 490).

241 C.   [*Tropaeum Traiani* - Moes. inf.]
scriba. — Popescu (1964) 188f. (*CIL* 3, 14214.02. *IScM*-04, 12).

242 [Ca]murtius [Se]verus   [*Paestum* - reg. iii]
scriba. — Mello (2012) (*AE* 2012, 407).

243 T. Cassius Mansuetus   [*Cularo* - Gall. Narb.]
scriba. — *CIL* 12, 2238 (*ILN* 05-02, 376).

244 C. Catius *L. filius Maecia (tribu)* Martialis   [*Libarna* - reg. ix]
scriba. — *CIL* 5, 7430 (*CLE* 1464).

245 Q. Ci[- - -] [Euty]ches   [*Antium* - reg. i]
scriba rei publicae. — *CIL* 10, 6676 (*ILMN* 01, 603).

246 Cinna   [*Mediolanum* - reg. xi]
scriba. — *CIL* 5, 5924.

247 Claudius Galonius   [*Mursella* - Pan. sup.]
scriba. — *CIL* 3, 4267 (*RIU*-02, 372).

248 Cocceius   [*Tropaeum Traiani* - Moes. inf.]
scriba. — Popescu (1964) 201 (*AE* 1964, 253. *CIL* 3, 7484. 12461. *ILS* 7183. *IScM*-04, 13).

249 Cornelianus   [*Neapolis* - reg. i]
scriba. — *CIL* 10, 1494 (*IG* 14, 803. *CIG* 5820. *IGI-Napoli* 02, 150).

250   P. Cornelius *P. filius* Proculus   [*Capua* - REG. I]
scriba duumviralis. — ILS 6315 (*RECapua* 42).

251   P. Cornelius *P. filius* Victorinus   [*Ostia* - REG. I]
decurialis scriba librarius coloniae. — CIL 14, 4290 (*ILS* 4369. SIRIS 538. RICIS-02, 503/1118). CIL 14, 343 (*SIRIS* 539. RICIS-02, 503/1119).

252   C. Curiatius *T. filius Sergia (tribu)* Secundus   [*Salona* - DAL.]
scriba. — CIL 3, 2019 (*ILS* 7161).

253   Deusdedit   [*Ravenna* - OSTROGOTHIC KINGDOM]
scriba. — CASSIOD. *Var.* 12. 21. 1–5.

254   A. Egrilius *A. filius* Plarianus   [*Ostia* - REG. I]
decurialis scriba cerarius. — CIL 14, 346 (*CIL* 10, 7955. *ILS* 6151).

255   A. Egrilius *A. filius* Secundus Threptianus   [*Ostia* - REG. I]
decurialis scriptus cerarius. scriba collegii fabrum tignuariorum. — CIL 14, 347 (*ILS* 6150).

256   L. Fabius *C. filius* Clemens   [*Salona* - DAL.]
scriba. — CIL 3, 2122 (*CIL* 3, 8593. *ILS* 7799).

257   L. Fabius *Sp. filius* Eutychus   [*Ostia* - REG. I]
scriba cerarius. librarius. — CIL 14, 353 (*ILS* 6148). CIL 14, 4642 (*AE* 1910, 181).

258   L. Feronius *L. filius Vellina (tribu)* Rufus   [*Auximum* - REG. V]
scriba. — CIL 9, 5858.

259   T. Flavius Aper   [*Sarmizegetusa* - DAC.]
scriba coloniae. — IDR 03-02, 457 (*CIL* 3, 1512. Ciongradi (2007) 205, B/S 6). IDR 03-02, 187 (*CIL* 3, 7914). IDR 03-02, 264 (*CIL* 3, 1580). IDR0302253 (*CIL* 3, 7917).

260   L. Fulvius Clemens   [*Cubulteria* - REG. I]
scriba rei publicae. — CIL 10, 4620 (*IATrebula* 96).

261   M. Gavius *M. filius Palatina tribu* Sabinus   [*Beneventum* - REG. II]
scriba aedilium iure dicundo. — CIL 9, 1646 (*ILS* 6498).

262   Q. Ingenus Maximinus   [*Mediolanum* - REG. XI]
scriba publicus. — CIL 5, 5866.

263   C. Iulius Ingenus   [*Aquincum* - PAN. INF.]
scriba civitatis. — TitAq-01, 239 (*CIL* 3, 14344a. *AE* 1899, 68a). TitAq-01, 242 (*CIL* 3, 14344b. *AE* 1899, 68b. CIMRM 02, 1759). TitAq-01, 240 (*CIL* 3, 14345). TitAq-01, 241 (*CIL* 3, 14346).

264   Iulius Nobilis   [*Tolosa* - GALL. NARB.]
scriba. — CAG-31-3, 335.

265   C. Iulius Socrates   [*Puteoli* - REG. I]
scriba. — CIL 10, 1953.

266 L. Laelius *Sp. filius* Herennianus   [*Ostia* - REG. I]
   scriba cerarius. — *AE* 1948, 28 (*AE* 1987, 202. *CCCA*-03, 387). *AE* 1948, 30 (*CCCA*-03, 390).

267 M. Licinius Privatus   [*Ostia* - REG. I]
   decurialis scriba librarius. — *CIL* 14, 374 (*ILS* 6165). *CIL* 14, 128 (*CIL* 6, 116. *ILS* 615).

268 Sex. Lucretius Apollonius   [*Augusta Taurinorum* - REG. XI]
   scriba. — *CIL* 5, 7033.

269 Cn. Marius *Cn. filius Tromentina (tribu)* Severus   [*Aesernia* - REG. IV]
   scriba. — *CIL* 9, 2675 (*Aesernia* 64).

270 P. Octavius *P. filius* Eu[- - -]anus   [*Sulmo* - REG. IV]
   scriba. — *CIL* 9, 3101.

271 L. Octavius Iustus   [*Sulmo* - REG. IV]
   scriba rei publicae. — *SupIt*-04-S, 46 (*AE* 1900, 184).

272 C. Ovinius *Palatina (tribu)* Antonianus   [*Ostia* - REG. I]
   scriba cerarius coloniae. — *AE* 1988, 195.

273 Paccius Lucianus   [*Puteoli* - REG. I]
   scriba. — *CIL* 10, 1955.

274 Cn. Papirius Claudianus   [*Potentia* - REG. III]
   scriba rei publicae. — *CIL* 10, 140.

275 Q. Petronius *Q. filius* Rufus   [*Asculum* - REG. V]
   scriba quinquennalicius. — *CIL* 9, 5190.

276 P. Plotius *P. filius Palatina (tribu)* Faustinus   [*Neapolis* - REG. I]
   scriba publicus aedilicius. — *IGI-Napoli* 01, 84 (*ILS* 6460. *AE* 1891, 163. 1892, 1. *IGRRP*-01, 452).

277 L. Pompeius Hermeros   [*Aquae Sextiae* - GALL. NARB.]
   scriba IIIIvirum. — *CIL* 12, 524 (*ILN* 03, 35).

278 Pontius Lupus   [*Siscia* - PAN. SUP.]
   scriba municipii. — *CIL* 3, 3974.

279 Sex. Publicius *Sex. filius Maecia (tribu)*   [*Hadria* - REG. V]
   scriba. — *CIL* 9, 5018.

280 Respectus   [*Tropaeum Traiani* - MOES. INF.]
   scriba. — Popescu (1964) 188f. (*CIL* 3, 14214.02. *IScM*-04, 12).

281 D. Rupilius Menander   [*Tibur* - REG. I]
   scriba rei publicae. — *CIL* 14, 3699 (*CIL* 15, 7892. *InscrIt* 04-01, 625).

282 T. Rustius Lysiponus   [*Caere* - REG. VII]
   scriba. — *CIL* 11, 3614 (*CIL* 11, 4347. *ILS* 5918a).

283 Rustius Numerius [*Puteoli* - REG. I]
scriba. — *CIL* 10, 1954.

284 T. Sabidius Victor [*Tibur* - REG. I]
scriba rei publicae. — *CIL* 14, 3699 (*CIL* 15, 7892. *InscrIt* 04-01, 625).

285 T. Sammius Tertiolus [*Cularo* - GALL. NARB.]
scriba aerarii. — *CIL* 12, 2212 (*ILN* 05-02, 335).

286 Saturius Gratus [*Puteoli* - REG. I]
scriba. — *CIL* 10, 1956.

287 C. Sentinatius *C. filius Lemonia (tribu)* Iustus [*Sentinum* - REG. VI]
scriba publicus. — *CIL* 11, 5760.

288 T. Sentius Men(- - -) [*Asculum* - REG. V]
scriba. — *CIL* 9, 5278.

289 Synda [*Sarmizegetusa* - DAC.]
scriba tabularii. — *IDR* 03-02, 386 (*CIL* 3, 7975. Ciongradi (2007) 267, T/S 7).

290 Temporinius Cerialis [*Nemausus* - GALL. NARB.]
scriba. — *AE* 1937, 221.

291 P. Terentius Felix [*Atella* - REG. I]
scriba. — *CIL* 10, 3737.

292 P. Tertius [*Mogetiana* - PAN. SUP.]
scriba municipii. — Alföldy (1990) 94, no. 8 (*AE* 1996, 1240). *CIL* 3, 4137; 10900. *CSIR*-U 08, 104. *RIU*-02, 328).

293 Ulpius Florentinus [*Forum Novum* - REG. IV]
scriba rei publicae. — *SupIt*-05-FN, 32 (*AE* 1990, 253).

294 Valentinus [*Tropaeum Traiani* - MOES. INF.]
scriba. — Popescu (1964) 192 (*AE* 1964, 251. *IScM*-04, 11).

295 L. Valerius Iulianus [*Puteoli* - REG. I]
scriba. — *CIL* 10, 1958.

296 M. Valerius Victor [*Venafrum* - REG. I]
scriba. — *CIL* 10, 4905.

297 Vatinius Priscus [*Capena* - REG. VII]
scriba publicus rei publicae. — *AE* 1954, 168.

298 Volumnius Serenus [*Concordia* - REG. X]
scriba. — FRONTO *amic.* 2. 7 (H176, N192).

299 [- - -]pius *C. filius* Cla[- - -] [*Puteoli* - REG. I]
scriba. — *CIL* 10, 1957.

Incerti

300 L. Apuleius Marcus [*Sarmizegetusa* - Dac.]
scriba. — Daicoviciu and Piso (1977) (*AE* 1976, 561. *IDR* 03-02, 11).

301 C. Licinius Proclus [*Neapolis* - reg. i]
τῆς πόλεως ἀναγραφεύων. — *CIL* 10, 1489 (*CIG* 5843. *IGI-Napoli* 01, 82. *IG* 14, 757. *IGRRP*-01, 450).

302 Seneca [*Raetinum* - Dal.]
scriba. — *AE* 2007, 1116.

303 T. Sevius [*Cara* - Hisp. Tarr.]
scriba. — *CIL* 2, 2972.

304 [- - -]inius *Quirina (tribu)* Urbanus [*Thisdra* - Afr. proc.]
scriba coloniae. — *ILPBardo* 84 (*ILTun* 111).

305 Anonymus [*Fulginae* - reg. vi]
scriba. — *CIL* 11, 5226.

A.3 Associations

Civic

306 P. Aelius *P. filius Palatina (tribu)* Bellenius Aristo
scriba tribus Palatinae corporis seniorum clientium perpetuum. — *CIL* 6, 10215 (*ILS* 6057).

Religious

307 P. Aelius Exuperatus
scriba collegii genii provinciae Pannoniae superioris. — *CIL* 3, 4168 (*ILS* 7118. *RIU*-01, 31).

308 T. Aurelius Peculiaris
scriba collegii genii provinciae Pannoniae superioris. — *CIL* 3, 4168 (*ILS* 7118. *RIU*-01, 31).

309 Fonteius Eutycho
scriba cultus Iovis Optimi Maximi Dolicheni. — *CIL* 6, 407 (*ILS* 4317. *CCID* 379).

310 Q. Gavius Zosimus
scriba cultus Iovis Optimi Maximi Dolicheni et Heliopolitani. — *CIL* 3, 11131 (*CIL* 3, 13447. *ILS* 4310. *CCID* 221).

Professional

311 **Antonius Capitolinus**
scriba corporationis. — *CIL* 6, 868.

312 **[M.] Aurelius** *Augg. libertus* **Plebeius**   [Albanum - REG. I]
scriba corporis scaenicorum Latinorum. — *CIL* 14, 2299 (*ILS* 5206. *AE* 2000, 270).

313 **T. Aurelius Telesphorus**
scriba medicorum. γραμματεὺς ἰατρῶν. — *CIL* 6, 9566 (*ILMN* 01, 140. *ILS* 7817). *SEG*-33, 786.

314 **Concordius Successus**   [Ravenna - REG. VIII]
scriba collegii. — Donati (1977) (*AE* 1977, 265b).

255 **A. Egrilius** *A. filius* **Secundus Threptianus**   [Ostia - REG. I]
scriba collegii fabrum tignuariorum. decurialis scriptus cerarius. — *CIL* 14, 347 (*ILS* 6150).

315 **Fabius Primus**   [Ostia - REG. I]
scriba numeri caligatorum collegii fabrum tignuariorum. — *CIL* 14, 4569 (*AE* 1928, 123).

316 **Flavius Tyrannus**
scriba collegii fabrum Romae. — *CIL* 6, 33856 (*ILS* 8935. *AE* 1900, 88. *AE* 1900, 89).

317 **Marsenus Castus**
scriba collegii fabrum tignariorum Romae. — *CIL* 6, 1060 (*CIL* 6, 33858. *ILS* 7225).

318 **Minisius Primitivos**
scriba collegii fabrum Romae. — *CIL* 6, 33856 (*ILS* 8935. *AE* 1900, 88. *AE* 1900, 89).

319 **Monnienius Tudienus**
scriba collegii fabrum tignariorum Romae. — *CIL* 6, 1060 (*CIL* 6, 33858. *ILS* 7225).

320 **Mustius**
scriba collegii fabrum tignariorum Romae. — *CIL* 6, 1060 (*CIL* 6, 33858. *ILS* 7225).

321 **Paccius Eleuther**
scriba collegii fabrum Romae. — *CIL* 6, 33856 (*ILS* 8935. *AE* 1900, 88. *AE* 1900, 89).

322 **Pactumeius Eutychianus**   [Narona - DAL.]
scriba collegii fabrum. — *Lupa* 24336.

323 **Plaetorius Primitivos**
scriba collegii fabrum Romae. — *CIL* 6, 33856 (*ILS* 8935. *AE* 1900, 88. *AE* 1900, 89).

324 **C. Similius Philocyrius**   [Ostia - REG. I]
scriba numeri militum caligatorum collegii fabrum tignuariorum. — *CIL* 14, 418 (*ILMN* 01, 565. *ILS* 6167). *CIL* 14, 419 (*CIL* 14, 4668).

325 **Terentius Fortunatus**   [Ravenna - REG. VIII]
scriba collegii. — Donati (1977) (*AE* 1977, 265b).

326 Terentius Geminus
scriba collegii fabrum Romae. — *CIL* 6, 33856 (*ILS* 8935. *AE* 1900, 88. *AE* 1900, 89).

327 Trebellius Modestus
scriba collegii fabrum Romae. — *CIL* 6, 33856 (*ILS* 8935. *AE* 1900, 88. *AE* 1900, 89).

328 Tuceius Hermes
scriba collegii fabrum tignariorum Romae. — *CIL* 6, 1060 (*CIL* 6, 33858. *ILS* 7225).

329 Valerius Karicus
scriba collegii fabrum tignariorum Romae. — *CIL* 6, 1060 (*CIL* 6, 33858. *ILS* 7225).

330 Valerius Ste[- - -]
scriba collegii fabrum tignariorum Romae. — *CIL* 6, 1060 (*CIL* 6, 33858. *ILS* 7225).

Military

331 Ul[pius] Amantius   [*Aquileia* - REG. X]
scriba collegii veteranorum. — *CIL* 5, 784 (*InscrAqu* 01, 247).

332 L. Ve[- - -]ius C[- - -]tus
scriba corporis immunium. — *AE* 1983, 42.

Familia Caesaris

333 Aelius Epaphroditus
scriba cocorum. — *CIL* 6, 9262 (*ILS* 7469. *IGLFriuli* 40).

334 L. Aelius Protus
scriba unctorum. — *CIL* 6, 9995 (*ILS* 7417).

335 P. Aelius *Aug. libertus* Threptus
scriba cubiculariorum. — *CIL* 6, 33770 (*ILS* 9030).

336 M. Aurelius *Aug. libertus* Fortunatianus
scriba cursorum. — *CIL* 6, 37753 (*ILS* 9031. *AE* 1903, 129).

337 Basilius
scriba collegii magni arkarum divarum Faustinarum matris et Piae. — *CIL* 6, 33840 (*ILS* 7455. FIRA 3, 142. Giovagnoli (2012a)).

338 *Imperatoris Caesaris Vespasiani servus* Cahallistus
scriba pedisequorum. — G. Mancini (1923) 31f. (*AE* 1923, 79. Ferrua (1944) no. 104. Feraudi-Gruénais (2003) no. 100).

339 Ti. Claudius Philargyrus
scriba ostiariorum. — *CIL* 6, 8961.

340 **Ti. Claudius** *divi Claudi libertus* **Philius**
scriba cubiculariorum. — AE 1946, 99 (Sinn 284).

341 **Claudius** *Actes libertus* **Storax**
scriba cubiculariorum. — CIL 6, 8767.

342 **Eutyches**
scriba. — CIL 6, 1025 (ILS 404).

343 **Felicianus**
scriba. — CIL 6, 1025 (ILS 404).

344 **T. Flavius** *Aug. libertus* **Myrtilus Ianuarianus**
scriba collegii magni Larum et imaginum. — CIL 6, 10252 (ILS 7349).

345 **Fortunatianus**
scriba. — CIL 6, 1025 (ILS 404).

346 **Hypurgus**
scriba collegii magni arkarum divarum Faustinarum matris et Piae. — CIL 6, 33840 (ILS 7455. FIRA 3, 142. Giovagnoli (2012a)).

347 *Domitiani Caesaris libertus* **Ianuarius**
scriba cubiculariorum. — CIL 6, 8768.

348 **Ianuarius**
scriba lecticariorum. — CIL 6, 8875.

349 *Augg. libertus* **Onesimus**
scriba collegii magni Larum et imaginum. — CIL 6, 10253 (ILCV 705a).

350 **Philumenus**
scriba. — CIL 6, 1025 (ILS 404).

351 **Quintius**
scriba. — CIL 6, 1025 (ILS 404).

352 **Saturio**
scriba lecticariorum. — CIL 6, 8875.

353 *Augusti libertus* **Vitalis**
scriba cubiculariorum. — CIL 6, 8769 (CIL 11, 155c*. Sinn 84).

Incerti

354 **Anonymus**   [*Caesarea* - Maur. Caes.]
scriba. — AE 1985, 908.

A.4 Naval Forces

Classis Augusta Alexandrina

355 **Apuleius Nepos**
scriba. — *CIL* 10, 3481 (*ILS* 2881). *CEL* 156 (*ChLA* III 204).

356 **Insteius Victorinus**
scriba classis liburna. — *CIL* 8, 9379.

Classis Flavia Pannonica

357 **Iulius Celer**
scriba classis. — *ILJug*-01, 278.

Classis Germanica

358 **Dionysius** *Plestharchi filius* **Trallianus**
scriba. — *CIL* 13, 8323 (*ILS* 2828. *IKöln* 395).

Classis Misenatium

359 **L. Atilius** *Xenonis filius* **Pudens**
scriba. — *CIL* 10, 3488.

360 **Q. Caesius Paternus**
scriba quadriere. — *CIL* 10, 3489.

361 **L. Calpurnius Rufus**
scriba classis praetoriae Misenensis. — *ILS* 2888 (*IK* 16, 2232a. *LIKelsey* 18. *EE* 8, 426).

362 **Cattius Sossius Felix**
scriba. — *CIL* 10, 3380.

363 **T. Claudius Paternus**
scriba. — *CIL* 10, 3490.

364 **L. Flavius Bitho**
ex scriba classis praetoriae Misenensis. — *AE* 1929, 145 (*AE* 1988, 310).

365 **C. Iulius** *C. filius Claudia (tribu)* **Maro**
ex scriba classis praetoriae Misenensis. — *AE* 1995, 311.

366 **Iulius Mummius**
scriba classis praetoriae Misenensis. — *AE* 1965, 145.

367   C. Iulius Saturninus
      scriba liburna. — *CIL* 10, 3491.

368   A. Iulius *Serri filius* Valens Diza
      scriba ex classe praetoria Misenense. — *CIL* 10, 8374a.

369   Metrod[orus]
      scriba ex classe praetoriae Misenense. — *CIL* 10, 3289 (*AE* 1990, 150. 1990, 156).

370   Minucius Aper
      scriba. — *CIL* 10, 3493.

371   Q. Naevius Propincus
      scriba. — *CIL* 10, 3492 (*ILS* 2887).

372   Q. Valerius Pollio
      scriba. — *CIL* 10, 3493.

Classis Ravennatium

373   L. Fulvius Severus
      scriba triere. — *CIL* 11, 59.

374   M. Marcius Menelaus
      ex scriba. — *CIL* 11, 77 (*ILS* 2892).

375   C. Seius Victor
      scriba triere. — *AE* 1980, 487.

376   M. Valerius *M. filius Claudia (tribu)* Colonus
      scriba. — *CIL* 11, 104 (*ILS* 2889).

377   T. Veturius Florus
      scriba. — *CIL* 11, 108.

A.5   Unassigned

378   T. Laticius Zeno   [*Trea* - REG. V]
      scriba. — *CIL* 9, 5648.

379   Lupercus   [*Ephesos* - As.]
      σκρείβας. — *I. Ephesos* 2283.

380   Saturninus   [*Karanis* - AEG.]
      scriba. — Strassi (2008) no. 2 (*P. Mich.* VIII 468. *CEL* 142. *ChLA* XLII 1217. *CEL* 143. *ChLA* V 299).

Falsi

381 **Serenus** [*Karanis* - Aeg.]
scriba. — Strassi (2008) no. 1 (*P. Mich.* VIII 467. *CEL* 141. *ChLA* XLII 1218). Strassi (2008) no. 2 (*P. Mich.* VIII 468. *CEL* 142. *ChLA* XLII 1217. *CEL* 143. *ChLA* V 299).

382 **Anonymus** [*Savaria* - Pan. sup.]
scriba. — *RIU*-01, 96 (*CIL* 3, 4195. *LapSav* 154).

383 **Anonymus** [*Minturnae* - reg. I]
scriba. — Coarelli (1989) 167, no. 44 (*AE* 1973, 198).

384 **Anonymus**
scriba. — *CIL* 6, 32284.

Incerti

385 **C. Iulius Agathopous** [*Ancyra* - Gal.]
ὑπογραφεύς. — *GLIA* 01, 64.

386 **Valerius**
scr(- - -). — *CECapitol* 4.

A.6 Falsi

Claudius Alcibiades
*scriba ab epistulis Latinis**. — *CIL* 6, 963* (*CIL* 6, 964*. *ILMN* 01, 635).

Ti. Claudius *Ti. Aug. libertus* **Arrius Claudionianus**
*scriba libel(- - -)**. — *CIL* 6, 3045*.

Livius Theona
*scriba a libris pontificalibus**. — *CIL* 6, 963* (*CIL* 6, 964*. *ILMN* 01, 635).

Sex. Numius *Sex. filius* **Ausenator**
*scriba**. — *ERAlavesa* 118*.

L. Oppius *C. filius Teretina (tribu)* **Priscus**
*scriba aedilicius**. — *CIL* 9, 258* (*Allifae* 188).

Sextia Xantha
*scriba libraria**. — *CIL* 6, 941*.

Bibliography

Sources

The editions of ancient texts used are, whenever possible, those of the 'Oxford Classical Texts (OCT) / *Scriptorum Classicorum Bibliotheca Oxoniensis*'. Other editions used as well as the translations cited are given below.

Appianos (1912–1913). *Historia Romana*. Roman History. Translated by Horace White. Loeb Classical Library. Cambridge: Harvard University Press.

Asconius, Q. Pedianus (2006). *Commentaries on Speeches of Cicero*. Ed. by A. C. Clark. Translated with Commentary by R. G. Lewis. Oxford: Oxford University Press.

Baviera, Johannes, ed. (1940). *Fontes iuris Romani antejustiniani. Pars altera. Auctores*. Florence: Barbèra.

Cassiodorus, Flavius Magnus Aurelius Senator (1886). *The Letters. Being a Condensed Translation of the Variae Epistolae of Magnus Aurelius Cassiodorus Senator. With an Introduction*. Ed. by Thomas Hodgkin. London: Henry Frowde.

Cassiodorus, Flavius Magnus Aurelius Senator (2014–2015). *Variae*. Ed. by Andrea Giardina. A cura di Andrea Giardina, Giovanni Alberto Cecconi, Ignazio Tantillo, con la collaborazione di Fabrizio Oppedisano. Rome: Bretschneider.

Cicero, M. Tullius (1900). *Epistulae*. Translated by Evelyn S. Shuckburgh. London: George Bell and Sons.

Cicero, M. Tullius (1917). *De natura deorum*. Ed. by Otto Plasberg and Wilhelm Ax. Bibliotheca Teubneriana. Leipzig: Teubner.

Cicero, M. Tullius (1927–1929). *Epistulae ad familiares*. The Letters to His Friends. Translated by W. G. Williams. Loeb Classical Library. London: Putnam's Sons.

Cicero, M. Tullius (1928). *De Re Publica. De Legibus*. Translated by C. W. Keyes. Loeb Classical Library. London: Heinemann.

Cicero, M. Tullius (1928–1935). *In Verrem*. The Verrine Orations. Translated by L. H. G. Greenwood. Loeb Classical Library. Cambridge: Harvard University Press.

Cicero, M. Tullius (1931). *Pro Milone. In Pisonem. Pro Scauro. Pro Fonteio. Pro Rabirio Postumo. Pro Marcello. Pro Ligario. Pro Deiotaro.* Translated by N. H. Watts. Loeb Classical Library. London: Heinemann.

Cicero, M. Tullius (1958). *Pro Sestio. In Vatinium.* Translated by R. Gardner. Loeb Classical Library. Cambridge: Harvard University Press.

Cicero, M. Tullius (1965–1970). *Epistulae ad Atticum.* Cicero's Letters to Atticus. 7 vols. Ed. by David R. Shackleton Bailey. Cambridge: Cambridge University Press.

Cornell, Timothy J., ed. (2013). *The Fragments of the Roman Historians.* Oxford: Oxford University Press.

Dio, Cassius (1914–1927). *Historia Romana.* Roman History. Translated by Earnest Cary, on the basis of Herbert B. Foster. Loeb Classical Library. Cambridge: Harvard University Press.

Dionysius, Halicarnassensis (1937–1950). *Antiquitates romanae.* The Roman Antiquities. Translated by Earnest Cary. Loeb Classical Library. Cambridge: Harvard University Press.

Eutropius (1995). *Breviarium ab urbe condita.* Ed. by Friedhelm L. Müller. Eutropius, kurze Geschichte Roms seit Gründung. Einleitung, Text und Übersetzung. Stuttgart: Steiner.

Festus, Sextus Pompeius (1913). *De verborum significatione quae supersunt cum Pauli epitome. Thewrewkianis copiis usus.* Ed. by Wallace M. Lindsay. Bibliotheca Teubneriana. Leipzig: Teubner.

Florus, Lucius Annaeus (1966). *Epitoma rerum Romanorum.* Epitome of Roman History. Translated by Edward Seymour Forster. Loeb Classical Library. Cambridge: Harvard University Press.

Frontinus, Sextus Iulius (1998). *De aquaeductu urbis Romae.* Ed. by Cezary Kunderewicz. Bibliotheca Teubneriana. Berlin: Teubner.

Fronto, M. Cornelius (1988). *Epistulae.* Ed. by Michael P. J. van den Hout. Bibliotheca Teubneriana. Schedis tam ed. quam ined. Edmundi Hauleri usus iterum editum. Stuttgart: Teubner.

Hohl, Ernst, ed. (1971). *Scriptores historiae Augustae.* Bibliotheca Teubneriana. Editio stereotypa correctior. Addenda et corrigenda adiecerunt Ch. Samberger et W. Seyforth. Leipzig: Teubner.

Horatius, Q. Flaccus (1926). *Sermones. Epistulae. Ars poetica.* Satires. Epistles. The Art of Poetry. Translated by H. Rushton Fairclough. Loeb Classical Library. Cambridge: Harvard University Press.

Iordanes (1991). *De origine actibusque Getarum.* Ed. by Francesco Giunta and Antonino Grillone. Rome: Istituto Storico Italiano per il Medio Evo.

Isidorus (2006). *Etymologiae.* The *Etymologies* of Isidore of Seville. Translated by Stephen A. Barney, W. J. Lewis, J. A. Beach and Oliver Berghof, with the collaboration of Muriel Hall. Cambridge: Cambridge University Press.

Josephus, Flavius (1888–1896). *Opera omnia.* Ed. by Samuel Adrian Naber. Leipzig: Teubner.

Keil, Heinrich, ed. (1857). *Grammatici Latini I. Flavii Sosipatri Charisii artis grammaticae libri V. Diomedis artis grammaticae libri III. Ex Charisii arte grammatica excerpta.* Leipzig: Teubner.

Lactantius, L. Caecilius Firmianus (1890). *Divinae institutiones et Epitome divinarum institutionum*. Ed. by Samuel Brandt. CSEL 19. Vienna: F. Tempsky.
Lamb, Charles (1935). *The Letters of Charles Lamb to Which Are Added Those of His Sister Mary Lamb. 3 Volumes*. Ed. by E. V. Lucas. London: J. M. Dent & Methuen.
Lancel, Serge, ed. (1972–1991). *Actes de la Conférence de Carthage en 411. 4 tomes*. Sources chrétiennes. Paris: Les Éditions du Cerf.
Lancel, Serge, ed. (1974). *Gesta Conlationis Carthaginiensis anno 411 accedit Sancti Augustini Breviculus conlationis cum Donatistis*. Corpus Christianorum. Turnhout: Brepols.
Lichtheim, Miriam, ed. (1975–1980). *Ancient Egyptian Literature*. Berkeley: University of California Press.
Livius, T. (1926). *Ab urbe condita*. History of Rome, Volume IV: Books 8–10. Translated by B. O. Foster. Loeb Classical Library. Cambridge: Harvard University Press.
Lydos, Johannes (1898). *De mensibus*. Ed. by Richard Wünsch. Leipzig: Teubner.
Lydos, Johannes (2006). *De magistratibus*. Des magistratures de l'état romain. Texte établi, traduit et commenté. Ed. by Michel Dubuisson and Jacques Schamp. Collection Budé. Paris: Belles Lettres.
Mommsen, Theodor and Paul Krueger, eds. (1890). *Fragmenta Vaticana. Mosaicarum et romanarum legum collatio*. Berlin: Weidmann.
Mommsen, Theodor and Paul Krueger, eds. (1985). *The Digest of Justinian. 4 vols*. English translation ed. by Alan Watson. Philadelphia: University of Pennsylvania Press.
Pharr, Clyde, ed. (1952). *The Theodosian Code and Novels and the Sirmondian Constitutions. A Translation with Commentary, Glossary, and Bibliography*. New York: Greenwood Press.
Plinius, C. Secundus (1938–1962). *Historia naturalis*. Natural History. Translated by H. Rackham, W. H. S. Jones and D. E. Eichholz. Loeb Classical Library. Cambridge: Harvard University Press.
Plutarchos (1914–1926). *Vitae parallelae*. Plutarch's Lives. Ed. by G. P. Goold, translated by Bernadotte Perrin. Loeb Classical Library. Cambridge: Harvard University Press.
Plutarchos (1961). *Ethika*. Moralia IX. Table-Talk, Books 7–9. Dialogue on Love. Ed. by Jeffrey Henderson, translated by Edwin L. Minar Jr, F. H. Sandbach and W. C. Helmbold. Loeb Classical Library. Cambridge: Harvard University Press.
Plutarchos (1969). *Ethika*. Moralia VIII. Table-Talk, Books 1–6. Ed. by Jeffrey Henderson, translated by P. A. Clement and H. B. Hoffleit. Loeb Classical Library. Cambridge: Harvard University Press.
Poe, Edgar Allan (1840). 'The Man of the Crowd'. In: *Graham's Magazine* 7.6, pp. 267–270.
Polybios (1922–1927). *Historiae*. The Histories. Translated by W. R. Paton. Loeb Classical Library. Cambridge: Harvard University Press.

Porphyrio, Pomponius (1874). *Commentarii in Q. Horatium Flaccum*. Ed. by Wilhelm Meyer. Leipzig: Teubner.
Sallustius Crispus, C. (1891). *Historiarum reliquiae*. Ed. by Bertold Maurenbrecher. Leipzig: Teubner.
Sallustius Crispus, C. (2013). *De coniuratione Catilinae. De bello Iugurthino*. The War with Catiline. The War with Jugurtha. Translated by J. C. Rolfe. Ed. by John T. Ramsey. Loeb Classical Library. Cambridge: Harvard University Press.
Scheid, John, ed. (1998). *Commentarii fratrum arvalium qui supersunt. Les copies épigraphiques des protocoles annuels de la confrérie arvale (21 av.–304 ap. J.-C.)* Roma Antica 4. Rome: École Française de Rome.
Seeck, Otto, ed. (1876). *Notitia Dignitatum accedunt Notitia Urbis Constantinopolitanae et Laterculi Provinciarum*. Berlin: Weidmann.
Servius (1881–1902). *In Vergilii carmina commentarii*. Ed. by Georg Thilo and Hermann Hagen. Leipzig: Teubner.
Stangl, Thomas, ed. (1912). *Ciceronis orationum scholiastae. Asconius, Scholia Bobiensia, Scholia Pseudasconii Sangallensia, Scholia Cluniacensia et recentoria Ambrosiana ac Vaticana, Scholia Lugdunensia sive Gronoviana et eorum excerpta Lugdunensia. Commentarii*. Vienna.
Strabon (2002–2011). *Geographika*. Ed. by Stefan Radt. Mit Übersetzung und Kommentar. Göttingen: Vandenhoeck & Ruprecht.
Strassi, Silvia (2008). *L'archivio di Claudius Tiberianus da Karanis*. Archiv für Papyrusforschung und verwandte Gebiete, Beiheft 26. Berlin and New York: de Gruyter.
Valerius Maximus (2000). *Factorum et dictorum memorabilium libri novem*. Memorable Doings and Sayings. Ed. and translated by David R. Shackleton Bailey. Loeb Classical Library. Cambridge: Harvard University Press.
Varro, M. Terentius (1938). *De lingua latina*. On the Latin Language. Translated by Roland G. Kent. Loeb Classical Library. Cambridge: Harvard University Press.
Varro, M. Terentius (1960). *De agricultura*. On Agriculture. Translated by W. D. Hooper, revised by H. B. Ash. Loeb Classical Library. Cambridge: Harvard University Press.
Vitruvius (1962). *De architectura*. On Architecture. Ed. from the Harleian manuscript 2767 and translated into English by Frank Granger. Loeb Classical Library. Cambridge: Harvard University Press.
Wessner, Paul, ed. (1931). *Scholia in Iuvenalem vetustiora*. Leipzig: Teubner.

References

Abbott, Frank Frost and Allan Chester Johnson (1926). *Municipal Administration in the Roman Empire*. New York: Russell & Russell.

Adak, Mustafa and Sencer Şahin (2004). 'Neue Inschriften aus Tlos'. In: *Gephyra* 1, pp. 85–105.
Alföldy, Géza (1964). 'Municipium Iasorum'. In: *Epigraphica* 26, pp. 95–106.
Alföldy, Géza (1990). 'Revidierte Inschriften aus der Gegend des Plattensees'. In: *Specimina Nova Universitatis Quinqueecclesiensis*, pp. 85–108.
Alföldy, Géza (1991). 'Augustus und die Inschriften: Tradition und Innovation. Die Geburt der imperialen Epigraphik'. In: *Gymnasium* 98, pp. 289–324.
Alföldy, Géza (2011). *Römische Sozialgeschichte*. 4th ed. Stuttgart: Steiner.
Alföldy, Géza, Juan Manuel Abascal, and Rosario Cebrián (2003). 'Nuevos monumentos epigráficos del foro de Segobriga. Parte primera: Inscripciones votivas, imperiales y de empleados del Estado romano'. In: *Zeitschrift für Papyrologie und Epigraphik* 143, pp. 255–274.
Ammirati, Serena (2013). 'The Use of Wooden Tablets in the Ancient Graeco-Roman World and the Birth of the Book in *Codex* Form: Some Remarks'. In: *Scripta* 6, pp. 9–15.
Andreae, Bernard (1957). 'Archäologische Funde und Grabungen im Bereich der Soprintendenzen von Rom 1949–1956/57'. In: *Jahrbuch des Deutschen Archäologischen Instituts*, pp. 110–358.
Andreau, Jean (1987). *La vie financière dans le monde romain. Les métiers de manieurs d'argent (IVe siècle av. J.-C. – IIIe siècle ap. J.-C.)* Rome: École Française de Rome.
Andreau, Jean (1999). *Banking and Business in the Roman World*. Cambridge: Cambridge University Press.
Andreau, Jean (2007). 'Registers, Account-Books, and Written Documents in the *de frumento*'. In: *Sicilia nutrix plebis romanae. Rhetoric, Law, and Taxation in Cicero's 'Verrines'*. Ed. by Jonathan R. W. Prag. Bulletin of the Institute of Classical Studies. Supplement No. 97. Institute of Classical Studies, University of London, pp. 81–92.
Armstrong, David (2010). 'The Biographical and Social Foundations of Horace's Poetic Voice'. In: *A Companion to Horace*. Ed. by Gregson Davis. Malden and Oxford: Blackwell, pp. 7–33.
Armstrong, David (2012). '*Juvenalis Eques*: A Dissident Voice from the Lower Tier of the Roman Elite'. In: *A Companion to Persius and Juvenal*. Ed. by Susanna Braund and Josiah Osgood. Malden and Oxford: Blackwell, pp. 59–78.
Ausbüttel, Frank M. (1982). *Untersuchungen zu den Vereinen im Westen des Römischen Reiches*. Kallmünz: Michael Lassleben.
Ausbüttel, Frank M. (1998). *Die Verwaltung des Römischen Kaiserreiches. Von der Herrschaft des Augustus bis zum Niedergang des Weströmischen Reiches*. Darmstadt: Wissenschaftliche Buchgesellschaft.
Badian, Ernst (1972). *Publicans and Sinners. Private Enterprise in the Service of the Roman Republic*. Ithaca, New York: Cornell University Press.
Badian, Ernst (1989). 'The *scribae* of the Roman Republic'. In: *Klio* 71.2, pp. 582–603.

Balty, Jean Ch. (1991). *Curia ordinis. Recherches d'architecture et d'urbanisme antiques sur les curies provinciales du monde romain*. Brussels: Académie Royale de Belgique.

Barbieri, Federico (1975). 'Tre nuove iscrizioni di Trevignano e nota sugli scribi'. In: *Rendiconti della Classe di Scienze morali, storiche e filologiche dell'Academia dei Lincei* 30, pp. 145–151.

Bats, Maria (1994). 'Les débuts de l'information politique officielle a Rome au premier siècle avant J. C.' In: *La mémoire perdue. A la recherche des archives oubliées, publiques et privées, de la Rome antique*. Ed. by Claude Nicolet et al. Histoire Ancienne et Médiévale, URA 994 30. Paris: Sorbonne, pp. 19–43.

Beard, Mary (1998). 'Documenting Roman Religion'. In: *La mémoire perdue. Recherches sur l'administration romaine*. Ed. by Claude Moatti et al. Collection de l'École Française de Rome 243. Rome: École Française de Rome, pp. 75–101.

Beltrán Lloris, Francisco (2015). 'The "Epigraphic Habit" in the Roman World'. In: *The Oxford Handbook of Roman Epigraphy*. Ed. by Christer Bruun and Jonathan Edmondson. Oxford: Oxford University Press, pp. 131–148.

Benner, Herbert (1987). *Die Politik des P. Clodius Pulcher. Untersuchungen zur Denaturierung des Clientelwesens in der ausgehenden römischen Republik*. Stuttgart: Franz Steiner.

Bertolazzi, Riccardo and Valeria Lamonaca (2010). '*Regio X (Venetia et Histria)*, parte occidentale: Vicetia, Mantua, Tridentum, Verona'. In: *Le tribù romane. Atti della XVI*^{e} *Rencontre sur l'épigraphie (Bari 8–10 ottobre 2009)*. Ed. by Marina Silvestrini. Bari: Edipuglia, pp. 281–292.

Birley, Anthony Richard (1997). 'Marius Maximus: The Consular Biographer'. In: *Aufstieg und Niedergang der römischen Welt (ANRW). Principat*. Ed. by Wolfgang Haase. Vol. 34.3. Berlin and New York, pp. 2679–2757.

Bloch, Herbert (1953). 'Regione I (*LATIVM ET CAMPANIA*). IX. – Ostia. – Iscrizioni rinvenute tra il 1930 e il 1939'. In: *Notizie degli scavi di antichità* 6, pp. 239–306.

Boge, Herbert (1973). *Griechische Tachygraphie und Tironische Noten. Ein Handbuch der antiken und mittelalterlichen Schnellschrift*. Berlin: Akademie.

Bönisch, Sophia and Andrew Lepke (2013). 'Neue Inschriften aus Patara II: Kaiserzeitliche Ehren- und Grabinschriften'. In: *Chiron* 43, pp. 487–525.

Bonner, Stanley F. (1977). *Education in Ancient Rome. From the Elder Cato to the Younger Pliny*. London: Methuen.

Bordenache Battaglia, Gabriella and Anna Maria Sgubini Moretti (1975). 'Rilievo funerario con tre busti'. In: *Nuove scoperte e acuisizioni nell'Etruria meridionale*. Ed. by Mario Moretti. Rome: Artistica di A. Nardini, pp. 251–253.

Bounegru, Octavian (1981–1982). 'T. Iulius Saturninus, conductor Illyrici utriusque et ripae Thraciae'. In: *Dacoromania. Jahrbuch für östliche Latinität* 6, pp. 121–132.

Bourdieu, Pierre (1986). 'The Forms of Capital'. In: *Handbook of Theory and Research for the Sociology of Education*. Ed. by J. G. Richardson. New York: Greenwood Press, pp. 241–258.

Bozič, Dragan and Michel Feugère (2004). 'Les instruments de l'écriture'. In: *Gallia* 61, pp. 21–41.
Brennan, T. Corey (2000). *The Praetorship in the Roman Republic*. 2 Volumes. Oxford: Oxford University Press.
Broughton, Thomas Robert Shannon (1951–1952). *The Magistrates of the Roman Republic. Two Volumes*. New York: American Philological Association.
Bruckner, Albert and Robert Marichal, eds. (1954–1998). *Chartae Latinae Antiquiores. 1–49*. Dietikon, Zurich: Urs Graf Verlag.
Brunt, Peter A. (1988). *The Fall of the Roman Republic and Related Essays*. Oxford: Clarendon Press.
Bücheler, Franz (1908). 'Mitteilungen. Inschriftliches und zu Plutarchs parall. min.' In: *Berliner philologische Wochenschrift* 28, pp. 510–511.
Buonocore, Marco (1984a). *Schiavi e liberti dei Volusi Saturnini. Le iscrizioni del colombario sulla via Appia antica*. Rome: Bretschneider.
Butler, Shane (2002). *The Hand of Cicero*. Abingdon: Oxon.
Camodeca, Giuseppe (1980). 'Richerche sui "curatores rei publicae"'. In: *Aufstieg und Niedergang der römischen Welt (ANRW). Principat* 13, pp. 453–534.
Camodeca, Giuseppe (1993). 'Nuovi dati dagli archivi campani sulla datazione e applicazione del "S. C. Neronianum"'. In: *Index* 21, pp. 353–364.
Camodeca, Giuseppe (2007). 'Il giurista L. Neratius Priscus *cos. suff.* 97. Nuovi dati su carriera e famiglia'. In: *Studia et Documenta Historiae et Iuris* 73, pp. 291–311.
Camodeca, Giuseppe (2010). 'Il patrimonio epigrafico latino e l'élite municipale di Cuma: parte prima'. In: *Il Mediterraneo e la Storia. Epigrafia e archeologia in Campania: letture storiche. Napoli 4–5 dicembre 2008*. Ed. by Laura Chioffi. Naples: Luciano, pp. 47–72.
Carrié, Jean-Michel (1998). 'Archives municipales et distributions alimentaires dans l'Égypte romaine'. In: *La mémoire perdue. Recherches sur l'administration romaine*. Ed. by Claude Moatti et al. Collection de l'École Française de Rome 243. Rome: École Française de Rome, pp. 271–302.
Castritius, Helmut (1982). 'Korruption im ostgotischen Italien'. In: *Korruption im Altertum. Konstanzer Symposium Oktober 1979*. Ed. by Wolfgang Schuller. Munich and Vienna: R. Oldenbourg, pp. 215–238.
Cencetti, Giorgio (1940). 'Gli archivi dell'antica Roma nell'età repubblicana'. In: *Archivi* S. II 7, pp. 7–47.
Cencetti, Giorgio (1953). 'Tabularium principis'. In: *Studi di paleografia, diplomatica, storia e araldica in onore de Cesare Manaresi*. Milan: Giuffrè, pp. 133–166.
Chantraine, Heinrich (1967). *Freigelassene und Sklaven im Dienst der römischen Kaiser*. Wiesbaden: Franz Steiner.
Chastagnol, André (1953). 'Le ravitaillement de Rome en viande au Ve siècle'. In: *Revue Historique* 210.1, pp. 13–22.
Chastagnol, André (1960). *La préfecture urbaine à Rome sous le Bas-Empire*. Publications de la Faculté des Lettres et Sciences Humaines d'Alger 34. Paris: Presses Universitaires de France.

Chioffi, Laura (1999). 'Schola: scribae librarii et praecones aedilium curulium'. In: *Lexicon topographicum urbis Romae*. Ed. by Eva Margareta Steinby. Vol. IV P-S. Rome: Quasar, pp. 257–258.

Christol, Michel (1981). 'Observations complémentaires sur les carrières de Marcus Aurelius Hermogenes et de Pontius Eglectus Iulianus: Procurator a studis et magister a studis'. In: *Zeitschrift für Papyrologie und Epigraphik* 43, pp. 67–74.

Ciongradi, Carmen (2007). *Grabmonumente und sozialer Status in Oberdakien*. Cluj-Napoca: Mega Verlag.

Cîrjan, Romeo (2010). 'Personnel municipal subalterne dans les provinces danubiennes de l'Empire Romain (Ier–IIIe siècles après J.-Chr.)' In: *Ephemeris Napocensis* 20, pp. 181–189.

Clanchy, Michael T. (1993). *From Memory to Written Record. England 1066–1307*. 2nd ed. Malden and Oxford: Blackwell.

Coarelli, Filippo, ed. (1989). *Minturnae*. Rome: NER.

Coarelli, Filippo (2011). *Roma*. 3rd ed. Rome: Laterza.

Cohen, Benjamin (1984). 'Some Neglected *Ordines*: The Apparitorial Status-Groups'. In: *Des Ordres à Rome*. Ed. by Claude Nicolet. Paris: La Sorbonne, pp. 24–60.

Collassero, Silvia (1985). 'Librārius'. In: *Thesaurus Linguae Latinae* VII.2, pp. 1347.3–1348.21.

Collingwood, R. G. et al., eds. (1990–1995). *The Roman Inscriptions of Britain. Volume II. Instrumentum Domesticum*. Oxford: Alan Sutton.

Colonna, Giovanni (1976). 'Scriba cum rege sedens'. In: *L'Italie préromaine et la Rome républicaine. Mélanges offerts à Jacques Heurgon*. Vol. 1. Rome: École Française de Rome, pp. 187–195.

Corbier, Mireille (1974). *L'aerarium Saturni et l'aerarium militare. Administration et prosopographie sénatoriale*. Collection de l'École Française de Rome 24. Rome: De Boccard.

Corbier, Mireille (1987). 'L'écriture dans l'espace public Romain'. In: *L'urbs. Espace urbain et histoire (Ier siècle av. J.-C. – IIIe siècle ap. J.-C.)* Collection de l'École Française de Rome 98. Rome: École Française de Rome, pp. 27–60.

Cornell, Timothy J. (1995). *The Beginnings of Rome. Italy and Rome from the Bronze Age to the Punic Wars (c. 1000–264 BC)*. London and New York: Routledge.

Coudry, Marianne (1994). 'Sénatus-consultes et *acta senatus*: rédaction, conservation et archivage des documents émanant du sénat, de l'époque de César à celle des Sévères'. In: *La mémoire perdue. A la recherche des archives oubliées, publiques et privées, de la Rome antique*. Ed. by Claude Nicolet et al. Histoire Ancienne et Médiévale, URA 994 30. Paris: Sorbonne, pp. 65–102.

Cribiore, Raffaella (2001). *Gymnastics of the Mind. Greek Education in Hellenistic and Roman Egypt*. Princeton and Oxford: Princeton University Press.

Crowther, N. B. (1973). 'The Collegium Poetarum at Rome: Fact and Conjecture'. In: *Latomus* 32, pp. 575–580.

Cugusi, Paolo, ed. (1992, 2002). *Corpus Epistularum Latinarum Papyris Tabulis Ostracis servatarum. Vol. I Textus, Vol. II Commentarius, Vol. III Addenda, Corrigenda, Indices rerum, Index verborum omnium*. Florence: Gonnelli.

Culham, Phyllis (1989). 'Archives and Alternatives in Republican Rome'. In: *Classical Philology* 84.2, pp. 100–115.
Culham, Phyllis (1996). 'Fraud, Fakery and Forgery: The Limits of Roman Information Technology'. In: *The Ancient World* 27.2, pp. 172–183.
Cuomo, Serafina (2011). 'All the Proconsul's Men: Cicero, Verres and Account-Keeping'. In: *L'insegnamento delle technai nelle culture antiche. Atti del convegno, Ercolano, 23–24 marzo 2009*. Ed. by Amneris Roselli and Roberto Velardi. Pisa and Rome: Fabrizio Serra, pp. 165–185.
Curchin, Leonard A. (1986). 'Non-slave Labour in Roman Spain'. In: *Gerión* 4, pp. 177–187.
Daguet-Gagey, Anne (2015). *Splendor aedilitatum. L'édilité à Rome (Ier s. avant J.-C. – IIIe s. après J.-C.)* Rome: École Française de Rome.
Daicoviciu, H. and Ioan Piso (1977). 'Sarmizegetusa et les guerres marcomannes'. In: *Revue Roumaine d'Histoire* 16.1, pp. 155–159.
Damon, Cynthia (1992). 'Sex. Cloelius, *Scriba*'. In: *Harvard Studies in Classical Philology* 94, pp. 227–250.
d'Arms, John H. (1976). 'Notes on Municipal Notables of Imperial Ostia'. In: *The American Journal of Philology* 97.4, pp. 387–411.
David, Jean-Michel (2007). 'Ce que les *Verrines* nous apprennent sur les scribes de magistrats à la fin de la République'. In: *La Sicile de Cicéron. Lectures des Verrines. Actes du colloque de Paris, 19–20 mai 2006, organisé par l'UMR 8585, Centre Gustave Glotz*. Ed. by Julien Dubouloz and Sylvie Pittia. Besançon: Pr. Universitaires de Franche-Comté, pp. 35–56.
Degrassi, Attilio, ed. (1954). *Fasti Capitolini*. Turin: Paravia.
Delbrueck, Richard (1907–1912). *Hellenistische Bauten in Latium. I. Baubeschreibungen. II. Baubeschreibungen, Geschichtliche Erläuterungen*. Strasbourg: Karl J. Trübner.
Delmaire, Roland (1995). *Les institutions du Bas-Empire romain, de Constantin à Justinien. I. Les institutions civiles palatines*. Paris: Cerf.
Demougin, Ségolène (1978). 'M. Sufenas M. f. Proculus'. In: *Latomus* 37.3, pp. 620–624.
Demougin, Ségolène (1988). *L'ordre équestre sous les Julio-Claudiens*. Collection de l'École Française de Rome 108. Rome: École Française de Rome.
Demougin, Ségolène (1992). *Prosopographie des chevaliers romains julio-claudiens (43 av. J.-C. – 70 ap. J.-C.)* Rome: École Française de Rome.
Demougin, Ségolène (1993). 'Appartenir à l'ordre équestre au IIème siècle'. In: *Prosopographie und Sozialgeschichte. Studien zur Methodik und Erkenntnismöglichkeit der kaiserzeitlichen Prosopographie. Kolloquium Köln 24. – 26. November 1991*. Ed. by Werner Eck. Cologne: Böhlau, pp. 233–250.
Devijver, Hubert (1976–2001). *Prosopographia militiarum equestrium quae fuerunt ab Augusto ad Gallienum*. Ed. by Ségolène Demougin and Marie-Thérèse Raepsaet-Charlier. Leuven: Universitaire Pers.
Dietz, Karlheinz (1980). *Senatus contra principem. Untersuchungen zur senatorischen Opposition gegen Kaiser Maximinus Thrax*. Munich: C.H. Beck.

Donati, Angela (1977). 'Cataloghi collegiali su un'iscrizione opistografa ravennate'. In: *Epigraphica* 39, pp. 27–40.
Düll, Rudolf (1943). 'Zur Apparitorenfrage'. In: *Zeitschrift der Savigny-Stiftung für Rechtsgeschichte, Rom. Abt.* 63.1, pp. 393–396.
Duncan-Jones, Richard (2016). *Power and Privilege in Roman Society*. Cambridge: Cambridge University Press.
Duthoy, Robert (1979). 'Curatores rei publicae en Occident durant le Principat. Recherches préliminaires sur l'apport des sources épigraphiques'. In: *Ancient Society* 10, pp. 171–238.
Eck, Werner (1972). 'Die Familie der Volusii Saturnini in neuen Inschriften aus Lucus Feroniae'. In: *Hermes* 100.3, pp. 461–484.
Eck, Werner (1978). 'Abhängigkeit als ambivalenter Begriff. Zum Verhältnis von Patron und Libertus'. In: *Memorias de Historia Antiqua* 2, pp. 41–50.
Eck, Werner (1979). *Die staatliche Organisation Italiens in der hohen Kaiserzeit*. Vestigia 28. Munich: C. H. Beck.
Eck, Werner (1983). 'Jahres- und Provinzialfasten der senatorichen Statthalter von 69/70 bis 138/139'. In: *Chiron* 13, pp. 147–237.
Eck, Werner (1995). 'Die Wasserversorgung im römischen Reich: Sozio-politische Bedingungen, Recht und Administration'. In: *Die Verwaltung des Römischen Reiches in der Hohen Kaiserzeit. Ausgewählte und erweiterte Beiträge. 1. Band*. Ed. by Regula Frei-Stolba and Michael Alexander Speidel. Basel: F. Reinhardt, pp. 179–252.
Eck, Werner (1998). 'Inschriften auf Holz. Ein unterschätztes Phänomen der epigraphischen Kultur Roms'. In: *Imperium Romanum. Studien zu Geschichte und Rezeption*. Ed. by Peter Kneissl and Volker Losemann. Festschrift für Karl Christ zum 75. Geburtstag. Stuttgart: Franz Steiner Verlag, pp. 203–217.
Eck, Werner (1999). '*Ordo equitum romanorum, ordo libertorum*. Freigelassene und ihre Nachkommen im römischen Ritterstand'. In: *L'ordre équestre. Histoire d'une aristocratie (IIe siècle av. J.-C. – IIIe siècle ap. J.-C. Actes du colloque de Bruxelles-Leuven (octobre 1995)*. Ed. by Ségolène Demougin, Hubert Devijver, and Marie-Thérèse Raepsaet-Charlier. Collection de l'École Française de Rome 257. Rome: École Française de Rome, pp. 5–29.
Eck, Werner (2002). 'Verwaltung. VIII. Rom. A. Republik. B. Kaiserzeit'. In: *Der Neue Pauly* 12/2, pp. 111–114.
Eck, Werner (2014). 'Documents on Bronze: A Phenomenon of the Roman West?' In: *Ancient Documents and their Contexts. First North American Congress of Greek and Latin Epigraphy (2011)*. Ed. by John Bodel and Nora Dimitrova. Leiden: Brill, pp. 127–151.
Eich, Peter (2005). *Zur Metamorphose des politischen Systems in der römischen Kaiserzeit. Die Entstehung einer 'personalen Bürokratie' im langen dritten Jahrhundert*. Berlin: Akademie.
Erman, Henri (1905). 'La falsification des actes dans l'antiquité'. In: *Mélanges Nicole. Recueil de mémoires de philologie classique et d'archéologie offerts à Jules Nicole*. Geneva: W. Kündig & Fils, pp. 111–134.

Eschenbach, Andreas Christian and Johann Christoph Spies (1687). *De scribis veterum Romanorum*. Jena: Bauhofer.
Fallu, Élie (1979). 'Les règles de la comptabilité publique à Rome à la fin de la République'. In: *Points de vue sur la fiscalité antique*. Ed. by Henri van Effenterre. Paris: La Sorbonne, pp. 97–112.
Fantham, Elaine (1996). *Roman Literary Culture. From Cicero to Apuleius*. Baltimore and London: The Johns Hopkins University Press.
Feraudi-Gruénais, Francisca (2003). *Inschriften und 'Selbstdarstellung' in stadtrömischen Grabbauten*. Libitina 2. Rome: Quasar.
Ferrua, Antonio (1944). 'Analecta Romana. II. – S. Sebastiano'. In: *Epigraphica* 5-6, pp. 3–26.
Ferrua, Antonio (1958). 'Giovanni Zaratino Castellini raccoglitore di epigrafi'. In: *Epigraphica* 20, pp. 121–160.
Fioretti, Paolo (2014). '*Scribae*. Riflessi sulla cultura scritta nella Roma antica'. In: *Storia della scrittura e altre storie*. Ed. by Daniele Bianconi. Bollettino dei Classici, Supplemento no. 29. Rome: Accademia Nazionale dei Lincei, pp. 337–362.
Flambard, Jean-Marc (1978). 'Nouvel examen d'un dossier prosopographique: le cas de Sex. Clodius / Cloelius'. In: *Mélanges de l'École Française de Rome, Antiquité* 90.1, pp. 235–245.
Florescu, Gr. (1927–1932). 'Fouilles et recherches archéologiques à Callachioi (Capidava?) en 1924 et 1926'. In: *Dacia* 3–4, pp. 483–515.
Fraenkel, Eduard (1957). *Horace*. Oxford: Clarendon Press.
Freyburger, Gérard (1986). *FIDES. Étude sémantique et religieuse depuis les origines jusqu'à l'époque augustéenne*. Paris: Belles Lettres.
Frier, Bruce Woodward (1979). *Libri Annales Pontificum Maximorum. The Origins of the Annalistic Tradition*. Papers and Monography of the American Academy in Rome 27. Rome: American Academy in Rome.
Fuchs, Michel E., Richard Sylvestre, and Christophe Schmidt Heidenreich, eds. (2012). *Inscriptions mineures: nouveautés et réflexions. Actes du premier colloque Ductus (19–20 juin 2008, Université de Lausanne)*. Bern: Peter Lang.
Fusco, Ugo (2008–2009). 'Iscrizioni votive ad Ercole, alle Fonti e a Diana dal sito di Campetti a Veio: ulteriori elementi per l'interpretazione archeologica'. In: *Rendiconti della Pontificia Accademia Romana di Archeologia* 81, pp. 443–500.
Gabba, Emilio (1983). 'Lineamenti di un commento alla *Lex Cornelia de XX Quaestoribus*'. In: *Athenaeum* 71, pp. 487–493.
Gallego Franco, Henar (2001). 'Los *scribae* en la vida municipal de las ciudades de la provincia romana de *Pannonia*'. In: *Norba* 15, pp. 117–120.
Galsterer, Hartmut (1976). *Herrschaft und Verwaltung im republikanischen Italien. Die Beziehungen Roms zu den italischen Gemeinden vom Latinerfrieden 338 v. Chr. bis zum Bundesgenossenkrieg 91 v. Chr*. Munich: C. H. Beck.
Garnsey, Peter (2010). 'Roman Patronage'. In: *From the Tetrarchs to the Theodosians. Later Roman History and Culture, 284–450 CE*. Ed. by Scott McGill, Cristiana Sogno, and Edward Watts. Yale Classical Studies 34. Cambridge: Cambridge University Press, pp. 33–54.

Gasperini, Lidio (2009). 'Epitafio latino inedito dal Blerano'. In: *Epigraphica* 71, pp. 372–375.
Gatti, G. (1906). 'Roma. Nuove scoperte nella città e nel suburbio'. In: *Notizie degli scavi di antichità* 3, pp. 299–304.
Gee, James Paul (2015). 'The New Literacy Studies'. In: *The Routledge Handbook of Literacy Studies*. Ed. by Jennifer Rowsell and Kate Pahl. London and New York: Routledge, pp. 35–48.
Giovagnoli, Maurizio (2012a). 'Un colono'. In: *Terme di Diocleziano. La collezione epigrafica*. Ed. by Rosanna Friggeri, Maria Grazia Granino Cecere, and Gian Luca Gregori. Milan: Electa, pp. 500–501.
Giovagnoli, Maurizio (2012b). 'Un *magister scribarum*'. In: *Terme di Diocleziano. La collezione epigrafica*. Ed. by Rosanna Friggeri, Maria Grazia Granino Cecere, and Gian Luca Gregori. Milan: Electa, p. 220.
Giovagnoli, Maurizio (2013). 'Un nuovo cavaliere proveniente da Alatri'. In: *Epigraphica* 75, pp. 187–194.
Giovannini, Adalberto (1998). 'Les livres auguraux'. In: *La mémoire perdue. Recherches sur l'administration romaine*. Ed. by Claude Moatti et al. Collection de l'École Française de Rome 243. Rome: École Française de Rome, pp. 103–122.
Giuliani, Luca (1989). 'Achill-Sarkophage in Ost und West: Genese einer Ikonographie'. In: *Jahrbuch der Berliner Museen* 31, pp. 25–39.
Gnoli, Franco (1975). 'Cic., Nat. deor. 3,74 e l'origine della "quaestio perpetua peculatus"'. In: *Rendiconti Istituto Lombardo, Accademia di Scienze e Lettere, Classe di Lettere, Scienze morali e storiche* 109, pp. 331–341.
Gnoli, Franco (1979). *Ricerche sul crimen peculatus*. Milan: Giuffrè.
Goody, Jack and Ian Watt (1963). 'The Consequences of Literacy'. In: *Comparative Studies in Society and History* 5.3, pp. 304–345.
Graff, Harvey J. (1986). 'The Legacies of Literacy: Continuities and Contradictions in Western Society and Culture'. In: *Literacy, Society, and Schooling. A Reader*. Ed. by Suzanne de Castell, Allan Luke, and Kieran Egan. Cambridge: Cambridge University Press, pp. 61–86.
Graff, Harvey J. (1987). *The Legacies of Literacy. Continuities and Contradictions in Western Culture and Society*. Bloomington and Indianapolis: Indiana University Press.
Granino Cecere, Maria Grazia (2012). 'Dedica a un cavaliere'. In: *Terme di Diocleziano. La collezione epigrafica*. Ed. by Rosanna Friggeri, Maria Grazia Granino Cecere, and Gian Luca Gregori. Milan: Electa, pp. 457–458.
Gregori, Gian Luca (2007). 'Un nuovo *magister scribarum*'. In: *Centocelle II. Roma S.D.O. Le indagini archeologiche*. Ed. by R. Volpe. Catanzaro: Rubbettino, pp. 435–436.
Gros, Pierre (2001). 'Les édifices de la bureaucratie impériale: administration, archives et services publics dans le centre monumental de Rome'. In: *Pallas* 55, pp. 107–126.
Guizzi, Francesco, Elena Miranda De Martino, and Tullia Ritti (2012). 'Acquisizioni epigrafiche: iscrizioni ritrovate o studiate nel triennio 2004–2006'. In: *Hierapolis di Frigia. Le attività delle campagne di scavo e restauro*

2004–2006. Ed. by D'Andria Francesco, Maria Piera Caggia, and Ismaelli Tommaso. Hierapolis di Frigia V. Istanbul: Ege Yayınları, pp. 657–678.

Hächler, Nikolas (2019). *Kontinuität und Wandel des Senatorenstandes im Zeitalter der Soldatenkaiser. Prosopographische Untersuchungen zu Zusammensetzung, Funktion und Bedeutung des* amplissimus ordo *zwischen 235–284 n. Chr.* Impact of Empire 33. Leiden and Boston: Brill.

Haensch, Rudolf (1992). 'Das Statthalterarchiv'. In: *Zeitschrift der Savigny-Stiftung für Rechtsgeschichte, Roman. Abt.* 109, pp. 209–317.

Haensch, Rudolf (1996). 'Die Verwendung von Siegeln bei Dokumenten der kaiserzeitlichen Reichsadministration'. In: *Archives et Sceaux du Monde Hellénistique. Archivi e Sigilli nel Mondo Ellenistico. Torino, Villa Gualino. 13–16 Gennaio 1993*. Ed. by Marie-Françoise Boussac and Antonio Invernizzi. BCH Supplément 29. Athens: École Française d'Athènes, pp. 449–496.

Haensch, Rudolf (1997). *Capita provinciarum. Statthaltersitze und Provinzialverwaltung in der römischen Kaiserzeit*. Kölner Forschungen 7. Mainz: Philipp von Zabern.

Haines-Eitzen, Kim (2000). *Guardians of Letters. Literacy, Power, and the Transmitters of Early Christian Literature*. Oxford: Oxford University Press.

Hammond, Mason (1938). 'Curatores tabularum publicarum'. In: *Classical and Mediaeval Studies in Honor of Edward Kennard Rand*. Ed. by Leslie Webber Jones. New York, pp. 123–131.

Harris, William V. (1976). 'The Development of the Quaestorship, 267–81 BC.' In: *Classical Quarterly* 26, pp. 91–106.

Harris, William V. (1989). *Ancient Literacy*. Cambridge: Harvard University Press.

Hartmann, Benjamin (2015). 'Die hölzernen Schreibtafeln im Imperium Romanum – ein Inventar'. In: *Lesen und Schreiben in den römischen Provinzen. Schriftliche Kommunikation im Alltagsleben. Akten des 2. Internationalen Kolloquiums von DUCTUS – Association international pour l'étude des inscriptions mineures, RGZM Mainz, 15.-17. Juni 2011*. Ed. by Markus Scholz and Marietta Horster. RGZM-Tagungen 26. Mainz: Verlag des Römisch-Germanischen Zentralmuseums, pp. 43–58.

Hartmann, Benjamin (2018). 'Schreiben im Dienste des Staates. Prolegomena zu einer Kulturgeschichte der römischen *scribae*'. In: *Literacy in Ancient Everyday Life*. Ed. by Anne Kolb. Berlin and Boston: DeGruyter, pp. 351–360.

Häussler, Ralph (2013). 'Literacy, Rome and Provinces'. In: *The Encyclopedia of Ancient History* 7, pp. 4104–4108.

Havelock, Eric A. (1986). *The Muse Learns to Write. Reflection on Orality and Literacy from Antiquity to the Present*. New Haven and London: Yale University Press.

Haynes, Sybille (2000). *Etruscan Civilization. A Cultural History*. Los Angeles: The J. Paul Getty Museum.

Heinzelmann, Michael (2000). *Die Nekropolen von Ostia. Untersuchungen zu den Gräberstrassen vor der Porta Romana und an der Via Laurentina*. Munich: Pfeil.

Hergött, Jacob Ernst and Johann Wolfgang Bürger (1668). *De scribis veterum Graecorum, Romanorum atque Germanorum*. Wittenberg: Matthaeus Henckel.

Herzog, Ernst (1884–1891). *Geschichte und System der römischen Staatsverfassung.* Leipzig: Teubner.
Himmelmann, Nikolaus (1973). *Typologische Untersuchungen an römischen Sarkophagreliefs des 3. und 4. Jahrhunderts n. Chr.* Mainz: Philipp von Zabern.
Hirschfeld, Otto (1905). *Die kaiserlichen Verwaltungsbeamten bis auf Diocletian.* Zweite neu bearbeitete Auflage. Berlin: Weidmann.
Horsfall, Nicholas (1976). 'The *collegium poetarum*'. In: *Bulletin of the Institute of Classical Studies* 23, pp. 79–95.
Horsfall, Nicholas (2003). *The Culture of the Roman Plebs.* London: Duckworth.
Houston, George W. (2014). *Inside Roman Libraries. Book Collections and Their Management in Antiquity.* Chapel Hill: University of North Carolina Press.
Huelsen, Christian (1888). 'Il sito e le iscrizioni della schola Xantha sul Foro Romano'. In: *Mittheilungen des Kaiserlich Deutschen Archäologischen Instituts. Römische Abtheilung* 3, pp. 208–232.
Huelsen, Christian (1902). 'Neue Inschriften vom Forum Romanum'. In: *Klio* 2, pp. 227–283.
Hugo, Herman (1738). *De prima scribendi origine et universa rei litterariae antiquitate.* Notas, opusculum de scribis, apologiam pro Wachtlero, praefationem et indices adjecit C. H. Trotz [1. ed. Antwerpen 1617]. Utrecht: Herman Besseling.
Humm, Michel (2005). *Appius Claudius Caecus. La république accomplie.* Rome: École Française de Rome.
Jacques, François (1983). *Les curateurs des cités dans l'Occident romain de Trajan à Gallien.* Paris: Nouvelles éditions latines.
Jarrett, Michael G. (1963). 'The African Contribution to the Imperial Equestrian Service'. In: *Historia* 12.2, pp. 209–226.
Jones, Arnold H. M. (1949). 'The Roman Civil Service (Clerical and Sub-Clerical Grades)'. In: *The Journal of Roman Studies* 39, pp. 38–55.
Jones, Arnold H. M. (1964). *The Later Roman Empire 284–602. A Social, Economic and Administrative Survey.* Oxford: Blackwell.
Jones, David (2006). *The Bankers of Puetoli. Finance, Trade and Industry in the Roman World.* Stroud: Tempus.
Jory, E. J. (1968). 'P. Cornelius P. L. Surus. An Epigraphical Note'. In: *Bulletin of the Institute of Classical Studies* 15, pp. 125–126.
Jory, E. J. (1970). 'Associations of Actors in Rome'. In: *Hermes* 98, pp. 224–253.
Kajanto, Iiro (1982). *The Latin Cognomina.* Rome: Bretschneider.
Karlowa, Otto (1885–1901). *Römische Rechtsgeschichte.* Leipzig: von Veit & Comp.
Kavanagh, Bernard J. (2001). 'The Conspirator Aemilius Regulus and Seneca's Aunt's Family'. In: *Historia* 50.3, pp. 379–384.
Kelly, Christopher M. (1994). 'Late Roman Bureaucracy: Going through the Files'. In: *Literacy and Power in the Ancient World.* Ed. by Alan K. Bowman and Greg Woolf. Cambridge: Cambridge University Press, pp. 161–176.
Kleijwegt, Marc (1994). 'Discord in an Italian Town. Fronto's Letter on *Concordia* (*Ep. ad Am.* II, 7)'. In: *Studies in Latin Literature and Roman History VII.* Ed. by Carl Deroux. Collection Latomus 227. Brussels: Latomus, pp. 507–523.

Koch, Guntram and Hellmut Sichtermann (1982). *Römische Sarkophage*. Munich: C.H. Beck.
Koch, Holger (2014). 'Neue Beobachtungen zum Geschichtswerk des Iulius Florus als eines spätaugusteischen Autors'. In: *Acta classica Universitatis scientiarum Debreceniensis* 50, pp. 101–137.
Kockel, Valentin (1993). *Porträtreliefs stadtrömischer Grabbauten. Ein Beitrag zur Geschichte und zum Verständnis des spätrepublikanisch-frühkaiserzeitlichen Privatportraits*. Mainz: Philipp von Zabern.
Koeppel, Gerhard M. (1986). 'Die historischen Reliefs der römischen Kaiserzeit IV'. In: *Bonner Jahrbücher* 186, pp. 1–90.
Kolb, Anne (2000). *Transport und Nachrichtentransfer im Römischen Reich*. Berlin: Akademie.
Kolb, Anne (2015). 'Bronze in Epigraphy'. In: *New Research on Ancient Bronzes. Acta of the XVIIIth International Congress on Ancient Bronzes*. Ed. by Eckhard Deschler-Erb and Philippe Della Casa. Zurich Studies in Archaeology 10. Zurich: Chronos, pp. 343–348.
Konrad, C. F. (1994). *Plutarch's Sertorius. A Historical Commentary*. Chapel Hill and London: The University of North Carolina Press.
Kornemann, Ernst (1921). 'Scriba'. In: *Paulys Realencyclopädie der Classischen Altertumswissenschaft* 2. R. 3. Hlb. Pp. 848–857.
Krause, August Wilhelm Ferdinand (1858). 'De scribis publicis Romanorum'. In: *Jahrbuch des Pädagogiums zum Kloster Unser Lieben Frauen in Magdeburg* 22, pp. 1–22.
Krebs, Elimar et al., eds. (1897–1898). *Prosopographia Imperii Romani I. II. III.* Berlin: G. Reimer.
Kunihara, Kichinosuke (1963). 'The History of the Collegium Poetarum at Rome'. In: *Istituto Giapponese di Cultura in Roma. Annuario* 1.1963–1964, pp. 85–99.
Kunkel, Wolfgang and Roland Wittmann (1995). *Staatsordnung und Staatspraxis der römischen Republik. Zweiter Abschnitt. Die Magistratur*. Handbuch der Altertumswissenschaft III 2.2. Munich: C. H. Beck.
Lambrechts, Roger (1959). *Essai sur les magistratures des républiques étrusques*. Brussels and Rome: L'Institut historique Belge de Rome.
Langford Wilson, Harry (1909). 'Latin Inscriptions at the Johns Hopkins University. II'. In: *The American Journal of Philology* 30.1, pp. 61–71.
Latte, Kurt (1936). 'The Origin of the Roman Quaestorship'. In: *Transactions and Proceedings of the American Philological Association* 67, pp. 24–33.
Le Roux, Patrick (1982). 'Les senateurs originaires de la province d'Hispania citerior au Haut Empire romain'. In: *Atti del colloquio internazionale AIEGL su epigrafia e ordine senatorio: Roma, 14–20 maggio 1981*. Tituli 4–5. Rome: Ed. di storia e letteratura, pp. 439–464.
Lebek, W. D. (1994). 'Domitians *Lex Lati* und die Duumvirn, Aedilen und Quaestoren in Tab. Irn. Paragraph 18–20'. In: *Zeitschrift für Papyrologie und Epigraphik* 103, pp. 253–292.
Lehmler, Caroline and Michael Wörrle (2002). 'Neue Inschriftenfunde aus Aizanoi III: Aizanitica Minora I'. In: *Chiron* 32, pp. 571–646.

Lesquier, M. Jean (1918). *L'armée romaine d'Égypte d'Auguste à Dioclétien.* Cairo: Institut français d'archéologique orientale.
Levi, Margaret (1988). *Of Rule and Revenue.* Berkeley and Los Angeles: University of California Press.
Lévi-Strauss, Claude (1955). *Tristes tropiques.* Paris: Plon.
Liebenam, Wilhelm (1900). *Städteverwaltung im römischen Kaiserreiche.* Leipzig: Duncker & Humblot.
Liebs, Detlef (1980). 'Nichtliterarische römische Juristen der Kaiserzeit'. In: *Das Profil der Juristen in der europäischen Tradition. Symposion aus Anlass des 70. Geburtstages von Franz Wieacker.* Ed. by Klaus Luig and Detlef Liebs. Ebelsbach: Rolf Gremer, pp. 123–198.
Liebs, Detlef (1993). *Römische Jurisprudenz in Africa. Mit Studien zu den pseudopaulinischen Sentenzen.* Berlin: Akademie.
Lindsay, Hugh (2009). *Adoption in the Roman World.* Cambridge: Cambridge University Press.
Lintott, Andrew (1981). 'The leges de repetundis and Associate Measures Under the Republic'. In: *Zeitschrift der Savigny-Stiftung für Rechtsgeschichte, Rom. Abt.* 98.1, pp. 162–212.
Lippold, Adolf (1991). *Kommentar zur Vita Maximini Duo der Historia Augusta.* Bonn: Habelt.
Lis, Catharina and Hugo Soly (2012). *Worthy Efforts: Attitudes to Work and Workers in Pre-industrial Europe.* Leiden and Boston: Brill.
Lo Cascio, Elio (2001). 'Il *census* a Roma e la sua evoluzione dall'età "Serviana" alla prima età imperiale'. In: *Mélanges de l'École Française de Rome, Antiquité* 113, pp. 565–603.
MacMullen, Ramsay (1982). 'The Epigraphic Habit in the Roman Empire'. In: *American Journal of Philology* 103.3, pp. 233–246.
MacMullen, Ramsay (1988). *Corruption and the Decline of Rome.* New Haven: Yale University Press.
Maier, Gideon (2005). *Amtsträger und Herrscher in der Romania Gothica. Vergleichende Untersuchungen zu den Institutionen der ostgermanischen Völkerwanderungsreiche.* Historia Einzelschriften 181. Stuttgart: Franz Steiner.
Manacorda, Daniele (1996). 'Nymphae, aedes'. In: *Lexicon topographicum urbis Romae.* Ed. by Eva Margaret Steinby. Vol. III H–O. Rome: Quasar, pp. 350–351.
Mancini, Gioacchino (1923). 'I. Roma. Scavi sotto la basilica di S. Sebastiano sull'Appia Antica'. In: *Notizie degli scavi di antichità* 20, pp. 3–79.
Mantovani, Dario (2000). 'Aspetti documentali del processo criminale nella Repubblica. Le *tabulae publicae*'. In: *Mélanges de l'École Française de Rome, Antiquité* 112.2, pp. 651–691.
Marchese, Maria Elena (2003). 'Monumenti equestri ad Ostia Antica'. In: *Mitteilungen des Deutschen Archäologischen Instituts, Römische Abteilung* 110, pp. 319–328.
Marino, Fabiana (2014). 'Viabilità e complesso termale nel territorio di *Trebula Suffenas* (Castel Madama, Roma)'. In: *Lazio et Sabina. 10. Atti del Convegno*

'Decimo Incontro di Studi sul Lazio e la Sabina', Roma, 4–6 giugno 2013. Ed. by Elena Calandra, Giuseppina Ghini, and Zaccaria Mari. Rome: Quasar, pp. 97–102.

Mastino, Attilio and Paola Ruggeri (1995). '*Claudia Augusti liberta Acte*, la liberta amata de Nerone ad Olbia'. In: *Latomus* 54.3, pp. 513–544.

Mayer, Emanuel (2012). *The Ancient Middle Classes. Urban Life and Aesthetics in the Roman Empire, 100 BCE–250 CE*. Cambridge and London: Harvard University Press.

Mazzei, Paola (2009). 'Tabularium – Aerarium nelle fonti letterarie ed epigrafiche'. In: *Rendiconti della Classe di Scienze morali, storiche e filologiche dell'Academia dei Lincei* 20 (s. 9), pp. 275–378.

Meiggs, Russell (1973). *Roman Ostia*. 2nd ed. Oxford: Clarendon Press.

Meissner, Burkhard (1997). 'Berufsbildung in der Antike'. In: *Berufliche Bildung – Geschichte, Gegenwart, Zukunft*. Ed. by Max Liedtke. Bad Heilbrunn: Julius Klinkhardt, pp. 55–99.

Mello, Mario (2012). '*[Ca]murtius, scriba* in una nuova iscrizione di *Paestum*'. In: *Pignora Amicitiae. Scritti di storia antica e di storiografia offerti a Mario Mazza. II*. Ed. by Margherita Cassia et al. Acireale: Bonnano, pp. 101–112.

Meyer, Elizabeth A. (2004). *Legitimacy and Law in the Roman World. Tabulae in Roman Belief and Practice*. Cambridge: Cambridge University Press.

Meyer, Elizabeth A. (2009). 'Writing Paraphernalia, Tablets, and Muses in Campanian Wall Painting'. In: *American Journal of Archaeology* 113.4, pp. 569–597.

Meyer, Hugo (1993). 'Ein Denkmal des Consensus Civium'. In: *Bullettino della Commissione Archeologica Comunale di Roma* 95, pp. 45–68.

Millar, Fergus (1963). 'The Fiscus in the First Two Centuries'. In: *The Journal of Roman Studies* 53.1–2, pp. 29–42.

Millar, Fergus (1964). 'The Aerarium and its Officials under the Empire'. In: *The Journal of Roman Studies* 54, pp. 33–40.

Millar, Fergus (1977). *The Emperor in the Roman World (31 BC–AD 337)*. London: Duckworth.

Mingazzini, Paolino (1923). 'Iscrizioni di S. Silvestro in Capite'. In: *Bullettino della Commissione Archeologica Comunale di Roma* 51, pp. 63–145.

Moatti, Claudia (1993). *Archives et partage de la terre dans le monde romain (IIe siècle avant – Ier siècle après J.-C.)* Rome: École Française de Rome.

Moatti, Claudia (1994). 'Les archives des terres publiques à Rome (IIE S. av.–IER S. ap. J.C.): le cas des assignations'. In: *La mémoire perdue. A la recherche des archives oubliées, publiques et privées, de la Rome antique*. Ed. by Claude Nicolet et al. Histoire Ancienne et Médiévale, URA 994 30. Paris: Sorbonne, pp. 103–119.

Moatti, Claudia et al. (1998). *La mémoire perdue. Recherches sur l'administration romaine*. Collection de l'École Française de Rome 243. Rome: École Française de Rome.

Moatti, Claudia et al. (2000). 'La mémoire perdue. III'. In: *Mélanges de l'École Française de Rome, Antiquité* 112.2, pp. 647–779.

Moatti, Claudia et al. (2001). 'Les archives du *census*: le contrôle des hommes. Actes de la table ronde, Rome, Ier décembre 1997'. In: *Mélanges de l'École Française de Rome, Antiquité* 113.2, pp. 559–764.
Mommsen, Theodor (1843). *Ad legem de scribis et viatoribus et De auctoritate commentationes duae*. Diss. Univ. Kiel. Kiel: C. F. Mohr.
Mommsen, Theodor (1848). 'De apparitoribus magistratuum Romanorum'. In: *Museum für Philologie* 6, pp. 1–57.
Mommsen, Theodor (1867). 'Decret des Proconsuls von Sardinien L. Helvius Agrippa vom J. 68 n. Chr.' In: *Hermes* 2.1, pp. 102–127.
Mommsen, Theodor (1887). *Römisches Staatsrecht*. Ed. by Joachim Marquardt and Theodor Mommsen. 3rd ed. Handbuch der Römischen Alterthümer 1. Leipzig: S. Hirzel.
Mommsen, Theodor (1891). 'I fasti dei *sex primi ab aerario*'. In: *Mittheilungen des Kaiserlich Deutschen Archäologischen Instituts. Römische Abtheilung* 6, pp. 157–162.
More, J. H. (1975). 'Cornelius Surus: Bureaucrat and Poet'. In: *Grazer Beiträge* 3, pp. 241–262.
Moreau, Philippe (1994). 'La mémoire fragile: falsification et destruction des documents publics au Ier s. av. J.-C.' In: *La mémoire perdue. A la recherche des archives oubliées, publiques et privées, de la Rome antique*. Ed. by Claude Nicolet et al. Histoire Ancienne et Médiévale, URA 994 30. Paris: Sorbonne, pp. 121–145.
Morgan, Teresa (1998). *Literate Education in the Hellenistic and Roman Worlds*. Cambridge: Cambridge University Press.
Morgan, Teresa (2015). *Roman Faith and Christian Faith. Pistis and Fides in the Early Roman Empire and Early Churches*. Oxford: Oxford University Press.
Mouritsen, Henrik (2011). *The Freedman in the Roman World*. Cambridge: Cambridge University Press.
Muñiz Coello, Joaquín (1982). *Empleados y subalternos de la administración romana. I. Los 'scribae'*. Huelva.
Mura Somella, Anna (1999). 'Tabularium'. In: *Lexicon topographicum urbis Romae*. Ed. by Eva Margareta Steinby. Vol. V T–Z. Rome: Quasar, pp. 17–20.
Nicolet, Claude (1994). 'A la recherche des archives oubliées: une contribution à l'histoire de la bureaucratie romaine'. In: *La mémoire perdue. A la recherche des archives oubliées, publiques et privées, de la Rome antique*. Ed. by Claude Nicolet et al. Histoire Ancienne et Médiévale, URA 994 30. Paris: Sorbonne, pp. V–XVII.
Nicolet, Claude (2000). *Censeurs et publicains. Économie et fiscalité dans la Rome antique*. Paris: Fayard.
Nicolet, Claude et al. (1994). *La mémoire perdue. À la recherche des archives oubliées, publiques et privées, de la Rome antique*. Rome: École Française de Rome.
Nisbet, Robin (2007). 'Horace: Life and Chronology'. In: *The Cambridge Companion to Horace*. Ed. by Stephen Harrison. Cambridge: Cambridge University Press, pp. 7–21.

Nollé, Johannes (1982). *Nundinas instituere et habere. Epigraphische Zeugnisse zur Einrichtung und Gestaltung von ländlichen Märkten in Afrika und in der Provinz Asia*. Subsidia Epigraphica 9. Hildesheim and Zurich: Georg Olms.
North, John A. (1998). 'The Books of the *pontifices*'. In: *La mémoire perdue. Recherches sur l'administration romaine*. Ed. by Claude Moatti et al. Collection de l'École Française de Rome 243. Rome: École Française de Rome, pp. 45–63.
O'Donnell, James J. (1979). *Cassiodorus*. Berkeley: University of California Press.
Ogilvie, Robert Maxwell (2000). *The Romans and Their Gods*. [1. edn. 1969]. London: Pimlico.
Ong, Walter J. (2012). *Orality and Literacy. The Technologizing of the Word*. 30th Anniversary Edition. With additional chapters by John Hartley. London and New York: Routledge.
Pagano, Mario (1990). *Sinuessa. Storia ed archeologia di una colonia romana*. Sessa Aurunca: Edizioni Duomo.
Palme, Bernhard (1999). 'Die *officia* der Statthalter in der Spätantike. Forschungsstand und Perspektiven'. In: *Antiquité Tardive* 7, pp. 85–133.
Panciera, Silvio (1986). 'Ancora sull'iscrizione di Cornelius Surus magister scribarum poetarum'. In: *Bullettino della Commissione Archeologica Comunale di Roma* 91.1, pp. 35–44.
Pap, Levente (2016). 'The Stenchy Piso. An Accusation Strategy in M. T. Cicero's "In Pisonem"'. In: *Analele Universității Ovidius din Constanța. Seria Filologie* 27.2, pp. 451–458.
Papi, Emanuele (1995). 'Forum Traiani: porticus porphyretica'. In: *Lexicon topographicum urbis Romae*. Ed. by Eva Margareta Steinby. Vol. II D–G. Rome: Quasar, p. 356.
Pavis d'Escurac, Henriette (1976). *La préfecture de l'annone. Service administratif impérial d'Auguste à Constantin*. Rome: École Française de Rome.
Peachin, Michael (2004). *Frontinus and the curae of the curator aquarum*. Stuttgart: Franz Steiner Verlag.
Peachin, Michael (2011). 'Introduction'. In: *The Oxford Handbook of Social Relations in the Roman World*. Ed. by Michael Peachin. Oxford: Oxford University Press, pp. 3–36.
Pennitz, Martin (1993). 'Angela Romano, Il *"collegium scribarum"*. Aspetti sociali e giuridici della produzione letteraria tra III e II secolo A. C. (= Pubblicazioni del Dipartimento di diritto romano e storia della scienza romanistica dell'Università di Napoli "Federico II", vol. III). Jovene, Napoli 1990, VIIII, 141 S.' In: *Zeitschrift der Savigny-Stiftung für Rechtsgeschichte, Romanistische Abteilung* 110.1, pp. 680–687.
Pensabene, P. (2008). 'Lucio Volusio Volusiano, un nuovo equo publico di Roma'. In: *Epigrafia 2006. Atti della XIVe Renconctre sur l'épigraphie in onore di Silvio Panciera con altri contributi di colleghi, allievi e collaboratori*. Ed. by Maria Letizia Caldelli, Gian Luca Gregori, and Silvia Orlandi. Rome: Quasar, pp. 1113–1117.
Perl, Gerhard (1969). 'Sallust und die Krise der römischen Republik'. In: *Philologus* 113, pp. 201–216.

Petraccia Lucernoni, Maria Federica (1988). *I questori municipali dell'Italia antica*. Rome: Istituto Italiano per la Storia Antica.
Pflaum, Hans Georg (1968). 'Les juges des cinq décuries originaires d'Afrique romaine'. In: *Antiquités africaines* 2, pp. 153–195.
Pflaum, Hans-Georg (1960–1982). *Les carrières procuratoriennes équestres sous le Haut-Empire romain*. Paris: Geuthner.
Platner, Samuel Ball (1965). *A Topographical Dictionary of Ancient Rome*. Compl. and rev. by Thomas Ashby. Rome: Bretschneider.
Popescu, Emilian (1964). 'Epigraphische Beiträge zur Geschichte der Stadt Tropaeum Traiani'. In: *Studii Clasice* 6, pp. 185–203.
Posner, Ernst (1972). *Archives in the Ancient World*. Cambridge: Harvard University Press.
Poucet, Jacques (1989). 'Réflexions sur l'écrit et l'écriture dans la Rome des premiers siècles'. In: *Latomus* 48.2, pp. 285–311.
Purcell, Nicholas (1983). 'The *Apparitores*: A Study in Social Mobility'. In: *Papers of the British School at Rome* 51, pp. 125–173.
Purcell, Nicholas (1993). '*Atrium Libertatis*'. In: *Papers of the British School at Rome* 61, pp. 125–155.
Purcell, Nicholas (2001). 'The *Ordo Scribarum*: A Study in the Loss of Memory'. In: *Mélanges de l'École Française de Rome, Antiquité* 113.2, pp. 633–674.
Radman-Livaja, Ivan (2014). *Tesserae Sisciensiae. Les plombs inscrits de Siscia. Olovne tesere iz Siscije*. Musei Archaeologici Zagrabiensis Catalogi et Monographiae 9.1/9.2. Zagreb: Archaeological Museum in Zagreb.
Ramsay, William Mitchell (1883). 'Unedited Inscriptions of Asia Minor'. In: *Bulletin de Correspondance Hellénique* 7, pp. 258–278.
Ramsay, William Mitchell (1916). 'Colonia Caesarea (Pisidian Antioch) in the Augustan Age'. In: *Journal of Roman Studies* 6, pp. 83–134.
Ramsay, William Mitchell (1967). *The Social Basis of Roman Power in Asia Minor*. Prepared for the press by J. G. C. Anderson. Amsterdam: Adolf M. Hakkert.
Rankov, Boris (1999). 'The Governor's Men: The *officium consularis* in Provincial Administration'. In: *The Roman Army as a Community. Including Papers of a Conference Held at Birkbeck College, University of London on 11–12 January, 1997*. Ed. by Adrian Goldsworthy and Ian Haynes. JRA Supplementary Series Number 34. Portsmouth: The Journal of Roman Archaeology, pp. 15–34.
Rebenich, Stefan (2002). *Theodor Mommsen. Eine Biographie*. Munich: C. H. Beck.
Reddé, Michel (1986). *Mare nostrum. Les infrastructures, le dispositif et l'histoire de la marine militaire sous l'empire romain*. Bibliothèque des Écoles Françaises d'Athènes et de Rome. Rome: École Française de Rome.
Reynolds, Joyce (1982). *Aphrodisias and Rome*. London: The Society for the Promotion of Roman Studies.
Richardson, J. S. (1987). 'The Purpose of the Lex Calpurnia de Repetundis'. In: *The Journal of Roman Studies* 77, pp. 1–12.
Rodríguez Neila, Juan Francisco (2008). '*Tabulae Publicae*'. *Archivos municipales y documentación financiera en las ciudades de la bética*. Madrid: Dykinson.

Romano, Angela (1990). *Il 'collegium scribarum'. Aspetti sociali e giuridici della produzione letteraria tra* iii *e* ii *secolo* a.c. Naples: Eugenio Jovene.
Rosen, Klaus (1985). 'Die falschen Numabücher. Politik, Religion und Literatur in Rom 181 v. Chr.' In: *Chiron* 15, pp. 65–90.
Rosenberger, Veit (2009). 'Verwehrte Ehre: Zur Wertigkeit des *triumphus in monte Albano*'. In: *Klio* 91.1, pp. 29–39.
Rosillo-López, Cristina (2010a). *La corruption à la fin de la république romaine (IIe-Ier s. av. J.-C.): aspects politiques et financiers*. Historia Einzelschriften 200. Stuttgart: Franz Steiner.
Rosillo-López, Cristina (2010b). 'La gestion des profits illégaux par les magistrats pendant la République romaine (IIe-Ier siècle av. J.-C.)' In: *Latomus* 69, pp. 981–999.
Rotondi, Antonella (2010). 'L'ara degli scribi e i colombari di via di porta S. Sebastiano'. In: *Il primo miglio della via Appia a Roma. Atti della Giornata di Studio Roma - Museo Nazionale Romano 16 giugno 2009*. Ed. by Daniele Manacorda and Riccardo Santangeli Valenzani. Atlante di Roma 3. Rome: Tre-Croma, pp. 137–152.
Royden, Halsey R. (1988). *The Magistrates of the Roman Professional Collegia in Italy from the First to the Third Century* AD. Pisa: Giardini.
Rüpke, Jörg (1995a). '*Fasti*: Quellen oder Produkte römischer Geschichtsschreibung?' In: *Klio* 77, pp. 184–202.
Rüpke, Jörg (1995b). *Kalender und Öffentlichkeit. Die Geschichte der Repräsentation und religiösen Qualifikation von Zeit in Rom*. Religionsgeschichtliche Versuche und Vorarbeiten 40. Berlin and New York: de Gruyter.
Rüpke, Jörg (2005). *Fasti sacerdotum. Die Mitglieder der Priesterschaften und das sakrale Funktionspersonal römischer, griechischer, orientalischer und jüdisch-christlicher Kulte in der Stadt Rom von 300 v. Chr. bis 499 n. Chr.* Band 2. Anne Glock Mitautorin für die Biographien christlicher Funktionsträger. Potsdamer Altertumswissenschaftliche Beiträge (PAwB) 12. Stuttgart: Franz Steiner Verlag.
Rüpke, Jörg (2011). *The Roman Calendar from Numa to Constantine. Time, History and the Fasti*. Malden and Oxford: Wiley-Blackwell.
Ryan, Frank (2002). 'Unterpontifex und Pontifikalkollegium'. In: *Res publica reperta. Zur Verfassung und Gesellschaft der römischen Republik und des frühen Prinzipats. Festschrift für Jochen Bleicken zum 75. Geburtstag*. Ed. by Jörg Spielvogel. Hermes. Sonderband. Stuttgart: Franz Steiner, pp. 67–89.
Saller, Richard P. (1982). *Personal Patronage under the Early Empire*. Cambridge: Cambridge University Press.
Salomies, Olli (1992). *Adoptive and Polyonymous Nomenclature in the Roman Empire*. Commentationes humanarum litterarum 97. Helsinki: Societas Scientiarum Fennica.
Saulnier, Christiane (1984). 'Laurens Lauinas. Quelques remarques à propos d'un sacerdoce équestre à Rome'. In: *Latomus* 43, pp. 517–533.
Schäfer, Thomas (1989). *Imperii insignia. Sella curulis und fasces. Zur Repräsentation Römischer Magistrate*. Mainz: Philipp von Zabern.

Scheid, John (2016). 'Réflexions sur la falsification et le faux dans la Rome antique'. In: *Comptes rendus de l'Académie des Inscriptions et Belles-Lettres* 1, pp. 91–103.
Scheid, John and Maria Grazia Granino Cecere (1999). 'Les sacerdoces publics équestres'. In: *L'ordre équestre. Histoire d'une aristocratie (IIe siècle av. J.-C. – IIIe siècle ap. J.-C. Actes du colloque de Bruxelles-Leuven (octobre 1995)*. Ed. by Ségolène Demougin, Hubert Devijver, and Marie-Thérèse Raepsaet-Charlier. Collection de l'École Française de Rome 257. Rome: École Française de Rome, pp. 79–189.
Scholz, Markus and Marietta Horster, eds. (2015). *Lesen und Schreiben in den römischen Provinzen. Schriftliche Kommunikation im Alltagsleben. Akten des 2. Internationalen Kolloquiums von DUCTUS – Association international pour l'étude des inscriptions mineures, RGZM Mainz, 15.–17. Juni 2011*. RGZM-Tagungen 26. Mainz: Verlag des Römisch-Germanischen Zentralmuseums, pp. 43–58.
Schulte, Claudia (1994). *Die Grammateis von Ephesos. Schreiberamt und Sozialstruktur in einer Provinzhauptstadt des römischen Kaiserreiches*. Heidelberger althistorische Beiträge und epigraphische Studien 15. Stuttgart: Steiner.
Schulten, Adolf (1926). *Sertorius*. Leipzig: Dieterich'sche Verlagsbuchhandlung.
Scramuzza, Vincent Mary (1937). 'Roman Sicily'. In: *An Economic Survey of Ancient Rome. Vol. 3*. Ed. by Frank Tenney. Reprint Boston: Octagon Books 1972. 1. edn. 1937. Baltimore: Johns Hopkins University Press, pp. 225–337.
Seibel, Wolfgang (2016). *Verwaltung verstehen. Eine theoriegeschichtliche Einführung*. Berlin: Suhrkamp.
Shackleton Bailey, David R. (1960). 'Sex. Clodius – Sex. Cloelius'. In: *The Classical Quarterly* 10.1–2, pp. 41–42.
Shackleton Bailey, David R. (1965). 'Rezension. Cicéron: Correspondance. T. 5: Les débuts de la guerre civile. P. 1–5 (14.10.50–25.3.49). Texte ét. et trad. par Jean Bayet. Paris: Belles-Lettres 1964. 315 z. T. Doppels. 1 Kt. 24 F. (Coll. des Univ. de France)'. In: *Gnomon* 37.1, pp. 48–51.
Shackleton Bailey, David R., ed. (1965–1970). *Cicero, M. Tullius. Epistulae ad Atticum. Cicero's Letters to Atticus*. 7 vols. Cambridge: Cambridge University Press.
Sinnigen, William Gurnee (1957). *The officium of the Urban Prefecture during the Later Roman Empire*. Papers and Monographs of the American Academy in Rome 17. Rome: American Academy.
Škegro, Ante (1994). 'Epigraphische Mitteilungen aus Bosnien und Herzegowina'. In: *Zeitschrift für Papyrologie und Epigraphik* 101, pp. 287–298.
Snow, Charles Percy (1998). *The Two Cultures*. 1. edn. 1964. Cambridge: Cambridge University Press.
Speidel, Michael A. (1992). 'Roman Army Pay Scales'. In: *The Journal of Roman Studies* 82, pp. 87–106.
Speidel, Michael A. (1996). *Die römischen Schreibtafeln von Vindonissa. Lateinische Texte des militärischen Alltags und ihre geschichtliche Bedeutung*. Veröffentlichungen der Gesellschaft Pro Vindonissa 12. Brugg: Gesellschaft Pro Vindonissa.

Stauner, Konrad (2004). *Das offizielle Schriftwesen des römischen Heeres von Augustus bis Gallienus*. Bonn: Habelt.
Ste Croix, Geoffrey E. M. de (1956). 'Greek and Roman accounting'. In: *Studies in the History of Accounting*. Ed. by A. C. Littleton and B. S. Yamey. Homewood: Richard D. Irwin, pp. 14–74.
Steel, Catherine (2007). 'The Rhetoric of the *de Frumento*'. In: *Sicilia Nutrix Plebis Romanae. Rhetoric, Law and Taxation in Cicero's Verrines*. Ed. by Jonathan Prag. Bulletin of the Institute of Classical Studies Supplement 97. London: Institute of the Classical Studies, pp. 37–48.
Stefano Manzella, Ivan di (2000). 'Accensi: profilo di una ricerca in corso (a proposito dei "poteri collaterali" nella società romana)'. In: *Cahiers du Centre Gustave Glotz* 11, pp. 223–257.
Street, Brian V. (1984). *Literacy in Theory and Practice*. Cambridge Studies in Oral and Literate Culture 9. Cambridge: Cambridge University Press.
Swan, Michael (1970). '*CIL* XIV 353 and S 4642: *Apparitores* at Ostia and Urso'. In: *Latomus* 29, pp. 140–141.
Syme, Ronald (1983). 'Bogus Authors'. In: *Historia Augusta Papers*. Oxford: Clarendon Press, pp. 99–108.
Talbert, Richard J. A. (1984). *The Senate of Imperial Rome*. Princeton: Princeton University Press.
Tan, James (2015). 'The Roman Republic'. In: *Fiscal Regimes and the Political Economy of Premodern States*. Ed. by Andrew Monson and Walter Scheidel. Cambridge: Cambridge University Press, pp. 208–228.
Tan, James (2017). *Power and Public Finance at Rome, 264–49 BCE*. Oxford: Oxford University Press.
Tarpin, Michel (1998). 'L'utilisation d'archives annexes pour les distributions de blé'. In: *La mémoire perdue. Recherches sur l'administration romaine*. Ed. by Claude Moatti et al. Collection de l'École Française de Rome 243. Rome: École Française de Rome, pp. 387–409.
Teitler, Hans Carel (1985). *Notarii and Exceptores. An Inquiry into Role and Significance of Shorthand Writers in the Imperial and Ecclesiastical Bureaucracy of the Roman Empire (From the Early Principate to c. 450 AD)*. Amsterdam: J. C. Gieben.
Tennant, P. M. W. (1991). 'Political or Personal Propaganda? Horace, *Sermones* 1.5 in Perspective'. In: *Acta Classica* 34, pp. 51–64.
Thomas, Rosalind (1992). *Literacy and Orality in Ancient Greece*. Cambridge: Cambridge University Press.
Thomasson, Bengt E. (1972–2009). *Laterculi Praesidum*. Goteborg: Bokförlaget Radius.
Thommen, Lukas (1989). *Das Volkstribunat der späten römischen Republik*. Historia Einzelschriften 59. Stuttgart: Franz Steiner.
Todisco, Elisabetta (1999). *I veterani in Italia in età imperiale*. Bari: Edipuglia.
Tomlin, Roger S. O. (2016). *Roman London's First Voices: Writing Tablets from the Bloomberg Excavations, 2010–14*. MOLA Monograph 72. London: Museum of London Archaeology MOLA.

Toynbee, Jocelyn M. C. (1971). *Death and Burial in the Roman World*. London: Thames and Hudson.
Treggiari, Susan (1969). *Roman Freedmen during the Late Republic*. Oxford: Oxford University Press.
Treggiari, Susan, ed. (1996). *Cicero's Cilician Letters*. 2nd ed. London: LACTOR.
Tucci, Pier Luigi (2005). '"Where High Moneta Leads Her Steps Sublime". The "Tabularium" and the Temple of Juno Moneta'. In: *Journal of Roman Archaeology* 18, pp. 6–33.
Tucci, Pier Luigi (2014). 'A New Look at the *Tabularium* and the Capitoline Hill'. In: *Rendiconti della Pontificia Accademia Romana di Archeologia* 86.2013–2014, pp. 43–123.
Vaglieri, Dante (1910). 'Regione I (*LATIUM ET CAMPANIA*). II. Ostia'. In: *Notizie degli scavi di antichità* 7, pp. 9–33.
Vaglieri, Dante (1900). 'Nuove scoperte e nuovi studii al Foro Romano'. In: *Bullettino della Commissione Archeologica Comunale di Roma* 28, pp. 266–298.
Virlouvet, Catherine (1995). *Tessera frumentaria. Les procédures de la distribution du blé public à Rome à la fin de la République et au début de l'Empire*. Rome: École Française de Rome.
Virlouvet, Catherine (1998). 'Les archives de l'administration du blé public à Rome à travers le témoignage des inscriptions'. In: *La mémoire perdue. Recherches sur l'administration romaine*. Ed. by Claude Moatti et al. Collection de l'École Française de Rome 243. Rome: École Française de Rome, pp. 247–266.
Vössing, Konrad (2003). 'Die Geschichte der römischen Schule – ein Abriss vor dem Hintergrund der neueren Forschung'. In: *Gymnasium* 110, pp. 455–497.
Wachtel, Klaus et al., eds. (1933–). *Prosopographia Imperii Romani saec. I. II. III*. Editio altera. Berlin: de Gruyter.
Walbank, Frank W. (1957–1979). *A Historical Commentary on Polybius. 3 Vols*. Oxford: Oxford University Press.
Weber, Max (2002). *Wirtschaft und Gesellschaft. Grundriss der verstehenden Soziologie*. Ed. by Johannes Winckelmann. 5th ed. Tübingen: Mohr Siebeck.
Werner, Shirley (2009). 'Literacy Studies in Classics. The Last Twenty Years'. In: *Ancient Literacies. The Culture of Reading in Greece and Rome*. Ed. by William A. Johnson and Holt N. Parker. Oxford: Oxford University Press, pp. 333–382.
Wesch-Klein, Gabriele (1993). *Funus publicum. Eine Studie zur öffentlichen Beisetzung und Gewährung von Ehrengräbern in Rom und den Westprovinzen*. Stuttgart: Steiner.
Williams, Burma P. and Richard S. Williams (1995). 'Finger Numbers in the Greco-Roman World and the Early Middle Ages'. In: *Isis* 86.4, pp. 587–608.
Williams, Gordon (1995). '*Libertino Patre Natus*: True or False?' In: *Homage to Horace. A Bimillenary Celebration*. Ed. by S. J. Harrison. Oxford: Clarendon Press, pp. 296–313.
Williamson, Callie (1987). 'Monuments of Bronze: Roman Legal Documents on Bronze Tablets'. In: *Classical Antiquity* 6.1, pp. 160–183.

Williamson, Callie (2016). 'Crimes against the State'. In: *The Oxford Handbook of Roman Law and Society*. Ed. by Paul J. du Plessis, Clifford Ando, and Kaius Tuori. Oxford: Oxford University Press, pp. 333–344.

Wiseman, Timothy Peter (1971). *New Men in the Roman Senate. 139 BC–AD 14*. Oxford: Oxford University Press.

Wolf, Joseph Georg (1980). 'Die literarische Überlieferung der Publikation der Fasten und Legisaktionen durch Gnaeus Flavius'. In: *Nachrichten der Akademie der Wissenschaften in Göttingen. I. Philologisch-historische Klasse* 2, pp. 11–29.

Wood, John T. (1877). *Discoveries at Ephesus. Including the Site and Remains of the Great Temple of Diana*. London: Longmans, Green, and Co.

Woolf, Greg (2000). 'Literacy'. In: *The Cambridge Ancient History. XI. The High Empire, ad 70–192*. Ed. by Alan K. Bowman, Peter Garnsey, and Dominic Rathbone. 2nd ed. Cambridge: Cambridge University Press, pp. 875–897.

Woolf, Greg (2009). 'Literacy or Literacies in Rome?' In: *Ancient Literacies. The Culture of Reading in Greece and Rome*. Oxford: Oxford University Press, pp. 46–68.

Woolf, Greg (2015). 'Ancient Illiteracy?' In: *Bulletin of the Institute of Classical Studies* 58.2, pp. 31–42.

Wrede, Henning (1981). 'Scribae'. In: *Boreas* 4, pp. 106–116.

Wrede, Henning (2001). *Senatorische Sarkophage Roms. Der Beitrag des Senatorenstandes zur römischen Kunst der hohen und späten Kaiserzeit*. Mainz: Philipp von Zabern.

Yakobson, Alexander and Hermann Horstkotte (1997). '"Yes, Quaestor." A Republican Politician versus the Power of the Clerks'. In: *Zeitschrift für Papyrologie und Epigraphik* 116, pp. 247–248.

Youtie, Herbert Chayyim and John Garrett Winter, eds. (1951). *Papyri and Ostraca from Karanis. Second Series*. Ann Arbor: University of Michigan Press.

Zevi, Fausto and Rosanna Friggeri (2012). 'Ara degli scribi'. In: *Terme di Diocleziano. La collezione epigrafica*. Ed. by Rosanna Friggeri, Maria Grazia Granino Cecere, and Gian Luca Gregori. Milan: Electa, pp. 355–362.

Zucca, Raimondo (2010). 'Μάρκος Σερουίλιος Πο(πλίου) υἱός, Παλατεῖνα, Εὔνεικος, ἔπαρχος σπείρας Σαρδῶν'. In: *Giornata di studi per Lidio Gasperini. Roma, 5 Giugno 2008*. Ed. by Adelina Arnaldi, Eugenio Lanzillotta, and Simona Antolini. Themata 4. Tivoli: Tored, pp. 29–44.

Index Locorum

Acquasparta
  3, 155
  5, 163
AE
  1888
    125, 56, 150
  1889
    99, 132, 150
  1891
    163, 167
  1892
    1, 167
  1895
    45, 156
  1899
    68a, 166
    68b, 166
  1900
    88, 170, 171
    89, 170, 171
    184, 167
  1901
    134, 75
  1903
    129, 171
  1907
    17, 155, 156
    131, 151
    132, 144, 150
  1908
    110, 75
  1909
    91, 151
  1910
    181, 154, 166
  1913
    20, 160
    37, 152
    113, 156
  1920
    19, 153
    75, 159
  1921
    39, 125, 157–159
  1923
    79, 171
  1925
    44, 127, 153
  1926
    43, 154
    121, 152
  1927
    101, 114
    112, 158
    125, 162
  1928
    123, 170
    153, 156
  1929
    145, 173
  1934
    107, 156
  1935
    169, 73, 161
  1937
    221, 168
  1939
    153, 75, 163
  1940
    59, 114
    60, 114
    101, 156
  1946
    99, 172
  1948
    28, 167
    30, 167
  1954
    168, 168
  1959
    147, 23, 75
  1960
    343, 156
    344, 156

AE (cont.)
  1961
    114, 157
  1964
    11, 164
    73, 155
    251, 168
    253, 165
  1965
    145, 173
  1973
    198, 175
  1974
    224, 162
    550, 165
    655, 39
  1975
    19, 158
    44, 158
    71, 161
    189, 163
    375, 155
    376, 152, 164
  1976
    138, 159
    561, 169
  1977
    265b, 170
  1980
    42, 145
    487, 174
  1983
    23, 162
    42, 171
    409, 160
    447, 154
  1985
    908, 172
  1987
    202, 167
  1988
    195, 167
    310, 173
  1989
    353, 154
  1990
    111, 162
    150, 174
    156, 174
    253, 168
    312, 160
    385, 152
  1991
    114, 74, 159
    115, 164
    116, 164
  1993
    836a–b, 154
  1994
    1238, 156
    1364, 165
  1995
    311, 173
  1996
    1240, 168
  1998
    349, 161
    668, 165
  1999
    571b, 44
    199, 162
  2000
    270, 170
    1243, 165
  2001
    239, 163
  2002
    1393, 157
  2003
    986, 83, 159
  2004
    1521, 157
  2005
    1518, 157
  2006
    1481, 164
  2007
    1116, 169
  2008
    239, 162
    528, 163
  2009
    336, 152
  2010
    305, 158
    1385, 156
    1601, 160
  2012
    407, 165
  2013
    211, 163
    1557, 54, 105
Aesernia
  64, 167
Allifae
  188, 175
Appian
  Bella civilia
    1.1.11–12, 56, 58
    3.1.5, 154

Index Locorum

Punica
9.66, 66
Asconius
  Pro C. Cornelio
    58, 58
  Pro T. Annio Milone
    test. 19, 46, 153

CAG
  31–3
  335, 166
CartNova
  59, 133, 134, 151
  60, 133, 151
Cassiodorus
  Variae
    5.21.1–3, 23
    5.22.1–5, 23
    12.21, 146
    12.21.1–5, 148, 166
Cassius Hemina
  Annales (frg.)
    F20, 13
    F35, 57, 158
CCCA
  03
    387, 167
    390, 167
CCID
  221, 169
  379, 169
CEACelio
  22, 163
CECapitol
  4, 82, 175
  328, 164
  331, 164
CECasapulla
  27, 165
CEL
  141, 175
  142, 174, 175
  143, 174, 175
  156, 173
ChLA
  III
    204, 173
  V
    299, 174, 175
  XLII
    1217, 174, 175
    1218, 175
Cicero
  Ad Atticum
    2.24.2, 81, 160
    5.11.4, 51
    5.4.1, 51, 161
    6.1.8, 1, 154
    6.6.2, 51
    13.3.33, 36
    13.33.3, 43, 44
  Ad Brutum
    290, 81
  Ad Quintum fratrem
    1.1.29, 20
  Ad familiares
    5.20.1–2, 52
    5.20.1–6, 161
    5.20.1–9, 52
    5.20.2, 52
    5.20.6, 135
  De domo sua
    74, 17, 50, 74, 109, 112
  De haruspicum responso
    12, 123, 153
  De lege agraria
    2.32, 46, 62, 65, 82
    2.37, 33, 98
  De legibus
    2.61–62, 67
    3.46, 46, 56, 57, 105
    3.48, 57
  De natura deorum
    2.7, 115
    3.74, 6, 38, 56, 57, 76, 78, 97, 98
  De officiis
    1.150, 20
    2.29, 123, 153
    3.104, 102
  De oratore
    1.186, 1, 154
  De re publica
    4.3, 18
  Divinatio in Q. Caecilium
    29, 91, 158
  In Catilinam
    4.15, 74, 89
  In L. Pisonem
    36, 33
    61, 32, 34, 48, 56
  In M. Antonium orationes Philippicae
    2.16, 48, 56, 66
    5.4, 98
  In P. Vatinium testem interrogatio
    34, 33, 35
  In Verrem
    2.1.119, 31
    2.1.150, 56, 105, 153
    2.1.157, 157
    2.1.158, 96

Cicero (cont.)
    2.1.36, 34
    2.1.57, 33
    2.1.60, 34
    2.1.92, 96
    2.2.27, 82, 91, 101
    2.2.101, 96
    2.2.101–106, 34
    2.2.104, 96
    2.2.104–105, 33, 35
    2.2.105, 96
    2.2.106, 35
    2.2.187, 96
    2.2.189, 96
    2.2.191, 96
    2.3.26, 56, 58, 81
    2.3.41, 96
    2.3.83, 98
    2.3.137, 158
    2.3.154, 158
    2.3.155–157, 104
    2.3.167–168, 109, 151, 160
    2.3.168–169, 107
    2.3.171–176, 107
    2.3.171–187, 157
    2.3.181, 108
    2.3.181–187, 82, 124
    2.3.182, 20, 68, 102, 104, 108, 157, 160
    2.3.182–183, 106
    2.3.182–184, 20, 74, 108
    2.3.183, 17, 48, 59, 70, 73, 102, 112
    2.3.183–184, 124
    2.3.184, 72, 88, 103, 108, 109, 112, 124
    2.3.185–187, 109
    2.3.187, 89
    2.4.44, 91
    2.5.10, 35
Pro A. Cluentio
    62, 33, 35
    126, 73, 90, 104, 105, 157
    147, 81
Pro Archia poeta
    8–9, 35
Pro C. Rabirio Postumo
    13, 101, 106
Pro C. Rabirio perduellionis reo
    8, 38
Pro L. Balbo
    8, 33, 35
    11, 33
Pro L. Murena
    25, 1, 154
    42, 74, 101, 103–105
Pro L. Valerio Flacco
    21, 97

Pro M. Fonteio
    2, 33, 35
Pro P. Sestio
    129, 33, 35
Pro P. Sulla
    41–43, 143
    42, 29, 46
    44, 56
Pro Sex. Roscio Amerino
    128, 33, 35
Pro T. Annio Milone
    73, 29, 30, 33, 35, 37
Scholia in Ciceronem Bobiensia
    87, 89
CIG
    5820, 165
    5843, 169
CIL
    1^2
        587, 66, 69
    1
        1299, 154
        1313, 155
        1356, 75
        1490, 160
        2640, 158
        3421, 152
        p. 459, 122, 152
    2
        2972, 169
        3423, 133, 151
        3424, 133, 151
        3596, 156
        5941, 133, 151
        5942, 133, 151
    3
        257, 154
        263.2*, 127, 151
        1512, 166
        1568, 156
        1580, 166
        2019, 166
        2122, 166
        3974, 167
        4137, 168
        4168, 169
        4195, 175
        4267, 165
        4720, 156
        7484, 165
        7914, 166
        7917, 166
        7975, 168
        8593, 166
        10900, 168

Index Locorum

11131, 169
12363, 156
12461, 165
12690, 160
13447, 169
14214.02, 165, 167
14344a, 166
14344b, 166
14345, 166
14346, 166
p. 958, 156

5
784, 171
1883, 82
5079, 156
5080, 156
5314, 165
5866, 166
5924, 165
7033, 167
7430, 165

6
103, 75, 152
116, 167
296, 156
407, 169
559, 156
868, 170
916, 36
941*, 175
963*, 175
964*, 175
967, 6
999, 82
1025, 172
1060, 170, 171
1068, 75, 152
1314, 38
1495, 77
1496, 77
1610, 155
1648, 128
1770, 145
1802, 150
1803, 150
1804, 151
1805, 151
1806, 151
1807, 150, 161
1808, 152
1809, 161
1810, 153
1811, 154

1812, 163
1813, 154
1814, 154
1815, 154
1816, 76, 155
1817, 156
1818, 157
1819, 56, 76, 157
1820, 158
1821, 158
1822, 158
1822a, 161
1823, 159
1824, 159
1825, 159
1826, 75
1827, 160
1828, 161
1829, 161
1830, 150, 161
1831, 162
1832, 162
1833a, 162
1833b, 162
1833c, 162
1834, 162
1835, 163
1836, 151
1837, 151, 152
1838, 127, 151
1839, 153
1840, 153
1841, 153
1842, 154
1843, 156
1844, 156
1845, 156
1846, 157
1847, 157
1848, 81, 164
1849, 160
1850, 160
1851, 161
1852, 159
1853, 56, 163
1854, 72
1855, 151
1856, 162
1858, 151
1859, 153
1860, 153
1861, 153
1861a, 163
1862, 154
1863, 155

Cicero (cont.)
 1864, 155
 1865, 157
 1866, 158
 1867, 159
 1867a, 161
 1868, 162
 1888a2, 157
 1945, 83
 2165, 162
 2176, 81, 164
 2184, 161
 2185, 161
 3045*, 175
 3871, 152
 3872, 159
 5722, 161
 8767, 172
 8768, 172
 8769, 172
 8875, 172
 8881, 158
 8961, 171
 9262, 171
 9566, 170
 9995, 171
 10215, 169
 10252, 172
 10253, 172
 10621, 78, 150
 19082, 155
 29752, 153
 30428.2, 150
 30692, 75, 152
 31034, 161
 31221, 82
 31927, 145
 32265, 151
 32266, 154
 32267, 81, 164
 32268, 72
 32269, 161
 32270, 77
 32271, 77
 32272, 78, 150
 32273, 152
 32274, 150, 161
 32275a, 163
 32276, 151
 32277, 153
 32278, 155
 32279, 157
 32280, 159
 32281, 164
 32282, 74, 161
 32283, 155
 32284, 175
 32289b, 157
 32294, 82, 83
 32455a, 161
 33251, 162
 33252, 164
 33421, 162
 33721, 143, 155
 33770, 171
 33840, 171, 172
 33856, 170, 171
 33858, 170, 171
 33910, 161
 37098, 144, 150
 37140a, 157
 37141, 77
 37142, 78, 150
 37143, 161
 37144, 77
 37145, 75, 79, 164
 37146, 72, 151
 37147, 156
 37148, 75
 37154, 152, 156, 164
 37753, 171
 40702, 73
8
 33.4*, 151
 270, 45, 56, 57, 155, 156
 8936, 77, 81, 156
 9052, 85
 9379, 173
 11033, 154
 11451, 45, 57, 155, 156
 23246, 43–45, 57, 155, 156
9
 258*, 175
 1193, 151
 1646, 166
 2454, 72, 75
 2675, 167
 3083, 160
 3101, 167
 4057, 83
 5018, 167
 5190, 167
 5278, 168
 5564, 122, 152
 5648, 174
 5858, 166
10
 64*, 161
 140, 167
 531, 161

Index Locorum

948.29*, 159
1074, 153
1088.33*, 151
1089.173*, 159
1489, 169
1494, 165
1723, 156
1725, 160
1953, 166
1954, 168
1955, 167
1956, 168
1957, 168
1958, 168
3289, 174
3380, 173
3481, 173
3488, 173
3489, 173
3490, 173
3491, 174
3492, 174
3493, 174
3737, 168
3906, 165
4620, 166
4643, 85
4737, 132, 152
4832, 82, 134, 154
4905, 168
6094, 162
6238, 130
6239, 130
6326, 154
6676, 165
6979, 165
7845, 165
7852, 31, 44, 55, 68, 154
7955, 166
8374a, 174

11
59, 174
77, 174
104, 174
108, 174
155c*, 172
205a*, 154
1355a, 165
1421, 33, 56
3101, 159
3259, 159
3614, 43, 55, 86, 167
3618, 152
3805, 72
4347, 43, 55, 86, 167

4358, 159
4572, 155
4575, 163
5226, 169
5760, 168
7541, 161
7555, 132, 150
7764, 152

12
524, 167
2212, 168
2238, 165

13
1750, 156
1810, 125
1815, 151
1864, 156
3636, 156
8323, 173

14
128, 167
172, 125, 158
251, 138
343, 166
346, 166
347, 166, 170
353, 71, 86, 138, 139, 154, 166
354, 154
374, 167
409, 86
418, 170
419, 170
617a, 138
618, 138
2108, 151, 159
2265, 158
2299, 170
2839, 159
2940, 162
3532, 132
3548, 162
3625, 153
3645, 160
3646, 160
3674, 131, 159
3699, 85, 132, 167, 168
3705a–b, 132
3706a, 132
3707, 132
3714, 158
3715, 158
3949, 157
4250, 162
4290, 166
4569, 170

Cicero (cont.)
    4642, 71, 138, 139, 154, 166
    4643, 139, 154
    4668, 170
    5340, 152
    5345, 125, 158
  15
    7904,1, 132
    7905,2, 132
    7907a, 132
    7191, 144
    7892, 85, 132, 167, 168
  16
    35, 39
CIMRM
  02
    1759, 166
    1847, 156
CLE
  1464, 165
Codex Iustinianus
  1
    55.9, 146
  10
    71.1, 146
Codex Theodosianus
  8
    2.1, 146
    2.3, 146
    9.1, 74, 108, 143
  11
    8.3, 146
  12
    1.31, 146
  14
    1, 69
    1.1, 23, 143
    1.2, 143
    1.3, 136, 143
    1.4, 143
    1.5, 143
    1.6, 143
    17.6, 109, 145
  gesta
    8, 143, 155
CSIR
  D-04-03
    26, 156
  U-08
    104, 168

Digesta
  1
    2.2.7, 1, 115, 154
  8
    2.10, 56

  48
    4.2.1, 35, 98
    10, 98
    10.1.4, 98
    10.1.13, 98
    10.16.2, 98
    11.27.pr, 95
    11.6.2, 95
    13.1, 95
    13.10.1, 98
    13.11.5, 98
    13.12.pr., 98
  50
    4.18.17, 72
    5.3, 95
    15.4.1, 33
Dio Cassius
  Historia Romana
    37.43.2, 56, 58
    43.48.3, 37
    54.36.1, 37
    55.25.6, 78
    57.16.2, 36, 77
    69.8.1^2, 6
Diodorus of Sicily
  Bibliotheca historica
    20.36.6, 1, 154
    24.1.5, 115
Diomedes
  Ars grammatica
    484, 67, 115
Dionysius of Halicarnassus
  Antiquitates Romanae
    1.74.5, 29
    5.28.2, 14
    5.29.1, 14
    5.8.2, 64
    5.9.1, 64
    11.21.6, 64

EAOR
  02
    12, 163
  04
    39, 86
  08
    6, 85
    37, 132, 152
EE
  8
    368, 150
    426, 173
ERAlavesa
  118*, 175

EURom
   87, 163
Eutropius
   Breviarium historiae Romanae
      9.19, 116

FCap cons.
   249, 114, 153
FCap triumph.
   172, 122, 152
Festus
   De verborum significatu
      168.10–11, 87
      168.8–9, 87
      272.5–15, 67
      28.19–21, 116
      333.19–22, 50
      446.26–29, 22, 47, 75
      490.28–31, 29
FIRA
   3
      142, 171, 172
Florus
   Epitoma de Tito Livio
      1.22.23–25, 66, 82
      1.6.3, 29
Fragmenta Vaticana
   124, 75, 76
Franchetti
   7, 162
Frat. Arv.
   80
   61–65, 45
Frontinus
   De aquae ductu urbis Romae
      2.100, 30, 48, 82
      2.100–101, 65
      2.101, 72
      2.96.1, 33
Fronto
   Ad Marcum Aurelium
      5.41, 46
   Ad amicos
      2.7, 85, 168
      2.7.4–6, 85

Gellius
   Noctes Atticae
      3.9.2–6, 160
      7.9.1–6, 1, 49, 154
      7.9.2–3, 48
      7.9.5–6, 121
   Gesta conlationis Carthaginiensis
      1.1, 145, 158, 159
      1.27, 145, 158
      1.148, 145, 159
      1.149, 145
      1.157, 145, 159
      1.163, 145, 159
      1.176, 145, 159
      1.207, 145, 159
      1.213, 145, 159
      1.214, 145
      1.216, 145, 158
      1.218, 145, 159
      1.219, 145
      2.1, 145, 158, 159
      2.43, 59
      3.1, 145, 158, 159
      3.171, 159
      3.172, 145
      3.173, 145
GLIA
   01
      64, 175
      180, 154
      181, 164
GLISwedish
   4, 156

Horace
   Epistulae
      1.1.54, 107
      1.3, 21
      1.3.15–20, 21
      1.8, 21
      1.8.1–2, 21, 82
      1.8.2, 151
      2.1.156–157, 24
      2.3, 21
   Saturae
      1.5.27–29, 130
      1.5.34–36, 130
      1.5.35, 152
      1.5.51–70, 160
      1.6.71–78, 16
      1.6.86, 19
      2.6, 107, 111
      2.6.35, 74
      2.6.36, 17, 155
      2.6.36–37, 111

I. Ephesos
   411, 161
   720, 161
   1540, 161
   2283, 174
   4123, 73, 161
IAnkara
   50, 164

IATrebula
  96, 166
ICUR
  08
    23064, 143, 155
IDR
  03-01
    35, 156
    60, 156
  03-02
    11, 169
    187, 166
    264, 166
    386, 168
    457, 166
  01
    54, 156
IDRE
  01
    115, 153
IG
  14
    757, 169
    803, 165
    1607, 152
    2171, 163
IGI-Napoli
  01
    82, 169
    84, 167
  02
    150, 165
IGLFriuli
  40, 171
IGLMessina
  60g, 165
IGRRP
  01
    450, 169
    452, 167
IGUR
  03
    1216, 152
IK
  16
    2232a, 173
  59
    24, 73, 161
  61
    409, 157
IKöln
  395, 173
ILAfr
  325, 160
  592, 68, 125, 157–159

ILAlg
  01
    2194, 153
ILBulg
  246, 156
  336, 156
ILCV
  705, 143, 155
  705a, 172
ILD
  490, 165
  566, 165
ILJug
  01
    278, 173
  02
    920, 156
    1132, 164
ILLRP
  773, 75
  811, 154
  812, 155
  813, 160
  814d, 158
ILLRP-S
  37, 74, 159
  38, 164
  39, 164
ILMN
  01
    140, 170
    565, 170
    603, 165
    635, 175
ILN
  05-02
    335, 168
    376, 165
  03
    35, 167
ILPBardo
  26, 155, 156
  84, 169
  188, 160
  370, 125, 157–159
ILS
  333, 82
  359, 161
  404, 172
  615, 167
  1033, 72, 75
  1382, 156
  1383, 156
  1384, 156
  1391, 162

Index Locorum

1429, 125, 158
1859, 156
1877, 158
1878, 161
1879, 75, 152
1880, 75, 152
1881, 151
1882, 157
1883, 156
1884, 159
1885, 160
1886, 132, 150
1887, 161
1888, 159
1889, 131, 159
1890, 151
1891, 158
1892, 163
1893, 158
1894, 159
1895, 155
1896, 157
1897, 75
1898, 152
1898a, 132, 152
1899, 157
1900, 153
1901, 163
1926, 154
1931, 162
1935, 158
1958, 143, 155
2699, 160
2706, 162
2727, 127, 151
2748, 150
2828, 173
2881, 173
2887, 174
2888, 173
2889, 174
2892, 174
4310, 169
4317, 169
4369, 166
4951a, 162
4971, 161
5053, 153
5206, 170
5918a, 86, 167
5947, 154
6057, 169
6107, 165
6146, 86
6148, 86, 138, 139, 154, 166

6150, 166, 170
6151, 166
6165, 167
6167, 170
6188, 161
6283, 162
6315, 166
6316, 165
6460, 167
6498, 166
6579, 72
6953, 133, 151
6954, 133, 151
7118, 169
7161, 166
7183, 165
7225, 170, 171
7227, 165
7349, 172
7417, 171
7455, 171, 172
7469, 171
7799, 166
7817, 170
8833, 161
8859, 160
8935, 170, 171
9030, 171
9031, 171
9036, 72, 151
9040, 75
9041, 144, 150
9505, 83
ILSanMichele
11, 156
ILTun
15, 154
111, 169
396, 155, 156
IMCCatania
379, 159
InscrAqu
01
43, 152
247, 171
InscrIt
01-01
11, 161
04-01
30, 160
47, 162
148, 162
156, 153
197, 131, 159
253, 158

InscrIt (cont.)
   625, 85, 132, 167, 168
  13-01
    1ab, 114, 153
    27, 77
    35, 152
IPOstia
  A
    50a, 154
  B
    339, 86
IRComo
  3, 165
IRPAlicante
  50, 156
IScM
  04
    11, 168
    12, 165, 167
    13, 165
  05
    10, 156
Isidore of Seville
  Origines
    6.14.2, 140
ISIS
  5, 154

John the Lydian
  De magistratibus
    2.30.4, 145
  De mensibus
    1.28, 145
Jordanes
  De summa temporum vel origine actibusque gentis Romanorum
    192, 66, 82
Josephus
  Antiquitates Judaicae
    14.219, 44, 153
Juvenal
  Saturae
    5.3, 160
  Scholia in Iuvenalis saturas
    5.3, 160

Lactantius
  Divinae institutiones
    1.22, 158
LapSav
  154, 175
lex agr.
  10, 33
  13, 33
  20, 33
  70, 33

lex Irn.
  18
    34, 84
    48, 101
    73, 85, 100
    30–31, 52
    31–36, 86
    31–47, 17, 47
    32–39, 33
    32–42, 17
    34–35, 17
    35–36, 17
    37–40, 59
    39–42, 100
    43–47, 84
    31, 20
lex Urson.
  62–63, 63
  62, 85, 106
    12–13, 46
    24–31, 69
    32–35, 47
    31, 20
  81, 85, 100
    14–25, 17
    15–17, 33
    17–23, 100
    17–29, 47
    20, 52
  130
    42, 33
  131
    3, 33
  134
    41–44, 33
Licinius Macer
  Annales (frg.)
    F24, 48, 154
LIKelsey
  18, 173
Livy
  Ab urbe condita
    1.8.3, 13, 63
    2.12.1–16, 13, 66
    2.27.6, 33
    3.55.13, 31, 37
    4.8.4, 30, 36, 66, 81, 99
    9.46.1–12, 1, 154
    9.46.2, 49
    9.46.2–3, 48
    9.46.10–12, 120
    21.63.3, 95, 101
    22.57.3, 67, 73, 152
    23.19.17–18, 131, 151
    26.36.11, 33, 56, 66, 82
    27.16.8, 56, 66, 81

27.37.7, 22
29.37.12–13, 29
29.37.7, 33
30.39.7, 37, 105
38.55.4–5, 68, 101, 105
38.55.5, 66
40.29.3–14, 57, 90, 158
42.1.5, 152
42.7.1–2, 122, 152
42.21.6–7, 122, 152
43.16.13, 37, 45, 81
45.15.10, 122, 152
45.17.4, 122, 152
per. 19, 114, 115, 153
per. 40, 158
per. 57, 33
per. 9, 1, 154
LMentana
47, 159
Lucian
 Apologia
  12, 36
Lupa
 24336, 170

Macrobius
 Saturnalia
  1.14.2, 155
  1.15.9, 1, 154
Martial
 Epigrammata
  8.38.1–16, 74

Nepos
 Eumenes
  1.5, 20
Notitia dignitatum
 Occ.
  18.2–14, 145
 Or.
  21.9, 142

P. Mich.
 VIII
  467, 175
  468, 174, 175
Paulus
 Sententiae
  5.25.6, 97
Petronius
 Satyrica
  44, 109
  85, 163

Piso Frugi
 Annales (frg.)
  F29, 1, 48, 49, 121, 154
Plautus
 Frg. inc.
  17.1, 87
 Trinummus
  419, 32
Pliny the Elder
 Naturalis historia
  7.183, 160
  13.84, 57, 158
  26.3, 163
  33.17, 115
  33.17–19, 1, 154
  33.32–33, 109
  35.7, 29
Pliny the Younger
 Epistulae
  1.10.9–10, 21
  3.1, 21
  3.5, 21
  4.12.2, 20, 89
  6.22.4, 45, 55, 68, 105
  10.48.1, 51
  10.7b.2, 51
Plutarch
 Aemilius Paullus
  37.4, 163
 Cato maior
  24.2, 164
 Cato minor
  16–18, 105
  16.1–2, 19
  16.2–3, 69
  16.3, 101
  16.3–6, 72
  16.4–10, 90, 99
  17.3–4, 33, 97
  18.2, 35, 99
  18.5, 45
  28.1, 56, 58
  34.3, 68
  34.3–4, 89
  38.2–3, 34
 Fabius
  22.5, 66
 Publicola
  12.2, 31
 Quaestiones convivales
  1.3.10, 81
 Sulla
  27.6, 38

Polybius
  Historiae
    1.49–51, 116
    1.49–52, 115
    1.52.2–3, 116
    3.26.1, 37
    6.56.13–15, 94
    6.56.6–12, 116
Porphyrio
  Commentum in Horatii epistulas
    1.3.1, 21, 156
  Commentum in Horatii saturas
    1.5.35, 130, 152
    1.5.66, 160
    2.6.36, 72, 155

Q. Cicero
  Commentariolum petitionis
    30, 75
Quintillian
  Institutio oratoria
    10.3.31, 96

RECapua
  42, 166
RICIS
  02
    503/1118, 166
    503/1119, 166
    515/1401, 156
    515/1402, 156
RIU
  01
    31, 169
    96, 175
  02
    328, 168
    372, 165

Sallust
  De bello Iugurthino
    41.1–5, 95
  Historiae
    1.55.17, 153
    3.83.1, 68, 157, 162
Schiavi
  6, 162
  8, 162
  34, 162
  55, 162
  56, 162
SCPP
  175, 42
  176, 33

Scriptores Historiae Augustae
  Aurelianus
    39.1, 6, 33
  Gordiani tres
    12.3–4, 144
  Probus
    2.1, 144
SEG
  33
    786, 170
  52
    1251, 157
  54
    1453, 157
  60
    1131, 160
Seneca the Younger
  Dialogi
    1.3.8, 33
    4.28.2, 33
    10.13.4, 40
Servius
  Commentarius in Vergilii Aeneida
    1.698, 68, 157, 162
  Commentarius in Vergilii Georgica
    2.502, 38
Sinn
  84, 172
  284, 172
SIRIS
  538, 166
  539, 166
  638, 156
  639, 156
Strabo
  Geographica
    5.4.13, 116
Suetonius
  Divus Augustus
    36.1, 35
  Divus Claudius
    16.1, 96
    38.2, 73
  Divus Iulius
    20.1, 35
  Divus Tiberius
    2.2, 115, 153
  Divus Vespasianus
    3, 155
  Domitianus
    14.3, 82
    9.3, 101, 108
  Nero
    17.1, 97

Vita Horatii
  24, 16, 48, 72, 83, 107, 155
SupIt
  04-S
    46, 167
  05-FN
    32, 168
  06-CI
    3, 160

Tab. Heracl.
  14, 33
  39–40, 33
  68–80, 48
  80, 46
  148–156, 33
tab. Vindon.
  1, 42
Tacitus
  Annales
    3.51.2, 35
    5.4.1, 143
    11.22.4, 66
    13.28.2, 33
    13.28.3, 36
    16.12.1, 63
  Dialogus de oratoribus
    39.1, 40
  Historiae
    3.72.3, 38
TitAq
  01
    239, 166
    240, 166
    241, 166
    242, 166

Valerius Maximus
  Facta et dicta memorabilia
    1.1.12, 158
    2.5.2, 1, 121, 154
    3.5.1, 122, 152
    3.7.11, 23
    4.1.10, 81
    4.1.10a, 58
    4.5.3, 81, 91, 122, 152
    5.7.ext. 2, 56, 81
    9.2.1, 33
    9.3.3, 1, 154
Varro
  De lingua Latina
    6.87, 47
    M 86–87, 81
  Res rusticae
    3.2.14, 46, 160
Vegetius
  Epitoma rei militaris
    2.7, 87
Vergil
  Georgica
    2.501–502, 38
Vitruvius
  De architectura
    7.9.2, 154

WT
  18, 87

General Index

[- - -]ammius (A.224), 164
[- - -]anius (A.225), 164
[- - -]cius, M. (A.200), 119, 162
[- - -]inius Thisdra (A.304), 169
[- - - i]us (A.202), 126, 163
[- - -]ius (A.226), 164
[- - -]lius Clemens (A.201), 82, 163
[- - -]nus (A.203), 163
[- - -]pius Cla[- - -] (A.299), 168
[- - -]usius (A.227), 164

ab actis senatus, 143
ab epistulis, 83
accensi, 2, 62, 67, 70, 85
accountability, 28, 34, 98
accounting, 15, 17, 19, 23, 25, 31, 33, 44, 52, 67
accounts, *see rationes*
Achaia (province), 133
Achilles, 137
acta
   diurna, 34
   senatus, 31, 143
Acte (Claudia Acte), 93
Ad Mercurium, 119, 142
Aeclanum, 119
aedes, see temple
aedilis
   at the *aerarium*, 37
   ἀγορανόμος, 37
   and corruption, 109
   and documentation, 31, 37
   as head of archive, 43
   and *senatus consulta*, 37
Aelius, L. (A.1), 78, 150
Aelius Aelianus, P. (A.232), 85–87, 107, 164
Aelius Agathoclianus, P. (A.2), 76, 81, 118, 129, 132, 150
Aelius Andri[- - -], P. (A.3), 119, 150
Aelius Bellenius Aristo, P. (A.306), 169
Aelius Domitianus Gaurus, C. (A.4), 56, 120, 126, 131, 150
Aelius Epaphroditus (A.333), 171

Aelius Exuperatus, P. (A.307), 169
Aelius Protus, L. (A.334), 171
Aelius Quintus, P. (A.233), 86, 165
Aelius Threptus, P. (A.335), 171
Aelius Victor, Sex. (A.5), 118, 150
Aemilianus (A.6), 119, 150
Aemilius Eucharpus (A.7), 143, 150
Aemilius Felicianus, M. (A.234), 86, 165
Aemilius Paullus, L., 122
Aemilius Proculus (A.8), 150
Aemilius Rectus, L. (A.9), 126, 133, 134, 151
Aemilius Regulus, 133
aerarium
   as archive, 29, 32, 37–39, 45, 77, 141
   as assembly place, 89
   and *rationes*, 32, 51
   and *senatus consulta*, 33, 57
   and *tabulae publicae*, 32
   and *tabularium*, 38
   as treasury, 30, 37, 66
aerarius, 73
aes apparitorum, 20
Aesernia, 86, 167
Africa (province), 125
Albanum, 119, 170
Albatius Verna, Q. (A.235), 86, 165
Albinovanus Celsus (A.10), 21, 82, 151
Albius Rufus, L. (A.11), 151
album, 75, 80
Aletius Lupus, C. (A.12), 119, 151
Alexandros (A.214), 163
Alfius Iustus, Q. (A.236), 86, 165
Allius Niger, C. (A.13), 72, 77, 119, 151
altar of Domitius Ahenobarbus (so-called), 41, 49
[Am]erimnus (A.237), 85, 86, 107, 165
amphitheatrum, 132
Ancyra, 175
Anicius, M. (A.14), 131, 151
annalistic tradition, 1, 2, 13, 62, 63, 103, 115
Annius Priscus, C. (A.15), 119, 134, 151
Annius Protectus, P. (A.16), 119, 151

216

General Index

Antiochos ('the Great'), 101, 105
Antistius, C. (A.17), 108, 116, 151
Antistius Maximus, M. (A.18), 151
Antistius Vetus, C. (A.238), 86, 165
Antium, 86, 165
Antoninus Pius (emperor), 82, 83, 127, 128
Antonius, M., 91
Antonius Capitolinus (A.311), 170
Antonius Rufus, M. (A.19), 75, 151
anulus aureus, 109, 126, 129
Apidius Proculus, C. (A.20), 151
Apidius Valerus (A.21), 119, 151
apparere ('to attend to' a magistrate), 61
apparitores
   and civil service, 61
   known as Bruttiani, 116
   Caesarum, 83, 128, 132
   Etruscan model, 13, 63
   imperial, 83
   and magistrates, 7, 62, 63, 65
   and the *ordo equester*, 125
   salaried, 46, 65, 106
   and servility, 116
   symbolic nature of, 61, 62
   system of, 4, 45
Apuleius Marcus, L. (A.300), 85, 107, 169
Apuleius Nepos (A.355), 173
Apusulenus Secundus (A.22), 77, 81, 151
Apusulenus Secundus, Q. (A.22), 118
Aquae Balissae, 86, 164
Aquae Sextiae, 86, 167
Aquileia, 119, 131, 171
Aquincum, 86, 166
Ara degli Scribi (so-called), 8, 39, 41, 45, 49, 117
architecti, 62
archives
   aerarium, 37, 43
   and archival practice, 32, 33, 36, 38, 44
   and archival policy, 34, 56
   and archival reform, 36
   architecture of, 39, 40
   Atrium Libertatis, 37
   of the *cura annonae*, 30
   destruction of, 30, 38
   materiality of, 4, 5, 41
   of the *plebs*, 37
   porticus porphyretica, 144
   provincial, 36
   of the senate, 144
   tablinum, 27
   tabularium, 27, 44
   temple of Ceres, 37
   temple of the Nymphs, 37
   temples as, 29
Argos, 133

armamentarium, 82
armarium, 39
Artoria, 136
Asculum, 86, 167, 168
Asia (province), 136
Asso, 133
Atella, 86, 168
Atellius Paetus, Sex. (A.23), 126, 151
Athens, 16, 51
Atiedius Dorus, L. (A.24), 119, 151
Atilius Pudens, L. (A.359), 173
Atinius Paternus, A. (A.25), 126, 127, 151
Atrium Libertatis, 29, 37, 38
Attidius Tuscus, 92
Aufidius, C. (A.26), 119, 131, 152
Aufidius Luscus (A.27), 116, 130–131, 152
Augusta Taurinorum, 86, 167
Augustales, 43, 72
Augustus (Imp. Caesar Augustus, emperor)
   and *acta diurna*, 35
   and archival reform, 36
   and corruption, 95
   and epigraphic habit, 25
   having *scribae*, 83
   and patronage, 16, 21
Aurelian (L. Domitius Aurelianus, emperor)
   cancelling debts, 6
Aurelius Fortunatianus, M. (A.336), 171
Aurelius Hermogenes, M. (A.28), 81, 118, 126–129, 132, 142, 152
Aurelius Marcianus (A.239), 86, 165
Aurelius Peculiaris, T. (A.308), 169
Aurelius Plebeius, [M.] (A.312), 170
Aurelius Telesphorus, T. (A.313), 170
Aurelius Viator (A.240), 86, 165
Auximum, 86, 166
Avidius Charito (A.29), 119, 152
Avillius Licinius Trosius, C. (A.30), 75, 119, 152

Baetica (province), 134
balneum, 132
Basilius (A.337), 171
Basti, 133
Bellicus (A.31), 152
Beneventum, 51, 86, 166
Bibulus, M., 81
Bovillae, 131
Bruttii, 116
bureaucracy, 28

C. (A.241), 86, 165
Caecilius Amandus, Q. (A.32), 119, 152
Caecilius Birronianus, Sex. (A.33), 92, 119, 132, 152

Caecilius Epagathus, Sex. (A.34), 83, 92, 119, 120, 129, 152
Caecilius Metellus, M., 55
Caecilius Niger, Q., 91
Caecilius Proculus, C. (A.35), 152
Caecilius Simplex, 56
Caere, 43, 55, 86, 167
Caesar (C. Iulius Caesar, emperor), 81, 91, 122
  and *acta senatus*, 143
  legislation against corruption, 51, 95
  publication of *acta diurna*, 34
  reform of the *aerarium*, 37
  reform of the calendar, 91
Caesarea, 127, 131, 134, 136, 172
Caesius Paternus, Q. (A.360), 173
Cahallistus (A.338), 171
calendar, 1, 57, 88, 91, 115
Caligula (C. Iulius Caesar Germanicus, emperor), 133
Calpurnius Piso Caesoninus, L., 32, 34
Calpurnius Piso Frugi, L., 44, 104
Calpurnius Piso, Cn., 41
Calpurnius Rufus, L. (A.361), 173
Campus Martius, 29
[Ca]murtius [Se]verus (A.242), 8, 53, 86, 165
Cantilius, L. (A.36), 73, 152
Canuleius Cilo (A.37), 152
Capena, 86, 168
capital (Bourdieu), 3
Capitolium, 29, 32, 38, 48, 78
Capua, 86, 165, 166
caput ('heading', in a document), 43, 44
Cara, 169
Caracalla (M. Aurelius Antoninus, emperor), 75
carmen, 58
Carsulae, 131
Carthago, 37, 95, 145
Carthago Nova, 133
Casae, 57
Cassienius (A.38), 152
Cassiodorus (Magnus Aurelius Cassiodorus Senator), 146
Cassius Mansuetus, T. (A.243), 85, 86, 107, 165
Cassius Priscus, L. (A.39), 152
Catholics, 59
Catiline (L. Sergius Catilina), 89
Catius Martialis, C. (A.244), 165
Cato the Younger (M. Porcius Cato Uticensis)
  archiving documents, 32, 97
  consulting archives, 35
  as *quaestor in Cyprus*, 89
  and *rationes*, 34
  reform of the *aerarium*, 19, 24, 45, 90
  as a Republican model, 105
  and *scribae*, 56, 68, 69, 99, 101

Cattius Sossius Felix (A.362), 173
censor
  and *cura tabularum publicarum*, 30, 36, 66
  and documentation, 38
  private archive of, 29
  and *scribae*, 30, 81
  and *tabulae censoriae*, 31, 37
censuales, 144
census, 29, 31, 33, 49, 67
centumviri, 72
cera (page, of a document), 44
cerarium (wax tax), 108
chartae (sheets of papyrus), 5, 30
chirographum, 57, 97
Ci[- - -] [Euty]ches, Q. (A.245), 86, 165
Cicereius, C. (A.40), 81, 91, 122, 152
Cicero (M. Tullius Cicero), 68, 89, 90
  and archival policy, 56
  consulting private archives, 34
  correspondence of, 50
  on corruption, 124
  defending a *scriba* in court, 73, 90, 105
  and the destruction of archives, 30
  and documentary evidence, 31, 35, 58
  on education, 20
  having senators keep the minutes, 46
  on the nature of the *tabulae publicae*, 35
  on nepotism, 123
  and the *ordo scribarum*, 74, 102, 104, 112
  and *rationes*, 51
  on the social status of *scribae*, 20
  on wage labour, 20
Cilicia (province), 50, 76, 82, 89, 90, 107, 135
Cinna (A.246), 86, 165
Circeii, 127
cista, 54
civil service, 61, 142
Civil Wars, 125
Claudius (Ti. Claudius Nero Germanicus, emperor), 93
Claudius, M. (A.216), 75, 163
Claudius Armiger, Ti. (A.41), 132, 153
Claudius Caecus, App., 1, 88, 103, 115, 121
Claudius Galonius (A.247), 86, 165
Claudius Glicia, M. (A.42), 6, 114–116, 121, 153
Claudius Helvius Secundus, Ti. (A.43), 92, 126, 127, 131, 134, 136, 153
Claudius Hispanus, Ti. (A.44), 118, 126, 131, 153
Claudius Paternus, T. (A.363), 173
Claudius Paulus (A.45), 126, 127, 153
Claudius Philargyrus, Ti. (A.339), 171
Claudius Philius, Ti. (A.340), 172
Claudius Pulcher, P., 6, 114, 116
Claudius Secundus Philippianus, Ti. (A.46), 93, 119, 120, 129, 153

General Index

Claudius Storax (A.341), 172
Clemens (A.201), 131
Clodius, A. (A.47), 153
Clodius Fortunatus (A.48), 153
Clodius Pulcher, P., 89, 90, 101
Cloelius, Sex. (A.49), 90, 116, 153
Cloelius Hermio, D. (A.50), 119, 153
Clusium, 63
[Clu]vius Formica (A.51), 74, 76, 129, 153
coactor, 19
Cocceius (A.248), 86, 165
codex, 42, 44
   accepti et expensi, 44
   ansatus, 31, 44, 55
   notarum, 59
   and *tabulae publicae*, 32
   typology of, 40, 43
collegium
   album of, 75, 79
   organisation of, 87
   poetarum, 23
   schola of, 75, 80
   scribarum histrionumque, 23
   scribarum librariorum, 74
   scribarum librariorum quaestoriorum, 75
   scribarum poetarum, 75
   sex primorum, 75, 76
colonisation, 24
comitia, 33, 95
commentarii, 31
   cottidiani, 43, 55
   as part of the *tabulae publicae*, 35, 55
   and *scribae*, 68
   structure of, 43, 44
Commodus (L. Aurelius Commodus, emperor), 126, 129
Comum, 86, 165
Concordia, 85, 86, 168
Concordius Successus (A.314), 170
concustodire ('to administer' a document), 52
conductor portorii, 128
consilium, 68
Constantine (Flavius Valerius Constantinus, emperor), 74, 142, 145
Constantinople, 145
Constantius II (Flavius Iulius Constantius, emperor), 23, 146
constitutional law (Mommsen), 9
consul
   and appointment to *decuriae*, 70
   and *scribae*, 81
contio, 100
Cor[- - -], Cn. (A.52), 153
Cora, 127

Cornelianus (A.249), 165
Cornelius, Cn. (A.53), 153
Cornelius, Q. (A.54), 90, 91, 116, 123, 153
Cornelius Proculus, P. (A.250), 86, 166
Cornelius Scipio Africanus, P., 81, 91, 122
Cornelius Scipio Asiagenes, L., 68, 101, 105
Cornelius Surus, 23, 75
Cornelius Terentianus, L. (A.55), 82, 129, 153
Cornelius Victorinus, P. (A.251), 86, 166
Cornificius (A.56), 105, 153
corruption, 88, 94–109
   and accountability, 98
   and documentary evidence, 96
   and *fides*, 102, 141
   legislation against, 95, 105
   in the provinces, 108
Corsi, 122
crimen, see corruption
   falsi, see embezzlement, extortion
   de peculatu, see embezzlement
   de repetundis, see extortion
Cubulteria, 86, 166
Cularo, 86, 87, 165, 168
Culcisius, T. (A.57), 153
Cumae, 131
cura
   annonae, 30, 31, 109, 145
   ludorum, 31
   tabularum publicarum, 30, 36, 77
   urbis, 31
curator
   aquarum, 30, 48, 65, 72, 82, 85, 132
   coloniae, 43
   fani Herculis Victoris, 132
   kalendarii, 127
   rei publicae, 128
   tabularum publicarum, 36, 77
   viarum Ostiensis et Campanae, 128
curia, 39
Curiatius Cosanus, 43
Curiatius Secundus, C. (A.252), 86, 166
Curius Servilius Draco, P. (A.58), 126, 154
cursus honorum, 61
Curtius, C., 38
Curtius Tutus, P. (A.59), 118, 154
Cutius Amemptus, M'. (A.60), 119, 154
Cyprus (province), 34, 89

debt relief
   by Aurelian, 6
   by Hadrian, 6, 41
decemviri
   agris dandis adsignandis, 65, 82
   stlitibus iudicandis, 82
Decumius Vaarus, N. (A.61), 116, 154

decuriae
  ab aerario, 75
  admission to, 70
  assignment to, 70, 89
  available for purchase, 16, 21, 71, 107, 111, 135
  and civil service, 62, 141
  of *collegia*, 87
  late antique, 23, 142
  maiores, 81
  minores, 81
  municipal, 86, 106
  and *ordines*, 73
  organisation of, 69–71, 79, 80
  privileges of, 69, 72
  of the *scribae*, 82
  as sinecures, 72, 107
  and social status, 73
  and wage labour, 70
decuriae urbis Romae, see decuriae
decuriales, 136, 143, *see* decuriae
decuriam emere ('to buy into a *decuria*'), 72
decuriones, 17, 71, 84
Delminium, 86, 165
δέλτος, *see tabula*
Deusdedit (A.253), 146, 166
dictator, 81
dignitas, 112
Diocletian (C. Aurelius Valerius Diocletianus, emperor), 5, 116, 142
Dionysius Trallianus (A.358), 173
documentary practice, 31–33, 41–44, 48–57
documentation, 27–44, 66, 96, 99, 144
documents, *see tabulae ceratae*
  access to, 1, 34
  and accountability, 28, 99
  archival of, 27, 29, 32, 40, 44, 97
  attestation of, 43
  censorial, 29, *see tabulae censoriae*
  destruction of, 6, 41
  as evidence, 35, 58
  financial, 2, 6, 32, 33, 41, 44, 45, *see rationes*
  forgery of, 96, 98
  importance of, 28, 31, 140
  judicial, 31, 33, 35, 55
  legal, 1, 2, 6, 24, 32, 33, 41, 55
  materiality of, 5, 26, 27
  private, 29
  public, 17, 27–29, *see tabulae publicae*
  publication of, 29, 34
  religious, 24
  sealing of, 97
  structure of, 43–44
  subscription of, 97
Domatius Sabinus (A.62), 154
Domitian (T. Flavius Domitianus, emperor), 108

Domitius Ahenobarbus, Cn., 41
Domitius Dexter, C., 92, 138
Domitius Fabius Hermogenes, C. (A.63), 71, 92, 118, 126, 131, 136–139, 154
dona militaria, 127
Donatists, 59, 145
Drepana, 115, 116
Durius, Q. (A.64), 154
duumvir, 132
  iure dicundo, 86
  quinquennalis, 132

education, 16–20
  elementary, 18
  Greek, 24
  higher, 16, 18, 19, 112
  levels of, 18, 25
  and social status, 20
Egnatius Fuscus, Cn. (A.65), 55, 154
Egrilius Plarianus, A. (A.254), 86, 87, 166
Egrilius Secundus Threptianus, A. (A.255), 86, 87, 166, 170
embezzlement, 5, 50, 88, 94, 95, 98–101, *see corruption*
Ennius, C. (A.66), 154
Ennius Vicetinus, M. (A.67), 131, 134, 154
Epaphroditus (Ti. Claudius Epaphroditus), 83
Ephesos, 73, 136, 174
epigraphy, 9, 117
  epigraphic habit, 25, 113
Eporedia, 119, 134
Eumenes of Cardia, 20
Eumolpus (A.215), 163
Eutyches (A.342), 172
exceptor, 59, 145, 146
  amplissimi senatus, 143
extortion, 94, 95, 99, *see corruption*

Faberius (A.68), 81, 91, 154
Fabius (A.217), 164
Fabius Africanus, Q., 92
Fabius Clemens, L. (A.256), 86, 166
Fabius Cytisus, Q. (A.69), 92, 119, 120, 129, 154
Fabius Eutychus, L. (A.257), 71, 86, 87, 136, 166
Fabius Largus (A.111), 72
Fabius Primus (A.315), 170
Fabrateria Nova, 127
Fabricius Caesennius Gallus, L. (A.70), 126, 131, 154
Faenius Alexander, L. (A.71), 118, 154
Faesulae, 128
fasces, 62
fasti, 1, 76, 78, 80, 103, 121, 138, *see calendar*
  consulares, 114
  triumphales, 122

General Index

Faustina the Younger (Annia Galeria Faustina), 127
Felicianus (A.343), 172
Feronius Rufus, L. (A.258), 86, 166
fides, 35, 48, 97, 102, 141, 148, *see* oath
finitores, 62
fistula, 85, 132
flamen
    divi Hadriani, 131, 138
    perpetuus, 131
Flaminius Severus, C. (A.72), 154
Flavius, Cn. (A.73), 1, 2, 24, 34, 49, 57, 67, 88, 103, 104, 115, 116, 121, 154
Flavius, M. (A.74), 91, 155
Flavius Aper, M., 83
Flavius Aper, T. (A.259), 86, 166
Flavius Bitho, L. (A.364), 173
Flavius Cominus, T. (A.75), 155
Flavius Laurentius (A.76), 155
Flavius Liberalis (A.77), 118, 155
Flavius Myrtilus Ianuarianus, T. (A.344), 172
Flavius R[ufin]ianus, T. (A.78), 72, 126, 128, 155
Flavius Tyrannus (A.316), 170
Florentia, 128
Floronia (Vestal Virgin), 73
Fonteius Claudianus, C. (A.79), 92, 118, 155
Fonteius Eutycho (A.309), 169
forensis, 146
forgery, 96–98, *see* corruption, documents
Formiae, 132
Fortunatianus (A.345), 172
Fortunatus (A.48), 119
Forum Clodii, 132
Forum Novum, 86, 168
Forum Romanum, 41, 75
Frontinus (Sex. Iulius Frontinus), 65
Fronto (M. Cornelius Fronto), 46, 85
frumentatio, 30
Fulginae, 169
[F]ulviu[s] (A.218), 164
Fulvius Clemens, L. (A.260), 86, 166
Fulvius Eros Modestus, T. (A.80), 119, 155
Fulvius Eunus, Q., 118
Fulvius Faustus, Q. (A.81), 8, 45, 117, 120, 155
Fulvius Priscus, Q. (A.82), 8, 47, 117, 155
Fulvius Severus, L. (A.373), 174
Fundi, 130
funus publicum, 136
Furius, A., 44
Furius Aculeo, C., 68
Furius Tiro, C. (A.83), 131, 155

Galillenses, 55
Gallienus (P. Licinius Egnatius Gallienus, emperor), 142
Gavius Capito Maximianus (A.84), 126, 129, 155
Gavius Sabinus, M. (A.261), 86, 166
Gavius Zosimus, Q. (A.310), 169
Germanicus (Iulius Caesar Germanicus), 41
γραμματεύς, 8
Granius [Eut]yches, L. (A.85), 119, 155
Gratian (Flavius Gratianus, emperor), 146

habere ('to keep' a document), 17
Hadria, 167
Hadrian (P. Aelius Hadrianus, emperor), 6, 93
Hannibal, 116
haruspices, 62, 85
Hellenius Rufus, Cn. (A.86), 155
Helvius Agrippa, L., 44, 55
Heracleia, 35
Herennius, L. (A.87), 76, 116, 155
Hierapolis, 54, 105
Hispalis, 140
Hispania Tarraconensis (province), 133, 134
histriones, 22
Horace (Q. Horatius Flaccus) (A.88), 6, 16, 18, 21, 72, 83, 107, 111, 124, 130–131, 155
humanitas (παιδεία), *see* education
Hypurgus (A.346), 172

Ianuarius (A.347), 172
Ianuarius (A.348), 172
illiteracy, 26
Illyricum (province), 128
imperium, 62
Ingenus Maximinus, Q. (A.262), 85, 86, 107, 166
inspicere ('to inspect' a document), 17
Insteius Victorinus (A.356), 173
instrumentum domesticum, 25, 26
interpretes, 62
Irni, 86
Isidore (Isidorus Hispalensis), 140
iudex quaestionis, 31, 82
iudicium populi, 95
Iulius Agathocles, Q. (A.89), 118, 155
Iulius Agathopous, C. (A.385), 175
Iulius Alexander, L. (A.90), 118, 156
Iulius Augustalis, C. (A.91), 83, 156
Iulius Canus, 133
Iulius Celer (A.357), 173
Iulius Florus (A.92), 21, 156
Iulius Fortunatus, C. (A.93), 156
Iulius Gelos, C., 72
Iulius Ingenus, C. (A.263), 86, 166
Iulius Iustus, C. (A.94), 81, 126, 156
Iulius Maro, C. (A.365), 173
Iulius Martialis (A.95), 156
Iulius Mummius (A.366), 173
Iulius Nobilis (A.264), 86, 166

Iulius Paulinus, Sex. (A.96), 156
Iulius Priscus, C. (A.97), 156
Iulius Receptus, C. (A.98), 156
Iulius Saturninus, C. (A.367), 174
Iulius Saturninus, T. (A.99), 83, 126–129, 156
Iulius Socrates, C. (A.265), 86, 166
Iulius Valens Diza, A. (A.368), 174
Iunius Achilles, T. (A.100), 92, 119, 156
Iunius Ami[- - -], Q. (A.101), 156
Iunius Auctus, M. (A.102), 119, 156
Iunius Brutus, L., 64
Iunius Brutus, M., 16, 112
Iunius Lyco, L. (A.103), 119, 156
Iunius Menander, [M.] (A.104), 75, 119, 120, 157
Iunius Pastor, A. (A.105), 92, 119, 126, 157
Iunius Pullus, L., 114
Iunius Rusticus, 143
Iunius Severus, T., 92
Iupiter, 100
ius civile, 1
ius iurandum, see oath
Iuvenitus Rixa, M., 55

Julian (Flavius Claudius Iulianus, emperor), 23
jurisprudence, 56
Justinian (Flavius Petrus Sabbatius Iustinianus, emperor), 147

Karanis, 174, 175
κήρωμα, *see* cera

Lacedaemon, 133
Laelius Herennianus, L. (A.266), 87, 167
Laodicea, 51
Laticius Zeno, T. (A.378), 174
Laurentius (A.76), 143
lead tablets, 26
lectio, 71, 73, 78, 89
legatus Augusti, 83
legere ('to designate' to a *decuria*), 70, 73
legis actiones, 1, 104, 121, *see* calendar
lex
    Calpurnia de repetundis, 34, 95, 104
    coloniae Genetivae Iuliae (Ursonensis), 7, 17, 46, 69, 84, 100, 106
    Cornelia de falsis, 98
    Cornelia de XX quaestoribus, 7, 9, 62, 66, 69, 70, 73, 76, 79, 112
    duodecim tabulae, 95
    Irnitana, 7, 17, 84
    Iulia de repetundis, 34, 51, 95
    Iulia municipalis, 7
    Iulia peculatus, 95, 98, 101
    latina tabulae Bantinae, 100
Libarna, 165

liber sententiarum, 43, 57
liberal arts, 23
liberti, 115
libraries, 39, 144
librarii, 22, 45–47, 71, 85, 136, *see scribae librarii*
Licinius Crassus, M., 101
Licinius Privatus, M. (A.267), 85, 86, 107, 131, 167
Licinius Proclus, C. (A.301), 169
lictores, 62, 67, 71, 83, 85, 125, 136
    curiatii, 138
literacy, 12, 140, *see* numeracy
    consequences of, 4, 11, 13–16
    Egyptian, 14
    functional, 18
    Greek, 15
    levels of, 4, 15, 22, 25, 26
    models of, 15
    Near Eastern, 14
    and power, 2, 14, 24
    Republic, 24
literary culture, 20, 24
literate culture, 16, 21, 25
literate practice, 16, 24
    and the aristocratic household, 24
    cultic, 25
    military, 25
    private, 25
    public, 21, 25, 27–60
literature, 111
liturae, 96
Livius Andronicus, 22
Lucius Verus (emperor), 127
Lucretius Apollonius, Sex. (A.268), 86, 167
Lucretius Quintianus, Q. (A.106), 119, 157
Lugdunum, 119
Luna, 86, 165
Lupercus (A.379), 174
lustrum, 47
Lutatius Catulus, Q., 38, 90, 99
Lycia and Pamphylia (province), 83

Macedonia (province), 32, 122
Madauros, 131
Maecenas (A.107), 68, 91, 116, 157
Maecenas, C., 16, 111
Maelius Flaccus, L. (A.108), 118, 157
Maevius (A.109), 6, 88, 102, 104, 106–109, 123, 157
magister
    census, 143
    scribarum poetarum, 23, 75
magistrates
    and *apparitores*, 7, 14
    and archives, 31

General Index

and clerical writing, 21
commentarii of, 31
and documents, 29–31
Etruscan, 14
and oath, 100, 102
and patronage, 88, 136
and *res publica*, 61
Mamilius, L. (A.110), 68, 104, 116, 157
Mamius Fabius Largus, L. (A.111), 126, 157
Marcius Menelaus, M. (A.374), 174
Marcus Aurelius (emperor), 125, 127
Marius Clementianus, T. (A.112), 129, 157
Marius Doryphorus, [L.] (A.113), 92, 118, 120, 126, 129, 157
Marius Maximus Perpetuus Aurelianus, 125
Marius Maximus, L., 92
Marius Perpetuus, L. (A.114), 68, 92, 125, 157
Marius Severus, Cn. (A.269), 86, 167
Marsenus Castus (A.317), 170
Matrinius, D. (A.115), 73, 90, 104, 105, 157
Maximinus Thrax (C. Iulius Verus Maximinus, emperor), 144
Mediolanum, 86, 165, 166
mercenarius, 20
merces, 20, 70, 106
Mercusenus Theodotus, P. (A.116), 118, 157
Mescinius Rufus, L., 51, 76
Messalina (Statilia Messalina, empress), 93
Messana, 86, 165
Metrod[orus] (A.369), 174
militiae, 127
Mindius, M., 52
Minisius Primitivos (A.318), 170
Minturnae, 175
Minucius Aper (A.370), 174
minutes, *see* documents
Modius Proculus, Q. (A.219), 81, 164
Moesia inferior (province), 127
Mogetiana, 86, 168
Monnienius Tudienus (A.319), 170
mons Albanus, 122
mos maiorum, 100, 103, 108, 114
Mucius Scaevola, C., 13
municipes, 17
Mursella, 86, 165
Mustius (A.320), 170
Mutilius Primus, Sex. (A.117), 157

Naevius Propincus, Q. (A.371), 174
Naevius Urbanus, L. (A.118), 56, 76, 119, 157
Nampius (A.119), 145, 158
Napoca, 86, 165
Narona, 170
Natronius Rusticus, M. (A.120), 72, 76, 158
Neapolis, 86, 165, 167, 169

negotium, 17, 20
Nemausus, 168
Nepet, 119
Neratius Priscus, L., 75
Nero (Nero Claudius Caesar, emperor), 36, 83, 93, 97
Nerva (M. Cocceius Nerva, emperor), 65, 127
Nigidius Sors, L. (A.121), 116, 158
notarius, 59, 145
Numa (Pompilius Numa), 57, 90
numen, 100
numeracy, 140, *see* literacy
consequences of, 4
functional, 18
levels of, 4, 15
Numpidius Philomelus, L. (A.122), 119, 158
Nysa, 136

oath, 17, 35, 47, 59, 84, 94, 97, 98, 100, 102, *see fides*
Octavia (minor), 93
Octavius Auctus, C. (A.123), 93, 119, 158
Octavius Eu[- - -]anus, P. (A.270), 86, 167
Octavius Iustus, L. (A.271), 86, 167
officiales, 108, 142
officium
 censuale, 143
 epistularum, 83
Onesimus (A.349), 172
orality, 24, *see* literacy
ordinare ('to organise' a document), 17, 52
ordo, 23, 70, 73
 equester, 5, 74, 109, 111, 125
 scribarum, 73, 74, 102, 109, 111, 112
 senatorius, 5, 74
ornamenta decurionalia, 85
Ostia, 71, 86, 87, 125, 131, 132, 136, 166, 167, 170
Ostrogoths, 146
otium, 17, 20
Ovinius Antonianus, C. (A.272), 87, 167

Paccius Eleuther (A.321), 170
Paccius Lucianus (A.273), 86, 167
Pactumeius Eutychianus (A.322), 170
Paestum, 8, 53, 86, 165
pagina ('page', in a document), 43
παιδεία (*humanitas*), 19, *see* education
Papienus Salutaris, P. (A.124), 68, 119, 158
Papirius, M. (A.126), 131, 158
Papirius Claudianus, Cn. (A.274), 86, 167
Papirius Maximus, Q. (A.127), 72, 76, 80, 126, 129, 158
Papirius Potamo, L. (A.125), 91, 116, 158
papyrus, 5, 30, 49
Parthian War, 127

224 General Index

Patara, 83
patronage, 4, 21, 88, 92, 93, 127, 132, 141
patronus, see patronage
Patulcenses Campani, 55
Peducaeus Saturninus, L. (A.128), 119, 120, 158
Penates, 100
perfectissimus, 128
periculum, 55
Perperna Fronto, A. (A.129), 118, 158
Perperna Quadra, T., 75
perscribere ('to enter' into public record), 32
Petilius, L. (A.130), 57, 90, 116, 158
Petilius Colonus, P. (A.131), 134, 136, 158
Petilius Spurinna, Q., 90
Petronius (A.220), 164
Petronius Melior, Q. (A.132), 75, 76, 125–128, 158
Petronius Rufus, Q. (A.275), 86, 167
Philippi, battle of, 16, 111
Philumenus (A.350), 172
Pituanius Eros, L. (A.133), 119, 158
Plaetorius Primitivos (A.323), 170
Plautius, A., 41
plebiscitum Claudianum, 95, 101
plebs, 1, 87, 115, 135
Pliny the Younger (C. Plinius Caecilius Secundus), 21
Plotius Faustinus, P. (A.276), 86, 167
Plutei Traiani, 41
poetae, 22
πόλις, 8
Pompeius Aemilianus, A. (A.134), 119, 158
Pompeius Baebianus, Sex. (A.135), 129, 159
Pompeius Carpus, A. (A.136), 119, 159
Pompeius Hermeros, L. (A.277), 86, 167
Pompeius Magnus, Cn., 101
Pompeius Mai[- - -], M. (A.137), 159
Pompeius Pylades, P. (A.138), 74, 159
Pompey (Cn. Pompeius Magnus), 46
Pomponius Carisianus, L. (A.139), 68, 119, 159
Pomponius Niger, L. (A.140), 159
Pomponius Rufus, Q., 92, 127
Pon[tius], M. (A.141), 72, 126
pontifex, 131
  Faesulis et Florentiae, 128
  minor, 67, 123
  Salius, 132
Pon[tius], M. (A.141), 120, 159
Pontius Lupus (A.278), 86, 167
Pontius Martialis, L. (A.142), 76, 159
Popillius Helenus, A. (A.143), 119, 159
Porcius, M. (A.144), 83, 159
Porcius Pollio, M. (A.145), 119, 120, 129, 159
Porsenna, Lars, 13
porta Capena, 117
porticus
  porphyretica, 144
  Purpuretica, 144
portorium, 128
Potaissa, 86, 165
Potentia, 86, 167
praecones, 58, 62, 69, 70, 76, 85, 125
praefectus
  Aegypti, 133
  aerarii, 21, 36, 43, 77, 86
  alae, 126
  annonae, 145
  cohortis, 126
  frumenti dandi, 30, 31, 65, 82
  praesidiorum et montis Berenicidis, 126
  urbi, 145
  vehiculorum, 127, 128
Praeneste, 131
praetor
  aerarii, 77
  and documentation, 31
  and *scribae*, 81
  tutelarius, 145
Prastina Fronto (A.146), 159
Priscus (A.297), 168
procurator, 127, 142
  a studiis, 128
  annonae, 125, 127
  ordinis, 74
  provinciarum Lugdunesis et Aquitanicae, 125
proscriptions, 112
prosopography, 10
provincia aquaria, 70
public administration, 28, 39
public service, 21, *see apparitores*
publicani, 74
Publicius, Sex. (A.279), 167
Publicius Malleolus, C., 89
pugillares, 41, *see tabulae ceratae*
Pulfennius Phileros, L. (A.147), 119, 159
pullarii, 62
Punic Wars, 115, 116
Puteoli, 86, 131, 166–168

quaestio, 81
  de repetundis, 34
  perpetua, 95
quaestor, 31, 37, 48, 51, 68
  as head of the *aerarium*, 19, 37
  and *senatus consulta*, 37
  urbanus, 45, 69, 70
quattuorvir, 131
  iure dicundo, 86, 131

General Index

quinquennalis, 74, 86, 128, 131, 132
Quintius (A.351), 172

Raetinum, 169
rationes, 31, 32, 34, 47, 50, 51, 108
   access to, 34
   archival of, 32, 34, 37, 51
Ravenna, 146, 166, 170
rector decuriarum, 23
recuperator, 95
referre ('to register' a document to public record), 17, 29, 32, 42, 97
res gestae, 29
Respectus (A.280), 86, 167
Ricinius Persa, Cn. (A.148), 87, 126, 159
Romilius, L., 75
Rostra, 75, 79
Rufinianus (A.149), 145, 159
Rufrae, 131, 135
Rupilius Menander, D. (A.281), 85, 86, 132, 167
Rustius Lysiponus, T. (A.282), 55, 86, 167
Rustius Numerius (A.283), 168

Sabidius Maximus, T. (A.150), 76, 131, 159
Sabidius Victor, T. (A.284), 85, 86, 132, 168
sacerdos
   Apollonis, 131
   Genii coloniae, 132
Saena, 127, 128
salarium, 20
Sallustius Virgula (A.151), 159
Salona, 86, 166
Salonius (A.221), 164
Sammius Tertiolus, T. (A.285), 86, 168
sarcophagus, 137, 142, 144
Sardinia (province), 44, 55, 122
Sarmentus (A.152), 116, 160
Sarmizegetusa, 86, 166, 168, 169
Saturio (A.352), 172
Saturius Gratus (A.286), 86, 168
Saturnia, 135
Saturninus (A.380), 174
Saufeius, D. (A.153), 116, 160
Savaria, 175
scheda, 59
schola, 75, 80
Scrasius Naeolus, P. (A.154), 118, 126, 160
scriba, see Appendix
   and accountability, 99
   aedilicius, 8, 39, 41, 80, 109, 117, 126
   aedilicius sex primus curatorum, 81
   aedilium iure dicundo, 86
   aerarii, 86
   at the *aerarium*, 69, 71, 109
   as *apparitor*, 7, 8
   appointment of, 4, 17, 88, 89
   as archivist, 5, 11, 32, 44, 49, 148
   authenticating documents, 43, 76, 97
   as bookkeeper, 5, 8, 32, 49, 51, 52, 54, 56, 66, 67, 104, 107, 141
   career paths of, 123, 124
   and *censuales*, 144
   cerarii, 136
   and *cerarium*, 108
   cerarius, 71, 86, 87
   and citizenship, 113, 118
   and civil service, 63, 142
   civitatis, 86
   collegium of, 74
   of *collegium*, 8, 87
   coloniae, 86
   copying documents, 56, 57
   and corruption, 4, 11, 94, 103–105, 108, 141
   criminal prosecution of, 99, 101, 105, 108, 109
   curatorum aquarum, 82
   decemvirum agris dandis adsignandis, 82
   decemvirum stlitibus iudicandis, 82
   as *decuriones*, 85
   depiction of, 39, 53
   as documentary specialist, 19, 49, 55, 56, 66, 99, 140
   and documents, 12, 145, 148
   duumvirum, 54, 86
   education of, 18
   and embezzlement, 37, 50, 99, 104
   of the emperors, 83
   Etruscan origin, 14, 63
   as expert of literate practice, 2–4, 11, 15, 19, 27, 121, 140, 149
   and *fides*, 48, 59, 102, 103, 148
   of the fleet, 8, 87
   and forgery, 99
   forming an *ordo*, 73
   as holder of sinecure, 11
   and jurisprudence, 56
   and knowledge, 2, 4, 11, 19, 57
   and late imperial administration, 142
   librarius, see scriba librarius
   and literary culture, 11, 21
   and magistrates, 68, 107, 141
   minuting in court, 56
   and moral suitability, 17, 20, 88
   municipal, 8, 84, 86, 146
   municipii, 86
   and *negotium*, 20
   and oath, 17, 47, 59, 100, 101
   and the *ordo equester*, 109, 112, 124–127
   and the *ordo senatorius*, 123
   and patronage, 4, 11, 105, 116, 121–124, 141

scriba (cont.)
  and *poetae*, 22
  pontificius, 67, 73
  and power, 2, 11, 14, 33, 88, 107
  praefecti frumenti dandi, 82
  princeps, 75
  privileges of, 143
  and procuratorial posts, 127
  professional requirements of, 17
  publicus, 86
  quaestorius, 16, 21, 50, 54, 55, 66–69, 75, 78, 80, 86, 109, 126
  quaestorius sex primus curatorum, 57, 76–78, 80, 97
  quattuorvirum, 86
  quinquennalicius, 86
  reading in public, 56, 58, 64
  registering documents, 32, 56
  rei publicae, 86
  self-perception of, 8
  in the senate, 64, 143
  senatus, 143
  σκρ(ε)ίβα(ς) in Greek, 8, 54
  and social mobility, 2–5, 11, 21, 22, 50, 109, 113, 121, 123–125, 141
  social origin of, 116–118, 121, 141
  and social relations, 2, 88
  and social status, 5, 47, 112, 114, 116, 121, 123, 141
  and *tabulae ceratae*, 49, 53, 55
  and *tabulae publicae*, 4, 20, 47, 48, 52, 56, 58, 59, 72–74, 99, 102, 112, 141, 148
  and tax farming, 108
  and trade, 101, 108
  tribunicius, 80, 126
  triumvirum mensarii, 82
  viginti(sex)virum, 82
  and wage labour, 20, 47, 84, 85, 106, 141
  at workplace, 8, 48, 54
  and writing, 49, 140
scriba librarius, see scriba, Appendix
  aedilicius, 80, 117
  as *apparitor*, 46
  career paths of, 120, 129
  collegium of, 74
  curatorum aquarum, 65
  freeborn, 119
  freedmen, 119
  and jurisprudence, 56
  and late imperial administration, 142
  and libertine ancestry, 119
  municipal, 86
  and the *ordo equester*, 127
  quaestorius, 68, 76
  in the retinue of a *proconsul*, 68
  in relation to *scriba*, 22, 45–47, 68
  tribunicius, 74
scribere ('to write, draft' a document), 17, 52
scribes
  Etruscan, 13, 22, 49, 66
  Greek, 8, 20
scrinium, 142
scriptum facere (to administer the office of *scriba*), 48
seal, 97
Segobriga, 83
Seius, Cn. (A.155), 160
Seius, M. (A.156), 46, 47, 119, 160
Seius Victor, C. (A.375), 174
sella, 7, 49
senate, 31
senatus consultum, 23, 31, 78
  archival of, 35, 37, 44
  de Aphrodisiensibus, 42, 44
  de nundinis saltus Beguensis, 43–45, 57
  referral to the *tabulae publicae*, 41
  tacitum, 144
Seneca (A.302), 169
Sentinatius Iustus, C. (A.287), 86, 168
Sentinum, 86, 168
Sentius Men(- - -), T. (A.288), 86, 168
Septimius, C. (A.157), 81, 116, 160
Septimius Libo, C. (A.158), 131, 160
Septimius Severus (L. Septimius Severus, emperor), 138
Septumius, P. (A.159), 76, 116, 160
Serenus (A.381), 175
Sergius, L. (A.160), 68, 89, 104, 116, 160
Sertorius, Q., 68, 91
Servilius, P. (A.162), 108, 116, 160
Servilius Draco (A.58), 72
Servilius Eunicus, M. (A.161), 119, 126, 136, 160
Servilius Isauricus, 136
Servilius Rullus, P., 46, 65
Severius Severus, D. (A.163), 126, 131, 160
Sevius, T. (A.303), 169
shorthand, 59
Sicelli, 133
Sicily (province), 6, 82, 88, 89, 91, 104, 108, 109
Similius Philocyrius, C. (A.324), 170
sinecure, 11, 83, 92
Sinuessa, 132, 135
sinus, 41
Siscia, 86, 167
slave, 45
social mobility, 1, 2, 10, 21, 22, 112, 120, 127, 129, 139
social relations, *see* patronage
social status, 3, 4

Social War, 35, 112
societas publicanorum, 108
Sorilius Bassus (A.164), 75, 160
Sosius, Q., 6, 38
sportula, 108
Statilius Messalinianus, T. (A.165), 93, 126, 129, 160
Statius Celsus, C. (A.166), 119, 126, 142, 160
Statius Optatus, P. (A.167), 77, 81, 160
Stertinius Maximus Eutyches (A.168), 92, 119, 126, 136, 161
Stertinius Maximus, C., 92
Stertinius Orpex, C. (A.169), 73, 92, 119, 136, 161
Struggle of the Orders, 1, 35, 38
Suessa Aurunca, 131
Sufenas Myro, P. (A.170), 92, 118, 126, 131, 161
Sufenas Severus Sempronianus, P. (A.171), 92, 118, 131, 161
Sufenas Verus, P., 92
suffragium, 107
Suillius Celsus, M'. (A.172), 92, 161
Suillius Rufus, P., 92
Sulla (L. Cornelius Sulla Felix), 62, 66, 69, 90, 91, 98, 123
Sulmo, 86, 131, 167
Sulpicius Olympus, C. (A.173), 119, 161
sumere ('to adopt' an *apparitor*), 70
Suovetaurilia, 58
Synda (A.289), 168
σύνκλητος, *see* codex

tablinum, 27, 29, 33, 34, *see* archive
tabula, *see* tabulae ceratae
Tabula Heracleensis, 46, 48
tabulae censoriae, 29, 31, 35, 37, 41
tabulae ceratae (wooden wax tablets), 27, 29, 30, 53, 140
  archival of, 44
  destruction of, 6, 41
  large-format, 4, 39, 41, 43, 49, 96
  materiality of, 5, 26, 40
  as part of a document, 44
  and sealing, 97
  small-format, 48
  survival of, 6
  symbolic nature of, 49, 64, 145
  writing surface of, 42
tabulae communes, *see* tabulae publicae
tabulae publicae, 4, 17, 27, 33, 34, 36, 42, 48, 66, 72, 77, 81, 140
  access to, 98
  archival of, 37, 39, 44
  authority of, 35
  destruction of, 41
  forgery of, 96, 100
  large-format, 41, 42
  materiality of, 40, 96, 97
  physical evidence of, 41
  as repository of public knowledge, 32, 35
Tabularium, 38, 39
tabularium, 6, 27, 33–35, 37, 38, *see* archive
  architecture of, 39, 40
  of the *censores*, 45
  epigraphic evidence of, 39
  local, 44
  as place of trial, 40
  principis, 39
  publicum, 38
  as workplace, 40
tabularius, 146
tabulas ponere ('to put down one's writing tablets', i.e. to quit one's position as *scriba*), 49
ταμιακαὶ δέλτοι, *see* tabulae publicae
ταμιεῖον, 37, *see* aerarium
Tarquitius Etruscus Sulpicianus, L. (A.174), 161
tax farming, 67, 108
Telegennus Anthus, C. (A.175), 119, 120, 161
temple, 131
  as archive, 29, 37
  of Ceres, 37
  of Iuno Moneta, 38
  of Jupiter, 38
  of Minerva, 22
  of Moneta, 122
  of the Nymphs, 29, 37
  of Saturn, 37, 38, 70, 75, 76, 78–80
Temporinius Cerialis (A.290), 168
Terentius Felix, P. (A.291), 86, 168
Terentius Fortunatus (A.325), 170
Terentius Geminus (A.326), 171
Terentius, Cn., *see* Petilius, L.
Tertius, P. (A.292), 86, 168
Tettienus Felix, T. (A.176), 92, 119, 120, 161
Tettienus Serenus, T., 92
Tettius Certus, P. (A.177), 119, 161
Theodosius (emperor), 146
Thisdra, 169
Thracia (province), 128
Tiberius (Tiberius Iulius Caesar Augustus, emperor), 21
  having scribae, 82
  and *senatus consulta*, 41
  and *tabulae publicae*, 36, 77
tibicines, 85
Tibur, 86, 131, 132, 167, 168
toga, 53
  praetexta, 114
Tolosa, 86, 166
tractare ('to manage' a document), 17

Trajan (M. Ulpius Traianus, emperor), 127
Trea, 174
Trebellius Modestus (A.327), 171
Trebula Suffenas, 44, 132
tribunus
   aerarii, 74
   militum, 16, 112, 126
   plebis, 1, 31, 37, 58, 81
tribus, 30, 134
tributum, 66
triumph, 122
triumviri mensarii, 82
Tropaeum Traiani, 86, 165, 167, 168
Tucci, 134, 136
Tuceius Hermes (A.328), 171
Tullius, M. (A.178), 50, 54, 76, 90, 107, 116, 135, 161
Tullius, Servius, 29
Tullius Cicero, M., *see* Cicero
tunica, 53
tutela, 76
Tyrannus (A.179), 93, 119, 161

Ul[pius] Amantius (A.331), 171
Ulpius Callistus, M. (A.180), 93, 119, 161
Ulpius Celsianus, M. (A.181), 74, 119, 161
Ulpius Florentinus (A.293), 86, 168
Ulpius Vesbinus, 43
Ummidius Quadratus, C., 77
Uselis, 86, 165

Valentinian II (emperor), 146
Valentinus (A.294), 86, 168
Valerian (P. Licinius Valerianus, emperor), 142
Valerianus (A.182), 119, 161
Valerius (A.183), 161
Valerius (A.386), 82, 175
Valerius (A.222), 164
Valerius, C. (A.184), 126, 162
Valerius Bassus, M'. (A.185), 76, 126, 162
Valerius Colonus, M. (A.376), 174
Valerius Hedymeles, M. (A.186), 119, 162
Valerius Iulianus, L. (A.295), 86, 168
Valerius Karicus (A.329), 171
Valerius Pollio, Q. (A.372), 174
Valerius Propolus, D. (A.187), 92, 119, 162
Valerius Ste[- - -] (A.330), 171
Valerius Victor, M. (A.296), 86, 168
Varro (M. Terrentius Varro), 46, 47
Varronius (A.223), 164

Varronius Capito, L. (A.188), 129, 132, 162
Vatinius Priscus (A.297), 86
Ve[- - -]ius C[- - -]tus, L. (A.332), 171
vectigal, 67
Veii, 72
Venafrum, 86, 168
Venusia, 16, 111
Verres, C., 6, 7, 34, 82, 88, 91, 96, 104, 109
Versius (A.189), 68, 91, 162
Veturius Crescens, T. (A.190), 119, 162
Veturius Florus, T. (A.377), 174
via Appia, 117
viatores, 37, 62, 69, 70, 76, 85, 105, 125, 132
Vibius Publilianus, C. (A.191), 126, 162
vicarius, 70, 72, 73
Vicetia, 131, 134
vicus, 30
viginti(sex)viri, 82
villa publica, 29
vir spectabilis, 23
Vitalis (A.353), 172
Vivius Iulianus, C. (A.192), 162
Volumnius Serenus (A.298), 85, 86, 168
[Volu]ntilius Macer (A.193), 129, 162
[Volusius] (A.194), 119
Volusius Hermes, L. (A.195), 92, 119, 162
Volusius Himerus, L. (A.196), 92, 119, 162
Volusius Plocamus Maior, L. (A.197), 92, 119, 162
Volusius Primanus, L. (A.198), 92, 119, 120, 162
Volusius Saturninus, L., 92
Volusius Volusianus P[- - -]anus, L. (A.199), 119, 126, 162
[Volusius - - -]us (A.194), 162

wage labour, 20, 111
   and social status, 20, 21
wax, 27, 35, 40, 96, *see tabulae ceratae*
wood, 30, 40, *see* tabulae ceratae
writing
   artisanal, 25
   clerical, 21, 22
   commercial, 25
   on *instrumentum domesticum*, 25, 26
   legal, 25
   literary, 21, 22
   private, 25, 29
   in public, 48
   religious, 25
writing material, 26, 30, 49, *see* documents, *tabulae ceratae*

Printed by Printforce, the Netherlands